Formative and Shared Assessment to Promote Global University Learning

José Sánchez-Santamaría
Universidad de Castilla-La Mancha, Spain

A volume in the Advances in Higher Education and Professional Development (AHEPD) Book Series

Published in the United States of America by
  IGI Global
  Information Science Reference (an imprint of IGI Global)
  701 E. Chocolate Avenue
  Hershey PA, USA 17033
  Tel: 717-533-8845
  Fax: 717-533-8661
  E-mail: cust@igi-global.com
  Web site: http://www.igi-global.com

Library of Congress Cataloging-in-Publication Data

Names: Sánchez-Santamaría, José, 1977- editor.
Title: Formative and shared assessment to promote global university
  learning / José Sánchez-Santamaría, Editor.
Description: Hershey, PA : Information Science Reference, [2023] | Includes
  bibliographical references and index.
Identifiers: LCCN 2022004184 (print) | LCCN 2022004185 (ebook) | ISBN
  9781668435373 (hardcover) | ISBN 9781668435397 (ebook)
Subjects: LCSH: Educational tests and measurements. | International
  education. | Competency-based education. | Teacher-student
  relationships.
Classification: LCC LB3051 .F646 2022 (print) | LCC LB3051 (ebook) | DDC
  371.26--dc23/eng/20220425
LC record available at https://lccn.loc.gov/2022004184
LC ebook record available at https://lccn.loc.gov/2022004185

This book is published in the IGI Global book series Advances in Higher Education and Professional Development (AHEPD) (ISSN: 2327-6983; eISSN: 2327-6991)

British Cataloguing in Publication Data
A Cataloguing in Publication record for this book is available from the British Library.

For electronic access to this publication, please contact: eresources@igi-global.com.

Advances in Higher Education and Professional Development (AHEPD) Book Series

Jared Keengwe
University of North Dakota, USA

ISSN:2327-6983
EISSN:2327-6991

MISSION

As world economies continue to shift and change in response to global financial situations, job markets have begun to demand a more highly-skilled workforce. In many industries a college degree is the minimum requirement and further educational development is expected to advance. With these current trends in mind, the **Advances in Higher Education & Professional Development (AHEPD) Book Series** provides an outlet for researchers and academics to publish their research in these areas and to distribute these works to practitioners and other researchers.

AHEPD encompasses all research dealing with higher education pedagogy, development, and curriculum design, as well as all areas of professional development, regardless of focus.

COVERAGE

- Adult Education
- Assessment in Higher Education
- Career Training
- Coaching and Mentoring
- Continuing Professional Development
- Governance in Higher Education
- Higher Education Policy
- Pedagogy of Teaching Higher Education
- Vocational Education

IGI Global is currently accepting manuscripts for publication within this series. To submit a proposal for a volume in this series, please contact our Acquisition Editors at Acquisitions@igi-global.com or visit: http://www.igi-global.com/publish/.

Titles in this Series

For a list of additional titles in this series, please visit: www.igi-global.com/book-series/advances-higher-education-professional-development/73681

The Impact of HEIs on Regional Development Facts and Practices of Collaborative Work With SMEs
Susana Rodrigues (CARME, ESTG, Polytechnic Institute of Leiria, Portugal) and Joaquim Mourato (Polytechnic Institute of Portalegre, Portugal)
Information Science Reference • © 2023 • 427pp • H/C (ISBN: 9781668467015) • US $215.00

Improving Higher Education Models Through International Comparative Analysis
Valerie A. Storey (Franklin University, USA) and Thomas E. Beeman (St. Joseph's University, USA)
Information Science Reference • © 2023 • 315pp • H/C (ISBN: 9781668473276) • US $215.00

Global Perspectives on the Difficulties and Opportunities Faced by Migrant and Refugee Students in Higher Education
Sameerah Tawfeeq Saeed (English Language Teaching Department, Faculty of Education, Tishk International University, Erbil, Iraq) and Min Zhang (UNESCO, Paris, France)
Information Science Reference • © 2023 • 328pp • H/C (ISBN: 9781668477816) • US $215.00

Accessibility of Digital Higher Education in the Global South
Pfano Mashau (University of KwaZulu-Natal, South Africa) and Tshililo Farisani (University of KwaZulu-Natal, South Africa)
Information Science Reference • © 2023 • 310pp • H/C (ISBN: 9781668491799) • US $215.00

Handbook of Research on Sustainable Career Ecosystems for University Students and Graduates
William E. Donald (University of Southampton, UK & Ronin Institute, USA)
Information Science Reference • © 2023 • 589pp • H/C (ISBN: 9781668474426) • US $280.00

Impact of Global University Ranking Systems on Developing Countries
Omwoyo Bosire Onyancha (University of South Africa, South Africa) and Adeyinka Tella (University of Ilorin, Nigeria)
Information Science Reference • © 2023 • 384pp • H/C (ISBN: 9781668482667) • US $215.00

Co-Constructing and Sustaining Service Learning in Graduate Programs Reflections from the Field
Rabia Hos (University of Rhode Island, USA) and Brenda Santos (University of Rhode Island, USA)
Information Science Reference • © 2023 • 300pp • H/C (ISBN: 9781668465332) • US $215.00

701 East Chocolate Avenue, Hershey, PA 17033, USA
Tel: 717-533-8845 x100 • Fax: 717-533-8661
E-Mail: cust@igi-global.com • www.igi-global.com

Table of Contents

Detailed Table of Contents

    Walter Nuninger, CNRS, Centrale Lille, CRIStAL Laboratory URM 9189, University of Lille,
        France
    Frédéric Hoogstoel, CNRS, Centrale Lille, CRIStAL Laboratory URM 9189, University of
        Lille, France
    Luigi Lancieri, CNRS, Centrale Lille, CRIStAL Laboratory URM 9189, University of Lille,
        France

In the framework of lifelong learning, learning outcomes target a set of skills for work based on contextualized previous experiences. Specially designed activities performed during the training path will become formative thanks to guiding and feedback, but also formative assessment before summative evaluation. Higher education learning performance motivates this learner-centered pedagogical choice that requires a real commitment from the audience. By relying on our practices in an engineering school and satisfaction surveys, the chapter puts the focus on how peer review during activities supports personal development. The authors present a gradual assessment process as a part of the pedagogical scenario for groups enrolled in initial and vocational trainings. This should provide a key lever to develop skills not only for the work but also for learning autonomy, commitment, human and social qualities, thanks to the external feedback from their peers and supervised debriefings. This process supports the satisfaction of all with respect to a common objective embodied by accepted and shared assessments.

    Purificación Cruz, Universidad de Castilla-La Mancha, Spain
    Javier Rodríguez, Universidad de Castilla-La Mancha, Spain
    Lorena López, Universidad de Castilla-La Mancha, Spain

These days, many authors ask whether having a high level of intellectual knowledge is a guarantee of success at university. The answer is no, at least not only with rational intelligence. Emotional intelligence is needed to cope with life. This emotional intelligence can be learned as another competence, and it will also allow us to acquire the rest of the competences required for personal and professional development. Therefore, the results in the assessments to which university students are "subjected" are closely linked to the emotional development of the individual.

Félix Enrique Lobo de Diego, Universidad de Valladolid, Spain
Laura Cañadas, Universidad Autónoma de Madrid, Spain

The purpose of this study is to analyse how the modality used (online vs. face-to-face) for the teaching and learning process influences the acquisition of professional competences in a formative assessment experience. An action-research study was implemented during two academic years in the 2019/2020 and 2020/2021. One teacher and sixty teacher education students of the third course of the Faculty of Education of Segovia (University of Valladolid, Spain) participated in this study. A questionnaire and two teaching staff reports were used to collect the information. Results show agreement of the utility of the formative assessment experience implemented to the development of teaching competences both in online and in face-to-face mode. As conclusion the authors highlight the need for rethinking the way formative assessment is delivered at Higher Education so that theory and practice are connected and contribute to develop professional competences.

Lucía Sánchez-Tarazaga, Universitat Jaume I, Spain
Aida Sanahuja Ribés, Universitat Jaume I, Spain
Francesc M. Esteve-Mon, Universitat Jaume I, Spain

The aim of this paper is to analyze the conception and use of formative assessment and feedback by faculty teachers in the context of a training course held at a Spanish university. Open-response data from 42 faculty teachers were analyzed using an inductively derived coding framework and thematic analysis. Analysis was organized around four main themes: 1) faculty teachers' beliefs about assessment, 2) main barriers or constraints that hinder feedback implementation, 3) associated benefits and 4) integration of digital technology to enrich formative assessment. The main results show different conceptions and myths about assessment and feedback, as well as a number of barriers to implementation. Furthermore, the training provided reveals that faculty teachers regard the feedback process, enhanced by digital tools, as beneficial.

Natalia Hipólito Hipólito, Universidad de Castilla-La Mancha, Spain
Irene Martínez Martín, Universidad Complutense de Madrid, Spain
María Teresa Bejarano Franco, Universidad de Castilla-La Mancha, Spain
Pia Rauff Krøyer, VIA University College, Denmark

This chapter aims to reflect on assessment practices in the context of university from a feminist and decolonial perspective. It is committed to a university education based on the principles of equity, social justice, and equality. Within this framework it becomes essential to rethink assessment systems. To do so, the chapter is divided into two parts: first, the epistemological construction of assessment from decolonial feminism and the skills and competences approach is discussed; and second, university experiences regarding assessment are described under the presented principles. As final proposals, an answer is given to the question of whether it is possible to transform assessment in the university by focusing on clarifying what the objective and the subjects of a feminist and decolonial evaluation are, as well as the strategies, techniques, and uses of transformative assessment.

Chapter 6

Carla Fernández Garcimartín, University of Valladolid, Spain
Teresa Fuentes Nieto, University of Valladolid, Spain
Víctor Manuel López-Pastor, University of Valladolid, Spain
David Hortigüela-Alcalá, University of Burgos, Spain
Miriam Molina Soria, University of Valladolid, Spain
Cristina Pascual-Arias, University of Valladolid, Spain

The aim of this chapter was to check the importance of the curricular alignment between the teaching methodology and the assessment system used, specifically between the use of tutored learning projects (TLP) and formative and shared-assessment (FandSA) systems, in terms of student participation in assessment. The assessment of students and lecturers on student participation in the FandSA processes is studied when they are associated with active learning methodologies such as TLP. The study sample consisted of 256 students and lecturers from higher education. The results obtained show a high level of satisfaction with the experience of good practice in developing TLP in groups and taking part in the assessment process. One of the advantages found is that student involvement in their learning was high, and an increase was observed in all the subjects. The main disadvantage that the students indicated was the high workload involved.

Chapter 7

Cristina Pascual-Arias, University of Valladolid, Spain
David Hortigüela-Alcalá, University of Burgos, Spain
Teresa Fuentes Nieto, University of Valladolid, Spain
Víctor M. López-Pastor, University of Valladolid, Spain
Carla Fernández-Garcimartín, University of Valladolid, Spain
Miriam Molina Soria, University of Valladolid, Spain

This chapter has two clearly defined objectives: (a) to analyse how higher education (HE) teachers participating in an in-service teacher education (ISTE) inter-level seminar evaluated the Action-Research (A-R) processes they carried out; (b) to determine the advantages that HE teachers find after carrying out formative and shared assessment (F&SA) processes, as well as the disadvantages and proposals for improvement to overcome them. For this purpose, a case study was conducted in an ISTE inter-level seminar on F&SA with 10 HE teachers. The teachers found the A-R processes very useful although they believed that they should systematise them continuously during the whole teaching-learning process; moreover, they considered that F&SA practices have many advantages and some disadvantages for which they proposed solutions to overcome them.

In March 2020, assessment in universities and colleges globally changed in radical and unprecedented ways when the Covid-19 pandemic closed campuses to students and staff, meaning that on-site, unseen, time-constrained exams could not take place. University management and staff had to move very fast to ensure that students could be assessed reliably and validly in crisis conditions. The authors' immediate and widely shared suggestions on pragmatic alternatives incorporating assessment-for-learning principles were well-received and prompted the development of a systematic and practical six-stage 'task-generator' to enable the creation of flexible context/scenario-based assessment activities for use off-campus. This chapter concludes by arguing why some of the changes implemented in crisis conditions have so much value in terms of student learning and engagement that universities must never revert to an over-reliance on former modes of assessment.

In this chapter the authors try to delve into the relationship between emotional education and social education in the context of higher education. To do this, the theoretical framework has been developed by referring to the interest of emotional education, as well as the importance of emotional competencies, within the educational work of the 21st century. In this way, the research carried out to know this relationship more in depth is justified, on the one hand, contemplating the perceptions of students and teachers from a questionnaire that raises the perceptions about the importance of this relationship and, on the other hand, identifying the content on education and emotional management in the educational programs of bachelor's degrees in social education at the Spanish universities, highlighting the importance of competencies assessment. The results are discussed with other studies and contributions on emotional education in socio-educational intervention, thus achieving the aims of the research.

The main objective of the study was to analyse the results of the implementation of formative and shared assessment (F&SA) systems in pre-service teacher education (PTE) classrooms with respect to the acquisition of student competencies, their academic performance and the advantages and disadvantages of the system. It is an "ex post facto" study with a sample of 333 students of a PTE subject in a Spanish public university. The data collection instruments were: (1) a structured report of best practices in higher education (HE); and (2) an anonymous questionnaire for the assessment of the best practice experience carried out and the assessment system used. The results show that F&SA had a positive influence on the acquisition of professional competencies and on the academic performance of students and that these systems present more advantages than disadvantages.

Chapter 11

The Covid-19 crisis not only had a global impact on the sanitary services, but also had economic and social repercussions, especially at the educational system; this last apex is to be dealt with in relation to the Ecuadorian higher education level reality. As it is so, this chapter's aim is to collect the tutoring experience as part of the shared and formative evaluation (F&SA) during the pandemic. For this process the phenomenological methodology of research was used, managing to consolidate teachers and university students focus groups, who made a contribution with derivate features from the university educational reality, coming to consider tutoring as a necessary tool to strengthen those weaknesses given during synchronous connections. In this way, it provides an evaluation that promotes participative training process, where favorable learning environments are generated.

Preface

Introduction

Formative and shared assessment (F&SA) implies a radical change in the way in which we understand the meaning and function of the assessment of university learning (Bearman, Boud & Ajjawi, 2020; Boud & Dawson, 2023). The competency approach has fostered an ideal scenario for providing content to the pedagogical function of assessment, as it is considered to be a learning task and not just an assessing task (Cañadas, 2023). In this sense, to a large extent, assessment is used to find out the degree of skills development of a student, but above all to turn assessment into a situation assessment is learning, i.e. it is not only about what the student learns, but also about how the student learns. This also means that any learning task involves making students aware of what and how they learn, and how to successfully use learning in the future (Ibarra-Sáiz, Rodríguez-Gómez & Boud, 2020).

Thus, in current debates on the assessment of university learning there is an essential question: *"Can we be sure that assessment in higher education meets the need of developing and assuring high quality learning outcomes?"* (Boud, 2020). The evidence gathered in recent years has informed that F&SA has played an essential role in the university setting. Its relevance lies in three dimensions: firstly, it allows estimating student learning; secondly, it contributes to the promotion of student participation in the learning process from autonomy and commitment around active methodologies; and thirdly, it has proved to be an essential ally for developing transversal competencies such as reflective, teamwork, ethical, oral skills, among others, hand in hand with the changes of the digital era in university teaching (Kaya-Capocci, O'Leary & Costello, 2022).

F&SA provides a set of pedagogical possibilities for improving teaching processes and learning outcomes for university students. F&SA has a set of pedagogical possibilities for improving teaching processes and learning outcomes for university students.

- F&SA can provide very useful information to teachers to plan and guide teaching decisions in relation to students' progress, challenges and difficulties in their learning (Boud & Dawson, 2023). The natural derivative of this type of information is to be able to incorporate improvements on teaching strategies adapted to the individual needs of the student body, and above all it allows the possibility of offering effective feedback, connected to the need and coherent with the demand of the student body.

- F&SA is equivalent to a feedback process oriented to meaningful, relevant learning for all. In other words, it is an action that stimulates student inclusion, which combined with appropriate strategies can be essential for the educational success of university students. All this enhances their ability to think about what they learn, but above all to think about themselves in relation to how they are learning.

- F&SA is not only about understanding assessment as learning, but also about promoting assessment as a facilitator of the participation of all in learning outcomes. In other words, an F&SA that does not involve students, does not allow them to learn and is not connected to the professional profile of university studies does not fulfill its function.

- F&SA is learning, therefore, it is not grading but knowing in order to understand what students learn and knowing in order to transform how students learn in relation to the proposed learning outcomes. In other words, not only is there a learning path to follow, but this path also has a meaning in terms of the function of evaluation as a learning activity. It is a way of learning, learning ahead (Sadler, Reimann & Sambell, 2022).

- The F&SA has demonstrated its potential to assess, and therefore, mobilize and expand the soft, transversal or invisible skills of the university student body. This is essential for the training of university students in the context of the current environmental, social and economic challenges highlighted by the 2030 Agenda.

- F&SA is inclusive, not only because it allows the participation of all, but also because it presents strategies, tools and resources that take into account the diversity of students: their different styles, their previous and own knowledge, their individual experiences. It establishes comprehensive and mobilizing frameworks for overcoming barriers to participation that limit relevant and meaningful learning.

Despite the evidence that informs the efficacy and rigor of the F&SA, there are pending challenges, in the sense that there are still important cultural resistances in many universities that limit the meaning and formative function of the F&SA, but above all its scope as participation in learning, beyond do-it-yourself. Technical problems are being overcome more easily and the need for resources for the implementation of this type of evaluation is progressively being met.

What is clear is the crucial role of F&SA in the education of university students. Overcoming these challenges will require the commitment of all: teachers, students, administrators, academic and policy makers, but the long-term benefits in terms of meaningful learning and personal development make it worth the effort, since its implications are pedagogical, but above all social and democratic.

Following in this wake, this book is an invitation to trace some of these challenges. Specifically, this work represents an attempt to contribute in a modest but rigorous way to the debate on the impact of F&SA on teaching-learning processes and practices at the university. This book gathers a total of 11 book chapters that combine research, proposals and experiences that contribute to shed some light on the debate on F&SA in higher education.

In the first chapter, authors Nuninger, Hoogstoel and Lancieri present a paper on progressive peer review to enhance formative learning. These authors focus attention on issues of trust and motivation for college student engagement. Based on internships in an engineering school and satisfaction surveys, this chapter highlights how peer review during activities supports personal development.

In the second chapter, professors Cruz, Rodríguez and López propose the importance of placing assessment evaluation as an exciting activity, so that we can have an assessment based on a true value with positive implications in university teaching processes. They open us to the world of emotions, in the sense of understanding evaluation from the double cognition-emotion axis oriented to action as meaningful learning.

The third chapter by Lobo de Diego and Cañadas is an interesting action-research study, which analyzes the development of competencies in online and face-to-face teaching modalities through a formative assessment experience. It is undoubtedly a relevant work for its implications on virtual teaching and its relationship with F&SA.

In the fourth chapter, along the same lines, the authors Sánchez-Tarazaga, Sanahuja and Esteve-Mon show the results of an experience on the training of university teachers in relation to formative assessment and feedback processes for the development of teaching skills in a digital world. It offers us, from a qualitative point of view, the perceptions, experiences and conceptions of a sample of Spanish teachers of interest to understand the impact of the F&SA in teacher training, a space that is beginning to have a greater projection, after having devoted much weight to the students' perspective.

The fifth chapter written by Hipólito, Martínez, Bejarano and Krøyer, brings together the work of three different universities around an innovative and necessary look at university evaluation and from a comparative framework between Spain and Denmark: the approach of feminist and decolonial pedagogies. It is an unusual look in European and American contexts, where the weight on F&SA has had a greater focus on the processes of self-regulation, feedback or assessment strategies or techniques.

The sixth chapter features an experienced group of researchers and academics in relation to F&SA. Fernández, Fuentes, López-Pastor, Hortigüela-Alcalá, Molina and Pascual-Arias address a crucial issue in F&SA. It is the internal coherence or constructive alignment between didactic methodologies and evaluation, specifically the proposal of tutored learning projects. In this survey research on good teaching practices, the potential for promoting student participation and engagement in their learning is evident.

The seventh chapter assumes an action-research approach, which is undoubtedly of great relevance since it goes beyond quantitative approaches and provides evidence from processes of conscious, systematic and reflective participation on F&SA in initial teacher training. The authors Pascual-Arias, Hortigüela-Alcalá, Fuentes, López-Pastor, Fernández and Molina contribute to assess results consistent with those obtained in other research on the advantages of F&SA in university teaching

The eighth chapter by two European F&SA referents, Brown and Sambell, presents us with an interesting proposal on how to adapt to the demands of Covid-19, but above all on the importance of having strategies that make us overcome dependence on meaningless assessment models. This is essential to address crisis situations that require flexible assessments based on learning and assessment scenarios beyond the classroom, beyond the campus.

The ninth chapter by authors Lirio, Medina, Fernández and Portal incorporates an emotional look at the training processes of education professionals linked to community services. Using a sequential mixed method they provide evidence that informs on the perceptions of these professionals in their training processes according to the emotional dimension and its relationship with F&SA.

The tenth chapter by Molina, López-Pastor, Hortigüela-Alcalá, Fuentes, Pascual-Arias and Fernández, highlights the importance of F&SA systems in initial teacher training according to the acquisition of competencies, academic performance and advantages and disadvantages. The results shared report the positive impact of good practices on competence development and, therefore, on the improvement of academic performance.

The eleventh chapter of this book, written by Rocha and Soria-Miranda, deals with the role of tutoring in times of Covid and its relationship with the F&SA, where we find that in times of crisis, the F&SA is also an ally for the participation and meaningful learning of students.

To sum up, the readers, academics and researchers have before them, a modest work but with scientific sense and pedagogical function to continue thinking about the F&SA as a valid, rigorous and necessary proposal for a conscious and committed development (López-Aguilar, Álvarez-Pérez & Garcés-Delgado, 2021) of the professional and personal competencies of university students in liquid (Ibarra-Sáiz, Rodríguez-Gómez, Boud, Rotsaert, Brown, Salinas & Rodríguez Gómez, 2020) and digital societies (Kaya-Capocci, O'Leary & Costello, 2022).

José Sánchez Santamaría
University of Castilla-La Mancha (Spain)

REFERENCES

Bearman, M., Boud, D., & Ajjawi, R. (2020). New Directions for Assessment in a Digital World. In *The enabling power of assessment* (pp. 7–18). Springer Nature. doi:10.1007/978-3-030-41956-1_2

Boud, D. (2020). Challenges in reforming higher education assessment: a perspective from afar. *RELIEVE – Electronic Journal of Educational Research and Evaluation, 26*(1). doi:10.7203/relieve.26.1.17088

Boud, D., & Dawson, P. (2023). What feedback literate teachers do: An empirically-derived competency framework. *Assessment & Evaluation in Higher Education, 48*(2), 158–171. doi:10.1080/02602938.2021.1910928

Cañadas, L. (2021). Contribution of formative assessment for developing teaching competences in teacher education. *European Journal of Teacher Education, 46*(3), 516–532. doi:10.1080/02619768.2021.1950684

Ibarra-Sáiz, M. S., Rodríguez-Gómez, G., & Boud, D. (2020). Developing student competence through peer assessment: The role of feedback, self-regulation and evaluative judgement. *Higher Education, 80*(1), 137–156. doi:10.100710734-019-00469-2

Ibarra-Sáiz, M. S., Rodríguez-Gómez, G., Boud, D., Rotsaert, T., Brown, S., Salinas, M. L., & Rodríguez, H. M. (2020). The future of assessment in Higher Education. *RELIEVE – Electronic Journal of Educational Research and Evaluation, 26*(1). doi:10.7203/relieve.26.1.17323

Kaya-Capocci, S., O'Leary, M., & Costello, E. (2022). Towards a Framework to Support the Implementation of Digital Formative Assessment in Higher Education. *Education Sciences, 12*(11), 823. doi:10.3390/educsci12110823

López-Aguilar, D., Álvarez-Pérez, P. R., & Garcés-Delgado, Y. (2021). Academic engagement and its impact on undergraduate student performance at the University of La Laguna. *RELIEVE – Electronic Journal of Educational Research and Evaluation, 27*(1). doi:10.30827/relieve.v27i1.21169

Chapter 1
A Progressive Peer Review to Enhance Formative Learning:
An Issue of Trust and Motivation for Commitment

Walter Nuninger

(iD) https://orcid.org/0000-0002-2639-1359

CNRS, Centrale Lille, CRIStAL Laboratory URM 9189, University of Lille, France

Frédéric Hoogstoel

CNRS, Centrale Lille, CRIStAL Laboratory URM 9189, University of Lille, France

Luigi Lancieri

CNRS, Centrale Lille, CRIStAL Laboratory URM 9189, University of Lille, France

ABSTRACT

In the framework of lifelong learning, learning outcomes target a set of skills for work based on contextualized previous experiences. Specially designed activities performed during the training path will become formative thanks to guiding and feedback, but also formative assessment before summative evaluation. Higher education learning performance motivates this learner-centered pedagogical choice that requires a real commitment from the audience. By relying on our practices in an engineering school and satisfaction surveys, the chapter puts the focus on how peer review during activities supports personal development. The authors present a gradual assessment process as a part of the pedagogical scenario for groups enrolled in initial and vocational trainings. This should provide a key lever to develop skills not only for the work but also for learning autonomy, commitment, human and social qualities, thanks to the external feedback from their peers and supervised debriefings. This process supports the satisfaction of all with respect to a common objective embodied by accepted and shared assessments.

DOI: 10.4018/978-1-6684-3537-3.ch001

INTRODUCTION

The European Association for Quality Assurance in Higher Education (AISBL) defines the European Standards and Guidelines for the learning performance of the training offer in Higher Education (ENQA, 2009). In compliance with the EU strategy "Europe 2020" and University Lifelong Learning accepted definition (Davies, 2007), the goal is to ensure the competences for the European citizen that support employability and mobility for socially integrated citizens. Thus, EU supports innovation and knowledge and a high level of employment partly based on digital evolution and lifelong skills development. The "future works" skills to be developed contribute to the autonomy of knowledge acquisition and the ability to use it to pursue specific goals and critical thinking. These are defined by Davies et al. (2011) as metacognitive abilities, collective and social intelligence, capability for virtual collaboration, computational thinking, cognitive load management and design mindset. The operational performance of HE Institutions (HEIs) requires a Community of Practice (CoP): a professional community of experts and partners for a better understanding of societal needs and working cultures. CoP supports an evolving and innovative educational culture based on trust, confidence, cross-boundary and collegial support (Trust & Horrock, 2019; Wenger, 2020). This professional learning network is regarded in a meso position with respect to education policies and training for relevance, flexibility, collaboration, support and scaffolding (Carpenter et al., 2021; Dille & Røkenes, 2021). The integration of digital technology should be seen as a means for facilitating work and learning. The assessment must be aligned with the chosen curriculum and pedagogy. In this framework, Work Integrated Learning (such as Continuous Vocational Training (CVT) and apprenticeship (Initial Vocational Training, IVT)) sounds like a key solution that merges learning at the university and learning in the company (Nuninger & Châtelet, 2020): work experience and active pedagogy support the personal reflection to enhance the learning ability. The aim is to support the commitment of all for knowledge ownership and to target professional skills in a specific field of expertise for the work. But the goal is also to gain in learning autonomy, in problem-solving skills and in social and collective intelligence (Goleman, 2007; Johnson, 2011). The chosen pedagogy must integrate core competences, the design of activities and situations, and support the reflexive learning to make such situations formative. Thus, it requires a formative assessment before final summative evaluation for a diploma.

In the following, the background focuses on formative activities and peer review to support learning performance, focusing on the concerns for our field of intervention. Then, in the framework of blended-oriented courses with collective projects, a 4-step gradual process of evaluation called SCPR for Self and Cross Peer Review is presented. The case study justifies motivation and improvements based on data processed between 2019 and 2022 with three groups enrolled in three different training paths of an engineering school. The satisfaction surveys related to the Teaching Units (TUs) show the relevance of SCPR, but also stress the concerns with today's generations. Finally, the conclusion brings out the key levers and perspectives of our solution that gives understanding and trust, develops positive criticism and supports the learning with the essential role of the trainer-mentor.

BACKGROUNDS

This chapter considers the Chartered Engineer training designed from a Coach-Leader-Manager professional skill-oriented repository. The underlying competences enable the individual to interact with the other parties for a shared purpose each day and in a disrupted context. This refers to the three categories proposed by Mintzberg (Chareanpunsirikul & Wood, 2002): interpersonal role (personal effectiveness to cope with challenges); information role (analysis and realization as an active observer); decision-making role (influence). In that respect, the training integrates professional situations such as internships, work placement or practical lessons to develop the professional style. This motivates the choice of an active pedagogy to reinforce reflective learning on the experience and the integration of peer assessment as a means to improve reflexive learning during projects, then learning performance. The challenge is to engage learners in the chosen pedagogy and facilitate their understanding of the learning outcomes for greater sustainability and rigorous assessment of competencies.

Learning Performance and Formative Activities

Operational performance based on Houssaye's pedagogical triangle (Bonicoli, 2008) is a balance between the relevance of the targeted learning outcomes, the effectiveness of the pedagogical resources mobilized and the effort expected from the learner to be recognized as competent. Formative learning activities support the personal evolution along the cone of learning experience by Dale (Lee & Reeves, 2007): from surface level of knowledge up to deep-learning characterized by the ability to act in new situations and transfer expertise. In this way, a high level of efficiency (actions/results), efficacy (results/objectives) and relevance (means/aim) are achieved (see Figure 1).

Figure 1. Triangle of operational performance of learning enriched by the learning pyramid (center) with pedagogical levers indicated (circles)

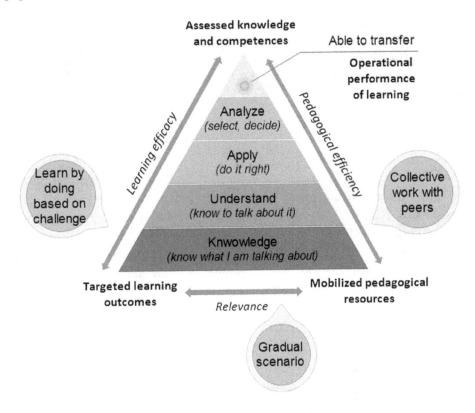

For aspiring professionals, this formative perspective targets learning and management capabilities for relevant behaviors in learning organizations. They are related to personal efficacy, leadership commitment, strategic intent, shared vision, systemic thinking, openness and creativity, team building and learning, and knowledge transfer (Wiklund & Wiklund, 2002; Jerez-Gómez et al., 2005). The pedagogical approach is therefore rooted in the following models recalled by Nuninger & Châtelet (2016):

- the **systemic recursive learning loop models** to acquire and reflect on the experience to correct, adapt, and transfer;
- **Kolb's dynamic learning circle** that supports the future professional style of learners through situational repetition seen as continuously improving learning (Kolb & Kolb, 2005; Raelin, 2008);
- and **the 8 Learning Events Model** of Leclercq & Poumay (2008) that focuses on meta-recognition to achieve the learning process.

Involvement in the training and active behavior are expected from the learners in reciprocal interaction with their peers and the teacher-trainer who is no longer the sole holder of knowledge. As shown in Figure 2, situated learning activities start with events (challenges) that incent the learner's perception. To make the activity formative, the issue of guidance and peer review are to encourage the motivational dynamic process (Viau, 2009): feedback and debriefings enhance the learners' development (Schein, 2013; Stone & Heen, 2014).

Figure 2. Motivational dynamic process during situated learning enriched by dialogic feedback to improve cognitive learning

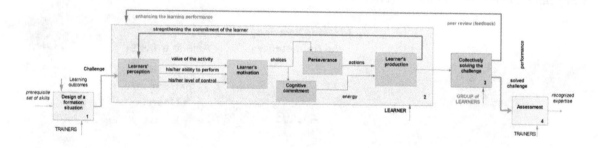

"*Learning by doing*" gives the individual the opportunity to learn to cope with their own difficulties and at their own pace while being supported by the collective commitment of the group and the trainer who guides and controls (Grzega, 2007). Confronting points of view require arguing and proving based on the experience observed and conceptualization: a reflexive ability useful for the individual to face complexity and uncertainties (Cendon, 2016). This active pedagogy focuses on the linkages beyond fragmented knowledge to develop analytical skills, problem-solving and intercultural skills. In this way, the activity becomes formative (Nuninger & Châtelet, 2020).

Learning Assessments and Mode of Evaluation

Gradual activities of increasing level, complemented by evaluation instructions (targeted assessment modes defined in the key terms), give momentum to the Kolb's dynamic learning circle for the individual and for the group. As drawn in Figure 3, **self-evaluation** (SE), **cross assessment** (CA) and **peers review** (PR) are levers to strengthen the experience-based learning process at each step: bringing questioning, dialogic feedback (Hattie & Timperley, 2007) and debriefing with a trainer-facilitator. In connection with the learning outcomes and the results of the activities, training in assessment is also a formative activity (Bloxham & Body, 2007). The challenge (individual and group learning situation) and the assessment instructions (process and learning outcomes) make the learner become aware of his own responsibility for the success of the collective goal and for the evolution of his/her professional skills. First, because SE is task-specific (feed up) and somehow summative, it is regarded as a self-regulated process of learning (Andrade, 2009). Second, with the discovery of his/her new autonomy (feed forward) incented by dialogic feedback during CA (Ajjawi et al., 2017). Third, in the assumption of a personal effort of reflexive learning, PR (Anderson et al., 2019) confronts learners with an external third party and engages the recognition of their growing transferable professional skills (collaboration, active listening, critical assessment...).

Figure 3. Kolb's dynamic learning circle enriched with gradual assessment instructions

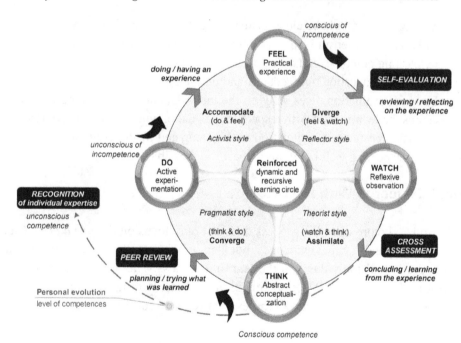

Deviations are due to the level of maturity and the interpersonal influences that can affect trusting relationships. Feedback and debriefings allow a measure in real-time to propose remedial activities and enrichment by building the learning regulation loop to comply with the learning outcomes specification. The active pedagogy is an efficient way to comply with competency referential, time-reduction constraints and the heterogeneous prior knowledge in larger groups (Roegiers, 2012). PR consolidates the knowledge and allows skill recognition through the results and the way to reach them, i.e., the observation of behaviors while working cooperatively for a shared production in teams (Biggs, 2003). PR supports formative learning and is part of the training experience and professional practices.

Peer review Built on Professional Practices

As far as research work is considered, peer-review (PR) is an assessment process to validate proposed scientific work by confronting argued opinions of a selected group of recognized experts in the field. The aim is scientific work quality based on a set of criteria related to: scientific approach and results, scope and limits, and considered publication standards. PR must lead to a shared and accepted compromise, with feedback to the authors. Despite the community concerns with respect to the level of recognized expertise, equity for researchers' careers and dissemination of results, the dialogue established within the community provides an opportunity to improve the knowledge and expertise in the field of research, confronting one's work with one's peers (Leduc & Molinié, 2020). In this way, PR is formative and values the final output. The underlying requirements are ethics and scientific rigor, values and economic or professional independence, thus transparency of criteria and of the peer decision in addition to profitable returns in their form and contents for progress. The same issue applies to the process of assessing learning outcomes by the students because one aim is to develop a professional behavior that supports the future professional style:

- first, the framing of PR should be clear (criteria, organization and functioning) to allow the group adhesion and confidence, ensure ethics and limit deviations, and enhance learning commitment;
- second, the learning outcomes must be developed through situational activities that become formative by motivating questioning, feedback and debriefing;
- third, as the act of evaluation gives value to the individual and is a learning experience in itself, the process must be incremental with respect to the goal of being a recognized and trusted expert;
- fourth, supervision ensures self-regulation in the group and by the group to support the evolution of individuals, respecting well-being in the best way possible.

Pedagogical Concerns With Peer Review

A robust, unbiased and more open PR process does not only focus on the *production* (i.e., the result of the work) which is one of factual evidences, but also on the way this *"masterpiece"* was produced collectively, integrating all individuals in the learning process. The underlying requirement covers three areas (Mottier Lopez et al., 2021): organization and tool, criteria and goal, and temporal steps. As for research work, giving credibility to the evaluation, self-confidence and true self-positioning require (Meissonier, 2017):

- observations and interactions with positive criticism;
- correction and progress with debriefing for a shared compromise at the time of skill evaluation.

As invested actors taking part in the evaluation, learners are expected to better identify learning expectations and measure their personal journey; changing their perception and conception with respect to the field of the Teaching Unit (TU) and the summative assessment. Thus, they can accept final evaluation in a more profitable way. Three assumptions motivate (Roy & Michaud, 2018; Girardet & Mottier Lopez, 2020):

- **learn by assessing** in the logical continuity of learning by doing;

- **gradual assessment activities** to support the learning loop and personal development; starting with self-evaluation (Legendre, 2005; Morrissette, 2010), then peer review (Topping, 2009);
- **benefits of reflexive experience** of a supervised committed learning group.

The decided PR process is locally dependent (forms and assessment instructions, steps and recursive phases) with respect to time constraint, targeted level of competences, prerequisites for the learning outcomes and maturity of the group. PR must lead to a reliable compromise on the levels of expertise. For reliability, it requests a personal experience of assessing, clarified rules with measurable criteria to make the expectations explicit but not necessarily exhaustive, then gives sufficient time to allow change based on fair and relevant feedback (Thomas et al., 2011). As a transformational leader, the trainer acts as a tutor-coach and a mentor who copes with the learners' resistance to change due to their personal conceptions and schemes, beliefs and values and learning strategy (Dembo & Seli, 2004). In this learning alliance between mentor and *protégé* as named by Alderfer (2014), roles change as the relationship evolves:

- first, the trainer-tutor is the one who initiates the process, acting as the referent who guides, gives advice, and demonstrates to motivate commitment;
- second, the trainer-coach regulates and supports, maintaining the learning momentum despite the learners' conflictual development;
- third, the trainer-mentor stabilizes the new balanced relationship as a newly recognized expert by learners, acting in a reciprocity manner.

Issues deal with well-being, assessment reliability and implementation. Indeed, the learner may feel uncomfortable and destabilized because of the questioning of their conception, especially of their reasoning patterns which may challenge their understanding. They may also fear receiving criticism, especially from peers whom they also judge. The modalities should be set rigorously to allow progression and confidence, but also transfer of expertise in the group.

Ethical and Professional Concerns

Supervision and self-regulation support factual judgment using explained criteria joint grids and mitigate possible collusive evaluations. The goal is to avoid the so-called free riders in the learning group who hinder the members but also participate in their own failure at final examination. On the contrary, a thorough PR process will prepare learners for success. Beyond the competition by the challenge which can shatter group building and cohesion, the comparison between individuals only makes sense to give them concerns about their behavior and learning strategy. By giving meaning, the involvement is on the learning effort and no longer on avoidance. The trainer-facilitator (see key terms) must establish a climate of trust in the group, helping auto-regulation without forgetting to provide the necessary knowledge and modus operandi. As the person in charge of knowledge and grading. They must accept to be questioned and to do so, they must motivate dialogue and argumentation. The aim is to make every learner in the group responsible for their personal evolution, but also in the achievement of the shared and validated production. Thus, the usual roles are redefined, changing the behavior in the light of collective intelligence. The group is given a free area of decision-making. It is necessary to train oneself to self-evaluation to better evaluate others; limiting judgment and allowing exchange upon the selected criteria for new perspectives (Sadler, 2010). The final individual test (for the diploma) will conclude on the sustainability of knowledge provided that the evaluation is aligned. The process influences the personal stance, or at least challenges it with concerns about assessment objectivity, independence but also personal data. The preventive actions that can be set up deal with:

- **a discovery phase** in a reassuring framework (to understand the task);
- **collaboration** rather than cooperation and internal competition;
- **transparency and clarity** of assessment criteria (relevant and easy to use);
- **trust, respect and fidelity** to the instructions which does not prohibit relational benevolence but maintains ethics and factual observations (Durand & Chouinard, 2012);
- **support of the change**.

The literature gives contrary points of view with respect to anonymity (of the person assessed and of the evaluator) in terms of instructional approach, purpose and social interaction that might lead to conflicts or avoidance. Anonymity seems appropriate in the case of a focus on invariable and context-independent results. On the contrary, the results of the project are expected to be innovative, without a priori solution, and to use a personal style developed by applying concepts and methods gradually. In this case, in situ observation, without anonymity, is a key to factually assessing personal expertise. More relevant, the evaluation is transparent and enriched by the differences of practices observed. This is our choice for learners enrolled in Chartered Engineer training who should develop positive criticism as future key actors in society, acting with values and ethics as reminded in the French Engineer Charter of Ethics (IESF, 2001). They must be able to contradict, explain and prove their results and competences for recognition in a collective environment. Obviously, the anonymity choice is context dependent based on a ratio of advantages to disadvantages that can vary due to jeopardy and the loss of learning and assessment quality.

GRADUAL SCENARIO TO ENHANCE COMMITMENT IN PEER REVIEW

Context of Intervention and Pedagogy

Our accredited engineering courses are three years in length and include on-the-job experience each year. They cover nine major industry areas. The curriculum is broken down into TUs scheduled as a series of lectures, tutorials and practical lessons throughout two semesters per year. Appendix 1 (see table 11) summarizes our fields of intervention for industrial production and food processing industry: computer programming and automation are two TUs that concern the three years of training and the three paths to the degree. The main learning outcomes are summarized in the field of these TUs of overlapping skills (see Figure 4) as *"the ability to understand and use problem-solving methods in order to define specifications and exchange with experts in the fields, then sign for works while being aware of constraints, risks and perspectives"*.

The standard pedagogical choice is that of a hybrid blended-oriented course. Whatever the group and TU, the course targets the flipped classroom and benefits from digital elements among which a Digital Support for Guided Self-Learning by Nuninger (2017) called ONAAG (see keywords). The scenario proposes learning activities during face-to-face lessons or at distance with individual and collective work, synchronous or not. The design of the activities aims at making the students work and evolve together:

Figure 4. Transversal and basic set of skills for the groups and TUs in the curriculum

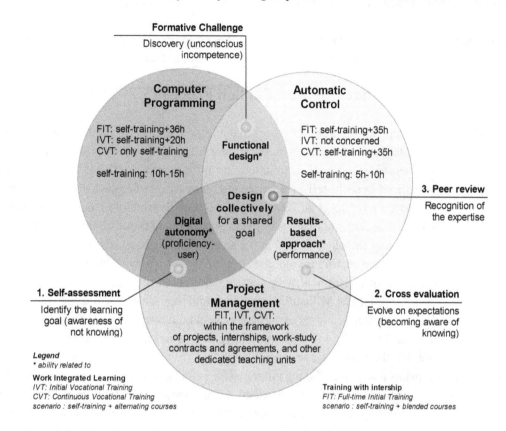

preparatory work, group cohesion, and collaborative project. The series choice depends on the allotted time and groups (see Appendix 1). In general terms, a challenge is proposed to the group split in smaller teams. Each team has to solve a specific project problem during 50% of the TU time on average (up to 2 thirds including estimated personal work). Despite no explanation given to learners, the activity is set over four basic phases that could be synchronous or asynchronous:

- **phase 1**: self-training when necessary to give confidence;
- **phase 2**: personal work for a worthwhile interaction in the classroom and/or work in pairs to favor a cooperative output and consolidate achievements;
- **phase 3**: collaboratively produce a merged solution for the shared goal based on the team's internally validated batch proposals and questioning;
- **phase 4**: externally confront and defend the consensus solution to the peers and the trainer for recognition.

Motivated by the generational changes during blended course previous experiences, authors sum up their decided hybrid method of mutual assessment under the acronym **SCPR** for **Self and Cross Peer Review process** to achieve the 3-goals in Chartered Engineer Training:

- **deep-learning** by giving meaning with self-evaluation (Thomas et al, 2011);

- **trust and empowerment** with intragroup cross feedback to motivate action and learning (Orsmond et al., 2000);
- **self-respect, knowledge ownership and competences** through reflexive learning based on a framed peer review to guarantee a relevant, reliable and fair evaluation (Fernandez, 2015).

Generational Changes Affect the Non-Explicit Process

The students' motivation depends on personal issues that compete in time and space. This is especially true for the demanding integrative alternation in vocational training. In our previous experiences, the learning process led learners to reflect on their practices, as did peer review, even if they were not aware of it or if it was not formalized as such: self-evaluation and comparison of one's level in the team or the group was simply a way to learn (Elliot et al, 2005). This is especially true for Gen X (born 1966-1977) at the acme of their professional career (a major part in the population of the community of trainers today and of expert managers; adding the older Gen Y at the start of their career). Even though there are no factual evidences of the main reason, things changed about ten years ago with increasing digitalization, less allocated time, evolution of recruitment with new generations of different needs, prerequisite and levels of knowledge (see Table 1). The Millennials (internet) and the Gen Z (mobile and social network) who make up the bulk of our group today, expect efficiency and quick expertise with turnkey solutions (i.e., the result and how to do it). They assume they have access to knowledge at any time and from anywhere with internet, but they are less aware and concerned with the selection and the validation of the information that remains a key issue for the citizen. This is an issue for engineers who must be able to apply understood and validated approaches in a new environment, then improve and innovate such methods for the goal considering unexpected issues. Today, the surprising trend observed among the youngest seems to be a wish and expectation to be guided by the hand through the learning process, with an apparent dependence or lack of effort. They also need incentive for action as we realized it during the COVID-19 crisis and Emergency Remote Teaching (ERT) on line during 2019/2020 and 2020/2021 (see Appendix 3). The trainer's challenge remains to drive the change with heterogeneous groups for a mutual understanding of the goal and collective intelligence.

Self and Cross Peer Review Process (SCPR)

Our proposal results from adaptations to better integrate the sharing of the evaluation task considered also as a means of learning. The strategy makes it possible to overcome misunderstandings and rejections and to avoid the underlying conflicts between peers; a phenomenon of higher incidence in vocational groups when learners are under great pressure at work and not able to manage the three lives (in the company, at school and in their personal life). From our experience and Roy et al. (2018), we identify in the following Figure 5 the major targeted goals of the SCPR process. For the trainer, it is a way to optimize the allotted time and the follow-up by sharing of the assessment with the learners for new perspectives that change habits. The expected benefits for the learners lie in the support from the group that facilitates the change of role and behavior based on a positive view of evaluation and satisfaction.

The process designed in Figure 6 is a new and improved proposal resulting from the merging of our two previous pedagogical scenarios. The first scenario introduced self-assessment (SE) and cross-assessment (CA) in pairs and teams, and between teams in the group, but without making an explicit peer review (PR), whereas the second one was a more formal implementation of PR and its expectations. The SCPR

Table 1. Main drivers of commitment encountered in our groups according to the definitions of generations for Europe (Thielfoldt & Scheef, 2004; Nuninger & Châtelet, 2020); the bias is the overlap of generations in our groups with Millennials covering the period 1977-1998 (*period and social markers may differ depending on part of the world)

Generation	Period*	Today enrolled in	Characterization	Lever for commitment
Xennials	1977-1983	CVT	More optimistic than the Gen X but less confident than Gen Y	Support confidence, provide guidance
Gen Y	1979-1995	CVT and apprentices (IVT)	Immediacy of needs, will to participate, interconnected, self-confidence, inventive and optimistic, life project and personal development, tolerant of differences, working less and better in opposition to previous generation (all is due)	Propose short and challenging activities in groups, give freedom to organize, support the questioning
Gen Z Gen C	>1995	IVT and Initial Training	Adopt IT technology, connected and rapid, share and collaborate in their group, network of friends, balance in life (individualism), entrepreneurship and hedonism, looking for employability and recognition, multiplying life experiences, rewrite style, killer lifestyle, irrelevance of institutions	Fully integrate digital technology into activities as a means of resources and interactions, accept less control, provide reinforced positive feedback when the need is expressed, with clear answers

provides a framework for practice through progressive assessment training with feedback to overcome individual barriers to cross-evaluation. It provides assessment tools for evidence-based decision making based on learners' production and measurable criteria. Our assessment criteria grid is based on the following items to facilitate common and shared definitions:

- **Identification** of evaluator and evaluated group;
- **Criteria set** with definitions (quality of deliverable, learning outcomes by topic and transversal skills like IT abilities and project management when it applies) with associated scales of skill level to tick that depends on scoring requirement for the group;

Figure 5. Targeted goals for the trainers and the learners with SCPR process

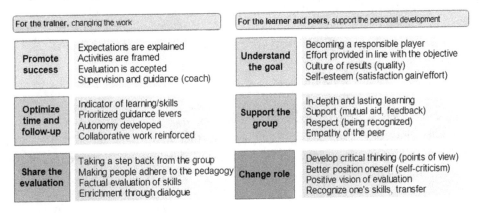

Figure 6. Self and cross peer review process

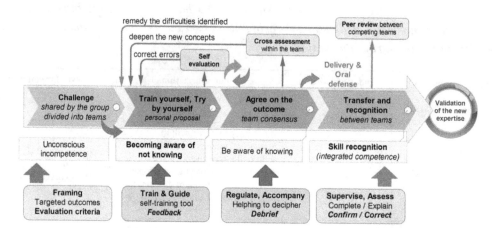

- **Collective and personal review** on results and progress with points for improvements;
- **Final decision** or mark with a summary of areas for improvement to those being evaluated.

Throughout this 4-step process, learners individually start and end a Hero's Journey from the Known towards the Unknown as illustrated in Table 2 for motivation and personal evolution (Campbell, 2008; Scharmer, 2009), evolving between consciousness and unconsciousness of their level of incompetence or competence as defined by Maslow:

- **discover** a challenge with prior analysis;
- **learn by trying** to solve the problem through questioning (SE);
- **receive positive feedback and interact** in their team in an improving learning loop based on cross social regulation (CA);
- **confront during debriefing and take a step back**, strengthening the reflexive learning loop which transforms and give recognition with external parties to their teams (PR).

The process provides the group with a clear and shared vision of the agreed-upon efforts, as well as task orientation for quality results. This covers the results of the project that the group must characterize and qualify, and the targeted expertise in the field. The guidance encourages autonomy and empowerment, while the supervision of the trainer-mentor provides the conditions for safe involvement and creativity. The recognition of the individuals in the group, transversal interactions through networking, responsibility, trust and adjustments are levers to learning efficiency impacted by the level on which team members interact.

The SCPR process generates several outputs:

- **the project production:** this factual result values the work of the group but is not sufficient to prove the individual competence though it gathers together all the material produced and validated;
- **a collective assessment and personal review on the experience** give awareness of the learning journey, stressing on the personal development and perspective;

Table 2. Hero's Journey and U-theory of change is supported by the SPCR process

SCPR process	Hero's Journey	Theory U
Challenge	*The ordinary world* (the known) 1. Call to adventure versus refusal of the call	*Protocols* for the agreement to the values, listen and observe
Learn and produce with self-evaluation in an area of freedom	2. Help by the mentor *Crossing the threshold to the new world* (the unknown) 3. Resistance and commitment	*Co-initiate* with full autonomy: feeling and testing, adapting
Improve with internal cross evaluation, assistance and reduce autonomy	4. The road of trials with challenge and temptations 5. The revelation *The return journeys.* 6. Transformation (new attitudes)	*Controversy* to confront and debate in an offset position, exchanging to explain, the "*presencing*" (presence and sensing) for action intention and change
Defend with external peer review for transfer	7. Atonement (the ultimate boon) 8. Starting a new journey, mastering the 2 worlds for freedom to live	*Generative conversation* (external position) for co-creation, integrating complementary future values for collective intelligence

- **a set of skills developed** during the process and recognized by the peers through defense and debriefings for a clear view of the level of expertise.

This set of deliverables forms are the materials for the trainer to validate the observed evolution and give the final mark. The final examination is the conclusion that confirms the sustainable knowledge and expertise or not. Throughout the process, learners are expected to make the difference between the project result, their personal approach to solve the issue and their decided choice in the collective framework.

EXPERIMENTATION WITH THREE TRAINING COURSES

Group characterization

The aim of this section is to illustrate and compare the effect of the SCPR changes on the learning of three different training promotions enrolled in different years of the engineering training pathway since 2019:

- average of 48 **full-time students enrolled in initial training** (FIT) entering the training 1st year (average 20 yrs in [19, 24]);
- **average of 20 apprentices in Initial Vocational Training** (IVT) in their second year (average 21 yrs on the periods);
- **average of 11 learners in Continuous Vocational Training** (CVT) with decreasing number, average and age limits (15 in 2019 of 36 yrs in [29,49] to 10 learners in 2021 of 32 yrs in [26, 38]).

For each group, the common framework is a standard blended-oriented scenario that integrates collective projects (different subjects) in the field of the TUs with PR in 2019 and SCPR in 2021. Project teams are of 6 to 12 students. Appendix 1 presents the groups characterization with scores in final examinations and rate of respondents to several satisfaction surveys made during the training to collect qualitative data (see Appendix 2). In 2019 and in 2020, pair programming was done online for all to avoid the unthinkable ubiquity of hybrid sessions with half part of the FIT group in the classroom and the other online. The Visio-conference tool favors the sharing of display, but puts in jeopardy the students with already low basics or without good remote access. The trainer provided more feedback, but mainly to the students who interacted and expressed themselves during sessions. This is not the case in 2021/2022 (back to normal). Less relevant data from the academic year 2020/2021 are not considered due to the consequences of COVID-19 crisis and Emergency Remote Teaching (see Appendix 3). Note that due to the small number in vocational groups or number of respondents, findings could be limited to the intervention setting.

New Trends With the Younger Millennials

Figure 7 shows the expressed previous experience in self-evaluation (SE), cross-assessment (CA) and peer review (PR) of the groups in 2019 and 2021 at the start of the TUs. In 2019, all groups seem to have the same previous experience whatever the kind of assessment (over 50%) and to be aware of SE (over 75%). The assumption is that they do not make a clear distinction between CA made in their team and PR made between competitive teams who had not worked all together. The distribution changes in 2021 but the survey better introduces each kind of evaluation. In 2021, the differences with the CVT group (older) are more pronounced. As employees in their last year of training, they are more used to working together for a goal and debating on their results, and therefore to CA. Their longer prior work experience in a technical position and their willingness to enter training explain that they were already aware of evaluating others (PR), rather than personal evaluation (SE). This is less obvious for young people, who are nevertheless, aware of cooperating (CA). Their reported low SE experience is a concern due to the impact of COVID-19 crisis (lockdowns and ERT), but it indicates a change in learning autonomy and ability. Their ability to reflect on their experience challenges personal development according to their priority goals (project and grade or learning outcomes) and might lead to jeopardy in the process of learning.

Quite unexpectedly, pre-course surveys show that the great majority of the audience (>70%), whatever the group and generation, prefers lectures followed by corrected exercises in order to learn. As shown in Figure 8, this trend remains true for vocational training groups. Only a few ones declare a more active behavior and a desire for accompaniment (<20% whatever the year). This is more consistent with the chosen active pedagogy and expected learning behavior. The elder learners (CVT) have always been observed as wanting interaction and active collaboration; but the average age decreases. The need for direct guiding by the trainer in the classroom is more present. This evolution is at odds with competence-based training specification and barriers due to the level of learning autonomy required for active pedagogy. The copycat attitude may be caused by gathering results with a false sense of control and knowledge, as well as the fact of not being guided but passively assisted without understanding for further use.

Groups in 2019 are nonetheless involved in the classroom and in teamwork (see Figure 9): not hesitating to ask and trying to find solutions, but with a trend to cooperate (a distribution of tasks between individuals that limits conscious interactions) rather than collaborate for higher transfer of expertise (with conscious interactions and communication for the joint objective). The risk is a final failure. A lack of step back on learning and 3-lives management issues may explain the higher rate in CVT. These are constant concerns for the teaching style and PR supervision. The lower number in CVT and lower number of respondents in IVT and FIT limit deeper comparison even if FIT respondents are 3 more numerous.

Figure 7. Previous experience between groups in 2019 and 2021 (no data for 2020)

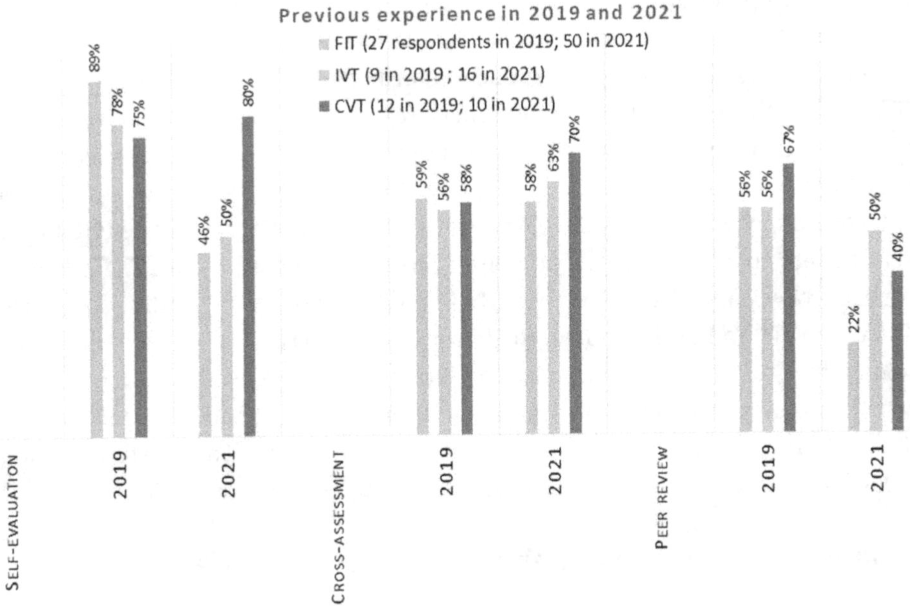

Previous experience in 2019 and 2021
- FIT (27 respondents in 2019; 50 in 2021)
- IVT (9 in 2019 ; 16 in 2021)
- CVT (12 in 2019; 10 in 2021)

Figure 8. Learning style declared at the start of the TU in 2019 and 2021

		FIT		IVT		CVT	
	number of respondents	27	50	9	16	12	10
	I prefer to learn (declared at the begining of the TU)	2019	2021	2019	2021	2019	2021
1 *(more passive)*	I prefer to learn by having a lecture, then solving exercises (tutorials), and doing practical lessons	89%	92%	89%	88%	75%	70%
2 *(more active behaviour)*	I prefer to learn from documents read before the lesson and the speaker's answers to questions from the class	-	-	11%	6%	8,33%	20%
3 *(prefer accompaniment)*	I prefer to be guided and to learn by completing exercises prepared with the group and as part of group projects	11%	8%	-	-	16,67%	10%

Students Main Feedback With Respect to Assessments

Despite the levers activated by the SCPR in 2021, obstacles remain, sometimes resulting in rejection.

Figure 9. Commitment and behavior declared at the end of the teaching unit

At the end of the university year		FIT		IVT		CVT	
	number of respondents	27	29	9	not asked	12	8
Commitment in the classroom		2019	2021	2019	2021	2019	2021
1	I always try to ask my questions to understand	30%	10%	44%		25%	13%
2	I try to solve the exercises and exchange with my colleagues	55%	83%	56%		75%	88%
3	I prefer to listen to others than to learn	11%	7%	-		-	0%
4	I try to make pass the time	4%	0%	-		-	0%
Personal behavior in collective work		2019	2022	2019	2021	2019	2022
1	I prefer to impose my point of view	4%	0%	0%		-	0%
2	I like to divide the tasks according to what we know how to do	19%	38%	56%		50%	13%
3	I prefer that we decide together and that we look for solutions	70%	62%	33%		50%	88%
4	I am used to working alone	7%	0%	11%		-	0%

Surprisingly, post-activity surveys show that the SCPR tends to reinforce the perceived difficulty felt in assessing the others except for the older students who have more confidence in assessing themselves or the others (see Figure 10). Direct observations in class with a closer guidance of the group during alternation (which is not the case for FIT) show a higher maturity due to work experience, age difference and commitment, then the role of the facilitator who supervises. A larger number of respondents have a more positive opinion in 2021 than in 2019 when PR was not framed by the SCPR. This is more obvious for the CVT group. For the youngest (FIT), the result is that SE is felt to be less motivating. Anonymization of personal data to comply with the General Data Protection Regulation in Europe (GDPR) and the lack of data prevent further conclusion for the youngest. First, the apprentices in IVT lacked commitment in the assessment process: they feel PR is easy (83%) but have no interest in the process and express a negative opinion (see Figure 11). Second, for the FIT group, the bias is partly due to the practical lessons always conducted by two different trainers (i.e., two professional styles that differ in 2019 and 2021) combined with imposed groups constituted by level in 2021 (i.e., not heterogeneous but with students with a low level of pre-requisites or with greater learning autonomy). Then, external disruptions over the period (social activities and collective projects thought to be priorities in 2021).

SCPR Challenges Students on Their Behavior and Beliefs

The SCPR allows for greater awareness of personal knowledge and expertise, but it also creates a fissure that can drive learning or hinder it if poorly accompanied. Indeed, open-ended questions reveal the fear of judgment from others, the lack of objectivity, then the reluctance of some to contradict the majority, and being identified with more or fewer skills. Goodwill and social skills with regard to the powers present in the group are highlighted by the following quotes in 2019: "*Evaluation belongs to the trainer*"; "*the judgment of peers is false*". Although we cannot generalize, these findings motivated a graduation of the assessment instruction. Such comments also remain in 2021 with SCPR, highlighting the time needed to manage the evaluation process with a facilitator and the necessary time to draw conclusions from the evaluation with the groups, deciphering positive aspects and points of improvement for each.

Table 3 and Figure 12 illustrate the mixed feelings and reveal unresolved conflicts in the groups. For instance, in 2019, apprentices who responded (almost half the group) find that their peers do not evaluate objectively. This is also the opinion of FIT and CVT but to a lesser extent whatever the year. These groups also identify positive aspects. The overall population asserted they had an active role (>6 on 1-to-10 level scale) except some who stayed back. The majority finds the grid of criteria useful. The grids of criteria differ and were modified in 2021. The trainers' observations show that the modified grid for the FIT is too complex and should be simplified so as not to discourage during SE. In all groups, some students still find that the evaluation is the trainer's job. Thus, the trainer's role is to establish a climate of trust for beneficial exchanges that can lead to an accepted compromise. Listening, empathy and commitment help build the group and are everyone's business.

Students' Concerns After Team Projects Incorporating PR

Figure 13 summarizes the most selected of the five proposed criteria in order of importance to respondent group members. In 2019, for vocational groups, the "*final score*" still remains the priority because of consequences of a not validated academic path upon their professional contract despite the worthwhile and expected feedback. With the new standard SCPR in 2021, whatever the group, the first selected

Figure 10. Difficulty felt in 2019 and 2021 in relation to the kind of assessment activity

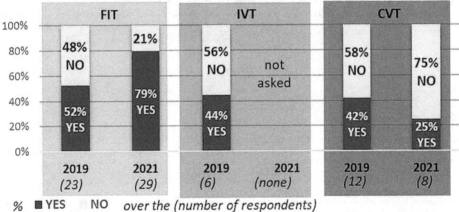

criterion is the "*personal understanding rather than marking*", then "*the personal feedback from the trainer*" and finally, the mark/grade explained. This tends to prove that the SCPR reinforces adhesion to the chosen pedagogy ("*learn by doing*") and emphasizes personal growth rather than grades.

Mixed Feelings Expressed by Students

For FIT (larger group of respondents), only limited criticisms are expressed in 2019/2020 mainly due to dissatisfaction with the personal level achieved. The apprentices (IVT) focus on the lack of time to finish projects the way they expected. Table 4 gives the surprising rejection quotes by the small CVT group (50% of the respondents) despite the fact that 25% of them engage in active behavior. Answers to open-ended questions reveal low understanding of the goal and low well-being with respect to the active pedagogy and in their team. Based on direct observations, concerns are about professional behaviors, learning autonomy after 3 years of training, and social intelligence.

In 2021, the apprentices (IVT) expressed the same type of rejection despite the return to face-to-face classes (no ERT for this group). The observed overall commitment of apprentices is low. At the start of

Figure 11. Impact of peer review process on the motivation and valorization of students in a group

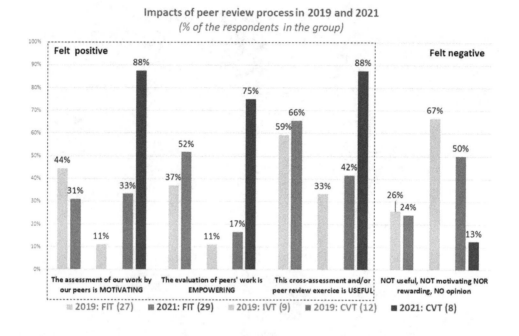

Table 3. Selected quotes to illustrate the mixed feeling about peer review in 2019

Group	Quote
FIT	I didn't find peer review very helpful
IVT	Distorted feedback from colleagues for fear of conflict
CVT	Colleagues' views are not always critical (benevolent and "biased")
CVT	As much as group work is enriching, assessing others does not bring me anything; not feeling competent
CVT	Peer evaluation does not have much added value because the group as a whole is benevolent. Their level does not make them legitimate to carry out this task. We are in class to learn knowledge for ourselves.

Figure 12. Main feeling expressed after the peer review experience in 2019 and 2021

		At the end the activity	FIT		IVT		CVT	
		number of respondents	22	29	6		11	8
		Mix feeling with respect to peer review	2019	2021	2019	2021	2019	2021
negative feelings	1	I don't need to evaluate myself	5%	3,5%	0%	not asked	0%	12,5%
	2	Evaluating others generates conflicts between us	5%	7%	0%		18%	12,5%
	3	Others do not evaluate us objectively	18%	17%	67%		36%	25%
	4	It is the provider's job to evaluate, not ours	36%	38%	33%		27%	25%
positive ones	5	Other: peer review improves our learning, is interesting	36%	34,5%	0%		19%	25%

	Evaluation grid for PR (2019) and SCPR (2021)	2019	2021	2019	2021	2019	2021
	number of respondents	27	29	6	none	12	8
	The grid is useful for understanding expectations	4%	83%	0%	not asked	33%	100%

	Behavior in the group (>6 on 1-to-10 level scale)	2019	2021	2019	2021	2019	2021
	number of respondents	23	29	6	none	12	8
	Actively participated and accepted a fair share of the group's work	65%	83%	83%		92%	88%

Figure 13. Priority concerns after peer review (in 2019 and in 2021)

		FIT (2019)	IVT (2019)	CVT (2021)	FIT and CVT (2021) *after SCPR*
rank 1	The most important	Personal feedback	Grade explanation	Personal feedback	Personal understanding rather than note
rank 2	Very important	Grade explanation	Personal feedback	Final mark	Personal feedback
rank 3	Important	Collective debriefing	Final mark	Collective debriefing	Final mark / grade explanation
rank 4	Less important	Personal understanding rather than note	Collective debriefing	Grade explanation	Collective debriefing
rank 5	The least important	Final mark	Personal understanding rather than note	Personal understanding rather than note	(not relevant)

Legend: sorted according to the most cited at rank 1, 2 and 3…

5 proposals Final mark: the overall final score for the TU (out of 20 or Validated)

(to sort) Grade explanation: details given according to the grid of criteria (level of expertise)

Personal feedback: comments given from the trainer

Collective debriefings: information shared and argued during defense exchange with the group and corrections

Personal understanding than note: if I understood, the notation is not so important

the TU, 25% of the 90% of respondents admit no use of IT at all, even if the majority want to understand the IT environment (60%) and be able to exchange with developers (10.5%). It is also assumed that some apprentices are under work pressure. Thus, the trainer gave priority to work as it suited them, even if their effort-saving strategy was not appropriate. Finally, apprentices confessed that the expected output of the pair teams during the project was not as complicated as they thought. In the end, they felt the work was feasible (56%) and that they all learned something (94%). Tables 5 and 6 summarize the main feedbacks after the Rapid Application Development (RAD) project with 82% of positive versus 18% of negative (or neutral) comments based on 76% of the respondents (group size is 21).

An overview of all groups (58% of respondents of which 56% explained their replies) shows that 49% of the difficulties deal with criteria, their knowledge or understanding of the goal. Then, 29.6% put the focus on social and human relations; not adding the 14.8% who refer to the lack of objectivity and the issue of not anonymous assessment. Such rejections motivate explicit deliverable with criteria grid and a gradual training of assessment with SCPR.

Final Results With SCPR Experienced With CVT and FIT Groups in 2021/2022

At the end of the university year, these groups have experimented SCPR twice. The first semester was the opportunity to discover PR and develop new assessment skills and collaboration. SCPR starts with

Table 4. Some quote of rejections expressed in CVT groups in 2019

	Expressed rejection of Peer Review by CVT in 2019
1	I don't know if peer review is interesting or appropriate for the group. If so, no improvement to be made.
2	I did not feel that peer review made a great contribution to my work.
3	My level is not sufficient to make a reliable analysis of the work done by others.
4	I can't comment about peer review because I am too far from the subject.
5	Defense of project with peer review can be suppressed: I did not get any benefit from it for the project.
6	It is not my role to evaluate other learners, being a learner myself. Certifications are issued by companies that will have an impartial judgment.
7	I am against peer review

Table 5. Main positive feedback of apprentices IVT

ID	Positive quotes
1	I thought the project in peers too complicated but finally I made the link between outcomes
2	I found the pedagogical approach interesting, helping a step-by-step learning. I feel I progress even if we did not finish the project
3	At the beginning, I had trouble understanding the functions and how to start coding. As time went by, I had a better vision of the possibilities of programming and understand a little bit better.
4	I learnt a lot
5	I consider having developed new competences
6	My logic of programming evolves positively
7	I am satisfied about the training received and will use the notions in my company

a first step of regular autonomous work with peers in a team; their productions receive feedback from the trainer before a defense of their improved proposal with the other teams during a tutorial or/and practical lesson (FIT). During the second semester, both groups reproduce the process in the framework of specific team projects. For the more autonomous CVT group, the activity ends with a final defense in front of the peers. For FIT group, the activity starts with pair programming as part of RAD method in a larger team: they have to self-assess their work, then validate the others' production (code review), and finally merge results (peer and mob programming) for a collective production to defend during PR.

Overview of the Evolutions

The intermediate surveys at the end of the first semester show that the great majority of members of these two groups express their satisfaction and consider that the set of collaborative activities should be kept (at distance or in the classroom): 72% and 81% of FIT and CVT respondents, respectively representing more than 67% and 60% of teams. All CVT learners agree that it helps them to understand better and deeper. Only one does not find it relevant after the activity. Note that 78% of FIT and 60% of CVT members had no previous experience of PR. Their replies to open-ended questions (all CVT respondents; 36% of FIT) show their interest in the pedagogical approach such as being active actors in the learning process and its evaluation, giving worthwhile comment for new perspectives.

CVT members emphasize on the faster progress thanks to the sharing of opinions and the heterogeneous skill levels, allowing correction and improvement. One member stresses on the "*motivation to evolve, avoiding blockage*". The main difficulty met lies in the availability of members for distance sessions all together. This confirms the different levels of involvement observed by the trainer during the course

Table 6. Main negative feedback of apprentices

ID	Negative or neutral
1	I feel technically very weak on programming, I felt completely drowned by the amount of information you were able to offer us.
2	I understand the code but I still see no interest in functional analysis as a programmer.
3	What slowed down the process was the lack of computer knowledge of my classmates and myself. Moreover, the fact that we were not invested at the same time "*complicated*" the thing.

of the various productions and returns. The final exam discredits the freeloaders in the groups. Indeed, of the 70% who validated after remediation (second attempt), 42% were at the lower level of expertise defined. On the contrary, 30% validated the higher level of expertise at their first attempt. At the end of the second semester, all validate at their first attempt with two levels identified (see Appendix 1).

Full time students (FIT) put the focus on the list of assessment criteria that helps. Even if it appears complex to use, members benefit from interaction that gives meaning. The assessment is felt to be more representative because it is done by the students, including those who have difficulties as well. Collective work is useful because it motivates being proactive for a better understanding. The main positive aspect is the sharing of views, which allows them to step back from the evaluation and see their progress better than they did before. The final examination is a way to confirm the appropriation of knowledge by FIT students. After the first semester with SCPR, the trend appears to be a decrease in standard deviation in the collective and individual scoring (see Appendix 1). It is not possible to conclude further for the second semester. The means values do not differ much over the 3 years despite the lower level observed at the beginning of the training, but the course organization changed. The guiding was different between FIT groups and other learning priorities have interfered and changed the involvement of some of the students: they mostly cooperate, oblivious of collaboration.

More Constructive Feedback

At the end of the first semester, the students (FIT) express difficulties with self-evaluation. A feeling mainly due to the fact that the practical project could not be finished because of a technical problem that could not be solved (2 teams out of 16). This focus on project output from younger students might lead to disappointment and frustration. For the CVT group, the rejection is illustrated by: "*(the project) is time consuming, and not an effective approach due to a too lower level in the field*". This reveals an awareness of personal skills on the part of professional adults, and an imbalance between the available time (despite a personal will) and the allocated training hours for integrated alternation. This is symptomatic of the 3-lives management during vocational training. The overall more positive feedback on the experience in 2021 compared to 2019 is illustrated in Tables 7 and 8 for both groups. Inspired by one learner in CVT, SCPR gives "*a different look (at results and expertise), thus a new vision (of the work and of the individuals)*". Indeed, instead of pretending not to be able to assess (not my role, not right level) and that it fails ethics due to conflicts or kindness like in 2019, the main comments point out positive aspects such as overall evaluation based on arguments (explicit and implicit), valorization of the work, recognition of the person, and the support of the peers.

STATEMENTS FOR A ROBUST SCPR

Students' suggestions for improvement

In 2019, the open-ended questions gave new perspectives for the PR, all intended to be integrated in the following SCPR dimensions (26%, 33% and 25% of proposals from FIT, IVT and CVT respondents respectively):

Table 7. Key comments of interest at the halfway point (67% of CVT respondents, and 17% of FIT)

Group	Quote at the end of the 1st semester
FIT	*I needed an additional session to verify my understanding.*
FIT	*I was able to benefit from the group, but I lacked personal work beforehand*
FIT	*Sharing with peers during assessment permits a cross support as in a collaborative team*
CVT	*The use of the software is not intuitive for me but I understand the main aspect. Evaluating the workload at the beginning was difficult, hence the delay in starting up.*
CVT	*The peer review was very good and useful. It is twice as positive: to quickly apprehend the new software and check the results proposed with the theory by the group.*
CVT	*The evolution passes by mixing the expertise in the group; without that the evolution is slower*
CVT	*This teaching method is new to me. The collective work at distance allowed us to share our knowledge but also to confront our disagreements. Despite the difficulties, we were able to provide quality work. The reversed pedagogy with the support of ONAAG is interesting and is a guide for the learning.*
CVT	*My level was very low at the start. The help of my colleague brought me towards a common goal, merging our solutions and correcting mistakes to understand and move forward together. At the end, I managed to bring my help and expertise after personal work. I really feel that I progressed a lot with a personal goal which is now feasible.*

- **organization** (31% of the proposals) with an earlier start for assessment training, smaller groups with heterogeneous prerequisites;
- **supervision** (31%) by the trainer with control on members' work, regulation of interaction in the group for the neutrality of internal debates, then personal feedback upstream of PR to support improved project outputs;
- **clarification of expectation** (23%) with explanation of PR goal and control of understanding of the assessment criteria;
- **scoring modality** (15%, from vocational groups) to give more importance to PR in the final mark of the TU with a confidentiality concern between groups;

This latter proposal denoted a lack of self-confidence and trust in the group in 2019.

In 2020/2021, despite conflicting situations and a lack of commitment (confessed by 13%) the apprentices show their positive step back on PR and help the identification of levers (see Table 9). Team and pair building (63%) is the main lever in order to mix different kinds of expertise, thus probably facilitating communication in the bigger teams (19%). For this audience, improving SCPR lies in a

Table 8. Main interesting feedback at the end of the 2nd semester for CVT and FIT

Group	Quote at the end of the 2nd semester
FIT	*This values involvement and participation in a way that is not based solely on results*
FIT	*SCPR allows you to be more interested in the work of others and take a step back.*
FIT	*Better understanding of the problem and sharing of knowledge*
CVT	*This is challenging.*
CVT	*A better knowledge of oneself and the work of others.*
CVT	*Validation and verification by peers allow for improvement*

Table 9. Underlying reasons that negatively affect peer programming based on the reply to open questions

Main reason	Relevant quote
Pair and team building (62.5%)	*I enjoyed sharing the lab sessions with my classmates, however the difference in level was far too obvious between us.*
Low communication in the group (18.8%)	*The group needed an additional session or lacked efficiency.* *I would say that it was the communication that held us back a bit.*
Insufficient personal commitment at the beginning (12.5%)	*What slowed down and caused concern in my group was myself (...) I could have participated much more in this project with a more consistent personal motivation. I realized this too late and spent more time catching up on my mistakes and limiting the damage than sharpening my skills in this subject.*
Deviation due to alternation (6%)	*One of the solutions would be for me to lengthen the practical session times and to bring the sessions closer together for a constant practice to assimilate.*

blocked week to maintain investment and meaning, avoiding the bias of long duration between sessions due to sandwich courses. Appendix 1 gives the scores for the TUs, showing larger standard deviations than in 2019 explained by two overlapping populations. A bias is due to pedagogical adaptations and the COVID-19 crisis.

In 2021, the new perspectives identified by the CVT for SCPR mostly focus on organization and final evaluation:

- **increase the time** dedicated to the project;
- **generalize the approach** from the beginning of the training;
- **integrate the PR mark** into the final score or make a collective final test instead of individual examination.

This last proposal questions the quality of the evaluation because of the difficulty of identifying individual expertise in the group. All the 12 proposals received from the 29 FIT respondents mainly focus on taking an extra time to better explain the issue of assessing the others and to give them more guidance. This points out a less facilitator role by one of the trainers involved in practical lessons, but also a lack of analytical skills, learning autonomy and other difficulties from some students (probably related to the effects of the COVID-19 crisis experienced when entering university). Indeed, two students show a lack of understanding of the role they had and one expressed rejection: "*Stop offering this teaching in our training!*". In one FIT group, some also criticize the lack of help from their more expert colleagues and the low commitment of others. But, on the overall point of view they consider that all were active and committed, analyzing all together and sharing expertise and solutions (72% of the respondents in CVT+FIT). Then, for 82% of the ones who express themselves (17 out of 37 respondents), the SCPR allows them to take a step back by exchanging with others and develop confidence. One student testifies to a real satisfaction for the collective intelligence: "*(the group had a) very good attitude. We helped each other out and worked for the time needed to get the job done right!*"

Main Challenges and Levers

The pedagogical aim is to motivate and give a learning rhythm, then to help learners realize their evolution, be satisfied and identify their personal area of progress. PR is context-dependent with a real time flexibility requirement. The SCPR is a more formalized timeline of gradual assessing activities integrated into collective activities to support and better control reflexive learning of groups with heterogeneous needs. The SCPR process implies the group and the individuals (holding together contradictions), gives sense (regulating conflicts) based on standards (shared criteria for factual measured indicators). The issue is to give the right synergy between steps to avoid consensus based on abstract evaluation summaries (Younès et al., 2020). SCPR requires overlapping knowledge and social intelligence, with relational dynamics to be supported. It is a more open approach in terms of dimensions such as time, transversality and value scale, explicit knowledge and implicit expertise. With a step back, the SCPR contributes to students' emancipation. The key levers are to generate the discrepancy in personal conceptions and the involvement in change, then the accompaniment for support. Based on free decision-making, the role of the facilitator is essential as it raises awareness of the heterogeneity of standards. Thus, SCPR could be a robust evaluation process if and only if a rigorous methodology:

- **drives the assessment approach** at each step (based on facts);
- **justifies the decisions** for ethics;
- **considers personal development** as a goal in itself (regardless of the gap between the current level of expertise and the previous one);
- and **does no harm**, tries to help and be helpful to the others.

In the framework of a diploma course with a final assessment at a given point in time, such an objective is sometimes delicate. SCPR initiates a never-ending personal process of transformation that questions and incents evolution. It invites ones to identify knowledge and skills thanks to: first, evaluate to understand; second, evaluate to appraise; third, evaluate to communicate; and finally, evaluate and learn (Mottier-Lopez et al., 2022). SCPR reveals the evolving interactions between the levels of confidence and competence; known as the Dunning-Kruger effect (Dunning et al., 2003): incompetent persons tend to overestimate their skill level and fail to recognize the competence of those who genuinely possess it, and also fail to realize their degree of incompetence; while the later underestimate themselves. Thus, if the training leads to a significant improvement in their competence, they will then be able to recognize and accept their previous shortcomings. SCPR is therefore a journey through situations and assessment methods that will lead to confidence and expertise consolidated by facts, confrontation and regulation.

Indicators for SCPR Deliverables

There are two sets of indicators: first, the ones to evaluate the project output with respect to quality (correct and relevant with respect to the challenge); second, the ones that allow the follow-up and evaluation of individuals and teams. Both measurements must enrich a learning dashboard (HMI); well thought-out visual displays based on collected and selected data, validated and processed. The aim is to permit correct decision-making by the users: the trainees for the project progress, and the trainer for recommendations through positive feedback, guiding during debriefings, level of adaptation and final marking. For a formative situation in relation to a targeted set of competences, the grid of selected criteria and indicators must be:

- set with respect to the project's intended results (quality of the group production) and targeted learning outcomes;

- be of sufficient number (for a quick and valid decision-making);
- observable to reflect the reality (easy to use and reliable);
- accurate and up-to-date (relevant and sensitive to incipient changes).

With the SCPR process, the learners are put into an operational realization context. They have to produce a result dealing with the field of expertise. They have to learn and apply knowledge for the goal. Quality production and learning outcomes require a minimum time to modify the personal perception, develop ownership and sustainable skills (deep learning). Future prospects must deal with digital issues to support learner production as a facilitation means, but also the tracking, collecting of materials and information, then analysis and selection of the data to be processed in order to improve the support to learners. The time allocated to the TU leads to define priorities being defined between activities.

Online Courses

As faced in 2020 with ERT, online lessons do not facilitate PR. Indeed, the trainer cannot be prescient as easily as during face-to-face interaction when he/she controls, catching the incipient signs from individuals in the work environment: the trainer adapts in real-time the planned course of events for desired, healthy and efficient interactions and relationships. The digital means to interact should be relevant for the process, supporting collective, social and emotional intelligence (Brackett et al., 2011):

- **a number of private rooms** for intergroup interactions with easy switching from one to the other for observation in real time and online feedback;
- **pre-scheduled collective debriefing times** to give freedom of organization;
- **digital online tools to facilitate** meta communication and collaborative real-time edition (like Etherpad, multi-user whiteboard and so forth), but also to track exchanges and to enrich the learning based on factual arguments and a dynamic and reflexive feedback loop on results;
- **shared remote spaces** for individual deposit and common work for transparent peer access and assessment of the outcomes;
- **and distance poll** based on assessment criteria to collect each individual review in an ethical manner and favor a personal step back on the experience and higher satisfaction level.

The aim is to generate worthwhile cooperation up to trust collaboration for a shared goal, based on courseware and assistance by the peer, and review with the peers for co-creation. The 6-phase model of professional development by Laferrière (Breuleux et al., 2002) emphasizes capacity building in a strong collaborative environment:

- **give awareness of the network** (connectivity, support and access);
- **master the proficiency-user IT skills for access** (DIGCOMP to handle information, communicate and create contents);
- **identify new possibilities for teaching and learning** (based on interactions and collaboration);
- **define new classroom management routine** (pre-organized content);
- **direct project-based learning**;
- **and develop knowledge-based communities**.

Figure 14. Spiral of group evolution with key SCPR control requirements

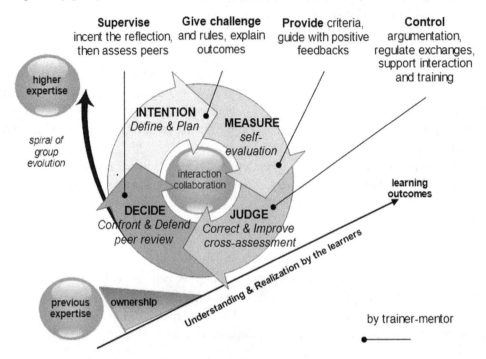

The Trainer-Mentor Role

The beneficial interactions of stakeholders can be summed up by a continuum of SCPR between:

- **Controlling and Reporting** (because the trainer is in charge and has to manage the group through a formative process of learning) towards;
- **Guiding and Evolving** (since the learners are the ones to be trained to assessment to give meaning to knowledge and to achieve a higher level of skills).

During the process, the trainer becomes somehow part of a new professional community network, identifying new perspectives in their practice while learners-peers give worthwhile feedbacks and enhanced knowledge. The SCPR is a new lever for professional style development. Indeed, the trainer must constantly change roles because of the demanding steps followed and repeated by the groups during this continuous improvement process (see Figure 14). The supervisor-trainer must focus on the following rules:

- **give a challenge** with clear objectives and planning;
- **provide a set of a priori criteria** for the project output and the learning outcomes;
- **incent communication** between pairs in a team to support peers work and cooperation;
- **give positive feedback on** the team's proposal if it is presented as a common consensus discussed beforehand;
- **authorize frank exchanges** of explained problem-solving approach between peers of different teams but forbid the hidden transmission of not argued turnkey solutions;

Table 10. The do's and don'ts of the trainer-mentor

Generation	Mentoring Do's	Mentoring Dont's
Millennials **Gen Z** **Gen Y**	Prepare for high expectations Support work environment and personalize Interact in the relationship Give quick recognition of results Show confidence and give freedom Give advice for time management Believe in creativity, focusing on results	Refuse closer collaboration Be unfriendly and pessimistic, nor confident Give insufficient advice nor provide concrete solutions, Lack reactivity Limit free decision-making Enforce feedback, thought-out Delay in giving peer recognition
Xennials	Needs of older Gen Y and younger Gen X	Same advice for older Gen Y and younger Gen X
Xennials **Gen X**	Involve in the task and develop flexibility Guide towards upstream thought-out solution; Adapt dynamically Enhance creativity and give confidence Act as a lever for decision-making Motivate a friendly work environment, with time and space to learn	Be too friendly or intrusive, mixing professional and private life Lack of commitment or reactivity Do not give support, understanding and show how Always agree instead of bringing contradictory element Refuse confrontation

- **maintain an area of freedom of action** during sessions in a state of mind that allows well-being at work;
- **supervise the collective debriefings** during peer review to comply with ethics and values.

Based on Thielfolds & Scheef (2004), table 10 gives the Do's and Don'ts of the trainer-mentor with respect to the generation met in our groups of intervention today.

CONCLUSION

Satisfaction of learners during the training path is at the core of the learning performance issues. Active pedagogy takes benefit from their previous experience. The presented gradual Self and Cross Peer Review process is a situated learning process that supports reflexive learning, confidence, sharing, deep learning and learning ownership. SCPR focuses on understanding and realization, thus self-reflection (SE), and the beneficial interactions within teams (CA) and between groups (PR) motivated by the project outcomes (challenge). Trainees must be guided with ethical support. Digital tools can help trainees' production. By taking into account the necessary time for skills development and knowledge ownership, data analysis could be a way to support supervision and learning autonomy despite the space and time distance. Future work will focus on IT solutions and adaptive learning dashboards (in time and content) to facilitate and ensure the commitment of individuals in the group to the shared collective goal. Online dashboards require data, including personal data. We note the SHEILA project (GCM, 2019) that targets a policy development framework to promote formative assessment and personalized learning; by taking advantage of direct involvement of stakeholders and digital data as they learn online in the development process. Of the 99 learning analytics policy feature statements, we emphasize the following set that complies with GDPR and is part of the SCPR process by essence (goal and process transparency, supervision with positive feedback and debriefings leading to accepted consensus based on factual arguments):

- **a clear strategy** and safeguarding;
- **safety, ethics, clarity and transparency** of purpose and usage (process) for individual benefit;
- **personal control** (agreement)
- **comprehensive visualization** (draw attention) for learning improvement (self-assessment) and collaboration based on decision-based evidence-making (cross evaluation);
- **support of meaningful relationships** to prevent misunderstanding and deviation based on data lacking contextual analysis (criteria grid);
- **encouraging actionable information and personalization** during the process, but recognizing limitations (peer review).

The final question is whether the evaluation shared with the peers and the trainer can be a valid evaluation for the diploma. PR implies a compromise between individual expectations and consensus faithful to the training specifications. The five key dimensions to sustain PR efficiency are the following that motivated the proposed SCPR:

- **Space** because the work environment impacts the collaboration between peers in a team and between teams with respect to the number of exchanges and level of interaction;
- **Scope of learning outcomes** must drive the setting of the project based on formative activity: decision-making focuses on gradual complexity of problem-solving issues and training with a corresponding set of evaluation criteria to assess personal control, and collective performance;
- **Allocated time** to propose a pre-set organization of synchronous and asynchronous periods;
- **Control** to comply with QA and learning performance, ensuring regulation and limit conflicts;
- **Supervision to ensure fairness,** respect of personal data and ownership of individual production, and peer review ethics for sustainable learning outcomes.

Finally, the SCPR process is an augmented project-based formative activity in a standard blended-oriented course that strengthens the situational intelligence (i.e., the ability of individuals to understand contexts and people in order to act in an informed way, so that any exchange is profitable and produces success as defined by Autissier (2013)). SCPR emphasizes the potential of peer review by triggering the levers for higher commitment and interaction. Clearly, this assessment process cannot be applied in all cases, but in situations where group activity is central to the tasks and skills to be assessed. Thus, peer assessment remains a promising complement to traditional knowledge assessment. But, the level of maturity of students and group cohesiveness are key information to prevent deviations and jeopardy. The quality of the trainer's follow-up of the groups over time and the CoP of the teaching team are keys to support this demanding process. To further our thinking on this topic, we are considering new experiments to better identify the factors influencing the added value of each step of the proposed SCPR. Identifying this taxonomy will allow for better comparison of evaluation methods and better determination of the most appropriate setting for their use.

REFERENCES

Ajjawi, R., & Boud, D. (2017). Researching feedback dialogue: An interactional analysis approach. *Assessment & Evaluation in Higher Education, 42*(2), 252–265. doi:10.1080/02602938.2015.1102863

Alderfer, C. (2014). Clarifying the meaning of mentor-protégé relationships. *Consulting Psychology Journal, 66*(1), 6–19. doi:10.1037/a0036367

Anderson, O., El Habbal, N., & Bridges, D. (2020). A peer evaluation training results in high-quality feedback, as measured over time in nutritional sciences graduate students. *Advances in Physiology Education, 44*(2), 203–209. doi:10.1152/advan.00114.2019 PMID:32243221

Andrade, H. (2019). A Critical Review of Research on Student Self-Assessment. *Frontiers in Education, 4*, 87. doi:10.3389/feduc.2019.00087

Autissier, D. (2013). *L'intelligence de situation - Savoir exploiter toutes les situations*. Ed. d'Organisation.

Biggs, J. B. (2003). *Teaching for quality learning at university*. The Open University Press.

Bloxham, S., & Boyd, P. (2007). *Developing effective assessment in higher education: A practical guide*. Open University Press.

Bonicoli, M. P. (2008). How to change learning process: Representation in Higher Education via distance-learning technology: the case study of a French continuing education center. In *Proceedings of the 2nd International Multi-Conference on Society, Cybernetics and Informatics: IMSCI 2008*. IIIS.

Brackett, M. A., Rivers, S. E., & Salovey, P. (2011). Emotional Intelligence: Implications for Personal, Social, Academic, and Workplace Success. *Social and Personality Psychology Compass, 5*(1), 88–103. doi:10.1111/j.1751-9004.2010.00334.x

Breuleux, A., Laferrière, T., & Lamon, M. (2002). Capacity building within and across countries into the effective uses of ICTs. In *Pan-Canadian Education Research Agenda Symposium*. Information Technology and Learning.

Campbell, J. (2008). *The hero with a thousand faces* (3rd ed.). New World Library.

Carpenter, J. P., Krutka, D. G., & Trust, T. (2021). Continuity and change in educators' professional learning networks. *Journal of Educational Change, 23*(1), 85–113. doi:10.100710833-020-09411-1

Cendon, E. (2016). Bridging Theory and Practice – Reflective Learning in Higher Education. In W. Nuninger & J.-M. Châtelet (Eds.), *Quality Assurance and Value Management in Higher Education*. IGI Global., doi:10.4018/978-1-5225-0024-7.ch012

Chareanpunsirikul, & Wood, R. C. (2002). Mintzberg, managers, and methodology: some observations from a study of hotel general managers. *Tourism Management, 23*(5), 551–556. doi:10.1016/S0261-5177(02)00016-X

Davies, A., Fidler, D., & Gorbis, M. (2011). *Future Work Skills 2020*. Institute for the Future for University of Phoenix Research Institute. www.iftf.org/uploads/media/SR-1382A_UPRI_future_work_skills_sm.pdf

Davies, P. (2007). *The Bologna Process and University Lifelong Learning: The State of Play and future Directions, Final report BeFlexPlus*. EUCEN Retrieved from http://www.eucen.eu/BeFlex/FinalReports/BeFlexFullReportPD.pdf

Dembo, M.-H., & Seli, H.-P. (2004). Student's Resistance to Change in Learning Strategies Courses. *Journal of Developmental Education, 27*(3), 2–11.

Dille, K. B., & Røkenes, F. M. (2021). Teachers' professional development in formal online communities: A scoping review. *Teaching and Teacher Education, 105*, 103431. doi:10.1016/j.tate.2021.103431

Dunning, J. K., Ehrlinger, J., & Kruger, J. (2003). Why People Fail to Recognize Their Own Incompetence. *Current Directions in Psychological Science, 12*(3), 83–87. doi:10.1111/1467-8721.01235

Durand, M.-J., & Chouinard, R. (2012). *L'évaluation des apprentissages. De la planification de la démarche à la communication des résultats*. Éditions Hurtubise.

Elliot, N., & Higgins, A. (2005). Self and peer assessment – does it make a difference to student group work? *Nurse Education in Practice, 5*(1), 40–48. doi:10.1016/j.nepr.2004.03.004 PMID:19038177

European Association for Quality Assurance in Higher Education - ENQA. (2015). *Standards and Guidelines for Quality Assurance in the European Higher Education Area (ESG)*. ENQA. www.enqa.eu/index.php/home/esg/

Fernandez, N. (2015). Évaluation et motivation, un couple gagnant pour soutenir l'apprentissage. Dans J. L. Leroux (dir.), Évaluer les compétences au collégial et à l'université: un guide pratique (p. 479-500). Montréal, QC: Chenelière Éducation/Association québécoise de pédagogie collégiale

Girardet, C., & Mottier Lopez, L. (2020). *La bienveillance à l'épreuve de l'évaluation entre pairs à l'université*. Revue Suisse des Sciences de l'Education.

Goleman, D. (2007). Social intelligence: the new science of human relationships. Reprint Editdion: Bantam

Grzega, J. (2007). *Learning By Teaching: The Didactic Model LdL in University Classes*. http://www.joachim-grzega.de/ldl-engl.pdf

Hattie, J., & Timperley, H. (2007). The Power of Feedback. *Review of Educational Research, 77*(1), 81–112. doi:10.3102/003465430298487

Jerez-Gómez, P., Céspedes-Lorente, J., & Valle-Cabrera, R. (2005). Organizational learning capability: A proposal of measurement. *Journal of Business Research, 58*(6), 715–725. doi:10.1016/j.jbusres.2003.11.002

Johnson, S. (2011). Making teamwork work: decreasing conflicts in Teams. In Orange Journ., 7(1), 1-14

Kolb, A. Y., & Kolb, D. A. (2005). Learning Styles and Learning Spaces: Enhancing Experiential Learning in Higher Education. *Academy of Management Learning & Education, 4*(2), 193–212. doi:10.5465/amle.2005.17268566

Leclercq, D., & Poumay, M. (2008). The 8 Learning Events Model and its principles. *LabSet*. http://www.labset.net/media/prod/8LEM.pdf

Leduc, M., & Molinié, A. (2020). *Les publications à l'heure de la science ouverte. Ethics Committee Report*. CNRS: France. ww.ouvrirlascience.fr/wp-content/uploads/2020/02/COMETS_Les-publications-a-lheure-de-la-science-ouverte_Avis-2019-40-1.pdf

Lee, S. J., & Reeves, T. C. (2007). Edgar Dale: A significant contributor to the field of educational technology. *Educational Technology, 47*(6), 56.

Legendre, R. (2005). Dictionnaire actuel de l'éducation (3e éd.). Montréal, QC: Guérin.

Meissonier. (2017). Évaluer un article: quels syndromes éviter? *Systèmes d'information & management, 22*(4), 3-8. doi:10.3917/sim.174.0003

Morrissette, J. (2010). Un panorama de la recherche sur l'évaluation formative des apprentissages. *Mesure et Évaluation en Éducation, 33*(3), 1–27. doi:10.7202/1024889ar

Mottier Lopez, L., Girardet, C., Bendela, P., Constenla Martinez, N., Elisme Pierre, E., Gibert, S., Lyu, X., Roth, M., Sauret, O., & Seguel Tapia, F. (2022). Quand la co-construction d'un référentiel devient un moyen d'apprendre. Expériences de doctorants et de doctorantes, le cas d'un référentiel pour évaluer des textes scientifiques. *La Revue LEeE, 3.* https://revue.leee.online/index.php/info/article/view/136

Mottier Lopez, L., Girardet, C., Broussal, D., & Demeester, A. (2021). EOC – une Evaluation Ouverte et Collaborative entre pairs: analyse critique du dispositif de La Revue LEeE. *La Revue LEeE, Numéro spécial.* doi:10.48325/rleee.spe.01

Nuninger, W. (2017). Integrated Learning Environment for blended oriented course: 3-year feedback on a skill-oriented hybrid strategy. HCI International, 9-14 July. In: Zaphiris P., Ioannou A. (eds). Learning and Collaboration Technologies. Novel Learning Ecosystems. Springer, Cham. doi:10.1007/978-3-319-58509-3_13

Nuninger, W., & Châtelet, J. (2016). Hybridization-Based Courses Consolidated through LMS and PLE Leading to a New Co-Creation of Learning: Changing All Actors' Behavior for Efficiency. In D. Fonseca & E. Redondo (Eds.), *Handbook of Research on Applied E-Learning in Engineering and Architecture Education* (pp. 55–87). IGI Global. doi:10.4018/978-1-4666-8803-2.ch004

Nuninger, W., & Châtelet, J. (2020). Key Processes for the Performance of Work-Integrated Learning in HE: Focusing on Talents with a Winning-Foursome. In W. Nuninger & J. Châtelet (Eds.), *Handbook of Research on Operational Quality Assurance in Higher Education for Life-Long Learning* (pp. 101–132). IGI Global. doi:10.4018/978-1-7998-1238-8.ch005

Orsmond, P., Merry, S., & Reiling, K. (2000). The use of student derived marking criteria in peer and self-assessment. *Assessment & Evaluation in Higher Education, 25*(1), 23–38. doi:10.1080/02602930050025006

Paudel, P. (2021). Online education: Benefits, challenges and strategies during and after COVID-19 in higher education. [IJonSE]. *International Journal on Studies in Education, 3*(2), 70–85. doi:10.46328/ijonse.32

Raelin, J. A. (2008). Work-based Learning. Bridging Knowledge and Action in the Workplace. San Francisco, CA: Jossey-Bass.

Roegiers, X. (2012). *Quelles réformes pédagogiques pour l'enseignement supérieur.* De Boeck.

Roy, M. et Michaud, N. (2018). Self-Assessment and Peer-Assessment in Higher Education: Promises and Challenges. *Formation et profession, 26*(2), 54-65. doi:10.18162/fp.2018.458

Sadler, D. R. (2010). Beyond feedback: Developing student capability in complex appraisal. *Assessment & Evaluation in Higher Education, 35*(5), 535–550. doi:10.1080/02602930903541015

Scharmer, C. O. (2009). *Theory U: Leading from the Future as It Emerges.* Berrett-Koeheler Publishers.

Schein, E. H. (2013). Humble Inquiry: The Gentle Art of Asking Instead of Telling. Berrett-Koehler Publishers.

Sheila Group Concept Mapping study-GCM. (2019). 99 learning analytics policy feature statements. *Sheila Project.* https://sheilaproject.eu/wp-content/uploads/2019/07/PolicyMa tters99GCMstatements.pdf

Societé des Ingénieurs et Scientifiques de France-IESF. (2001). *Engineer Charter of Ethics.* IESF. https://www.iesf.fr/752_p_49680/charte-ethique-de-l-ingenieu r.html

Stone, D., & Heen, S. (2014). Thanks for the feedback: The Science and Art of Receiving Feedback. Viking.

Thielfoldt, D., & Scheef, D. (2004). Generation X and the Millennials: What You Need to Know About Mentoring the New Generations (pp. 1-7). The Learning Café.

Thomas, G., Martin, D., & Pleasants, K. (2011). Using self- and peer-assessment to enhance students' future-learning in higher education. *Journal of University Teaching & Learning Practice, 8*(1), 1–17. http://ro.uow.edu.au/cgi/viewcontent.cgi?article=1112&contex t=jutlp. doi:10.53761/1.8.1.5

Topping, K. (2009). Peer Assessment. *Theory into Practice, 48*(1), 20–27. doi:10.1080/00405840802577569

Trust, T., & Horrocks, B. (2019). Six key elements identified in an active and thriving blended community of practice. *TechTrends, 63*(2), 108–115. doi:10.100711528-018-0265-x

UNESCO. (2020). *COVID-19 Educational disruption and response.* UNESCO. https://en.unesco.org/themes/educationemergencies/coronaviru s-school-closures

Viau, R. (2009). La motivation en contexte scolaire. De Boeck.

Wenger, E. (2000). Communities of Practice and Social Learning Systems. *Organization, 7*(2), 225–246. doi:10.1177/135050840072002

Wiklund, H., & Wiklund, P. S. (2002). Widening the Six Sigma concept: An approach to improve organizational learning. *Total Quality Management, 13*(2), 233–239. doi:10.1080/09544120120102469

Younès, N., Gremion, C. & Sylvestre, E. (2020). *L'évaluation, source de Synergies.* Presses de l'ADMEE

KEY-TERMS AND DEFINITIONS

Assessments (SE, CA and PR): These are conceptualized in this chapter within a formative educational perspective. Self-evaluation (SE) leads the individual to make a judgment about their own work, production and results. By continuity beyond this task-specific personal evaluation, cross-assessment (CA) between members of the same team (regarded as a unitary system) encourages sharing and incent dialogic feedback that helps the team progress toward the learning goal. Peer review (PR) between teams allows for confrontation between new actors and the opportunity to trust judgment in the dialogue between new experts.

Code review: This is as software Quality Assurance activity that allows a group to valid a computer application with respect to specifications. Developers check the algorithm and source code, reading the sequences and testing to limit interruption due to not predictable errors. The concept supports quality, transfer of expertise, mutual responsibility and collective ownership of the final code.

Hybrid blended-courses: This pedagogical strategy mixes different pedagogical approaches, materials and means (including digital) for knowledge ownership. It favors *"learning by doing"* and the creation of individuals' Personal Learning Environment, giving the students control over the time, place and pace of learning. It enhances commitment and collective debriefings. The activities, prepared beforehand, can be carried out remotely, during the face-to-face course at the school, but also during the virtual classroom. In that case, it requires tailored IT tools and an adequate time division to enhance the training momentum and ensure the co-presence of trainer and trainees. Hybridization of means promote flexibility for more Open Distance Learning (ODL); a point of view not to be confused with so-called *"hybrid lesson"* and ERT quickly promoted during COVID-19 pandemic, not specifying the true training modalities and requirement.

Integrative alternation: This is an organizational choice taking into account the available time and external constraints to find the best way to break down the time allocated to face-to-face sharing and self-directed activities. It is not an affixing of two contexts but an act of collaboration with commitment

ONAAG: French acronym for *"Outil Numérique d'Appui de l'Auto-Formation Guidée"* proposed to students to consolidate prerequisite mastery, facilitate new knowledge acquisition and understanding, then autonomy with respect to time management and collaborative work. The core of the pedagogical device is a set of learning activities of gradual complexity synchronized on Moodle with: hypertext lecture with educational videos, solved examples and self-assessment tests. The use of the pedagogical device by the trainer with asynchronous feedback and synchronous lessons in the classroom aims to incent worthwhile interaction in the group.

Pair programming: This refers to joint (i.e., by two people) operational development of a computer application, sharing the display of the workstation: one codes the previously thought-out functional solution, while the second controls the typed sequences in real time. They do so in an alternating manner, interacting and transferring expertise (SE and CA). During Rapid Application Development by a bigger team, peer-programming and mob-programming (PR) focuses on delayed code review while output and priority are argued during progress review respecting agile principles.

Teacher, Trainer, Tutor or Mentor: In the framework of active pedagogy, these terms refer interchangeably here to the facilitator experts who guide, support, give feedback, supervise debriefing and control the collective learning activity; the choice is related to the role that differs according to the stage of the SCPR process and the evolution of the groups.

Table 11. Our groups with course information and *SCPR project (**organization change in 2020 or 2021)

Group (age)number	Year	Field	TU of the 1st semester	TU of the 2nd semester
FIT (20 yrs) <50	1st	Biological and Food engineering	**Automation (34h)** Lecture: 10h; Tutorials (11h+8h) +preparatory work* (6-student team, collective debriefings) +5h PLC experimental bench* (3-student team, 2 teams as peers)	**Computer Programming** (36h)** Lecture: 8h; Tutorial: 11h +1h serious game* (1/4 of group) +16h RAD projects* (pair programming, code review in team (6), 12 peers)
IVT (21 yrs) <26	2nd	Production	**Computer Programming (20h)** Tutorial: 9h +1h serious game* (half a group) +10h RAD projects* (3-person team, half group of peers)	No intervention
CVT (over 32 yrs) <15	3rd	Production	**Automatic Control (20h)** Lesson and tutorial: 20h +asynchronous projects* (5-peer team)	**Automatic Control* (15h)** Lesson: 5h +synchronous projects*: 10h (5-person team, 2 teams: peers are the whole group)

APPENDIX 1: GROUP CHARACTERIZATION

APPENDIX 2: SURVEYS' CONTENTS

For better understanding of data, this part clarifies our surveys. Since 2020, all groups benefit from the same surveys supported by ONAAG as a standard. Specific questions are added with respect to the group. At the beginning of the TU, two surveys help the trainer to characterize the members in the group and motivate their personal questioning: previous path and expectations about the field. Then, the focus is put on prerequisites in relation to project management, IT skills and mathematics. Personal questions are asked about native language, age and gender and the way they prefer to learn (see Table 12).

Figure 15. Data about the Full-time Initial Training (FIT) between 2019 and 2022 (two TUs)

	TU: Automation FIT in their first year 1st semester			TU: Computer Programming FIT in their first year 2nd semester		
	2019-2020	2020-2021	2021-2022	2019-2020	2020-2021	2021-2022
Number in the promotion	47	48	48	46	46	50
Declared gender (% of female)	no data	no data	85%	76%	88%	89%
Average age between [min, max]	no data	no data	20 yo [19, 24]	20 yo [19, 22]	19.8 yo [19, 23]	20 yo [19, 24]
Survey at the start of the TU Mandatory answer after reading the instructions	94%	79%	94%	96%	83%	84%
Survey before starting self-training with ONAAG Required for access	not done	not done	100%	89%	96%	100%
Survey AFTER training with ONAAG device Unconstrained after completion (%)	after 2nd semester	after 2nd semester	after 2nd semester	15%	15%	10%
New intermediate quick survey on peer review (2021)	not done	not done	75%	x	x	x
Final survey on peer review after the TU (2020)	x	x	x	57%	24%	58%
Context of peer review (changes)	only homework in teams	only homework in teams	new pratical lesson with peer review	peer programming 100% online	peer programming 100% online	face-to-face peer programming sessions only
Satisfaction survey at the END of the EU On a voluntary basis (before return of grading)	x	x	13%	26%	24%	28%

Figure 16. Data for Vocational Training groups between 2019 and 2022 (IVT and CVT, 1 TU for each)

	IVT	TU: Computer programming in their second year 3rd semester		CVT	TU: Automatic Control in their thrid (last) year 5th and 6th semester	
		2019-2020	2020-2021	2021-2022	2019-2020	2020-2021	2021-2022
Number in the promotion	22	16	21	15	8	10
Declared gender (% of female)	9%	19%	14%	20%	0%	0%
Average age	22yo	23 yo	21 yo	36 yo	34 yo	32 yo
between [min, max]	[20,27]	[21, 27]	[20, 24]	[29, 49]	[26, 42]	[26, 38]
Survey at the start of the TU Mandatory answer after reading the instructions	100%	81%	90%	100%	100%	100%
Survey before starting self-training with ONAAG Required for access	64%	94%	76%	100%	100%	100%
Survey AFTER training with ONAAG device Unconstrained after completion (%)	9%	6%	not asked	non activée en 2020	38%	60%
New intermediate quick survey on peer review (2021)	x	x	76%*	x	x	70%
Final survey on peeer review after the TU (2020)	41%	6%	not asked	80%	38%	80%
Context of peer review (changes)	late survey (4th semester)	peer programming in the classroom	*specific after project, SCPR not made	Collective project (60% online)	Collective project (0% online)	Collective project (0% online)
Satisfaction survey at the END of the EU On a voluntary basis (before return of grading)	5%	not asked	not asked (lots of abs)	67%	not asked	70%

The aim of the intermediate survey is to quickly point out the learners' immediate feelings with respect to the peer review activity proposed: *not useful, help understanding the course, better or in a more autonomous way, and self-confidence.* Then in 2021 about SCPR experience (defined to them in 2021 as: *producing, self-assessing, confronting and deciding in the group, consulting and assessing peers and*

Figure 17. Groups average scores in relation to SCPR project, individual examination and TUs

FIT		2019-2020	2020-2021	2021-2022
	Number in the promotion	47	48	48
TU: Automation in their first year 1st semester	Final score to the SCPR project: average (std)	X	X	15.4 (1.2)
	between [min, max]	no activity	no activty	[13 ; 18]
	Individual score at the final examination: average (std)	9.9 (3.6)	11.7 (3.8)	10.3 (2.4)
	between [min, max]	[3.7 ; 17.7]	[5 ; 19.75]	[5 ; 15]
	Note of the group for the Teaching Unit: average (std)	10.7 (3.0)	13.79 (2.7)	11.6 (1.8)
	between [min, max]	[4.4 ; 17.5]	[8 ; 19]	[7.7 ; 15]
TU: Computer Programming in their first year 2nd semester	Final score to the SCPR Project: average (std)	15.6 (1.0)	14 (1.3)	14.1 (1,3)
	between [min, max]	[14 ; 17]	[12 ; 17.5]	[11 ; 16]
	Individual score at the final examination: average (std)	12.1 (2.1) ERT	11.8 (5.3)	11,2 (2,9)
	between [min, max]	[7.1 ; 17.2]	[0.5 ; 19.8]	[5 ; 16,5]
	Note of the group for the Teaching Unit: average (std)	not relevant	not relevant	new
	between [min, max]	merge results	merge results	organization

Remark: scores are upon 20 points for FIT (validation >10)

IVT		2019-2020	2020-2021	2021-2022
	Number in the promotion	22	16	21
TU: Computer Programming in their second year 3rd semester	Final score to the SCPR Project: average (std)	14.6 (0.6)	16.5 (0.5)	13.9 (1.5)
	between [min, max]	[12.5 ; 15]	[16 ; 17]	[10 ; 15.8]
	Individual score at the final examination: average (std)	10 (2.7)	11 (4.04)	12.4 (4.1)
	between [min, max]	[4.5 ; 14.5]	[5.3 ; 17.9]	[4.8 ; 19.5]
	Note of the group for the Teaching Unit: average (std)	11.9 (1.7)	13.8 (2.1)	13.2 (2.3)
	between [min, max]	[9.4 ; 15.7]	[10.6, 17.40]	[9 ; 16.9]

Remark: scores are upon 20 points for IVT (validation >10)

CVT		2019-2020	2020-2021	2021-2022
	Number in the promotion	15	8	10
TU: Automatic Control in their thrid (last) year 5th and 6th semester	Final score to the SCPR project: average (std) upon 5 level of expertise	V 3 levels	V 1 level	V 2 levels
	Individual score at the final examination (1st examination) upon 5 level of expertise	69% V at 1st try	50% V at 1st try	30% V at 1st try
	Note of the group for the Teaching Unit (final examination) upon 5 level of expertise	100% V	100% V	100% V at 1st try

Remark: score ar validate (V) or not (NV) for CVT

Table 12. Proposed learning style preferred (to be ticked)

ID	I prefer to learn by (proposals)	Refers to the following behaviors and teaching
1	having a lecture, then solved exercises, and practical work	Passive learners while the teacher disseminates the knowledge with low collaboration, but assistance
2	completing exercises prepared with the group and as part of group projects	More active learners who cooperate in pairs and try to collaborate during tutorials, but still expect the trainer to give the solution
3	reading documents before the lesson and the speaker's answers to questions from the class	Active behavior with learning autonomy that is appropriate for flipped classroom with exchange and knowledge input in interaction with an expert-mentor.
4	Other: please specify	Any personal learning autonomy expected

conversely submitting to them and being assessed) with the following two questions plus open questions to identify brakes and levers:

- Have you ever been confronted with this mode of evaluation in the past? (Yes or no)
- Today, what do you think of the PR experienced in your group? (4-point Likert scale covering the relevance to the learning goal (knowledge, expertise, evolution…) plus a possible no opinion ticked;

At the end of the TU, it is complemented by a survey exploring the following areas: learning style, previous experience, satisfaction, feeling about self-evaluation and cross-assessment, then reason of rejection and roles (see Table 13). The end-of-year survey focuses on overall satisfaction of the training and confidence in the reflexive learning.

APPENDIX 3: ERT SWITCH DURING COVID-19 CRISIS

Since the first lockdown in 2019, May 17th in France, the state of health emergency implemented by the law of May 31, 2021, applies until July 31, 2022. Training switched to ERT to comply with the continuity of education (UNESCO, 2020). The burst of digital practices showed that teaching and learning practices must change to limit the cognitive workload that affects all and improve well-being with more interaction and communication despite the accessibility issue (Paudel, 2021). The emphasis was put on the transfer of knowledge rather than on reflexive learning based on collectively lived experience. PR was put on hold due to constantly evolving work conditions and no convenient IT tool for the purpose. The vocational groups had to cope with external constraint: pressure at their professional workplace, family priority (for the older students) and non-identified personal issues that affect the group adhesion and momentum. Thus, the final examinations of the groups met in 2020 showed an average level below expectations, despite the apparent involvement of students. In 2021, there is less mastery of the prerequisites for younger students, and often a lack of autonomy.

Table 13. Different areas explored in the PR satisfaction survey

ID	Dimensions	Targeted information
1	Learning style	To identify the learning style declared
2	Commitment in a course	To split active and passive behavior and confirm reality
3	Felt personal role in previous projects	To separate directive role, cooperative, team player and work alone
4	Previous assessment experience	Self-evaluation, cross-assessment, peer review
5	SCPR process and assessment grid after this year experience	To confirm usefulness of the criteria grid to support understanding and SCPR for motivation and make one feels valued
6	Difficulty felt to assess	In relation to self-evaluation and evaluation of others
7	Personal feeling about evaluation	To identify learning behavior and maturity: no need to self-evaluate, source of conflict, lack of objectivity, it's the trainer's job to evaluate (not ours).
8	Open questions to justify the judgement	To identify levers and brakes
9	What is important during assessment	To split importance given to final mark, scoring level, feedback received, joint debriefing to progress, or understanding rather than the grade
10	Personal behaviors in SCPR activities	Ten points Likert scale for a 9-set of proposals
11	Feeling about the attitude of colleagues	Open question to compare feeling and role in teams
12	Open question	To have feedback on innovative perspective for SCPR

Chapter 2
An Exciting Assessment Towards an Exciting Education:
The True Value of Assessment in University Education

Purificación Cruz
Universidad de Castilla-La Mancha, Spain

Javier Rodríguez
https://orcid.org/0000-0003-1029-5562
Universidad de Castilla-La Mancha, Spain

Lorena López
Universidad de Castilla-La Mancha, Spain

ABSTRACT

These days, many authors ask whether having a high level of intellectual knowledge is a guarantee of success at university. The answer is no, at least not only with rational intelligence. Emotional intelligence is needed to cope with life. This emotional intelligence can be learned as another competence, and it will also allow us to acquire the rest of the competences required for personal and professional development. Therefore, the results in the assessments to which university students are "subjected" are closely linked to the emotional development of the individual.

INTRODUCTION

According to Ayala (2015), one of the first contributions we find in the field of education is by the author Lafourcade (1986), who defines evaluation as a stage in the educational process that aims to systematically check to what extent the results expected in the objectives specified in advance have been achieved. As we can see, for this author, evaluation is simply a way of checking whether learners have achieved the proposed goals. Following his way of thinking, the assessment process would end with this verification.

DOI: 10.4018/978-1-6684-3537-3.ch002

Subsequently, other authors define it as a process that involves at least the following phases: collecting information, evaluating the information collected and making decisions. The next phase was to affirm that evaluation is a set of systematic processes of collecting, analysis, and interpretation of valid and reliable information, which in comparison with a reference or criterion allows us to reach a decision that promotes the improvement of the evaluated object. Subsequent contributions from university professors highlight, in some way, the role of the teacher in this whole process, as they specify the necessary use of strategies or instruments, as well as the proposal of a series of challenges to better understand what the student needs (Alsina, 2010). De Díaz (2006), provides the following definition: "A planned and comprehensive process that is relevant to the competences to be achieved. It is developed through the posing of tasks or challenges that the student must solve, requiring an integrated set of knowledge, skills and attitudes" (p. 26). We consider this definition to be accurate within a constructivist and holistic approach. Apart from standards, achievements, decimals, and boxes to be filled that seek to transform our students into assessable learning machines, we must not overlook the competency objectives set out in our teaching guides, which should be the reference point for our actions (Ricoy and Fernández-Rodríguez, p. 26). (Ricoy and Fernández-Rodríguez, 2013). As indicated by Zabalza and Lodeiro (2019), the assessment of competences emerges at the end of the degree as an expression of the overall training received.

Assessment as an essential component of the learning process must be integrated with the principles of freedom, integration, inclusion, and participation, as pointed out by Hernández (2002). From this perspective, why do we try to turn this process into something non-educational, something in which quantitative results are given more importance than the quality of the process? Why do we insist on teaching innovation only to seek methodological strategies, working from competences and putting the student at the center of learning, and why do we not do the same with assessment?

Emotions are an indispensable component for an adequate cognitive evaluation process, as they arouse curiosity and attract attention to help in the learning and evaluation process. They help to store all the information received in long-term memory. However, emotions are not only important for students, but they are also important for teachers, as they must know themselves to be aware of the emotions that their students evoke in them and how it affects their teaching (Boroel Cervantes et al, 2018). Following neurological studies, all learning that is carried out with emotion remains engraved forever in the brain, consequently, it is necessary to create an educational practice based on the emotional sphere, although this concept still generates a great deal of uncertainty among professionals on university campuses. In accordance with the report by the National Center for Clinical Infant (Ibarrola, 2013), this is the relationship between the emotional component and learning, which are closely related to the results in the assessment process (Table 1):

Emotional intelligence "is the ability to discern and respond appropriately to the moods, temperaments, motivations and desires of others" (Goleman, 2006). In other words, we all possess an emotional intelligence that will help us to find answers at certain moments in our lives in an appropriate way. Appropriate and determined responses that are the objective of any educational, personal, and global assessment. Emotions are useful, according to Mora (2017) to protect us from harmful stimuli or to bring us closer to pleasant stimuli; to make responses versatile and flexible; to activate the individual by activating multiple cerebral, endocrine, cardiovascular systems, etc.; to maintain interest and curiosity in new things; to communicate quickly and effectively with other individuals; to help store and evoke memories in a more efficient way and for decision making (Gambarini & Cruz, 2017).

Emotions "are multidimensional phenomena characterised by four elements: cognitive (how it is called and what it means what I feel), physiological (what biological changes I experience), behavioural

Table 1. Emotional components and learnings elicited

Emotional component:	Elicits	Emotional component:	Elicits
Confidence	Feeling of not failing in what is proposed	Relationship	Being understood and understanding others
Curiosity	Discovering new things that lead to pleasure	Ability to communicate	Confidence and understanding
Intentionality	Effective competence	Cooperation	Balancing one's own needs with the needs of others
Self-control	Feeling of internal control	Others: *assertiveness, empathy...*	

(where each emotion directs my behaviour) and expressive (through what bodily signals it is expressed)" (Ibarrola, 2013). They are responsible for facilitating the adaptation of individuals to the social environment in which they live, carrying it out through a series of functions. Nevertheless, not all emotions are the same; they can be classified into different types:

- Primary or innate emotions are produced by the amygdala and their function is adaptive by reacting automatically to a stimulus: anger, fear, joy, surprise, disgust, and sadness, although each of them can occur at different levels or intensities.
- Secondary emotions that are conscious and are acquired through the influence of our society, so they are different in each culture. They are present in the events and occurrences of everyday life.
- There are also the emotions that are in the background, which are those emotions that are felt according to the mood. They are emotions that can vary according to the intensity of the moment, but last longer over time. An example is the pupil who is angry at the end of an assessment task because he/she is not happy with the result obtained, he/she is going to have a bad day, he/she will be more tense with his/her classmates, he/she will be annoyed by the comments made by the teacher, and so on.

The more positive and affective the emotions that surround learning are, the easier it will be for them to remain in the memory. We must not forget, according to the latest neuroscience studies, that the learning processes are themselves shaping the brain, reinforcing the most active neuronal networks, and eliminating the less used ones. This could be used in universities to formulate curricula that promote maximum brain development and student learning without the need to rely on trial-and-error processes. However, this science also has its limitations, as it is not possible to observe the reactions and ways of dealing with problems of each individual learner. Moreover, we are still at the beginning of learning about all the possibilities and functions of the brain and its response capabilities.

When pupils are asked for a specific response or action in an individualized way, they are insecure, quieter and on alert. Their reptilian brain is acting in response to a situation that it considers dangerous, thus keeping it on alert. When the reptilian brain is activated, it is advisable to activate the emotional part, that is, the pupils' limbic system, to bring it out of this state and help it to adapt to the situation it has read as dangerous. This requires creating a comfortable, non-threatening environment and an assessment based on competences and not only on knowledge (Borjas, 2017).

The limbic brain is the area of affection and emotions. It is made up of different parts. The main ones are the amygdala, the hippocampus, the thalamus, and the hypothalamus. The limbic system controls the impulsivity of the reptilian brain and is where the motivations that will be maintained over time originate, due to the rewards that will provoke their repetition. Furthermore, it is in the limbic system, exactly in the hippocampus, where the long-term memory (LTM) resides, which will lead the brain to act in a certain way in search of the same experiences it remembers. These situations cause the brain to block itself in the event of repeated bad memories and to fail to respond to questions that the learner knows in principle. This would be the typical " I went blank in the exam" in a situation that provokes stress, panic, or anxiety. These blocks can be avoided by giving space and time for the student to decide. Sometimes they are forced to answer quickly when they would answer more confidently and thoughtfully with more time. Recognition for effort or for work well done is the most effective.

The neocortex brain is made up of the cerebral cortex, the two cerebral hemispheres, which in turn can be divided into occipital, frontal, parietal and temporal lobes, and the corpus callosum, which links the various hemispheres. It is the most evolved brain and the one that performs intellectual and emotional functions at a higher and more creative level. The neocortex is not prepared to focus attention on the same thing, action, or activity for a constant time, but seeks different stimuli that challenge it; it is a balancer of the two previous brains, the reptilian and the limbic. The knowledge of how the brain operates and what variants are involved should help teachers to develop a more effective assessment system, to find strategies to motivate, to create enthusiasm for the results obtained and for knowledge to reduce frustration, and even to prevent failure.

The brain must perform a cognitive learning process, which is slow, easy to forget, requires time and effort and is conscious; and an emotional learning process, which is fast, permanent, effortless, unconscious, and automatic (Tomas, 2013). Both are necessary for students to acquire the different competences in their university training. These competences are related to cognitive, technical, relational, and emotional competences. The problem is that currently there are few methods that assess the totality of competences, with the emotional competence being the most disadvantaged one in general. (table 2)

A search of recent national and international research reveals numerous reports that address the assessment of emotional intelligence in students, but we have not found any document that clarifies the emotional effects that assessment produces. We found some research that linked the emotion of fear with assessment, or the dependence of self-confidence and positive results of an assessment process, however, there are no studies that highlight the methodological treatment of assessment in relation to the emotional needs of students:

- Ricoy and Fernández-Rodríguez (2013). University students' perception of assessment: a case study. The research was carried out at the University of Vigo, Spain. Its participants were 32 students of the master's degree in Compulsory Secondary Education, Vocational Training and Language Teaching. Qualitative case study. The results show the feeling produced by the evaluation: mostly negative: nervousness, stress, anguish, anxiety, fear, uncertainty.
- Porto (2006). The evaluation of university students from the perspective of their protagonists. With a sample of students in the final year of degrees in the five areas of knowledge of the University of Santiago de Compostela and directors of the Department that teach in these degrees. The results of the research show that the conception of evaluation can be summarized in checking the level of

Table 2. Competences and general characteristics

CHARACTERISTICS		COMPETENCES			
		Cognitive	Technical	Relational	Emotional
	Main function	Think	Do	Communicate	Feel
	Mode of operation	Logical and Rational	Motor and Intellectual	Verbal and non-verbal	Irrational and Impulsive
	Type of learning	Cognitive	Procedural	Experimental	Associative
	Memory	Declarative	Procedural	Rational	Emotional
	Brain structure	Hippocampus and cortex	Gyrus fusiform cortex and cerebellum	Cortex	Amygdala and prefrontal lobe

basic cognitive abilities. In addition, most of the students affirm that the (final) exam is the instrument most used by teachers for the evaluation processes; the research concludes that the practices studied do not allow to improve communication and facilitate learning. The use of self-assessment and co-assessment is not perceived.

- Tlaseca (2010). The assessment of learning as seen by students: Contributions for didactics. Carried out by students from the Faculty of Psychology, Educational Area. Autonomous University of Queretaro. The results of the research show that 37% of students have a conception of the current use of assessment as an administrative one, with functions of control, certification, accreditation, or promotion of degree. The research concludes that the evaluative practices carried out in the area and within the line of psycho-pedagogical training are not entirely relevant or congruent with the cognitive and constructivist theoretical-methodological precepts.

- Zabalza and Lodeiro (2019). The Challenge of Evaluating by Competences at the University. Reflections and Practical Experiences. The aim of this article is to offer a reflection on competency-based assessment in higher education. It consists of two parts. The first part analyses the meaning and didactic conditions applicable to each of the three central concepts that organize this contribution (assessment, competence, and competence assessment). In the second, two specific experiences of competence assessment in our universities are presented: one in which competences are linked to the various subjects in the curriculum; another in which competence assessment appears at the end of the degree as an expression of the overall training received: the ECOEs of the Faculties of Medicine.

Emotional inclusion and competency-based assessment, therefore, covers strategies for developing these emotional competencies and the role they play in the processes of attention, memory, and learning, which are essential activators in assessment. Attention is not constant all the time, and there are attentional curves. For effective work, it is necessary to focus attention on a specific stimulus and disregard others, that is, concentration. This concentration is necessary for the message to reach the grey cells exclusively. On the other hand, the only proof that something has been learned is the memory. Memory is influenced by the same factors as learning. Memorization involves the hippocampus, where acquired and little-used information is forgotten to save neuronal networks and to transfer it to those that are used.

To assimilate this information from a neurobiological point of view, an order must be followed: First the appropriate neural network must be excited, then it must be actively retained, and finally it must be left to rest. This phase is the consolidation phase, where the information is registered in our brain, and the information is integrated into what we already had. This work is more difficult if what we have just learned is contrary to what we already knew. This whole process is a complex system where the input goes to the working memory and from there it is integrated into the MLP as meaningful learning. All this is done through a system of memories according to the information we acquire and its complexity.

The relationship between memory and emotion is clear. Those facts with a high emotional charge help us to consolidate and remember better. This emotional climate is what we should try to look for in evaluative tests. In studies (Barragán et al., 2014), it was concluded that the information best remembered was that associated with a positive emotional context where the hippocampus was activated, while a negative context activated the amygdala, recovering the memory incompletely. Thus, emotional states created by fear or stress should be avoided, as they will provoke emotional demands that will have repercussions on cognitive functions and, therefore, on performance (Verdaguer, 2017).

There is a relationship between emotion and motivation. The brain seeks motivation in everything that is new or unfamiliar or in exciting actions that fall inside its personal potential and that develop its intrinsic motivation. Marina (2011) shows us some strategies to use in assessment processes: setting goals that students are familiar with so that they can focus on them, influencing students' successes positively, increasing their confidence and possibilities, and controlling emotional regulation through different activities that match various learning styles.

Nowadays, university teaching has many challenges arising from changes in the profile of the university student; organizational, methodological, and learning assessment changes; the existence of new spaces where students also learn and which are outside the classroom, even outside the university, and so on. All of these are consequences of new forms, modes and actions that condition our teaching, by questioning us as teachers about what and how we can do to ensure that motivation contributes to generating successful learning processes, in the sense that students are committed to their learning and that the learning they experience can be integrated in relation to the training profile of the university degree they are studying. (Barreto, Fernandez, Sánchez-Santamaría, & Fernández, 2021).

For this reason, in this chapter, we would like to present an assessment experience carried out in the Faculty of Education in Toledo at the University of Castilla-La Mancha, where, in addition to assessing by competences, special care is taken in the methodological approach to the test to be taken, with the aim of making students feel comfortable, confident, able to express their talent through their learning style, having at their disposal all the technical and personal resources they would have in their professional future and being an integrative assessment of all the knowledge and aspects worked on in the subject. The results obtained could be described in one sentence from a student: "It is the most difficult exam I have ever taken in my life, but the one I have learnt the most from and I feel very satisfied with myself".

METHODOLOGY

Following Medina et al. (2014) the methodological complementarity becomes necessary for the solution of didactic problems and educational innovation processes, following this idea, the characteristics of the study and the design foreseen follows the parameters of a mixed methodology since it is a research design that involves quantitative and qualitative methodology, intertwining and mixing (Osorio et al.,

Table 3. Assessment criteria for the subject under investigation

3. CRITERIOS DE EVALUACIÓN Y VALORACIONES			
Sistema de evaluación	Evaluación continua	Evaluación no continua*	Descripción
Valoración de la participación con aprovechamiento en clase	10.00%	10.00%	Participación en las actividades desarrolladas en el aula, foros, debates y a través de la plataforma virtual
Trabajo	30.00%	30.00%	Prácticas, trabajos de investigación y estudio de casos que conformarán un p@rtafolios digital compartido.
Prueba final	60.00%	60.00%	Prueba final consistente en la aplicación, en un caso práctico, de todos los contenidos trabajados en la asignatura
Total	**100.00%**	**100.00%**	—

Source: Virtual Campus of the subject Treatment of Learning Difficulties of the Degree in Early Childhood Education at the University of Castile-La Mancha.

2021), being more than the sum of both, because it implies their interaction and empowerment, either in a particular study or in several studies within a research programme (Tashakkori and Teddlie, 2003). Mixed-methods research uses both quantitative and qualitative data collection and analysis in the methods that are part of the study. It is carried out in a parallel manner without any significant combination, as the questions posed and the inferences made are often qualitative or quantitative in nature without being combined (Tashakkori and Teddlie, 2003), and on other occasions inferences are made from all the information collected (meta-inferences), with the aim of achieving a greater understanding of the object of study (Hernández-Sampieri and Mendoza, 2008).

Our research is considered field research because the data is collected directly from the study environment, which in this case is represented on the one hand by the teachers responsible for the subject and, on the other hand, by the students of the subject who undertake the new form of assessment.

When reflecting on the topic, contexts, processes as well as resources, there are five main purposes that lead us to orient our research towards a mixed research design:

1. Triangulation, in other words, the search for convergence and corroboration of the results of different methods and models that study the same phenomenon.
2. Complementarity, that is, the search for collaboration, improvement, illustration and clarification of the results of one method with the results of the other method.
3. The discovery of paradoxes and contradictions leading to the reworking of the research question.
4. The development of how the results of one method are used to help explain the other method.
5. Expanding or seeking the breadth and scope of the research by using different methods for different components of enquiry.

Qualitative Phase

We used the subject Educational Treatment of Learning Difficulties and Diversity of Specific Needs, from the 3rd year of the Degree in Early Childhood Education at the Faculty of Education of the University of Castilla-La Mancha. The sample consisted of 47 students. Following the e-guide, the evaluation proposal for this subject is as follows: (Table 3)

As can be seen, the assessment consists of a practical part in which participation and use of the class is assessed, a part of practical and research work and a part, which is worth 60% of the final mark, consisting of a final test. In our case, we are interested in focusing on the final exam and addressing its process and development.

From the beginning of the subject, when the topic of the evaluation is addressed, it is explained that the test will start three days before the scheduled date and that it will end on the day set in the official calendar. They will have to work on two case studies (one dealing with a learning difficulty and the other with a case study of a disability). They will have to analyze the data provided, carry out the action protocol and resolve a specific learning situation. All based on the contents offered in the subject, the blogs made and shared by all and the consultation of the sources they consider appropriate. It will be as close as possible to the work that a teacher carries out in their daily practice and the cases will be taken (respecting anonymity) from the school reality.

Three days before the date of submission of the test, an assignment is opened in Moodle with all the indications and the two case studies. They will be oriented towards the most recent bibliography and the one recommended in the e-guide of the subject. They will have this time to complete their work individually, with a limit of three pages plus annexes and placing special emphasis on the references consulted. On the day of the test, all the reports must be "uploaded" to the Moodle platform by the established deadline.

One of the most important issues for us, as we are immersed in a competence-based learning system, is the analysis of which competences are worked on in this type of test and what transferences are produced to competences in other subjects. From this approach, we have examined each of the competences set out in the e-guide and their relationship with the process of developing the proposed test. The results, shown in the following table, demonstrate the intrinsic relationship between the two variables analyzed. (Table 4)

Finally, the relationship with the competences proposed in other subjects of the same degree was carried out, highlighting the bidirectionality with those marked in Practicum I (PI), Practicum II (PII), and Final Degree Project (TFG). Concluding the transfer of the contents worked on, as can be seen in the following table: (Table 5)

The second part of the research was carried out through the qualitative analysis of a questionnaire of open questions answered by the students once the test was over. The questions for this purpose were:

What did you think of the typology of the assessment test?

Most of the responses received (67%) rated the innovative proposal very positively, with time being a key factor in consolidating learning. On the other hand, although it is not significant (5%), but it should be considered, they expressed a certain feeling of uncertainty until they had seen how the test would go and had checked that there was no "trap".

From your point of view, which type of test promotes learning and why?

A high percentage of interviewees value this type of innovative test as it makes them aware of the following aspects that enhance their learning:

- Tranquility and reduction of pressure
- Awareness of the importance of the bibliography.
- The importance of continuous classroom work
- Re-reading and revision of productions.
- Appreciation of ICT in everyday life

What difficulties did you encounter and how did you feel emotionally?

Table 4. Relationship between the subject competences and the learning activities proposed in the assessment test

COMPETENCES	LEARNING ACTIVITIES
2.6.II.04 To recognize the identity of the stage and its cognitive, psychomotor, communicative, social, affective, and psychomotor characteristics.	Reading Orderly search of information Analysis and comparison of data
2.6.II.13 To know how to analyze the data obtained, critically understand the reality, and draw up a report of conclusions.	Organization and systematization of data Application of contents studied in the subject Arguing decision making
CB02 Students can apply their knowledge to their work or vocation in a professional manner and possess the competences usually demonstrated through the elaboration and defense of arguments and problem solving within their field of study.	Elaboration of reports according to an established model Assessing the importance of futurology and change Drawing conclusions
CB03 Students can gather and interpret relevant data (usually within their field of study) to make judgements that include reflection on relevant social, scientific, or ethical issues.	
CG01 To know the objectives, curricular contents, and evaluation criteria of Early Childhood Education.	
CT04 Ethical commitment and professional ethics.	

The answers show an initial feeling of anxiety up to the moment of learning about the cases to be developed. But once the evaluation process has begun, the feelings are of calmness, motivation, inter-

Table 5. Transfer to PI, PII, and TFG competences

Transfers		
Subjects	**Competences**	
Practicum I **Practicum II**	Control and monitor the educational process and the teaching and learning process by mastering the necessary techniques and strategies.	1.3.II.03
	Students can apply their knowledge to their work or vocation in a professional manner and possess the competences usually demonstrated through the elaboration and defense of arguments and the resolution of problems within their area of study.	CB02
	Students can gather and interpret relevant data (usually within their field of study) to make judgements which include reflection on relevant social, scientific, or ethical issues.	CB03
TFG	Students can apply their knowledge to their work or vocation in a professional manner and possess the competences usually demonstrated through the development and defense of arguments and problem solving within their field of study.	CB02
	Students can gather and interpret relevant data (usually within their field of study) with a view to making judgements that include reflection on relevant social, scientific, or ethical issues.	CB03
	Students have developed those learning skills necessary to undertake further study with a high degree of autonomy.	CB05

est, know-how, the need to learn more, enjoy the process and feel protagonist of the organization, work, and result.

Inevitably, in addition to the improvement of the students' emotions, we must know whether this type of test achieves the expected results and even whether these results improve in relation to the traditional test carried out in the previous academic year (consisting of 25 multiple-choice questions and a proposal to be developed). To this end, the results of the two consecutive academic years were examined using the Wilcoxon test, since this is a variable that can be measured on an ordinal scale and can be superimposed on continuous populations. The data shown in the table below confirm the good results obtained. (Table 6)

Table 6. Quantitative phase: analysis and comparison of results

TRADITIONAL TEST (2020)			INNOVATIVE TEST (2021)		
GOOD	34,89	15	GOOD	65.116%	28
OUTSTANDING	11.63%	5	OUTSTANDING	25.581%	11
PASS	37,20%	16	PASS	6.977%	3
FALLING GRADE	16.28%	7	FALLING GRADE	0%	0
HONORS QUALIFICATION	2.3%	2	HONORS QUALIFICATION	2.3%	2

CONCLUSION

Bisquerra et al. (2012) define emotional competence as "the set of knowledge, abilities, skills and attitudes necessary to understand, express and appropriately regulate emotional phenomena" (p. 73). This definition shows us that emotional competence can be learned and should be taught, avoiding being dominated by our reptilian brain. The development of a good emotional competence in students will constitute a meta-skill to face the evaluation or control of the acquired contents. This will be the one that regulates the level that the student will reach with respect to a teaching or subject, showing the importance that emotions have in learning, to the point that the cognitive and affective cannot be understood separately, since what they feel will determine what they think.

The emotional climate of the classroom is a determining factor in achieving positive student performance. This climate is composed of the relationship between teacher and students, the type of relationship and the climate that arises from this relationship (Yankovic, 2011). Students need to have a relationship of trust and security to learn well and to show this learning in the assessment process. According to Ibarrola (2013), there are five types of relationships that influence the classroom climate.

- The teacher's relationship with the subject or content studied. The subject proposed by the teacher must be interesting, otherwise the pupil will lose interest. When there is a lack of interest, there is a lack of predisposition to learning.
- The student's relationship with the subject or content studied. When designing an assessment activity, it is assumed that it will be interesting for students, but this does not necessarily have to be the case. Generally (Cruz, 2020), students are only motivated by the extrinsic motivation of the

qualification and consider the exam as the way to pass the subject, often far from the interest or need for training for their professional future.

- The teacher's relationship with himself/herself. It is essential for teachers to be aware of their own thoughts, experiences, attitudes, and so on, in other words, they have to develop their own emotional competence so that they can achieve an adequate development of their pupils.
- The teacher's relationship with the pupil. The pupil must feel that he/she is respected and understood by the teacher. This relationship is difficult to carry out with the ratio that many university classrooms have.
- The relationship between students. The teacher must ensure a good relationship between all of them, a situation that does not occur when there is a poor relationship between classmates, rivalry, physical absence, and so on.

The aim is to seek a pedagogy created with the students and not for them, developing their full potential. According to Tortosa et al. (2016), teachers must assume four aspects to favor the classroom climate and have a positive impact on the evaluation process: They must create communication, where the teacher must be able to interpret the non-verbal messages of the students, their fears, needs and apprehensions. They also must generate motivation, both from them towards their work and from the pupils towards their own confidence. Additionally, they must be adaptable to personal aptitudes and attitudes, being creative to cope with any unexpected situation. And finally, self-control. They must have control over themselves to face any reality that may arise.

In short, creating an emotionally positive and trustworthy environment, where all participants give the best of themselves (Goleman calls it resonance), bearing in mind the need to know how to manage a neural structure through appropriate emotional management, which will provide truly significant learning, with highly satisfactory evaluative results that will excite all students. And the most appropriate methodology, to achieve this emotionally positive environment, is the use of different assessment methods where the student can show their abilities, skills, and abilities (definition of competence) and try not to relegate the assessment to a simple final exam.

Assessment is one of the most important parts of any teaching-learning process, as it allows us to identify the competences acquired by the student in a specific subject, and at the same time it serves as feedback to check what aspects need to be changed in the methodological and didactic approach to the subject (De Miguel, 2006). Regarding the role of the teacher in the classroom, Ibarrola (2013) makes a proposal for improving student motivation, dealing with assessment in a positive way and achieving adequate emotional competence:

- To know what the origins of the student's lack of motivation are to discover elements that foster their intrinsic motivation.
- To give them the necessary tools to be able to answer: Why, what for and how?
- To create a relaxed and calm atmosphere in the classroom.
- To evaluate the work and not the students, so that their self-esteem remains intact.
- To value the whole learning process and not only the final mark.
- To encourage self-confidence to overcome failure, turning objectives into sub-objectives.
- To relate all learning to real life and especially to the professional performance they will face in the future.
- To make learning less dramatic by dressing it up with satisfaction, joy, and so on.

- To create successful practices so that they activate the reward center and get positive reinforcement.
- To make it very clear what is expected of the students, through rubrics.
- To offer the resolution of the tasks, after the test, so that they continue to learn from their successes or mistakes.
- To encourage students' self-reflection so that they can find out what needs they have.
- The teacher must always be motivated, because what he/she feels is what he/she will pass on to the students.
- To offer them different assessment strategies where they can reflect not only content, but also procedures and attitudes.
- To set motivating and interesting challenges for the students.
- To encourage cooperative work as opposed to competitive work, and not to overuse the latter.
- To encourage creativity and allow tasks to be carried out in a different way.

It is pertinent that the teacher reflects deeply on whether the current university is inclusive. Within the framework of international policies, institutions are asked to adapt to make effective the rights to education, participation, and equal opportunities for all. For this assessment to be achieved for all, it is essential that teachers transform their epistemological, ethical, political, and pedagogical positions, influenced by their previous beliefs and experiences, so that, when constructing the value judgements inherent to the assessment process, they have the subject and not knowledge as a reference point, accompanied by excellent preparation and training in the handling of instrumental content and formal skills (Casanova, 2011).

A particularly noteworthy fact is that for some time now, the university systems of the different Latin American countries have been in tension due to the serious mismatch between the actions taken in the sphere of quality assessment and the concept of quality that is held. This tension is reflected in the fragmentation and reduction of the areas of quality evaluated and the increasing comprehensiveness required and requested of the concept of educational quality to be achieved (Murillo, 2010).

We advocate, as Santiuste and Arranz (2009) indicate, a rigorous but motivating assessment, a conceptual assessment but at the same time a competency-based assessment, an assessment where the student can show the contents learned but also their predisposition to research, enquiry and problem solving, an assessment where time and space are not the emotional marker, an assessment where the professional reality provides the "know-how" and the "know-how to be", an assessment where fear, tension and frustration are eliminated by motivation and the desire to give the best of oneself to continue learning.

When evaluation with an emphasis on control and measurement of results has punitive purposes, associated with survival, fear will be triggered by the expectation of results (Tortosa et al., 2016). However, if assessment has a formative and humanistic intention, it becomes an ally of students and teachers. Our reality in most university classrooms indicates that assessment is not well received by those being assessed, even though it is installed as a compulsory process (Borjas, 2017). We advocate for an evaluation where the process is the most important because of its formative component, where individual mistakes are shared and used as part of the development, where the results serve to improve the teaching-learning process. And where the competence objectives are the protagonists. An emotionally appropriate evaluation that makes training exciting.

REFERENCES

Alsina, J. (2010). *Evaluación por competencias en la universidad: las competencias transversales. Cuadernos de docencia universitaria.* Octaedro.

Ayala, M. (2015). *Evaluación según sus agentes.* Atencion. https://n9.cl/0gdu6

Barragán, E., & Ahmad, R. Morales, M., & Cinthya, I. (2014). Psicología de las emociones positivas: generalidades y beneficios. *Enseñanza e Investigación en Psicología.* Consejo Nacional para la Enseñanza en Investigación en Psicología. https://www.redalyc.org/pdf/292/29232614006.pdf

Bisquerra, R. (2012). *¿Cómo educar las emociones? La inteligencia emocional en la infancia y la adolescencia.* Espligues de Llobregat (Barcelona): Hospital San Joan de Déu.

Borjas, M. (2017). Ludoevaluación en Educación Infantil. *Verbum.*

Boroel Cervantes, B. I., Sánchez-Santamaría, J., Morales Gutiérrez, K. D., & Henríquez Ritchie, P. S. (2018). Educación exitosa para todos: La tutoría como proceso de acompañamiento escolar desde la mirada de la equidad educativa. *Revista Fuentes, 20*(2), 91–104. doi:10.12795/revistafuentes.2018.v20.i2.06

Casanova, M. A. (2011). Evaluación para la Inclusión Educativa. *Revista Iberoamericana de Evaluación Educativa, 4*(1), 78–89.

Chabot, D., & Chabot, M. (2014). *Pedagogía Emocional. Sentir para Aprender.* Alfaomega.

Cruz, P., Borjas, M. P., & López, M. (2020). Ludoevaluación de la emoción del miedo en educación infantil. *Revista Latinoamericana De Ciencias Sociales, Niñez Y Juventud, 19*(1), 1–21. doi:10.11600/rlcsnj.19.1.4184

De Miguel Díaz, M. (2006). Metodologías para optimizar el aprendizaje. Segundo objetivo del Espacio Europeo de Educación Superior. *Revista Interuniversitaria de Formación de Profesorado,* 20-41. https://www.redalyc.org/pdf/274/27411311004.pdf

Gambarini, M. F., & Cruz, P. (2019). Habilidades docentes en comunicación eficaz. Ejercicio de liderazgo centrado en la misión docente. *Aularia, 8*(1), pp. 9-20. http://cort.as/-ME77

Goleman, D. (2006). *Inteligencia social.* Kairós.

Hernández, R. (2002). El juego en la infancia. *Revista Chilena de Pediatria, 4*(21-22), 134–137. doi:10.4067/S0370-41062008000500014

Hernández Sampieri, R., & Mendoza, C. P. (2008). El matrimonio cuantitativo cualitativo: el paradigma mixto. En *6º Congreso de Investigación en Sexología. Congreso efectuado por el Instituto Mexicano de Sexología.* A. C. y la Universidad Juárez Autónoma de Tabasco, Villahermosa, Tabasco, México.

Ibarrola, B. (2013). *Aprendizaje emocionante. Neurociencia para el aula.* SM.

Marina, J. A. (2011). Los secretos de la motivación. *Ariel.*

Medina, A., Herrán, A., & Domínguez, M. C. (2014). *Fronteras en la investigación de la Didáctica.* UNED.

Mora, F. (2017). *Sólo se puede aprender aquello que se ama*. Alianza Editorial.

Murillo, F. J. (2010). *Retos en la evaluación de la calidad de la educación en América Latina*. CUTT. https://cutt.ly/RePXTI0

Osorio González, R., & Castro Ricalde, D.Osorio–González. (2021). Aproximaciones a una metodología mixta. *Novarua, 13*(22), 65–84. doi:10.20983/novarua.2021.22.4

Porto, M. (2006). *La evaluación de estudiantes universitarios vista por sus protagonistas*. Educatio Siglo XXI, 24, 167–188. https://revistas.um.es/educatio/article/view/156

Ricoy, M., & Fernández-Rodríguez, J. (2013). The University students» perception of the evaluation: a case study. *Educación XX1. 16*(2), 321-341. doi: 10.5944/educxx1.16.2.2645

Barreto, I. M. G., Fernandez, R., Sánchez-Santamaría, J., & Fernández, C. (2021). A Global Competence Approach to Teaching Development for Intercultural Education. In Barreto, I.M.G. (ed) Handbook of Research on Promoting Social Justice for Immigrants and Refugees Through Active Citizenship and Intercultural Education (pp. 268-287). https://doi.org/10.4018/978-1-7998-7283-2.ch014

Santiuste, V., & Arranz, M.ª L. (2009). Nuevas perspectivas en el concepto de evaluación. *Review of Education, 350*, 463–476.

Tashakkori, A., & Teddlie, Ch. (Eds.). (2003). *Handbook of mixed methods in social and behavioral research*. Sage.

Tlaseca, M. (2010). *La evaluación del aprendizaje vista por los estudiantes: Aportes para la didáctica*. Universidad Autónoma de Querétaro.

Tomás, U. (2013). *Neuroeducación. Educar con emociones*. Alianza editorial. https://www.alianzaeditorial.es/primer_capitulo/neuroeducacion.pdf

Tortosa, M. T., Grao, S., & Álvarez, J. D. (coords.). (2016). *XIV Jornadas de Redes de Investigación en Docencia Universitaria. Investigación, innovación y enseñanza universitaria: enfoques pluridisciplinares*. Universitat d'Alacant, Institut de Ciències de l'Educació, pp. 1466-1480. http://hdl.handle.net/10045/57093

Verdaguer, S. (2017). *El arte de dar clases*. Plaza y Valdes.

Yankovic, B. (2011). *Emociones, sentimientos, afecto. El desarrollo emocional*. CUTT. https://cutt.ly/0eOnvtT

Zabalza, M. A., & Lodeiro Enjo, L. (2019). El Desafío de Evaluar por Competencias en la Universidad. Reflexiones y Experiencias Prácticas. *Revista Iberoamericana De Evaluación Educativa, 12*(2), 29–48. doi:10.15366/riee2019.12.2.002

Chapter 3
Analysis of Competences Development in Online and Face-to-Face Teaching Modalities Through a Formative Assessment Experience

Félix Enrique Lobo de Diego
https://orcid.org/0000-0002-5469-2052
Universidad de Valladolid, Spain

Laura Cañadas
Universidad Autónoma de Madrid, Spain

ABSTRACT

The purpose of this study is to analyse how the modality used (online vs. face-to-face) for the teaching and learning process influences the acquisition of professional competences in a formative assessment experience. An action-research study was implemented during two academic years in the 2019/2020 and 2020/2021. One teacher and sixty teacher education students of the third course of the Faculty of Education of Segovia (University of Valladolid, Spain) participated in this study. A questionnaire and two teaching staff reports were used to collect the information. Results show agreement of the utility of the formative assessment experience implemented to the development of teaching competences both in online and in face-to-face mode. As conclusion the authors highlight the need for rethinking the way formative assessment is delivered at Higher Education so that theory and practice are connected and contribute to develop professional competences.

DOI: 10.4018/978-1-6684-3537-3.ch003

INTRODUCTION

Teacher education should contribute to the development of competences that students will need in their future work (Cañadas et al., 2019). Competences are defined as a complex and comprehensive construct that includes knowledge, skills, techniques, abilities, dispositions, attitudes, and values, among others (Moreno-Olivos, 2021). For this purpose, the different subjects that are part of the curricula must generate teaching and learning processes that allow their development to the greatest extent possible. Methodology and assessment will be essential for this purpose. Specifically, the role of assessment in student learning has been increasingly recognized over the last three decades as an important element of the quality in the teaching and learning process (Baird et al., 2017; Black et al., 2006, López-Pastor et al., 2013; López-Pastor & Sicilia, 2017).

However, during COVID-19 pandemic situation the teaching and learning processes have had to be adapted to different scenarios depending on the teaching model to be adopted by the specific health situation in which we find ourselves, and with them, the assessment processes (Carrillo & Flores, 2020; Flores, 2020; Flores & Gago, 2020). During the situation caused by COVID-19, numerous doubts and difficulties have arisen to ensure a fair, sustainable and quality assessment process for the development of the competences of the degrees (Cañadas, 2020).

Given this framework, the purpose of this chapter is to analyse how the modality used for the teaching and learning process influences the acquisition of professional competences in a formative assessment experience carried out in the academic years 2019-2020 in online modality by the health emergency derived from COVID-19, and 2020-2021 in face-to-face modality at the Faculty of Education of Segovia (University of Valladolid). In addition, we explore the advantages and disadvantages of the application of a formative assessment system. Specifically, we study how the implementation of an Oriented Project Learning (OPL), in which students have to design and implement a learning proposal, in two different teaching contexts marked by the health situation arising from COVID-19 has influenced the development of professional competences of future teachers and their experience lived in a formative assessment practice.

FORMATIVE ASSESSMENT

Traditionally, assessment was oriented to the certification of academic results (Knight, 2006). Its main objective was to assess the degree of achievement of the planned objectives at the end of a teaching period, using a grade as an act that ratifies what is learned (Black et al., 2002). This conception was characterized by the search for objectivity to measure in the most reliable way possible the products of the students at the end of the teaching and learning process (Álvarez, 2011). In this conception, assessment is matched with grading, limiting the assessment to taking an exam and the teaching staff being the only one responsible for assessing and the students the only object of the assessment (Calderón & Escalera, 2008). However, during the last decades a different way of assess has been increasing its presence in teaching and learning processes. It is called by different denominations, but one of the most extended is formative assessment. Andrade et al. (2019) defined formative assessment:

As part of a planned assessment system, formative assessment supports teachers' and students' inferences about strengths, weaknesses, and opportunities for improvements in learning. It is a source of information that educators can use in instructional planning and students can use in deepening their understandings, improving their achievement, taking responsibility for, and self-regulating, their learning. Formative assessment includes both general principles, and discipline-specific elements that comprise the formal and informal materials, collaborative processes, ways of knowing, and habits of mind particular to a content domain (p. 14).

Under this definition, assessment should be used to improve not only students learning but also teaching processes. Information derived from assessment process should serve not only for upgrade students' assignments but mainly for improve and self-regulate their learning, improving their capabilities to recognize their strengths and weaknesses.

For this purpose, some authors have studied what are the strategies to apply a truly formative assessment process. Wiliam and Thompson (2007) and Wiliam and Leahy (2015) indicate five key strategies for this purpose: (a) clarifying, sharing, and understanding goals for learning and criteria for success with learners; (b) engineering effective classroom activities and tasks that elicit evidence of students' learning; (c) providing feedback that moves learning forward; (d) activating students as owners of their own learning; and (e) activating students as mutual learning resources.

FORMATIVE ASSESSMENT AND COMPETENCES DEVELOPMENT

Recent studies have put the focus in the use of formative assessment in Higher Education. They have shown that formative assessment improves students' motivation, involvement, and learning (Atienza et al., 2016; Hortigüela et al, 2018); it contributes to the development of their competences, specifically, teacher competences in teacher education studies (Cañadas, in press; Cañadas et al., 2021; Panadero et al., 2018); and it let them self-regulate their learning (Clark, 2012). In the last years, some researchers have focus on how the implementation of formative assessment process during teacher education improve the grade of development of teaching competences (Asún-Dieste et al., 2019; Cañadas, in press; Cañadas et al, 2018, 2021; Gallardo-Fuentes et al., 2018, 2020; Gómez-Gasquet et al., 2018; Hortigüela et al., 2018; Romero-Martín et al., 2017). All these studies have found that after the application of formative assessment experiences the development of teaching competences improve. For example, Hortigüela et al. (2018) study shown that the use of formative assessment has a great impact on generic competences development (4 out of 5 competences studied improve). Same results are found by Gómez-Gasquet et al. (2018). Romero-Martín et al. (2017) study has shown that the implementation of formative assessment processes contributes to raise the levels of involvement during teamwork, improve the competence development and recognize feelings of justice in grading process. Cañadas et al. (2021) study show that 35 out of 45 competences studied improve after the use of formative assessment and Gallardo-Fuentes et al. (2020) study show an improvement in 15 out of 45 competences studied after the application of a formative assessment system based on deliveries throughout the course and constant feedback. Pla-Campas et al. (2016) study showed that those students involved in a participatory formative assessment system seems to achieve better academic results.

In the context of COVID-19, there is not some much research that has analyzed what are the implications of online and semi-presential teaching for students learning. The studies have mainly focus on the development of digital competences or in describing the experiences developed by teachers to adapt their teaching (Pérez-Escoda et al., 2021; Sá & Serpa, 2020). Some studies have also analyzed how the modality used for teaching and assessment affects the development of competences. Specifically, the study of Cañadas & Lobo-de-Diego (2021) analyzed the grade of development of teaching competences of Early Childhood and Primary Education Degree students after the implementation of didactics proposals in virtual and blended learning formats and whether there are differences in the grade of development of those competences depending on if the subject has been taught in online or blended learning format. They found that after the development of training subjects in those formats, 31 out of 45 competences improved their development. Regarding the second objective, it was found that the fact of developing teaching in one or the other modality affects the development of a reduced number of competences (7 out of 45).

FORMATIVE ASSESSMENT: ADVANTAGES AND DISADVANTAGES

Along with the role that formative assessment plays in the development of competences and learning in teacher education, there is also another issue that has been the focus of attention in recent years: the advantages and disadvantages that the application of these assessment systems have for both students and teachers. There are some studies that have focused on this issue (Atienza et al., 2016; Gallardo & Carter, 2016; Hortigüela, et al., 2015; Lorente-Catalán & Kirk, 2016; Martos-García et al., 2017). Cañadas (2018) carries out a review of these studies concluding the main advantages and disadvantages found, among which we have:

- Advantages: Students become the protagonists of their own learning, their motivation increases, academic performance improves, feedback improves learning and allows them to learn more, autonomous learning competences are developed and promotes metacognitive processes, among others.
- Disadvantages: a greater workload is perceived, both for teachers and students, it requires continuous effort and compulsory attendance, there is little custom in its implementation, and it is thought that it is a soft assessment system and undemanding

METHOD

Design

A retrospective study design was carried out. An action-research study was implemented during two academic years to change and improve teacher students' education at the local level. This methodological choice responds to the need to understand and generate knowledge about educational practices and their complexities (McAteer, 2013).

Participants

Sixty teacher education students of the third course of Primary Education Degree and Joint Study Programme Bachelor's Degree in Primary Education and Bachelor's Degree in Early Childhood Education of the Faculty of Education of Segovia (University of Valladolid, Spain) participated. Specifically, 40 students took the course in an online format in 2019-2020 academic year and 20 students took it in a face-to-face format in 2020-2021 academic year. They were aged between 19 and 26 years old with an average of 21.32 years ± 1.59. Of these, 30% were men and 70% were women.

The teacher in charge of carrying out the experience in the two academic years studied, was a Graduate Teaching Assistant taking a PhD in Education with three years of teaching experience at university level. The Graduate Teaching Assistant was in charge of the design, elaboration and development of the good practice, advising and supervising the students in its development.

Instruments

Two instruments were used to collect information for this study: (i) the quantitative Questionnaire on the "Experience of Good Practice" and its assessment (Cuestionario sobre la "Experiencia de Buena práctica" y su evaluación) developed and validated by the Spanish Network for Formative and Shared Evaluation in Education (Authors) that was completed by teacher education students; and (ii) two qualitative reports on the development of the good practice in the years studied completed by the teacher in charge.

i. The questionnaire it is composed for 46 items that help us understand the experience lived by students and their degree of agreement on the assessment system employed. It has 13 specific questions on the development of good practice and 33 on the subject in general. It was answered with a five-point Likert scale from 0 (disagree) to 4 (strongly agree). We obtained adequate reliability indices with a Cronbach's alpha of 0.737 for the part of the questions on the development of the good experience, and 0.956 Cronbach's alpha for the questions on the subject in general, which allow us to ensure reliable measures.

ii. Two Final reports of the formative assessment practice of the years studied have been chosen to examine teachers' opinion, academic results, changes and evolution of the Oriented Project Learning practice.

Procedure

This research was structured in 8 phases: (1) Study design: Before the beginning of the second semester of the academic year 2019-2020, we designed the formative assessment practice and the research phases that guided data collection; (2) Explanation of the research to the participants and the aim of the formative assessment practice; (3) Development and exposition of the Oriented Project Learning that participants designed; (4) First round of data collection; (5) Analysis of gathered data and final report writing; (6) modifications to the proposal of the practice in formative assessment before beginning of first semester of 2020-2021 academic-year; (7) Explanation of the research to participants and development and implementation of designed proposals; (8) Data collection; and (9) Analysis of the information, final report writing and comparative of the two rounds of implementation of the formative assessment practice. In this research, the anonymity of the participants has been guaranteed in accordance with national and international ethics standards.

In both academic years, students had to carry out, as a learning activity for the good formative assessment experience, the development of an OPL in which they had to design and elaborate a proposal for the teaching of Physical Education contents. This work was carried out in small groups of 4-5 students

Table 1. Items of the questionnaire grouped

Related to the Good practice experience	1.1 Was the use of this experience in the subject negotiated at the beginning of the subject?	
	1.2 Do you think that this experience has helped you to acquire professional competences?	
	1.3 Does the assessment that has been proposed favour the acquisition of professional competences?	
	1.4 Do you consider what you have learned from this experience to be useful?	
	1.5 Innovative, because it develops new or creative solutions?	
	1.6 Effective, because it demonstrates a positive and tangible impact of improvement?	
	1.7 Sustainable, because it is maintained over time and can produce long-lasting effects.	
	1.8 Replicable, because it can be used as a model to be developed in other contexts.	
	1.9 How do you value the support received by the teacher?	
	1.10 How do you rate the help received from classmates?	
	1.11 Indicate your overall satisfaction with the experience.	
	1.12 Indicate your overall satisfaction in relation to the evaluation of the experience.	
Related to the subject development	Advantages of the use of formative assessment	2.1 What is the degree of difficulty of the experience?
		2.2 There is a pre-agreed, negotiated and consensual contract for the assessment system.
		2.3 Requires participation in my own assessment
		2.4 Is process focused, importance of daily work.
		2.5 The student is an active learner.
		2.6 Teamwork is approached in a collaborative way.
		2.7 Learner is more motivated, learning process is more motivating.
		2.8 Grading is fairer.
		2.9 Improves academic tutoring (monitoring and help to the student).
		2.10 Allows functional learning.
		2.11 Enables meaningful learning.
		2.12 Much more learning is achieved.

who were supervised at all times by the teaching staff. Likewise, the OPL was put into practice, firstly, with university classmates to improve aspects of content, group control, verbal and non-verbal expression and communication techniques, teamwork, etc., and then with primary school students, as was the case in the 2020-2021 academic year with the face-to-face modality. After this, the university students had to make a presentation and defence of their work to their classmates.

Data Analysis

After collecting the information of the two academic years, we proceeded to analyse it. Quantitative data from the questionnaire were descriptively analysed using SPSS version 24. Differences in means have also been calculated using the statistic U-Mann-Whitney ($P < 0.05$) to detect whether there are significant differences between academic years. For the analysis of the qualitative information of the Final Reports we have carried out a deductive documentary analysis (Cohen et al., 2018) with the software

Atlas.ti version 7.5.4. based on the following deductively determined categories (Table 3). After both, quantitative and qualitative analysis, the information has been connected.

Table 2. Continuation of the questionnaire items grouping

Related to the subject development	Advantages of the use of formative assessment	2.13 Improves the quality of the work required.
		2.14 There is an interrelationship between theory and practice.
		2.15 It assesses all possible aspects (knowledge, know-how, know-how and being).
		2.16 There is feedback on documents and activities.
		2.17 There is the possibility of correcting mistakes in documents and activities.
		2.18 There is a more individualised follow up.
	Disadvantages of the use of formative assessment	2.19 Requires more responsibility.
		2.20 Requires compulsory and active attendance.
		2.21 Has unfamiliar work dynamics, lack of habitus.
		2.22 Requires continuity.
		2.23 Needs to be understood beforehand.
		2.24 Requires more effort.
		2.25 It is difficult to work in a group.
		2.26 A lot of work can accumulate in the end.
		2.27 There is a disproportion between tasks/credits.
		2.28 The grading process is more complex, and sometimes unclear.
		2.29 It creates insecurity and uncertainty, doubts about what to do.
		2.30 It is unfair compared to other assessment processes.
		2.31 The corrections have been unclear.
		2.32 The assessment of the work is subjective.

Table 3. Categories used for the documentary analysis

Assessment of the experience	Assessment of the teaching and learning process
	Student's motivation
	Student's participation
	Advantages
	Difficulties and disadvantages
	Learning outcomes and transfer

Figure 1. Scores obtained on some of the items on good practice experience
Note. Item 1= Do you think that this experience has helped you to acquire professional competences?; Item 2= Does the assessment that has been proposed favour the acquisition of professional competences?; Item 3= Do you consider what you have learned from this experience to be useful?; Item 4= Innovative, because it develops new or creative solutions?

RESULTS

In Relation With the Development of the Good Practice Experience

Table 4 shows the results about the "Good practice experience". Participants obtained scores above three points out of four on the acquisition of professional competences through this experience of formative assessment. The results obtained in the online mode are higher than in face-to-face mode. Likewise, students in both academic years agree that the formative assessment system favours the development of professional competences with averages of 3.42 and 3.00 (Table 4 and Figure 1). In both the online and face-to-face modalities, students consider that what they have learned is quite useful with scores above 3.62. However, we found significant differences in this aspect (p= .049), being higher in online modality. Online and face-to-face participants agree that the experience was innovative with means above 2.72, although we found significant differences (p=.005), being higher, again, in the online modality. In addition, 68.3% of the participants had previously taken part in experiences of good practice in formative assessment in other subjects at the university. This is stated by teaching staff as "For those students who are already familiar with this type of experience, it may also have been innovative for them, since the format (guidelines that guide the preparation of the work) vary with respect to other subjects that have taken and used this type of experience." (Final Report 2, p.10).

Participants from both modalities agree that through this type of experience there is a positive impact and improvement with scores above 3.32 (Table 4). In this sense, participants consider that this type of experience generates results that are maintained over time and can produce long-lasting effects, with the highest score obtained in the online modality with an average of 3.32. Participants in both modalities consider it to be replicable with scores above 3.30 out of four.

Table 4. Descriptive statistics (mean and standard deviation) and U-Mann Whitney for the good practice experience grouping items

About the Good Practice Experience	19/20 (Online)	20/21 (Face-to-face)	P
	M (SD)	M (SD)	
N	40	20	
1.1 Was the use of this experience in the subject negotiated at the beginning of the subject?	3.05 (0.80)	2.70 (0.94)	0.288
1.2 Do you think that this experience has helped you to acquire professional competences?	3.57 (0.59)	3.31 (0.82)	0.238
1.3 Does the assessment that has been proposed favour the acquisition of professional competences?	3.42 (0.59)	3.00 (0.81)	0.284
1.4 Do you consider what you have learned from this experience to be useful?	3.75 (0.49)	3.63 (0.49)	**0.049**
1.5 Innovative, because it develops new or creative solutions?	3.38 (0.63)	2.73 (0.87)	**0.005**
1.6 Effective, because it demonstrates a positive and tangible impact of improvement?	3.45 (0.55)	3.33 (0.68)	0.609
1.7 Sustainable, because it is maintained over time and can produce long-lasting effects	3.32 (0.65)	3.05 (0.70)	0.156
1.8 Replicable, because it can be used as a model to be developed in other contexts.	3.57 (0.50)	3.31 (0.67)	0.163
1.9 How do you value the support received by the teacher?	3.77 (0.47)	3.31 (0.74)	**0.008**
1.10 How do you rate the help received from classmates?	3.25 (0.66)	3.10 (0.99)	0.793
1.11 Indicate your overall satisfaction with the experience	3.55 (0.55)	3.36 (0.76)	0.466
1.12 Indicate your overall satisfaction in relation to the evaluation of the experience	3.47 (0.67)	3.05 (0.97)	0.098

Regarding the assessments of the help received from the teaching staff, we find that both modalities are quite in agreement that this has been adequate, with scores above 3.30. The highest score was obtained in the online modality with an average of 3.77. In this aspect we found significant differences (p=.008). In the same way, the participants agree quite strongly that the help received from colleagues has been adequate with scores of 3.25 and 3.10 respectively (Table 4). Regarding satisfaction with the experience, participants in both modalities are quite satisfied, obtaining scores above 3.35, with students in the online modality obtaining the highest score with an average of 3.55. In this line, the participants are also satisfied with the assessment system applied in the OPL experience, with scores above 3.04. Students in the online modality are the most satisfied with a score of 3.47.

In Relation With the Development of the Subject

Regarding to the development of the subject, the results are presented in Table 5. In both academic years the participants show that it is not a very difficult experience, with scores almost identical and below 1.77. However, teaching staff found some difficulties like the "Lack of adequate resources for videoconferencing with all students" (Final Report 1, p.12) or "The number of students in each practice group and the capacity allowed for sports practice in the capacity permitted in the facilities where the

Table 5. Descriptive statistics (mean and standard deviation) and U-Mann Whitney for the development of the subject

About the subject	19/20 (Online)	20/21 (Face-to-face)	P
	M (SD)	M (SD)	
N	40	20	
2.1 What is the degree of difficulty of the experience?	1.76 (0.54)	1.77 (0.54)	0.920
2.2 There is a pre-agreed, negotiated and consensual contract for the assessment system.	3.30 (0.76)	3.31 (0.74)	1.000
2.3 It offers alternatives to all students.	3.45 (0.63)	3,00 (0.68)	**0.020**
2.4 Requires participation in my own assessment.	2.94 (0.84)	3.50 (0.70)	**0.018**

practical classes were held" (Final Report 2, p.11). In both modalities we find that the participants agree that in both modalities they have had to participate in their own assessment, with scores above 2.93 and with a higher assessment obtained by students in the face-to-face modality. In this aspect we find significant differences (P=0.018).

Advantages of the application of formative assessment

The students are quite in agreement that alternatives in the development of the subject have been favoured, although we find that the score is higher in the course 2019/2020 (Table 6). Significant differences in the scores are found (p = 0.020). In both years, the participants agree that the assessment systems used in the subject have been negotiated and agreed in advance with the teaching staff. In fact, students strongly agree that the subjects developed focus on the process, although the score given by the 2019/2020 students

Figure 2. Scores on some of the items on the benefits of the application of formative assessment
Note. Item 1= Is process focused, importance of daily work; Item 2= The student is an active learner; Item 3= Learner is more motivated, learning process is more motivating; Item 4= Improves the quality of the work required

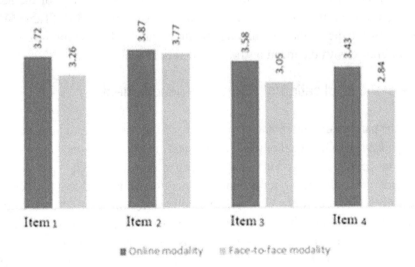

is 0.46 higher than the 2020/2021 with a mean of 3.72 (Figure 2). In both years the students strongly agree that the subjects and the development of the OPL is focused on an active learning process, this being the aspect that obtains the highest scores in this study with scores of 3.87 and 3.77 respectively (Figure 2). This is recorded in Final Report 1 when it is stated that "The main methodological principle that has governed the modifications has been the active learning of the students" (Final Report 1, p.11).

Likewise, students are quite in agreement that the work developed is approached from a collaborative perspective. In both years, students consider that they tend to be more motivated in their learning with the implementation of this type of experience, although students in the online modality are more satisfied with an average of 3.58 (Table 6). This is stated by teaching staff as they think that "the use of formative and shared assessment is quite positive, not only for the teachers but also for the students, who have been very motivated and involved in the subject during the confinement situation" (Final Report 1, p. 13). However, we found significant differences in this aspect (p=0.017). Related to this, the students are quite in agreement that they acquire significant and functional learning, improve the quality of the work required by the teaching staff, and improve academic tutoring, with scores above 2.83 in both academic years (Table 6), with the highest scores in the online modality. This is consistent with teaching staff Reports that consider that the experience has "optimized their learning thanks to the continuous supervision and advice they receive in the seminars and e-mails with the teachers" (Final Report 1, 13). However, we found significant differences in these aspects.

Students agree that in the development of both subjects and the OPL there has been an interrelation between theory and practice and that all possible knowledge is evaluated in them, with averages above 3.21. This coincides with what is expressed by the teaching staff reports "as the thematic blocks developed in the subject can be transferred to other contexts as they have been converted into a didactic resource and proposal" (Final Report 2, p.14). Similarly, we found that the participants agree that there is feedback from teaching staff in the tasks and activities of the subject they have to carry out, with higher scores for the course that experienced the subject in online format. This is consistent with teaching staff as there has been a process of continuous supervision and advice from the teachers at all times, which has allowed the quality of the work to improve considerably with the contributions and feedback received before, during and at the end of the implementation of practical sessions and the OPL" (Final Report 2, p.11). However, we found significant differences for this aspect (p = 0.047).

In both modalities the participants agree that corrections and improvement of the activities are allowed, being the highest score in the face-to-face modality with a mean of 3.42 (Table 6). However, the participants consider that in the online modality a more individualized follow-up was given with a mean of 3.55 and 0.71 difference with the mean of the face-to-face modality.

Disadvantages of the Application of Formative Assessment

In both modalities the participants agree that responsibility is required, although the average is higher in the online modality (Table 7). On the other hand, participants in the face-to-face mode score higher than those in the online mode in terms of compulsory and active attendance. The students of both courses agree that the work dynamics followed in the subject is not unfamiliar to them, obtaining scores below 1.97 and being lower in the face-to-face modality with an average of 1.33. In both courses, we found that the participants agree that the subject requires continuity on the part of the students, with averages above 3.35. Furthermore, the participants consider that it is necessary to understand the tasks beforehand in order to be able to carry them out successfully, with the score obtained in the 2020/2021 academic

Table 6. Descriptive statistics (mean and standard deviation) and U-Mann Whitney for the advantages of the use of formative assessment

About the subject	19/20 (Online)	20/21 (Face-to-face)	P
	M (SD)	M (SD)	
N	40	20	
2.4 Is process focused, importance of daily work.	3.72 (0.45)	3.26 (0.93)	0.057
2.5 The student is an active learner.	3.87 (0.33)	3.77 (0.42)	0.340
2.6 Teamwork is approached in a collaborative way.	3.70 (0.46)	3.72 (0.46)	0.865
2.7 Learner is more motivated, learning process is more motivating.	3.58 (0.54)	3.05 (0.91)	**0.017**
2.8 Grading is fairer.	3,47 (,64)	2.83 (1.04)	**0.020**
2.9 Improves academic tutoring (monitoring and help to the student).	3.62 (0.54)	3.11 (0.99)	**0.050**
2.10 Allows functional learning.	3.55 (0.55)	3,27 (0.46)	0.053
2.11 Enables meaningful learning.	3.72 (0.45)	3,42 (0.60)	**0.049**
2.12 Much more learning is achieved.	3.71 (0.45)	3.22 (0.54)	**0.002**
2.13 Improves the quality of the work required.	3.43 (0.68)	2.84 (0.95)	**0.016**
2.14 There is an interrelationship between theory and practice.	3.65 (0.48)	3.50 (0.70)	0.575
2.15 It assesses all possible aspects (knowledge, know-how, know-how and being).	3.45 (0.63)	3.22 (0.80)	0.321
2.16 There is feedback on documents and activities.	3.75 (0.43)	3.21 (1.08)	**0.047**
2.17 There is the possibility of correcting mistakes in documents and activities.	3.23 (0.77)	3.42 (0.90)	0.225
2.18 There is a more individualised follow up.	3.35 (0.69)	2.84 (1.06)	0.085

year being significantly higher than in the 2019/2020 academic year. In this aspect we found significant differences (P= .020). Likewise, students in both years consider that the subject requires a greater effort, with the score for the face-to-face mode being higher than for the online mode.

On the other hand, the participants agree that there is little difficulty in working in a group, with averages below 1.88. In fact, teaching staff report that "in some groups there has been a conflict in working in groups and carrying out group work (field notebook, OPL) due to the means and resources available to some group members (e.g. poor internet connection)" (Final Report 1, pp. 8-9). There is some discrepancy among students regarding the possibility of accumulating tasks at the end of the course, with online students considering that few tasks can be accumulated with an average of 1.75, while face-to-face students consider that work can be accumulated at the end with an average of 2.46. Along these lines, the participants in the online mode agree that there is no disproportion between the work sent by the teachers and the ECTS credits of the subject with an average of 1.36; while the participants in the face-to-face mode agree that there is some disproportion with an average of 2.09. In addition, students in the face-to-face mode consider the grading system to be more complex with an average of 2.11, while the assessment of students in the online mode is lower with an average of 1.39. However, in both years we find that participants agree that the use of formative assessment systems is less unfair compared to other assessment systems with scores below 1.34. In both modalities, students agree that the development of the subject and OPL do not generate or generate little uncertainty about what they have to do in the subject, with scores below 1.65. However, teaching staff recorded that "The overall experience has been quite positive despite the uncertainty that some students felt when designing their didactic proposal given the limitations of some materials or all the safety measures to be fulfilled" (Final Report 2, p. 11).

The students consider that the feedback and corrections received by the teaching staff have been quite clear, with the score obtained in the 2019/2020 academic year being better than in 2020/2021. Along these lines, the students in the online mode consider that the assessment of the work carried out was not very subjective with an average of 1.43, while the students in the face-to-face mode consider it to have been somewhat subjective with an average of 2.18.

Table 7. Descriptive statistics (mean and standard deviation) and U-Mann Whitney for the disadvantages of the use of formative assessment

About the subject	19/20 (Online)	20/21 (Face-to-face)	P
	M (SD)	M (SD)	
N	40	20	
2.19 Requires more responsibility.	3.56 (0.59)	3.36 (0.68)	0.277
2.20 Requires compulsory and active attendance.	3.30 (0.61)	3.44 (0.61)	0.418
2.21 Has unfamiliar work dynamics, lack of habitus.	1.96 (1.04)	1.33 (0.65)	0.059
2.22 Requires continuity.	3.37 (0.66)	3.36 (0.68)	0.971
2.23 Needs to be understood beforehand.	2.43 (0.91)	3.05 (0.91)	**0.020**
2.24 Requires more effort.	2.76 (0.71)	3.17 (0.80)	0.070
2.25 It is difficult to work in a group.	1.65 (0.66)	1.87 (1.14)	0.907
2.26 A lot of work can accumulate in the end.	1.75 (0.87)	2.46 (1.30)	0.079
2.27 There is a disproportion between tasks/credits.	1.36 (0.59)	2.09 (1.22)	0.096
2.28 The grading process is more complex, and sometimes unclear.	1.39 (0.78)	2.11 (1.45)	0.192
2.29 It creates insecurity and uncertainty, doubts about what to do.	1.30 (0.55)	1.64 (0.92)	0.246
2.30 It is unfair compared to other assessment processes.	1.33 (0.61)	1.20 (0.44)	0.729
2.31 The corrections have been unclear.	1.87 (1.08)	2.00 (1.05)	0.694
2.32 The assessment of the work is subjective.	1.43 (0.66)	2.18 (1.16)	0.051

DISCUSSION

The purpose of this chapter was to analyse how the modality used for the teaching and learning process influences the acquisition of professional competences in a formative assessment experience carried out in the academic years 2019-2020 in online modality by the health emergency derived from COVID-19, and 2020-2021 in face-to-face modality at the Faculty of Education of Segovia (University of Valladolid). We also explore the advantages and disadvantages of the application of a formative assessment system.

This study found that there is a totally agreement of the utility of the formative assessment experience implemented to the development of teaching competences both in online and in face-to-face mode. This is according with previous research which has shown that this kind of proposals are positively valued by students, contributing in an important way to the development of the competences of the degree

(Asún-Dieste et al., 2019; Cañadas, in press; Cañadas et al, 2018, 2021; Gallardo-Fuentes et al., 2018, 2020; Gómez-Gasquet et al., 2018; Hortigüela et al., 2018; Romero-Martín et al., 2017). However, it is necessary to highlight that are some indicators related with the formative assessment experience that are more valued in online teaching. Specifically, students consider that learning was more useful, more innovative and that there was more help from the teacher during online formative assessment experience. This perception may be derived from the fact that perhaps not all teachers have been able to make significant adaptations during the online teaching period because of COVID lockdown and comparing with other teachers, with higher ICT skills, students may assess this experience more positively (Carrillo & Flores, 2020; Flores, 2020; Flores & Gago, 2020). In view of this, we should be cautious and bear in mind that during the lockdown, teachers had many difficulties in implementing assessment systems that would guarantee quality learning (Cañadas, 2020).

Moreover, the positive appreciation that students make of the formative assessment system during the course also stands out. This research shows that the proposal carried out satisfies students, in both modalities. This points to the versatility of the application of formative assessment systems in different contexts. This is interesting since in the emergency situation derived by COVID, uncertainty was constant in the development of the subjects. Despite this, formative assessment has enabled students to benefit from its advantages in their learning outcomes. Previous research such as that of Atienza et al. (2016), Gallardo et al. (2020), Hortigüela et al. (2015) and Martínez-Mínguez et al. (2015) also found that the use of these assessment systems has numerous advantages for students. Among the items studied in this block "Grading is fairer" and "Improves the quality of the work required", highlight especially in the face-to-face modality. Both items obtain values below 3 points. However, in previous research such as that of Atienza et al. (2016) and Gallardo et al. (2020) both obtain higher values. It would be important to delve into why students have this perception, analysing whether it is necessary to carry out further monitoring or support for the students to change this vision. Another aspect to highlight is the significant difference in the item "There is feedback on documents and activities" perception. It obtains 3.75 points in online mode compared to 3.21 points in the face-to-face modality. Again, it may have to do with the perception that students have regarding other subjects that were being developed in the face-to-face period and where there was no constant feedback from teachers. Conversely, in the online modality, it has been a period where students have focused a lot on their positive assessment of those teachers who have been most involved with the aim of making teaching and learning process work. This had made they value it positively with a higher score.

Regarding the disadvantages perceived in the assessment system, in general values are obtained below 2 points. Those that are above this score are the items that have a strong relationship with the daily work, the involvement in the assessment system and students' effort. Same results are found by Gallardo et al. (2020) and Atienza et al. (2016) in their respective studies. It also stands out that the items that present significant differences between both courses are the prior understanding of the assessment system and that it requires participation in the assessment itself, with the highest average values in the face-to-face modality. Perhaps this could indicate that having to implement the OPL in the face-to-face modality makes the task somewhat difficult, requesting a greater students' involvement. Perhaps this may be because in the COVID online context the students did not have to do the practical part and the following year they had to follow a series of health measures to be able to do it safely in the case of having permission from the school to carry out their proposal with schoolchildren.

Finally, the results found differ from those found in the study by Cañadas and Lobo-de-Diego (2021). Their study finds that in a general way it is valued that both in blended and online modalities the use of a formative assessment process reported similar values in the development of teaching competences. In cases where this did not occur, it was the blended modality the one that obtained the highest values. This may be due to the differences between the two assessment systems implemented, and therefore, when requesting different elements from the students, there may be a different perception of the learning development in the different modalities. This is one of the main limitations of the study. Only a specific assessment system implemented in a single subject by a single teacher is included, which makes it difficult to know if there may be other reasons that, together with the assessment system, are modifying students' perception of the items studied. The main strength lies in the novelty of the study, since there is hardly any literature that verifies whether the adaptation of the assessment processes to the teaching modalities derived from the COVID-19 situation has changed the perception of the students about its usefulness for competences development of the subjects involved.

FUTURE RESEARCH DIRECTIONS

After having related the results of this study with the main scientific research, the future lines of research that open up from the findings of this study should be to see the long-term effects on the training of these students and whether they are subsequently able to carry out didactic proposals in the educational context, study the real grade of development of the professional competences necessary for the teaching, etc., and compare with other students that have completed or will complete the subject in one of each modalities. It would also be interesting to know in depth the opinion of these students and to find out whether they would have preferred to take the course in one modality or another, whether the learning acquired has helped them in their internship period in the following academic year.

Another line of research that has been opened by this study is to make comparisons with subjects taken in other universities with a similar formative assessment philosophy to develop professional competences and to compare the information obtained in each context.

CONCLUSION

This study evidence that a formative assessment experience contributes to the development of professional competences in different teaching modalities. Interestingly, students in the online mode perceive that they have acquired more professional competences than the face-to-face modality, despite the fact that in the online mode they did not have the experience of putting into practice with schoolchildren what they had developed in the subject. This means that we may have to rethink which teaching modality may be the most appropriate or the way in which the teaching is delivery.

For its part, Oriented Project Learning showed to help to get students engaged in their learning process as active learners while developing professional competences. Interestingly, we find that in the face-to-face modality the scores are lower than in the online modality, in which participants were able to do the practical part of the experience. We also find high satisfaction with the experience, and the improvement of the quality of the tasks done by students which indicates the potential of formative assessment at Higher Education level when it comes to get significant learning outcomes. This highlights the need of rethinking the way formative assessment is delivered at Higher Education and how future teachers experience formative assessment, so that theory and practice are connected, and students' education enriches and allows to develop in them the needed professional competences for their professional future.

ACKNOWLEDGMENT

This research received no specific grant from any funding agency in the public, commercial, or not-for-profit sectors.

REFERENCES

Álvarez Méndez, J. M. (2011). *Evaluar para conocer. Examinar para excluir*. Ediciones Morata.

Andrade, H. L., Bennet, R., & Cizek, G. J. (2019). *Handbook of formative assessment in the disciplines*. Routledge. doi:10.4324/9781315166933

Asún-Dieste, S., Rapún, M., & Romero-Martín, M. R. (2019). Percepciones de Estudiantes Universitarios sobre una Evaluación Formativa en el Trabajo en Equipo. *Revista Iberoamericana de Evaluación Educativa*, *12*(1), 175–192. doi:10.15366/10.15366/riee2019.12.1.010

Atienza, R., Valencia-Peris, A., Martos-García, D., López-Pastor, V. M., & Devís-Devís, J. (2016). La percepción del alumnado universitario de educación física sobre la evaluación formativa: Ventajas, dificultades y satisfacción. *Movimento (Porto Alegre)*, *22*(4), 1033–1048. doi:10.22456/1982-8918.59732

Baird, J., Andrich, D., Hopfenbeck, T., & Stobart, G. (2017). Assessment and learning: Fields apart? *Assessment in Education: Principles, Policy & Practice*, *24*(3), 317–350. doi:10.1080/0969594X.2017.1319337

Black, P., Harrison, C., Lee, C., Marshall, B., & Wiliam, D. (2002). *Working inside the black box: assessment for learning in the classroom*. King's College.

Black, P., McCormick, R., James, M., & Pedder, D. (2006). Learning How to Learn and Assessment for Learning: A theoretical inquiry. *Research Papers in Education*, *21*(2), 119–132. doi:10.1080/02671520600615612

Calderón, C., & Escalera, G. (2008). La evaluación de la docencia ante el reto del Espacio Europeo de Educación Superior. *Educación (Lima)*, *XXI*(0), 11, 237–256. doi:10.5944/educxx1.11.0.316

Cañadas, L. (2018). *La evaluación formativa en la adquisición de competencias docentes en la formación inicial del profesorado de Educación Física*. [Tesis Doctoral Inédit,. Universidad Autónoma de Madrid].

Cañadas, L. (2021). Contribution of formative assessment for developing teaching competences in teacher education. *European Journal of Teacher Education*. Taylor and Francis. https://doi.org/ doi:10.1080/02619768.2021.1950684

Cañadas, L., & Lobo-de-Diego, F. E. (2021). Desarrollo de competencias en docencia online y semipresencial en la formación en fundamentos en educación física. *Journal of Supranational Policies of Education*, *14*, 57–70. doi:10.15366/jospoe2021.14.004

Cañadas, L., Santos-Pastor, M. L., & Castejón, F. J. (2019). Competencias docentes en la formación inicial del profesorado de educación física, *Retos. Nuevas Tendencias en Educación Física. Deportes y Recreación, 35*, 284–288. doi:10.47197/retos.v0i35.64812

Cañadas, L., Santos-Pastor, M. L., & Castejón, J. (2018). Desarrollo de competencias docentes en la formación inicial del profesorado de Educación Física. Relación con los instrumentos de evaluación. *Estudios Pedagógicos (Valdivia), 44*(2), 111–126. doi:10.4067/S0718-07052018000200111

Cañadas, L., Santos-Pastor, M. L., & Ruíz, P. (2021). Percepción del impacto de la evaluación formativa en las competencias profesionales durante la formación inicial del profesorado. *Revista Electrónica de Investigación Educativa, 23*(e03), 1–14. doi:10.24320/redie.2021.23.e07.2982

Carrillo, C., & Flores, M. A. (2020). COVID-19 and teacher education: A literature review of online teaching and learning practices. *European Journal of Teacher Education, 43*(4), 466–487. doi:10.1080/02619768.2020.1821184

Clark, I. (2012). Formative assessment: Assessment is for self-regulated learning. *Educational Psychology Review, 24*(2), 205–249. doi:10.100710648-011-9191-6

Cohen, L., Manion, L., & Morrison, K. (2018). *Research Methods in Education*. Routledge.

Flores, M. A. (2020). Preparing Teachers to Teach in Complex Settings: Opportunities for Professional Learning and Development. *European Journal of Teacher Education, 43*(3), 297–300. doi:10.1080/02619768.2020.1771895

Flores, M. A., & Gago, M. (2020). Teacher Education in Times of COVID-19 Pandemic in Portugal: National, Institutional and Pedagogical Responses. *Journal of Education for Teaching, 46*(4), 507–516. doi:10.1080/02607476.2020.1799709

Gallardo, F., & Carter, B. (2016). La evaluación formativa y compartida durante el prácticum, en la formación inicial del profesorado: Análisis de un caso en Chile. *Retos, 29*(29), 258–263. doi:10.47197/retos.v0i29.43550

Gallardo-Fuentes, F., López-Pastor, V. M., & Carter-Thuillier, B. (2018). Efectos de la Aplicación de un Sistema de Evaluación Formativa en la Autopercepción de Competencias Adquiridas en Formación Inicial del Profesorado. *Estudios Pedagógicos (Valdivia), 44*(2), 55–77. doi:10.4067/S0718-07052018000200055

Gallardo-Fuentes, F. J., López-Pastor, V. M., & Cartier-Thuillier, B. (2020). Ventajas e Inconvenientes de la Evaluación Formativa, y su Influencia en la Autopercepción de Competencias en alumnado de Formación Inicial del Profesorado en Educación Física. *Retos, 38*(38), 417–424. doi:10.47197/retos.v38i38.75540

Hortigüela, D., Palacios, A., & López-Pastor, V. M. (2018). The impact of formative and shared or co-assessment on the acquisition of transversal competences in higher education. *Assessment & Evaluation in Higher Education, 44*(6), 933–945. doi:10.1080/02602938.2018.1530341

Hortigüela, D., Pérez-Pueyo, Á., & Abella, V. (2015). ¿De qué manera se implica el alumnado en el aprendizaje? Análisis de su percepción en procesos de evaluación formativa. *Revista de Investigación Educacional, 13*(1), 88–104.

Knight, P. (2006). The local practices of assessment. *Assessment & Evaluation in Higher Education*, *31*(4), 435–452. doi:10.1080/02602930600679126

López-Pastor, V. M., Kirk, D., Lorente-Catalán, E., MacPhail, A., & Macdonald, D. (2013). Alternative assessment in physical education: A review of international literature. *Sport Education and Society*, *18*(1), 57–76. doi:10.1080/13573322.2012.713860

López-Pastor, V. M., & Sicilia, Á. (2017). Formative and shared assessment in higher education. Lessons learned and challenges for the future. *Assessment & Evaluation in Higher Education*, *42*(1), 77–97. doi:10.1080/02602938.2015.1083535

Lorente-Catalán, E., & Kirk, D. (2016). Student teachers' understanding and application of assessment for learning during a physical education teacher education course. *European Physical Education Review*, *22*(1), 65–81. doi:10.1177/1356336X15590352

Martínez-Mínguez, L., Vallés, C., & Romero-Martín, R. (2015). Estudiantes universitarios: Ventajas e inconvenientes de la evaluación formativa. *@tic. Revista d'Innovació Educativa*, *14*, 59–70.

Martos-García, D., Usabiaga, O., & Valencia-Peris, A. (2017). Percepción del alumnado sobre la evaluación formativa y compartida: Conectado dos universidades a través de la Blogosfera. *Journal of New Approaches in Educational Research*, *6*(1), 68–74. doi:10.7821/naer.2017.1.194

McAteer, M. (2013). *Action Research in Education*. Sage. doi:10.4135/9781473913967

Moreno-Olivos, T. (2021). Cambiar la evaluación: Un imperativo en tiempos de incertidumbre. *Alteridad*, *16*(2), 223–234. doi:10.17163/alt.v16n2.2021.05

Panadero, E., Broadbent, J., Boud, D., & Lodge, J. M. (2018). Using formative assessment to influence self- and co-regulated learning: The role of evaluative judgement. *European Journal of Psychology of Education*, *34*(3), 535–557. doi:10.100710212-018-0407-8

Pérez-Escoda, A., Lena-Acebo, F., & García-Ruíz, R. (2021). Digital Competences for Smart Learning During COVID-19 in Higher Education Students from Spain and Latin America. *Digital Education Review*, *40*(40), 122–140. doi:10.1344/der.2021.40.122-140

Pla-Campas, G., Arumí-Prat, J., Senye-Mir, A. M., & Ramírez, E. (2016). Effect of using formative assessment techniques on students' grades. *Procedia: Social and Behavioral Sciences*, *228*, 190–195. doi:10.1016/j.sbspro.2016.07.028

Romero-Martín, M. R., Castejón-Oliva, F. J., López-Pastor, V. M., & Fraile-Aranda, A. (2017). Evaluación formativa, competencias comunicativas y TIC en la formación del profesorado. *Comunicar*, *52*. Advance online publication. doi:10.3916/C52-2017-07

Sá, M. J., & Serpa, S. (2020). COVID-19 and the Promotion of Digital Competences in Education. *Universal Journal of Educational Research*, *8*(10), 4520–4528. doi:10.13189/ujer.2020.081020

Wiliam, D., & Leahy, S. (2015). *Embedding formative assessment: Practical techniques for K-12 classrooms*. Learning Sciences International.

Wiliam, D., & Thompson, M. (2007). Integrating assessment with instruction: What will it take to make it work? In C.A. Dwyer (Coord), The Future of Assessment: Shaping Teaching and Learning (pp. 53-82). Lawrence Erlbaum Associates.

Chapter 4
Formative Assessment and Feedback in Higher Education:
Preparing Spanish Academics to Teach in a Digital World

Lucía Sánchez-Tarazaga
iD https://orcid.org/0000-0003-0927-5548
Universitat Jaume I, Spain

Aida Sanahuja Ribés
Universitat Jaume I, Spain

Francesc M. Esteve-Mon
iD https://orcid.org/0000-0003-4884-1485
Universitat Jaume I, Spain

ABSTRACT

The aim of this paper is to analyze the conception and use of formative assessment and feedback by faculty teachers in the context of a training course held at a Spanish university. Open-response data from 42 faculty teachers were analyzed using an inductively derived coding framework and thematic analysis. Analysis was organized around four main themes: 1) faculty teachers' beliefs about assessment, 2) main barriers or constraints that hinder feedback implementation, 3) associated benefits and 4) integration of digital technology to enrich formative assessment. The main results show different conceptions and myths about assessment and feedback, as well as a number of barriers to implementation. Furthermore, the training provided reveals that faculty teachers regard the feedback process, enhanced by digital tools, as beneficial.

INTRODUCTION

Assessment conditions of what and how students learn (Henderson et al., 2019). A poor choice of as-

DOI: 10.4018/978-1-6684-3537-3.ch004

sessment activities leads to poor learning and distorts what students are eventually capable of doing. At university there is still a predominance of summative and little practice of formative assessment (López-Pastor, 2017), despite it being known that students do not learn from grading but from assessment processes. One of the reasons for this practice lies in academics' beliefs, as will be addressed later.

Formative assessment also known as assessment for learning. According to Black and William (2009), formative assessment refers "to the extent that evidence about student achievement is elicited, interpreted, and used by teachers, learners, or their peers, to make decisions about the next steps in instruction that are likely to be better, or better founded, than the decisions they would have taken in the absence of the evidence that was elicited" (p.9). These authors state that formative assessment can be conceptualized as consisting in five strategies: 1) clarifying and sharing learning objectives and criteria for success; 2) articulating effective learning tasks that elicit evidence of student understanding; 3) providing feedback that moves learners forward; 4) activating students as instructional resources for one another; and 5) activating students as the owners of their learning. Moreover, when done well, this type of assessment promotes student satisfaction, since students have a better understanding of the learning path (McConlogue, 2020).

Thus, feedback is an integral part of formative assessment (Hamodi et al., 2015; Wiliam, 2018) and one of the determining factors in student learning (Cano et al., 2020; Gibbs & Simpson, 2009; Hattie, 2008). Although it has been widely defined, below is a clear, concise definition by authors working in this area: "feedback is a process through which learners make sense of the information from various sources and use it to enhance their work or learning strategies" (Carless & Boud, 2018, p. 1315). In recent decades, feedback has been reconceptualized and is no longer seen simply as comments delivered from the teacher to the student, but as a process which implies student engagement (Boud & Dawson, 2021).

According to the systematic review of the literature by Morris et al. (2021), feedback in higher education should be included in the evaluative practice of faculty teachers as it helps to develop students' competences and learning (Hattie & Timperley, 2007). Additionally, in an interconnected and technological context in which the university is immersed, the digital competence of the teacher is vital. Moreover, using new technologies is often seen as a way to make feedback more effective (Cumming & Rodriquez, 2017; Yuan & Kim, 2015).

Despite its evident importance, this issue has been little studied in educational practice and research (Boud & Dawson, 2021). Nowadays, integrating feedback into teaching–learning processes is a challenge (Jensen et al., 2021), due to the absence of adequate training (Sanahuja & Sánchez-Tarazaga, 2018) and teachers' beliefs and myths around this concept (Boud & Molloy, 2013). We would like to make a further point about beliefs.

The way teachers conduct formative assessment is strongly influenced by their beliefs and values about the importance of feedback within the context of a learning process (Brown, 2018; Karim, 2015). Prior studies show the impact of teachers' conceptions on their assessment and teaching practices (Amhag et al., 2020; Asghar, 2012; Brown et al., 2011; Myyry et al., 2022; Panadero & Brown, 2017). Designing feedback processes takes place within a complex interaction of intrapersonal, interpersonal, and contextual influences. As stated by Winstone and Carles (2020), this interaction creates feedback 'cultures'. Assessment practices thus become influenced by different factors such as class size, the importance allocated to teaching and research, or predisposition to experimentation versus conforming to normative assessment practices.

To move forward in obtaining more evidence on this concept, academics should review their own conceptualizations around assessment, ensuring they match their beliefs about the relationship of feedback to learning (Jensen et al., 2021). Thus, this paper seeks to analyze the conception and use of formative assessment and feedback by faculty teachers. This general aim is split into the following objectives:

O1. To understand academics' beliefs, regarding assessment and feedback.
O2. To describe the main barriers or constraints that hinder feedback implementation.
O3. To explain the associated benefits when giving feedback.
O4. To know how academics are integrating digital technology to enrich formative assessment.

METHOD

Methodologically, this is a descriptive study of a qualitative nature: "the goal of qualitative descriptive studies is a comprehensive summarization, in everyday terms, of specific events experienced by individuals or groups of individuals" (Lambert & Lambert, 2012, p.255). A semantic content analysis was performed (Miles & Huberman, 1994; Saldaña, 2009), following an inductive procedure, using ATLAS. ti software and an Excel spreadsheet, and a documentary analysis was made (Albert, 2007; Flick, 2014). The data source was teachers' reflective reports (42 reports) and contributions to virtual fora (personal reflections and comments).

Context of the Study

The Jaume I University (UJI) is a public higher education and research institution in the north of the Valencian Community (Spain), on the European Mediterranean coast. UJI was founded in 1991 and has about 1.500 members of teaching and research staff (approx. 47% women and 53% men) and close to 14.000 students (57% women and 43% men). For the 2021/2022 academic year, UJI offers 34 undergraduate courses, 6 international double degrees, 42 university master's degree courses, and 22 doctoral programmes.

In this context, the course "Accompanying students and effective feedback with digital tools for continuous assessment" was created for faculty staff from the UJI.

The course is specially designed so that academics can reflect on the possibilities of feedback and how to integrate it into their teaching. The main contents addressed in the course focus on these topics:

1. Evaluation under debate: assessment for learning or assessment for grading.
2. Formative assessment: concepts, advantages and possibilities in higher education.
3. Strategies for giving effective feedback: why, who, how, when.
4. Digital tools in teaching for giving feedback.
5. Practical experiences of feedback in university classes.

The course also includes a module of digital tools for good feedback and practical experiences at university. A validated questionnaire based on the European framework for the Digital Competence of Educators (Redecker & Punie, 2017) revealed a lack of digital competence at this Spanish university. According to the general results, faculty teachers perceive themselves as having an intermediate level of digital teaching competence (3.70 out of 5). Specifically, the area of evaluation and feedback of this competence shows that the use of ICT is lower for collecting evidence and analyzing students' learning progress (3.66) and for student empowerment (3.30) (Viñoles Cosentino et al., 2021).

The course is online and lasts for 10 hours of personal work, combined with formative pills and practical experiences, selected readings, practical work, and tutoring. At the end of the course, the university in-service teacher training department sent an evaluation questionnaire. Overall satisfaction of the participating teachers (n=21) was positive (M=4.5, SD=0.5), with particular reference to the relevance of the training for their work as educators (M=4.6; SD=0,5) and mastery of the content by the course facilitators (M=4.8; SD=0.4).

Participants

A total of 42 faculty teachers (64.3% women; 35.7% men) volunteered for the training in 2021. The sample is organized as follows, by field of knowledge: (1) Arts and Humanities: 9 (21.4%); (2) Sciences: 5 (11.9%); (3) Social and Legal Sciences: 18 (42.9%); (4) Engineering and Architecture: 5 (11.9%); and (5) Health Sciences: 5 (11.9%). The sample also comprises all the teaching staff, who represent 18 university departments: 11 (26.2%) were associate lecturers; 17 (40.5%) (pre- and post-doctoral) research staff in training; 8 (19.0%) assistant/doctoral assistants; 2 (4.8%) contracted doctors; 2 (4.8%) senior lecturers; 1 (2.4%) professor and 1 (2.4%) technician for teacher training. The course was given twice with 22 (52.4%) and 20 (47.6%) participating teachers, respectively. To ensure participant anonymity, a code system was used for identification purposes. For example, [E2_P25] Edition 2, participant number 25.

RESULTS

The results are set down below, according to the objectives outlined in the research:

To understand academics' beliefs, regarding assessment and feedback (O1)

The authors followed two procedures to answer this question. Firstly, a content analysis using the metaphor technique (Todd & Low, 2010) was conducted to explore faculty staff's conceptions about assessment (O1a). This analysis strategy is supported by educational research to conceptualize abstract concepts and has already been used in other research related to assessment and feedback (e.g., Jensen et al., 2021). Secondly, the authors wanted to discover the main teacher myths about feedback (O1b). For that purpose, a frequency analysis of teachers' reflections was performed with illustrative examples.

Understanding the meaning that teachers give to assessment (O1a)

Specifically, 38 contributions from participating teachers were analyzed out of a total of 42 registered. Four contributions were discarded because they were blank or because they responded to a question other than the one asked. The answers were collected from the virtual forum, which was the initial activity of the course. The question asked was "What does assessment mean to you?"

The results are shown in Table 1, in which each of the metaphors is summarized. For this purpose, a literal example sentence is included to illustrate the meaning, the type of assessment it is associated with according to purpose (formative or summative), the agent on whom the action mainly falls, the role assumed for the learner and the frequency of repetition (low: 2 times; medium: 3–5; high: 6 or more). The information has been arranged according to the degree of frequency, starting with the meanings that occurred least.

In total, 13 metaphors associated with the meanings of the assessment have been constructed. At the lowest level of frequency is assessment as teaching improvement and help. At an intermediate level is assessment as accompaniment, learning, correction, justice and fairness, as well as difficulty. Finally, the most frequently repeated metaphors are assessment as checking, improvement, evaluation, continuous process, testing and grading.

In terms of purpose, a large majority of metaphors could belong to the formative type (especially those in the medium and low frequencies). However, the summative purpose is more present in metaphors with a higher number of repetitions.

As far as roles and agents are concerned, it is noteworthy that there is unanimity in all the teacher-oriented proposals and that students assume a passive role in receiving the assessment (whether in terms of help received, as a test recipient or as correction to an assignment, among others).

Table 1. Meaning that faculty teachers attach to assessment

Assessment as TEACHER IMPROVEMENT	
Sample sentence	*IMPROVE my work as a teacher [E1_P3]* *Discovery is mutual. The students raise doubts and pose challenges where I had considered none, and I suggest possibilities that they hadn't contemplated. There is always room for surprise! [E1_P14]*
Purpose of the assessment	Formative
Agent on whom the action falls	Teacher
Role of the learner	Passive
Frequency of occurrence	Low
Assessment as HELP	
Sample sentence	*I believe assessment helps students achieve the objectives of the subject [E1_P10]* *I try to be a support so that my students can evolve at their own pace, according to their interests and needs [E1_P14]*
Purpose of the assessment	Summative and formative
Agent on whom the action falls	Teacher
Role of the learner	Passive
Frequency of occurrence	Low
Assessment as ACCOMPANIMENT	
Sample sentence	*This process helps me give them feedback, but essentially it is for them to feel accompanied in the learning process [E1_P2]* *Accompaniment is a process of moving together through diverse learning scenarios, ensuring that they don't feel alone along the way [E1_P14]*
Purpose of the assessment	Formative
Agent on whom the action falls	Teacher
Role of the learner	Passive
Frequency of occurrence	Medium
Assessment as LEARNING	
Sample sentence	*To try and improve the learning process, by strengthening interaction with the students [E1_P9]* *To continue learning [E1_P15]*
Purpose of the assessment	Formative
Agent on whom the action falls	Teacher
Role of the learner	Passive

continued on following page

Table 1. Continued

Assessment as **TEACHER IMPROVEMENT**	
Frequency of occurrence	Medium
Assessment as DIFFICULTY	
Sample sentence	*I find it very difficult to carry out this process of accompaniment with all students in a continuous manner [E1_P2]* *I also believe that having large numbers of students (between 120 and 130) in my main subject hinders accompaniment [E2_P40]*
Purpose of the assessment	Formative
Agent on whom the action falls	Teacher
Role of the learner	Passive
Frequency of occurrence	Medium
Assessment as CORRECTION	
Sample sentence	*When I return the corrected tasks to the students, I pinpoint the mistakes using Track changes (depending on the type of error, I underline, highlight in yellow or correct it and give the answer; I also add comments [E2_P23]* *What I do is correct the work [E2_P42]*
Purpose of the assessment	Summative and formative
Agent on whom the action falls	Teacher
Role of the learner	Passive
Frequency of occurrence	Medium
Assessment as JUSTICE AND FAIRNESS	
Sample sentence	*Fairness. Establishing a fair and accurate assessment of students' knowledge [E1_P8]* *Justice [E2_P32]*
Purpose of the assessment	Summative and formative
Agent on whom the action falls	Teacher
Role of the learner	Passive
Frequency of occurrence	Medium
Assessment as IMPROVEMENT	
Sample sentence	*It is also important to help students improve [E1_P13]* *Feedback to document weaknesses, strengths and actions for improvement [E2_P27]*
Purpose of the assessment	Formative
Agent on whom the action falls	Teacher
Role of the learner	Passive
Frequency of occurrence	Medium
Assessment as EVALUATION	
Sample sentence	*"Assess" (because grading feels very limited) with comments, questions that invite reflection and advice [E1_P5]* *For me, evaluating students consists in assessing the skills or competences acquired in the subjects I teach [E2_P26]*
Purpose of the assessment	Summative and formative
Agent on whom the action falls	Teacher
Role of the learner	Passive
Frequency of occurrence	Medium
Assessment as A CHECK	
Sample sentence	*To check the extent of student learning [E1_P3]* *To check whether students have obtained the skills, knowledge and competences in agreement with the results [E1_P15]*
Purpose of the assessment	Summative and formative
Agent on whom the action falls	Teacher
Role of the learner	Passive
Frequency of occurrence	High

continued on following page

Table 1. Continued

Assessment as TEACHER IMPROVEMENT	
Assessment as a CONTINUOUS process	
Sample sentence	*Assessment must be continuous, along with attendance and participation in class [E1_P18]* *I carry out continuous assessment, evaluating participation in class, the work done and attendance at seminars and practicals [E2_P26]*
Purpose of the assessment	Summative and formative
Agent on whom the action falls	Teacher
Role of the learner	Passive
Frequency of occurrence	High
Assessment as POSTING EXAMS	
Sample sentence	*At the end of the subject, I give them a final exam to which I add (never subtract) the grades for the exercises done in class. [E2_P24]* *Test: the type of exam common to all subjects in the degree [E2_P21]*
Purpose of the assessment	Summative
Agent on whom the action falls	Teacher
Role of the learner	Passive
Frequency of occurrence	High
Assessment as GRADING	
Sample sentence	*For the first essays, the grade is "done/or not done", although more often than not I give a grade because the students ask for one [E2_P23]* *The first consists in handing in completed exercises; the second is two partial exams and the third is the final exam. I think it is a summative assessment [E2_P25]*
Purpose of the assessment	Summative
Agent on whom the action falls	Teacher
Role of the learner	Passive
Frequency of occurrence	High

To describe the main teaching myths about feedback (O1b)

For this section, 35 responses were analyzed in the virtual forum (seven people did not answer or answered generically). After a synchronous session in which the main myths about feedback were explained, at the end of the session, participants were asked a reflection question entitled "What myths about feedback have been dispelled?" Table 2 includes the seven myths that were worked on during training, their frequency and some teachers' reflections to illustrate each case. Each teacher was asked to respond with the myth(s) they had about this issue.

The graph in Figure 1 gives a more visual version of the responses.

The findings reveal that faculty teachers have numerous myths about feedback. The most common are those relating to the way in which feedback is given, since 28.8% of the responses refer to the sandwich format as being most suitable. They have also realized that not all feedback is good (17.1%) or that the more feedback, the better (17.1%), because it can generate a significant cognitive load and lead to dependence on the teacher. Another relevant question is that good feedback consists in providing students with comments on an assignment, accompanied by a grade (14.6%). Finally, the authors wish to highlight teachers' views of feedback as an isolated task and not as a process. One fact that supports this is that feedback consists in only giving specific information (12.2%), which ends once received by the students (7.3%), with no consideration being given to what the learner does with that information.

Table 2. Myths that faculty teachers have about feedback

Myths	n (%)	Examples of reflections
The order of appropriate feedback is sandwich feedback (positive-negative-positive)	11 (26.8%)	*In my case, a fallen myth is the one about the order of feedback (positive-negative-positive), because I believed it to be a good order for achieving higher motivation in students.* [E1_P4] *I was surprised that positive-negative-positive feedback was not advisable. When I listened to the explanation and reasons for not implementing it, it made total sense.* [E1_P5]
All feedback is good	7 (17.1%)	*The main myth about feedback that has been dispelled for me is believing that it should always be positive.* [E1_P18] *The main concept I was mistaken about is concerned with phrases that supposedly give "positive reinforcement". When the work is good, I usually write things like "good work" or "well done". And it's true that these comments contribute nothing to the student.* [E1_P21]
The more feedback, the better	7 (17.1%)	*This sentence by Wiliam has opened my eyes: "Feedback should be more work for the recipient than the donor". I think I was sometimes guilty of giving too much feedback.* [E1_P10] *The fallen myth for me is "the more feedback, the better", because I have always been (and am) very attentive to the students. I think this makes them more dependent and perhaps reinforces their insecurities.* [E1_P16]
Feedback makes sense when it is accompanied by a qualification	6 (14.6%)	*I was very surprised to learn that if you only give comments as feedback, there is more improvement than if you gave a grade and comments. I thought that comments and a grade would be more motivating for students to improve.* [E2_P25] *This consideration points to a way of modifying certain activities with exercises that carry no grades as a way of preparing future exercises for the student to work on those modifications.* [E2_P27]
Feedback is about giving information	5 (12.2%)	*I thought that giving feedback was giving information. I didn't think about the subsequent use of this information.* [E1_P6] *I realize that I myself have believed some of the myths that have been presented, such as, for example, that giving feedback consists in giving information and after that the feedback is over. I think that's one of the mistakes I've been making.* [E1_P20]
The feedback concludes once the information has been given	3 (7.3%)	*I realize that my feedback process often ends when I've given the information.* [E1_P2] *I also didn't realize the importance of what the students were doing with this feedback.* [E1_P15]
Feedback is given to improve an assignment	2 (4.9%)	*Moreover, the fact that feedback is not only given to improve a specific task but can be extrapolated to other academic, personal or professional fields has enabled me to be more aware of the need to provide effective feedback.* [E1_P1] *What has surprised me most is "Feedback is provided to improve a specific task". The concept I had in mind was "this exercise is done like this" or "these concepts are the ones you need to learn".* [E2_P29]

Figure 1. Myths that faculty teachers have about feedback
Source: Authors

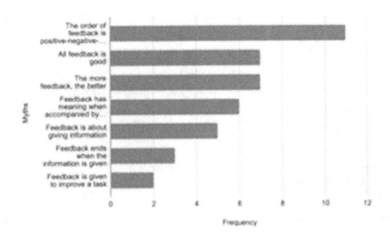

To Describe the Main Barriers or Constraints That Hinder Feedback Implementation (O2)

The categories referring to the barriers or negative conditioning factors identified by the teaching and research staff when implementing feedback in their teaching are shown in Table 3.

Table 3. Barriers or negative conditions identified by faculty teachers when using feedback in their teaching practice

Categories	n	%
1. Lack of student involvement/participation (process)	12	16.9
1.1. Work overload for students	4	5.6
1.2. Diversity/heterogeneity of levels	3	4.2
1.3. Lack of evaluative judgement (students)	10	14.1
2. Organizational barriers		
2.1. High student-to-faculty ratios (crowded classes)	9	12.7
2.2. Time management (lack of and delays)	13	18.3
2.3. Shared subject (teaching coordination)	4	5.6
2.4. Technological access	4	5.6
3. Work overload for teachers	12	16.9
TOTAL	71	100%

The percentages of the categories obtained from the reports analyzed reveal a series of barriers or conditioning factors that hinder feedback delivery in university classes according to the faculty teachers participating in this research. One of the main organizational barriers (18.3%) lies in time management issues, which lead to delays. The same percentage of responses (16.9%, respectively) reveals students' lack of involvement or participation throughout the teaching–learning process and the work overload for teachers when delivering this type of feedback. Students' lack of evaluative judgement stands at 14.1%. In 12.7% of the responses, teachers also refer to the high student-to-faculty ratios in university classes. A lower percentage of responses was linked to work overload for the students, teaching coordination and problems accessing technology (all at 5.6%, respectively), and the heterogeneity of levels in the classroom (4.2%).

For teachers, the lack of student involvement and participation represents a hindrance to accompanying students throughout the learning process.

"For accompaniment to be effective, students have to work throughout the term and not leave it till the last minute" [E2_P35].

Some students' lack of attention to learning is also pinpointed.

"[...] they want to do as little as possible to pass, and grabbing their attention is not easy" [E2_P25].

Another concern of teachers when delivering feedback is not overloading students with work.

"Regulate the workload students will have" [E2_P25].

"Having to 'rework' their assignment after feedback will involve more work for students" [E1_P13].

Similarly, some teachers perceive heterogeneity of levels as a barrier.

"Heterogeneous level of English. A group with different levels can hinder peer feedback because it is given orally" [E1_P1].

Also, teachers who carry out practical peer assessment highlight some students' lack of evaluative judgement.

"Peers give little, incorrect or disrespectful feedback" [E1_P20].

"Little objectivity from the student: possible 'favouritism' towards friends rather than peers" [E2_P30].

As for organizational barriers, faculty teachers indicate high student-to-faculty ratios (crowded classes) as a negative condition that hinders accompaniment and feedback focused on assessment as learning.

"High numbers of students in class for individual feedback" [E2_P28].

This high number of students in class results in delayed feedback and disrupts time management.

"Delays in delivering feedback because it involves more work" [E1_P4].

"The time and way the course is organized. Sometimes individual feedback to the previous questions arrives after the corresponding practical session" [E2_P39].

For some teachers, giving shared subjects is an added difficulty because of the lack of teaching co-ordination when systematizing feedback.

"The subject is shared, which means reaching a consensus for feedback among all the teaching staff involved in the practical sessions " [E1_P7].

Some teachers are aware of their low digital competence.

"I also have very limited knowledge of managing the virtual classroom and using the digital tools available" [E2_P26].

And problems with internet connections.

"In some virtual classes, several students had problems connecting" [E2_P34].

The last barrier that calls for comment is the work overload for the teacher to introduce effective feedback in their subjects.

"It can entail an extra workload for the teacher" [E1_P6].

For many teachers these are novel ideas and have not been formally incorporated into their teaching practice, resulting in additional work.

"These new ideas make more work for me" [E1_P2].

Moreover, some of the teachers are associate lecturers.

"As an associate lecturer I have a core job, which means I have less time to prepare the teaching component at home. That might improve if I gained more knowledge about using feedback and managing technology" [E2_P26].

To Explain the Benefits Associated When Implementing Feedback (O3)

To respond to the third objective of this study, the authors focus on fragments of the self-reports categorized as benefits that emerge from delivering feedback in higher education (see Table 4).

Table 4. Benefits of implementing feedback in higher education

Categories	n	%
1. Follow-up and accompaniment in the teaching–learning process	10	8.2
1.1. Feed up: prior information	4	3.3
1.2. Internalization of content (procedural)	7	5.7
1.3. Greater student involvement (active role)	13	10.7
2. Formative assessment: focused on improvement	34	27.9
2.1. Functional learning	4	3.3
2.2. Group skills (peer learning)	13	10.7
2.3. Promotion of critical thinking and evaluative judgement	8	6.6
3. Personalized teaching and motivation	13	10.7
4. Use of digital tools (real time)	16	13.1
TOTAL	122	100%

The percentages show that the most frequently named benefit in the self-reports (27.9%) corresponds to the idea of formative assessment, that is, improvement and learning. The responses (13.1%) refer to the benefits of delivering feedback rapidly and in real time using digital tools, thereby enabling students to incorporate it before submitting their final work. Identical percentages (10.7%, respectively) are given to involving students in adopting an active role in their learning process, growing cooperative skills when feedback is delivered by peers and personalizing teaching to fit student needs and motivations through feedback. The categorized comments (8.2%) refer to the benefits to student learning from follow-up and accompaniment in the learning process, which enables them to better internalize knowledge of the different subjects (5.7%). How feedback helps encourage the critical thinking and evaluative judgement of future professionals receives 6.6%. Finally, a lower percentage (3.3%) indicates the benefits of feeding up students at the beginning of the process and getting them to undertake functional learning for the profession they are training in.

The importance of follow-up and accompaniment in the teaching–learning process is also underlined.

"Both for group work and practicals, a follow-up by the teacher before final submission makes students feel more motivated to learn, improve and do group work, and not leave everything until the last minute" [E1_P3].

This accompaniment must be academic but must also focus on socio-emotional aspects.

"To achieve academic and emotional accompaniment for the students" [E2_P34].

Furthermore, feed up at the beginning of the process ensures students receive prior information about what is expected of them in the subject.

"The main advantage of feed up is that working teams will have information before doing the activity, which they can utilize to produce better work with no ambiguity about what they are expected 'to produce'" [E2_P37].

This enables students to internalize content better (throughout the process).

"Students are more aware of their learning throughout the course, because feedback is effective and motivating" [E2_P38].

Another significant benefit is greater student involvement (active role).

"This way they can incorporate actions to increase their participation in course activities as a major milestone on the road to reaching their learning goals" [E2_P38].

As already mentioned, the benefit with the highest percentage focuses on formative assessment and not on grading, thereby enabling students to gradually improve and learn throughout the subject.

"We do not give grades until the end of the subject. This means that students are only focused on improving their learning and not on obtaining a better grade" [E1_P6].

"In the case of weekly feedback, students can be more aware of the learning process and gradually improve during the term without paying so much attention to their grades" [E1_P9].

Likewise, another point in favour of introducing feedback is that it leads to more functional learning.

"Assignments are more aligned with the objective of the subject, which should increase the utility of the activity" [E1_P16].

Some teachers who use peer learning in their subjects highlight the fact that students also learn group skills.

"The group reflects on the work of each small group and tries to find and contribute solutions" [E2_P42].

Student participation and involvement encourages their critical thinking and evaluative judgement.

"Students develop their own evaluative judgement" [E2_P24].

"They develop their critical thinking by analyzing the information included in the texts, images and multimedia tools, and judging them autonomously and creatively" [E1_P1].

"Students become observers and develop their critical thinking to evaluate and observe their peers' correct answers and mistakes" [E2_P30].

Another benefit that emerges from this study is personalizing teaching through feedback and teacher accompaniment. By not doing the assessment at the end of the process, teachers can adapt the subject to their students' needs.

"We adapt to the diversity of learning styles" [E2_P34].

"It enables teachers to recognize the needs of each group and actively assist students with their specific problems" [E2_P29].

Generally speaking, this increases students' motivation to learn.

"Students feel more motivated to learn" [E1_P3].

Finally, mention must be made of using digital tools to deliver effective feedback to students.

"The forum enables me to answer general questions that usually appear in all groups. [...] Feedback over Google Group Meet allows me to give feedback without a grade while providing some direct accompaniment, which is difficult in large groups" [E1_P2].

To Know How Academics Are Integrating Digital Technology to Enrich Formative Assessment (O4)

To respond to this fourth objective, the authors focus on analysis of the digital tools used to enrich the feedback given by the participants in their self-reports. Table 5 shows that these fall into three main categories: tools from the university's virtual classroom, tools from Google's educational suite and other specific tools.

Among their main tools for providing feedback, most participants (69%) mentioned the virtual classroom or virtual teaching–learning environment. In the specific case of UJI, it was Moodle: a free distribution platform and modular architecture, for creating different types of activities. Specifically, assignment submission activities are the most frequently mentioned by teachers, who highlight that not only do they allow students' work or artefacts to be collected, they also provide feedback from the teacher. Forum (19%) and workshop activities (4.8%) are also virtual classroom tools used to discuss, reach consensus or provide feedback, either by the teacher or among the students themselves.

"Practical work is submitted, checked and the errors highlighted, but the work is not graded. It is handed back through the virtual classroom as a task, so that comments can be added and the submission edited. A forum is also created for each practical, so that some students' doubts can solve those of others" [E1_P6].

"Assignments are submitted online (in the virtual classroom), so they can be returned with feedback and comments. That way students can improve their final assignment (10% of the final grade)" [E2_P26].

Table 5. Main digital tools used to provide feedback

Digital tools	n	%
1. Virtual classroom or virtual teaching–learning environment (Moodle)	29	69.0
1.1. Handing in assignments	11	26.2
1.2. Forum	8	19.0
1.3. Document or video repository	7	16.7
1.4. Questionnaire or test	6	14.3
1.5. H5P Activity	3	7.1
1.6. Workshop	2	4.8
2. Google or Google Apps	20	47.6
2.1. Google Meet	15	35.7
2.2. Google Drive	12	28.6
2.3. Jamboard	3	7.1
2.4. Gmail	3	7.1
3. Other tools for feedback and participation	9	21.4
3.1. Padlet	3	7.1
3.2. Mentimeter	3	7.1
3.3. Genially	3	7.1
3.4. Other	6	14.3

Other university teachers mention tests and questionnaires (14.3%) or interactive and self-correcting H5P activities (7.1%) as the main feedback tools, especially for self-assessment, review and feedback. Likewise, the use of the virtual classroom as a repository of materials (16.7%), for distributing documents or videos for reflection, or for publishing assessment rubrics, are other practices mentioned by faculty teachers.

"Tasks are added online (not graded) to reinforce theoretical concepts through self-assessment. These tasks will be based on tools in the virtual classroom, particularly H5P, which provides a useful setting for self-assessment and content overview" [E2_P29].

Moreover, 47.6% of participants mentioned one of Google's tools among those they use for feedback and training assessment. The most prominent is the Google Meet videoconferencing service (35.7%), used for explanations, tutoring sessions and queries, either for the whole group, small groups or individually. Linked to this tool, some faculty members highlight the possibility of creating and working in small groups or breakout rooms or using Google Jamboard (7.1%) to generate ideas and interaction or for consensus on assessment criteria.

"Oral tutorial, through Google Meet: each week teachers meet each group to comment on specific doubts and plan work for the next session" [E2_P34].

Continuing with Google applications, the different Drive tools (especially documents and presentations) are also highlighted by 28.6% of teachers. These services, which enable the collaborative creation of materials, are used for sharing and feedback, through shared folders and documents, and for publishing comments by classmates and by university staff, in particular.

"Each working group creates its own reports in Google Drive and shares them with me through a link. That way I can comment on their work while it is being done and not afterwards" [E1_P4].

"They do the technical reports in a document in Google Drive that the teachers can access to give feedback in the form of questions, before submission to the virtual classroom" [E1_P17].

In addition to these main tools, other teachers mention email or Gmail, the calendar tool for setting up tutorials or, to a lesser extent, tools such as Google Maps, in specific cases related to the Arts and Humanities.

Finally, the third category concerns other types of tools for feedback and participation (21.4%). On the one hand, tools such as Padlet (used in a similar way to Jamboard), Mentimeter or Genially (7.1% each) are mainly used to encourage participation, to collect feedback from students or to visualize information more effectively. Other types of digital services are also mentioned by 14.3% of teachers, although in a more ad hoc or varied way. For example, online services such as Formative or Socrative, for participation and feedback, office tools (PowerPoint, audio or video tools, or PDF editors in which to add notes and comments) or specific applications for certain degrees or fields of knowledge.

Although there is no single pattern of use, the vast majority of faculty teachers use these tools to provide feedback to their students, either on tasks carried out during the course or on final assignments. In the same way, there are no noticeable differences between the practices carried out by teachers according to their areas of knowledge, with especially teacher-centred and not student-centred practices being identified in all areas.

DISCUSSION

Formative assessment is one of the most important determinants of student learning (Gibbs & Simpson, 2009; Hattie, 2008; Henderson et al., 2019). It is therefore necessary for academics to know how to use feedback as an integral part of this type of assessment (Wiliam, 2018). In higher education, the literature finds that faculty staff often have some knowledge of feedback but do not always apply it correctly in their feedback practices (Boud & Dawson, 2021), which represents a gap. The aim of this paper was to analyze the conception and use of formative assessment and feedback by faculty teachers, in the framework of a training course held at a Spanish university.

Objective 1 was to analyze teachers' predominant beliefs around this topic. On the one hand, the main results reflect different conceptions around assessment: up to 13 metaphors have been identified. Although there were many references to assessment for formative purposes (assessment as improvement, accompaniment and learning), the summative purpose is more present in metaphors with a greater number of repetitions (assessment as marking and setting exams). This shows that despite teaching experience, the concept is not solid and leads to confusion.

Previous studies (e.g., Panadero & Brown, 2017; Winstone & Carles, 2020) emphasized the relationship between academics' conceptions regarding assessment and their teaching practice. University faculty are not obliged to provide evidence of teacher training qualifications at most European higher education institutions, and this might undermine their evaluative competence. University faculty rarely apply new teaching methods (including assessment strategies) because they may lack confidence and prefer approaches that reproduce models that they experienced as students. They usually feel safer about giving numerical marks and grades that are formally recorded by the end of the learning process. This entails an opportunity to develop effective professional development programmes, especially tailored to early-career faculty (Sánchez-Tarazaga et al., 2022).

In addition, another striking fact is the excessive weight assumed by the teacher in the assessment: all the contributions consider the students as passive agents who receive the assessment and lack empowerment. This is a major limitation in the teaching–learning processes in university classrooms in which students should play an active role in assessment but are reluctant to carry out any tasks which are not graded (Broadbent et al., 2018). A challenge ahead for university faculty is to generate feedback that is not only useful to the student, but also actionable (Hepplestone & Chikwa, 2016). In other words, it should be linked to learning outcomes and to the next (future-oriented) assessment task. Moreover, additional courses are required for teaching strategies to empower students to learn to self-regulate and develop their evaluative judgement. The successful inclusion of this perspective would be a step towards more proficient and sustainable assessment, as pointed out by Boud (2020), resulting in better student learning.

For Objective 2, the main barriers or negative conditioning factors identified by the faculty teachers when giving feedback in their teaching were detected. They focused on the students (lack of student involvement/participation, work overload for students, heterogeneity of levels and lack of evaluative judgement); on organisational barriers (high ratios, lack of time or delays in providing feedback, problems in teaching coordination and technological access); and on work overload for university faculty staff. These results partially coincide with other studies (Henderson et al., 2019). For example, Sanahuja and Escobedo (2021) conducted research focused on detecting barriers when implementing peer assessment in the university classroom within the Spanish context. It reveals that the conditioning factors that hinder this type of practice are associated with overcrowded classes or very high ratios, the lack of teaching coordination, the lack of participatory culture of students in the university context and time limitation, above all, in master's degree subjects.

Findings for Objective 3 show the benefits of implementing feedback in the university classroom. It has been noted that all the benefits mentioned by university teaching staff focus on student learning (better accompaniment and monitoring: feedback, internalization of content and involvement; formative assessment: functional learning, group skills and promotion of evaluative judgement and critical thinking; and personalization of teaching). Only one category refers to the organizational benefits of using digital tools to provide swifter feedback in real time. Incorporating feedback in higher education also benefits the learning process. It responds to principles of Universal Design for Learning (Alba-Pastor et al., 2015), an inclusive approach that affects teachers' assessment practice and curriculum delivery in two ways: improving capacity to monitor progress and providing targeted feedback.

Despite these benefits, the success of feedback can only be proven once it is implemented. Therefore, further research is needed to gain data to examine how feedback is delivered after the course and to measure the real impact on student learning.

Technology facilitates the process of collecting evidence of learning and, as this research shows, is one of the benefits of giving feedback. However, in accordance with Sanmartí (2020), there is no point in using digital tools if a traditional assessment will be carried out for a solely summative purpose. Objective 4 shows that tools such as virtual classrooms not only fulfil an informative and practical function, allowing teachers to share content and generate tasks, but also have communicative, tutorial and evaluative functions (Area & Adell, 2009). Similarly, tools such as Google applications or other digital platforms facilitate communication, participation, information exchange or reflection (Esteve & Llopis, 2018). These are positive indications of the training received, given the influence of technology-enhanced feedback on student learning (Yuan & Kim, 2015).

CONCLUSION

Although the main limitation of this work is that it is a specific experience in the Spanish context, it does contribute to expanding scientific knowledge about academics' conceptions about assessment and feedback use. Myths about assessment practices are deep-rooted and difficult to combat with the organizational barriers in place, including work overload, at universities today. Moreover, digital tools facilitate the delivery of effective feedback to students. Learning how to use them for these purposes should therefore be encouraged. Finally, as Panadero and Brown (2017) advocate, understanding the reasons and experiences academics use to implement assessment strategies provides insights into both policy and professional development processes.

ACKNOWLEDGMENT

This research was supported by University Jaume I (Grant Ref. UJI-A2020-18), IP1: Francesc M. Esteve-Mon, IP2: Lucía Sánchez-Tarazaga; and Universitat Jaume I (Grant Ref. UJI-B2021-44). IP1: Odet Moliner, IP2: Aida Sanahuja.

REFERENCES

Alba-Pastor, C., Zubillaga del Río, A., & Sánchez-Serrano, J. M. (2015). Technology and Universal Design for Learning (UDL): Experiences in the university context and implications for teacher training. *Revista Latinoamericana de Tecnología Educativa-Relatec, 14*(1), 89–100. doi:10.17398/1695-288X.14.1.89

Albert, M. J. (2007). *La Investigación Educativa: Claves Teóricas.* McGraw Hill.

Amhag, L., Hellström, L., & Stigmar, M. (2019). Teacher Educators' Use of Digital Tools and Needs for Digital Competence in Higher Education. *Journal of Digital Learning in Teacher Education, 35*(4), 203–220. doi:10.1080/21532974.2019.1646169

Area, M., & Adell, J. (2009). E-Learning: Enseñar y aprender en espacios virtuales. In J. De Pablos (Ed.), *Tecnología educativa: la formación del profesorado de la era de internet* (pp. 391–424). Ediciones Aljibe.

Asghar, M. (2012). The lived experience of formative assessment practice in a British university. *Journal of Further and Higher Education*, *36*(2), 205–223. doi:10.1080/0309877X.2011.606901

Black, P., & William, D. (2009). Developing the theory of formative assessment. *Educational Assessment, Evaluation and Accountability*, *21*(1), 5–31. doi:10.100711092-008-9068-5

Boud, D. (2020). Challenges in reforming higher education assessment: A perspective from afar. *RELIEVE*, *26*(1), M3. Advance online publication. doi:10.7203/relieve.26.1.17088

Boud, D., & Dawson, P. (2021). What feedback literate teachers do: An empirically-derived competency framework. *Assessment & Evaluation in Higher Education*. doi:10.1080/02602938.2021.1910928

Boud, D., & Molloy, E. (2013). *Feedback in Higher and Professional Education. Understanding it and doing it well*. Routledge.

Broadbent, J., Panadero, E., & Boud, D. (2018). Implementing summative assessment with a formative flavour: A case study in a large class. *Assessment & Evaluation in Higher Education*, *43*(2), 307–322. doi:10.1080/02602938.2017.1343455

Brown, G. T. L. (2018). *Assessment of student achievement*. Routledge.

Brown, G. T. L., Hui, S. K. F., Yu, F. W. M., & Kennedy, K. J. (2011). Teachers' conceptions of assessment in Chinese context: A tripartite model of accountability, improvement, and irrelevance. *International Journal of Educational Research*, *50*(5-6), 307–320. doi:10.1016/j.ijer.2011.10.003

Cano, E., Pons-Seguí, L., & Lluch, L. (2020). [*'Educació Superior*. Universitat de Barcelona.]. *Feedback*, l.

Carless, D., & Boud, D. (2018). The development of student feedback literacy: Enabling uptake of feedback. *Assessment & Evaluation in Higher Education*, *43*(8), 1315–1325. doi:10.1080/02602938.2018.1463354

Cumming, T. M., & Rodriquez, C. D. (2017). A meta-analysis of mobile technology supporting individuals with disabilities. *The Journal of Special Education*, *51*(3), 164–176. doi:10.1177/0022466917713983

Esteve, F., & Llopis, M. A. (2018). Experiencia con GSuite en los grados de Maestro/a de Educación Infantil y Primaria. In *II Jornadas de innovación educativa DIMEU*. Universitat Jaume I.

Flick, U. (2014). *Qualitative Data Analysis*. SAGE Publications.

Gibbs, G., & Simpson, C. (2009). *Condiciones para una evaluación continuada favorecedora del aprendizaje*. Octaedro.

Hamodi, C., López, V. L., & López, A. T. (2015). Medios, técnicas e instrumentos de evaluación formativa y compartida en Educación Superior. *Perfiles Educativos*, *XXXVII*(147), 146–161. doi:10.22201/iisue.24486167e.2015.147.47271

Hattie, J. (2008). *Visible Learning: A Synthesis of Over 800 Meta-Analyses Relating to Achievement*. Routledge. doi:10.4324/9780203887332

Hattie, J., & Timperley, H. (2007). The Power of Feedback. *Review of Educational Research*, *77*(1), 81–112. doi:10.3102/003465430298487

Henderson, M., Ryan, T., & Phillips, P. (2019). The challenges of feedback in higher education. *Assessment & Evaluation in Higher Education*, *44*(8), 1237–1252. doi:10.1080/02602938.2019.1599815

Hepplestone, S., & Chikwa, G. (2016). Exploring the processes used by students to apply feedback. *Student Engagement and Experience Journal*, *5*(1), 1–15. doi:10.7190eej.v5i1.104

Jensen, L., Bearman, M., & Boud, D. (2021). Understanding feedback in online learning - A critical review and metaphor analysis. *Computers & Education*, *173*, 104271. doi:10.1016/j.compedu.2021.104271

Karim, B. H. H. (2015). The impact of teachers' beliefs and perceptions about formative assessment in the university ESL class. *International Journal of Humanities, Social. Sciences and Education*, *2*(3), 108–115.

Lambert, V. A., & Lambert, C. E. (2012). Qualitative descriptive research: An acceptable design. *Pacific Rim International Journal of Nursing Research*, *16*, 255–256.

López-Pastor, V. M. (2017). Evaluación formativa y compartida: Evaluar para aprender y la implicación del alumnado en los procesos de evaluación y aprendizaje. In V. M. López-Pastor & A. Pérez-Pueyo (Coords.), Evaluación formativa y compartida en Educación: experiencias de éxito en todas las etapas educativas (pp. 34–68). Universidad de León.

McConlogue, T. (2020). *Assessment and feedback in Higher Education: A Guide for Teachers*. UCL Press. doi:10.2307/j.ctv13xprqb

Miles, M. B., & Huberman, A. M. (1994). *Qualitative data analysis*. Sage Publications.

Morris, R., Perry, T., & Wardle, L. (2021). Formative assessment and feedback for learning in higher education: A systematic review. *Review of Education*, *9*(3). doi:10.1002/rev3.3292

Myyry, L., Karaharju-Suvanto, T., Virtala, A.M., Raekallio, M., Salminen, O., Vesalainen, M. & Nevgi, A. (2022). How self-efficacy beliefs are related to assessment practices: a study of experienced university teachers, *Assessment & Evaluation in Higher Education, 47*(1), 155-168. doi:10.1080/02602938.2021.1887812

Panadero, E., & Brown, G. T. L. (2017). Teachers' reasons for using peer assessment: Positive experience predicts use. *European Journal of Psychology of Education*, *32*(1), 133–156. doi:10.100710212-015-0282-5

Redecker, C., & Punie, Y. (2017). European Framework for the Digital Competence of Educators. DigCompEdu. JRC Science Hub, European Commission.

Saldaña, J. (2009). *The coding manual for qualitative researchers*. Sage Publications Ltd.

Sanahuja, A., & Escobedo, P. (2021). Seminario de innovación educativa sobre formación para una ciudadanía crítica: la evaluación entre iguales en el aula universitaria. In *M. Pallarés, J. Gil-Quintana y A. Santiesteban (Coord.), Docencia, ciencia y humanidades: hacia un enseñanza integral en la universidad del siglo XXI* (pp. 610–631). DYKINSON.

Sanahuja, A., & Sánchez-Tarazaga, L. (2018). La competencia evaluativa de los docentes: Formación, dominio y puesta en práctica en el aula. *Revista Iberoamericana de Educación*, 76(2), 95–115. doi:10.35362/rie7623072

Sánchez-Tarazaga, L., Ruiz-Bernardo, R., Viñoles Cosentino, V., & Esteve-Mon, F. (2022). University teaching induction programmes. A systematic literature review. *Professional Development in Education*, 1–17. doi:10.1080/19415257.2022.2147577

Sanmartí, N. (2020). *Evaluar y aprender: un único proceso*. Octaedro.

Todd, Z., & Low, G. (2010). A selective survey of research practice in published studies using metaphor analysis. In L. Cameron & R. Maslen (Eds.), *Metaphor analysis: Research practice in applied linguistics, social sciences and the humanities* (pp. 26–41). Equinox.

Viñoles Cosentino, V., Esteve-Mon, F. M., Llopis-Nebot, M. A., & Adell-Segura, J. (2021). Validación de una plataforma de evaluación formativa de la competencia digital docente en tiempos de Covid-19. *RIED. Revista Iberoamericana de Educación a Distancia*, 24(2), 87–106. doi:10.5944/ried.24.2.29102

Wiliam, D. (2018). Feedback: At the heart of - but definitely not all of - formative assessment. In A. Lipnevic & J. Smith (Eds.), *The Cambridge handbook of instructional feedback* (pp. 3–28). Cambridge University Press. doi:10.1017/9781316832134.003

Winstone, N., & Carless, D. (2020). *Designing Effective Feedback Processes in Higher Education: A Learning-Focused Approach*. Routledge.

KEY TERMS AND DEFINITIONS

Digital Tools: Software or applications that facilitate various tasks or activities using digital technology.

Feedback: The information given to a learner, typically by a teacher or mentor, that provides them with insight into their performance or understanding of a task or subject matter.

Formative Assessment: It refers to an ongoing process used to monitor the student learning by identifying areas of strength and weakness and guiding instructional decisions.

Mark: An indicator of the level of proficiency demonstrated by the learner in the subject or skill area covered by the qualification.

Myth: False beliefs or ideas that are often passed down through tradition or culture. They can relate to a variety of subjects and can be based on superstition, misinformation, or misinterpretation of facts.

Qualification: Formal certification or recognition of a learner's achievement in a particular field of study or skillset.

Universal Design for Learning: A framework for planning and delivering instruction that supports and engages all learners by providing multiple means of representation, expression, and engagement.

Chapter 5
How Can We Transform Assessment in University Classrooms From Feminist and Decolonial Pedagogies in Spain and Denmark?

Natalia Hipólito Hipólito
https://orcid.org/0000-0002-9255-9201
Universidad de Castilla-La Mancha, Spain

Irene Martínez Martín
Universidad Complutense de Madrid, Spain

María Teresa Bejarano Franco
Universidad de Castilla-La Mancha, Spain

Pia Rauff Krøyer
VIA University College, Denmark

ABSTRACT

This chapter aims to reflect on assessment practices in the context of university from a feminist and decolonial perspective. It is committed to a university education based on the principles of equity, social justice, and equality. Within this framework it becomes essential to rethink assessment systems. To do so, the chapter is divided into two parts: first, the epistemological construction of assessment from decolonial feminism and the skills and competences approach is discussed; and second, university experiences regarding assessment are described under the presented principles. As final proposals, an answer is given to the question of whether it is possible to transform assessment in the university by focusing on clarifying what the objective and the subjects of a feminist and decolonial evaluation are, as well as the strategies, techniques, and uses of transformative assessment.

DOI: 10.4018/978-1-6684-3537-3.ch005

INTRODUCTION

Following the historical contributions of critical pedagogies, feminist and decolonial pedagogies are committed to rethinking and transforming the foundations of education, including assessment. At the center of this transformation, Bell Hooks (2021) places: care, cooperative work, the collective construction of knowledge, educational praxis as a form of resistance, dialogue and joint reflection, the inclusion of body, emotions, and diverse identities in all educational spaces, as well as the construction of knowledge from the sidelines of the dominant knowledge. All this has direct implications in the construction of feminist and decolonial assessments.

If we think about how to connect this with university teaching models and their development to date, we have to stop and think about the creation of the European Higher Education Area (EHEA) and the so-called Bologna Plan that began with the Bologna Declaration in 1999. In accordance with the Knowledge Society, this plan was committed to a new educational model adapted to the society of the moment and a future vision based on teaching-learning processes centered around competence. Having had enough time to evaluate the direction of this process and with the teaching and research experience that accompanies us we want to rethink the competence assessment models that were proposed and investigate alternative assessment processes from a feminist, decolonial, and critical perspective. At the same time, we seek to approach other skill assessment processes that are perfectly compatible with the mentioned pedagogies. We are talking then, of not only assessing competence but also moving towards models that are consistent with assessing skill, including those that are necessary to train and educate on the principle of equality.

These skills are associated with arts and humanities: the ability to think critically, the ability to transcend local loyalties and approach global issues as a 'citizen of the world', and the ability to comprehensively visualize the situation of others or of overcoming gender inequalities, among others.

Starting from this framework, this chapter offers a state of the art of feminist and decolonial epistemology and how it influences assessment practices in the context of university. In addition, it aims to intersect feminist epistemology with skills and competence assessment approaches and to reflect on how, from a construction of non-hegemonic knowledge, we can evaluate the teaching-learning processes. In other words, rethinking what De Sousa Santos (2018) calls the monoculture of knowledge and rigor (2011a).

Thus, as critical feminist educators and teachers at the University we try to respond to some of our concerns: In our assessment practices, do we accommodate the diversities and intersections that appear in university classrooms? What is excluded from the dominant assessment? Is competence assessment put into dialogue at the University with the skill assessment models from the Southern epistemology? What contributions are made from feminist and decolonial pedagogies to the construction of a transformative assessment of skills and competences? What assessment best practices do we find at the University from feminist and decolonial perspectives? And what elements intersect in these practices that can define a feminist and decolonial assessment?

To do this, this chapter is divided into two fundamental parts: first, a collection and discussion of the theoretical framework and state of the art surrounding feminist and decolonial pedagogies and their contributions to the construction of transformative university assessments, as well as their intersection with the skills and competences assessment approach in both Spain and Denmark; and second, a description of two experiences of educational action in the Spanish and Danish university environment, with an emphasis on feminist and decolonial assessment practices. This chapter concludes by highlighting the key elements that interrelate in these selected practices and that will define feminist and decolonial assessment models in university settings.

BACKGROUND

Where Do We Come From? From Hegemonic Assessment to Transformative Perspectives in Education

"Tell me how you evaluate, and I will tell you how you teach." With this prominent phrase we want to call attention to the need to rethink university educational practices from the point of view of assessment procedures. Educational assessment is usually marked by a dominant and hegemonic tradition approach, giving rise to obsolete and not very innovative practices and banking models. We refer, for example, to assessment being a synonym of tests aimed at objectively measuring rote knowledge such as numerical evaluations whose ultimate objective is to establish labels and categories, decontextualized evaluations, or evaluations based on fear, control, and punishment. As teachers, thinking about these assessment processes implies not only focusing on how students are evaluated, but also on what use we ourselves are making of these evaluations and how we contribute to transferring new knowledge to the students. In addition, it implies taking into account the social and educational consequences of certain types of assessment. In other words, we should question whether our evaluation practices reproduce or transform socio-educational inequalities and violence.

Recovering words from Freire (2006) or Giroux (2018), education is not neutral and, therefore, it should become a political act of transformation and resistance to inequality and violence. In this same sense, Álvarez (2001) already questioned whether, "we evaluate to understand or test to exclude" (p.1) wondering who the subject and object of all educational assessments should be. In this work, we contribute a reflection from a university teacher perspective and ask ourselves about the object and subject of assessment or in other words we ask ourselves why we evaluate. With this we join the discussion that has been taking place in recent decades from critical pedagogies and emancipatory educational paradigms where processes are located at the center of the pedagogical debate.

The previously mentioned author refers to the need to distinguish between assessment as a synonym of testing which results in exclusion and formative evaluations. Following this reflection, we make a distinction between evaluation systems that are contextualized in rational and positivist educational paradigms where values related to individualism, competitiveness, memorization, quantitative comparison, and categorization prevail; and evaluations derived from emancipatory and critical paradigms where constructive, cooperative, reflective values are highlighted, allowing for multiple forms of representation of learning. In Giroux's words, "Tests steal childhood creativity and imagination."[1]

Álvarez (2001) urges us to ask ourselves: Why do we evaluate? Who do we evaluate? How do we evaluate? At whose service is this evaluation? What do we put at the center of the teaching and learning process? And what is a fair assessment?

Following the binarism of the traditional paradigms of education, we find that in a hegemonic evaluation we evaluate to exclude, as this practice is subject to numerical categorization, the comparison between students, and limited to the extent of a supposedly objective academic performance (reaching or not the external assessment criteria, competences, and imposed content). In addition, it is limited to assessing the student body always from an external or top-down perspective as a form of exercise of power/control of the educator towards the learner. The error, the failure, is punishment and never the possibility of improvement. Learning is built from fear, anxiety, insecurity, and the stress generated by the assessment. If we focus on how we evaluate, we notice that the practices are immobile and not very innovative such as the use of standardized tests or time and procedure limited practices (multiple choice, reduced time, memorization, short answers...). Finally, it should be noted that in this paradigm, assessment becomes an evaluation tool at the service of the institution, the teaching staff, and the system that excludes, but is never at the service of the student body, its diversity, and their learning. Therefore, at the center of education we are placing the fulfillment of external criteria, the idea of normalization in education (we educate for a stereotyped normality), competitiveness, individualism, and memorization as prevailing values in society. We are leaving out diversity, multiple intelligences, subjectivities, creativity, inclusion, dynamic teaching and learning processes, emotional education, the ability to ask intelligent questions, and the possibility of learning from mistakes from a constructivist and dialogic perspective.

Thus, we need to continue questioning what a fair assessment should look like. To do this, in this chapter we are going to focus on a post-critical paradigm (Sancho, et. al, 2020) in an educational setting in which we reference the proposals of feminist and decolonial epistemologies that provide other more inclusive, diverse, critical, innovative, and social justice approaches to evaluation systems.

EPISTEMOLOGICAL DIALOGUE IN EDUCATION

Assessment by Skills and Competences

The skills approach, although originally intended to conceive another model of human development and to reduce poverty, has been extensively studied to apply it to many different fields, including education. Skills, with regard to education, can be considered as "the real opportunities that students have in order to acquire the performance that they value" (Boni et al., 2010, p. 124). The skills approach looks at what each person is capable of doing and being, unlike the competences approach that, based on what we have been observing in the academic world, only assesses what students are capable of doing. At first, the competences approach proposed in the Bologna Plan posed a considerable change to previous models of teaching and learning and was intended to put the student body at the center, but over time we have seen how on many occasions these educational processes remained merely instrumental. Lozano (2012, p. 77) argues that the "dominant competences approach has important shortcomings, especially in regard to the comprehensive training and responsibility of professionals. Some deficiencies that could be overcome to a great extent by the skills approach". Therefore, we understand that the interweaving of both models (competences and skills) could be a perfect combination to work on both educational and instrumental processes as well as on a holistic training that incorporates a global approach focused on knowing, doing, being-feeling, and questioning hegemonic, colonial, heteropatriarchal, and normative knowledge.

For Nussbaum "education is the key to all human capabilities" (2006, p. 322), although she also considers that we are in a global educational crisis, in which education has been described to follow an economic development perspective based on basic skills, literacy, and numeracy and in which critical thinking could become a handicap for economic growth (Nussbaum, 2016). The skills approach aims for subjects to reach higher levels of freedom. This approach applied to university training proposes education to be a vehicle to achieve that freedom based on what students are capable of doing and being. This implies an open, flexible, and critical higher education model in which training not only serves to adapt to today's society, but also allows reflection, thinking, and having a critical capability to also understand how certain knowledge continues to be colonial, hegemonic, and heteropatriarchal.

In this sense, De Sousa Santos (2012) considers that we must transform the university setting into a creative, democratic, and emancipatory place that echoes and takes into account the social demands not only of the established powers but also of those who are outside of the power groups. To this end, we must understand that the knowledge we name as colonial, hegemonic, and heteropatriarchal and that is pre-eminently considered valid, hides other knowledge and that the latter not only "must gain a voice from practices and social struggles, but that the educational institution needs to commit to stop ignoring them and put them at the center of the knowledge that we learn, that we transmit, and we pass on" (Hipólito and Martínez, 2021). Therefore, an education for freedom only takes place if it is created to build free citizens regardless of their place of birth or their wealth, an education that intends for students to be masters of their own thought, of their own voice, beyond their social position (Nussbaum, 2005). In other words, "its purpose is to enable people to possess certain skills that facilitate a dignified, decent, «happy» life" (Guichot-Reina, 2015, p. 55).

After studying the postulates of Sen and Nussbaum, Melany Walker (2007, pp. 112-113) proposed a provisional list of skills based on the optimal conditions and opportunities for learning in Higher Education:

- Critical thinking. Being able to make well-reasoned, informed, critical, independent, intellectually sharp, socially responsible, and thoughtful choices aimed at practical and moral ends. Being able to build a personal life project by critically comparing human goods and purposes and reflectively establishing their hierarchical classification in the life plan itself.

- Educational resilience. Being able to navigate study, work, and life. Ability to negotiate risk, persevere academically, to be sensitive to educational opportunities, and to adapt to obstacles. Self-confidence. Having aspirations and hopes for a better future.

- Knowledge and imagination. Being able to acquire knowledge on any subject of interest –disciplinary and/or professional– its inquiry method and academic standards. Being able to apply critical thinking and imagination to understand the perspectives of others and form unbiased judgments. Being able to debate complex problems. Being able to acquire knowledge for pleasure and personal development, for work purposes and economic opportunities, for political, cultural, and social action and participation in the world. Knowledge of ethical debates and moral problems. Being open to new ideas and concepts. Being able to understand science and technology in public policies.

- Social relationships and social networks. Being able to participate in group learning, working with others to solve problems and carry out tasks. Being able to work with others to form effective participatory learning groups. Being able to form networks of friendship and belonging for the purpose of educational support and recreation. Mutual trust.

- Respect, dignity, and recognition. Feeling respect for oneself and others, treating oneself and others with dignity, not being belittled or devalued due to gender, social class, religion, or race. Valuing other languages, religions, and spiritual and human diversity practices. Showing empathy, compassion, honesty, and generosity. Being able to listen and take into account the points of view of another person in dialogue and debate. Acting in an inclusive and sensitive manner to human needs. Being competent in intercultural communication. Having communication abilities to participate effectively in learning; speak, debate, and persuasion; as well as being able to listen.

- Emotional integrity. Not falling prey to anxiety or fear that diminishes learning. Being able to develop emotions that foster imagination, understanding, empathy, knowledge, and discernment.
- Body integrity. Being free and safe from harassment in the classroom or in educational exchanges between teachers and students, as well as between students, and in the middle of campus.

According to Latorre (2020), in order to work from this skills and competence assessment perspective these skills and competences can only be evaluated if we have programmed the educational action based on their core elements, the students have worked on them in class, they understand those that are at stake in their teaching-learning process, and they clearly understand what they mean and what difficulties they entail.

Feminist and Decolonial Assessment

In this section we are going to offer key strategies to continue building transformative, feminist, and decolonial assessments following the contributions of skills and competence assessments since the breakdown of the monoculture of knowledge.

According to Hooks (2021), Walsh (2013), Martínez (2016), Ramos, *et al.* (2020) and Bejarano, *et al.* (2019, 2021) feminist and decolonial pedagogies seek to transform the structures of oppression and privilege that are reproduced in educational systems and that are represented in the day to day of teaching and learning processes. Feminist and decolonial pedagogies respond to the key principles of critical pedagogies, adding a gender perspective to the understanding of inequality and violence related to differentiated socialization, the reproduction of said structures, the imposition of a homogeneous narrative, the over-representation of privileges in knowledge, and the under-representation of diversities in said process. Thus, all dimensions of education are considered: institutional and legislative narratives, teacher training, the use and organization of spaces, and the basic aspects of the curriculum (languages, organization, content, methodologies, materials, and assessment).

This knowledge dialogue makes it possible for us to present the principles for the construction of a feminist and decolonial assessment in the university context:

- Gender and intersectional inequalities that generate social injustice and violence are placed at the center of assessment. These inequalities are understood as systemic and structural.
- Assessment is a political act (like education) given that it is not a neutral activity. The way in which we evaluate has a direct consequence on the development of the learners and on the general educational process. It is a subjective act influenced by the personal experiences, perspectives, and characteristics of the person who evaluates, the instruments used, and the contexts of application, as well as the analyses and uses of its results.
- Knowledge, its access, processing, and expression are not unique or universal, they are cultural, social, and contextual. There are multiple ways of knowing, doing, expressing... knowledge. Thus, it must be a resource of and for the people who create, build, feel, reflect, and share knowledge production processes.
- Evaluation is intersectional. There are multiple ways of knowing and expressing and one must be aware that some of them are privileged. In other words, with intersectional evaluation the unequal construction of oppressions and privileges influences access to knowledge (depending on social class, gender, place of birth, ethnicity, culture, capacities, identity...) and its production becomes

visible. Diverse references are made invisible, there is an under-representation of certain discourses that remain on the sidelines, and an over-representation of other privileged discourses that build the hegemonic channels of circulation of knowledge. Let us remember that "what we do not see, we do not name, does not exist".[2]

- Evaluating is not applying fixed techniques, filling out decontextualized questionnaires, comparing or memorizing, giving a score to categorize, disaggregating by sex, or making a report with no global sense, among others.

- The assessment content is related to the agency and empowerment of the people involved, the feminist agenda, by taking into account priority elements related to, for example, diversity and inclusion, the visibility and awareness of androcentrism present in the construction of knowledge, the promotion of autonomy, respect for diversity against the imposition of sexist roles and stereotypes, the use of languages, and inclusive resources.

If we compare the skills and competences approach with feminist and decolonial pedagogies, we come to the conclusion that they intersect at various points and that they aim to put the individual and their educational, professional, and future needs at the center, fleeing from a traditional teaching-learning model as a vertical process from top (those who know) to bottom (those who learn). At this point, we can summarize some of the common aspects and those to take into account for an alternative assessment model, understanding that we evaluate to find out if the student body is able to:

Having explained the skills assessment approach, we believe it is necessary to complement it with the competences approach, given that it is the one that has been "imposed" according to the philosophy of the European Higher Education Area. This curricular element needs to be included in the evaluation processes with its three types of knowledge: cognitive, procedural, and attitudinal. To which we add skills. From feminist and decolonial pedagogies, we introduce competence in sexuality and equality in the teaching curriculum as a vector axis of learning that must be newly evaluated in the professional teaching profile. The transformation of educational practice towards formal contexts of social equity happens by attributing this competence and these skills to the educational professional.

Evaluating Sexuality and Equality Competence in Teachers' Higher Education

Introducing an assessment system with a gender and decolonial perspective in Higher Education becomes essential to decode the androcentric codes that are being perpetuated in university knowledge. It is also necessary to review the practical contributions of critical pedagogies that seek to reverse the sexist and heteropatriarchal tendencies into other more inclusive and democratic discourses and practices. We found that in initial teacher training programs in Spain there is a lack of knowledge from feminist research and narrative, as well as of competences based on sexuality and equality education. This contributes to the naturalization of a professional profile scripted by androcentric knowledge where historically constructed sexual segregation allows the reproduction of gender codes (Ballarín et al., 2009) and learning about hyper-masculinized culture.

This diagnosis has been reported by different investigations (Anguita and Torrego, 2009) and raises the issue of training teaching professionals with a gender perspective. Initial teacher training continues to be marked by discrimination and inequality, despite the progress of formal equality in the context of Higher Education in Spain.

Table 1. Criteria for feminist and decolonial skills and competences assessment

Common elements	Transformative assessment criteria
Carry out critical, informed, free reflections.	Question the discourses and elaborate and justify own creative proposals for the construction of collective and individual knowledge.
Assume coherent teaching-learning and evaluation processes adapted to their needs, opportunities, and projections.	Disseminate, transfer the knowledge acquired to everyday and interdisciplinary situations.
Recognize and apprehend diverse knowledge, not only the hegemonic one.	Take into account the pillars of education: learn to be, to do, to feel, to know, from diversity.
Acquire useful knowledge for their global development.	Do situated, applied and experiential learning. Give feedback and rehearse reflective self-assessment processes.
Actively participate, work in a team, listen and respect other knowledge and constructs from an intercultural perspective.	Learn to work collectively, experiencing joint success.
Learn to manage the teaching-learning process in a healthy way.	Learn to learn, materialized in being aware of the learning goals and objectives, planning the learning processes, being strategic and capable of obtaining successful results.
Build emotional and bodily security.	Learn the co-responsibility of collective care as the center of the educational process, breaking the hegemonic stereotypes of normative masculinity and femininity.
Recognize gender and intersectional inequalities in this diverse knowledge.	Include narratives, references, materials ... diverse in gender, class, ethnicity ...
Establish dialogic processes.	Use inclusive language, without hate speech, both symbolic and subjective as well as direct language.
Accept, know, and identify situations of both privilege and oppression.	Offer alternatives that work, elements of resistance and transformation to violence and inequality.

Source: Own elaboration

Introducing a feminist and decolonial assessment discourse focuses on generating indices and criteria that assess whether knowledge exists and is present in terms of theoretical-practical knowledge based on sexuality and equality competence. The invisibility of non-binary references in knowledge continues to be a contrasted trend regarding a hetero-patriarchal society that relegates these groups to the margins of professional success, decision-making, and scientific and technical advances. Therefore, the need to attend educationally to the different ways of being, defining, and identifying ourselves is defended. In this regard, designing curriculum artifacts with a gender perspective constitutes a useful tool for transferring references and contributions. From the field of Sociology and Anthropology, an artifact is understood as any object that is the result of applying a technique with scientific or social interest that contributes meaning and knowledge to the culture to which it is applied (Isava, 2009). The design of curriculum artifacts of practical application with a gender perspective must be carried out through a systematic process adapted to educational requirements and, in our case, to other requirements that include the gender perspective based on the sexuality and equality competence.

Our proposal is to present the sexuality and equality competence as a vector axis of professional learning, which organizes itself based on the knowledge, skills, and attitudes collected in the concept of sexuality defined by UNESCO (2009). This agency reminds us that sexuality is present in all human dimensions (in its different stages or ages, and in all its diversity), and contributes to the development of social identity. This competence supports the principle of equality, and highlights the different behaviors, aspirations and needs of women and men and other identities equally.

What should competence in sexuality and equality embrace? Bejarano and Mateos (2016) defined the content of this curricular element by studying the different epistemological axes reported by the scientific literature following a historical-critical course and provided the following parameters: educate in equality; sex-gender systems; sexuality; sexuality education; affective-sexual relationships; educate in tolerance; educate for health and self-care; body and bodily changes; sexual identities; sexual diversities; sexual abuse/violence; sexual practices; affectivity/pleasure; family diversity.

The presence of this competence must be made effective in each initial teacher training course but with more emphasis on those that address teaching procedures. It is not enough to apply it from epistemological approaches, it is necessary to evaluate it from those educational practices applied to learning contexts, for example the design of curriculum materials and through techniques that include instruments developed to record progress in theoretical knowledge-practices with a gender perspective.

Next, we present two practical experiences that have been assessed using the previously explained approaches. One of them contextualized in Spain and another in Denmark. Both were designed with an educational commitment of subscribing to decolonial, feminist, and critical pedagogies. They have been evaluated taking into account gender perspectives and their purpose is educational transformation by entrusting teaching professionals with new educational tasks.

SOLUTIONS AND RECOMMENDATIONS: NARRATION OF PRACTICAL ASSESSMENT EXPERIENCES WITH A GENDER AND DECOLONIAL PERSPECTIVE IN THE UNIVERSITY ENVIRONMENT

Assessment Through Curriculum Artifacts

An educational practical course is approached from a gender perspective with two purposes. On the one hand, to design a curriculum artifact with a story format. This format has a high socializing power that is able to spread social representations that contribute to normalizing the normative constructs of being a man as opposed to being a woman (Etxaniz, 2011). On the other hand, to evaluate two related competences, a first one related to comprehensive sexuality and equality and a second one based on the design of curriculum materials with an applied-critical dimension. This practical course is presented to students enrolled in the bachelor's degree in Primary School Education. It is part of the subjects offered by the Department of Pedagogy, specifically, in those with applied educational content in the first and fourth year of the degree. It is carried out with a collaborative-investigative sub-group strategy. The objective of the story design is to incorporate the keys involved in the transmission of knowledge freed from sexist stereotypes at all levels of curriculum development, namely: title, narrative structure, images, sexed or non-sexed characters, positions of the characters, their functions, etc. Students are asked to link the plot (story) with a recognized subject from the primary school curriculum and to a specific content block. For the story development process, the students form collaborative subgroups and start by studying scientific materials that reflect the need to incorporate narratives and models with a gender perspective in curriculum materials. Seminars with specific thematic axes are used to study the articles and chapters of collective research. The topics included: inclusion of diverse narratives, counter-hegemony, depatriarchalizing the curriculum, counter-hegemonic references, coeducational model as an axis to introduce alternative knowledge (Bejarano and Martínez, 2019). The students also used co-educational and orientation guides dedicated to designing non-sexist stories and materials.

The story format proposal ends with a guide of educational activities that can be implemented using transformative critical pedagogies. The curricular creation process is supervised by a working document that expresses the guidelines that must be included in the design of this curriculum artifact based on education in sexuality and equality (Bejarano and Marí, 2019). As a result, a curricular proposal is obtained that helps overcome the stereotyped and reified barriers surrounding gender and sexual identities and that constitutes an alternative of subversive learning with cultural messages that are closer to current sexual realities with equal contributions and free of sexism.

The assessment procedure is carried out using two techniques, on the one hand, a rubric is elaborated from the paradigm of feminist pedagogy and taking into account the parameters of competence in sexuality and equality previously exposed. Each epistemological axis of the competence is broken down into descriptive criteria. An example of it:

Diverse sexuality: *heteronormativity is appreciated; characters are constructed from the "commonly accepted trinomial" body/gender/sexuality; a binary narrative is provided from the sexual perspective.*

The second technique is carried out through what is called individual monitoring. Each member of the group reflects on what the creation of this curriculum artifact has contributed to them. Self-monitoring revolves around the following questions that return inclusive learning:

- What prior knowledge do I identify regarding issues of sexuality and equality in my initial teacher training?
- By developing this material have I reversed any sexist social label that I had not self-monitored?
- What has this practical course contributed to my professional and civic training?

The evaluation of competence in sexuality and equality through the creation of curriculum artifacts, in this case in story format, provides the students in training with self-efficacy beliefs that consist of a self-perception about their own capacities to carry out a specific task: apply the feminist critical perspective to curriculum materials that allow the coeducational model to be introduced into the teaching practice through the dissemination of alternative knowledge. On the other hand, the confidence that the future professional has to develop certain curriculum materials is contrasted. These beliefs allow people in training to exercise control over their own thoughts, feelings and, consequently, over their own actions, which in this case means contributing a gender perspective. Applied rubric assessment techniques and self-monitoring allow students to generate their own beliefs of self-efficacy through their capacity for self-reflection, a matter supported by Bandura's (1986) social cognitive theory and supported by the theories of critical pedagogies.

Experiences From the Social Education of Denmark: The "Killjoy"-Trouble and How to Strengthen Antiracist and Antisexist Educational Environments

Where do you come from? - A story from the classroom

"During one of my lectures at The Social Education we deal with the concept of ethnocentrism, otherness and racial practices. In this context I addressed how "otherness" and racial practice is spoken and done. Fx by the statement "Where do you come from?" David, one of my first-year students, nods approvingly to how the statement "Where do you come from?" potentially evokes emotions and experiences of otherness in the person who are asked. David is born and raised in Denmark, but his parents is from Nigeria. He tells the class how he repeatedly experiences how people - the majority ethnical Danes - always ask him "Where do you come from?", or "You speak so good Danish". I use David's example to address how questions like these - even though it´s from the curious majority person´s perspective seems to be a common small talk question to ask – potentially can dismantle the person who are asked, to only be about the persons skin-collar. Fx when David is asked the question, the question addresses David's skin-collar, and not David as an individual. Another student from the class, an older white female student, is obviously provoked by David's statement, and don't understand why David don't understand that the question "Where do you come from?" is out of curiosity and the intention is not ...etc. etc. David tries to explain that he of course knows that. But he still finds it irrelevant and racial to be asked. The female student clearly becomes irritated and rolls her eyes. I try to enlarge David experience to the rest of the class, and use it as an example of majority blindness, and how white people (including myself) rarely are asked about ethnicity, hair structure or, as David added "good at dancing". The mood in the class changes and becomes tense and awkwardly silenced. The female student sits back in here chair with her arms crossed."

I wrote this story after one of my lectures at "Modul 2: Gender, sexuality and diversity", which all students attend during their first year at The Social Education in Denmark. The objective of the module is for the students to gain knowledge about how gender and identity are unfolded, negotiated and handled in pedagogical practice. The module contains different perspectives on gender, sexuality, equality and family structures. The module contains different perspectives on gender, sexuality, equality and family structures. The module is, approximately 6 weeks, and is finished by an oral and written evaluation.

My educational objective with the module is among other things to create a space for theoretical and empirical exploration of race, otherness, whiteness and gender through critical questions. Referring to decolonial and feminist theories and studies (Fx Fanon, 1952; Said 1978; Crenshaw 1991; Ahmed 2012; Butler 1990), The aim is to work pedagogically towards critical thinking, self-reflection and analysis of personal and societal power dynamics and structural privileges. This kind of approach can also be characterized as antiracist and antisexist pedagogy: by disrupting the exiting stereotypes you try to foster students' analytical skills through collaborative learning techniques (Koshimoto 2018). The story is an example one, how I as an educator try to do this by a biographical-narrative method: By inviting the personal or lived reality of the student into the classroom - in this case David's personal story - and analyze the story with concepts and theoretical perspectives from the module. In this way, I seek through collaboration with the students, to deal with and analyze the personal stories on an academic level of critique and reflection.

The Killjoy and the Awkward Silence

The above story is also one of many I have experienced during my lectures, where a classroom gets full with tension, emotion and awkward silence, when we talk about gender, race, discrimination, whiteness and privileges – A classroom I imagine many feminists and decolonial educators have experienced when addressing these issues. With Sara Ahmed you can call the silence and the tension in the classroom the effect of the "killjoy" (Ahmed 2018). The "killjoy" is both a person who calls the racist og sexist action or utterance in the room, and leaves the party - primarily the white majority - in a tense emotional state. In the above story, David is the killjoy. He calls, informed by my theoretical and analytical points, the racist action, and leaves the white female student and the majority of class in tension and awkward silence. As for me, a white female educator, I also experience the situation in the classroom intense and challenging, due to the affective reaction, and I sometime also experience a kind of resistance towards my authority as a teacher in the sense of not getting through to my students. In this case, the white female students.

White Innocence in the Classroom

The Danish psychologist and educational researcher Iram Khawaja (2021 (work in progress)) describes how there seems to be a generalized tendency of tabooing race in most Scandinavian countries including Denmark, which seems to be connected with the tendency of overlooking the colonial past and its power relational implications. This has also been termed the Nordic or Danish racial exceptionalism (Danbolt 2017). Referring to Gloria Wekker (2016), Iram Khawaja address this phenomenon, as an expression of "white innocence" meaning, that there is a a prevailing understanding that we, the Danes, have moved beyond race and racism, and that it is more appropriate to talk about cultural, religious and ethnic differences. "Race and racism are viewed as volatile concepts, and most commonly associated with Nazism, Holocaust and other historical events and movements we would like to believe we have moved beyond." (Khawaja 2021 (in press)). This "denial process" has more broadly been termed as silencing of race and whiteness (Castagno 2008). Other studies also describe a resistance amongst students in higher education when dealing with questions relating to racialization and privilege in educational contexts. Discussions on race and othering in regard to whiteness and structural privilege end in awkward silences and repressed anger. From a teacher point of view: a sense of not getting through to the students (Khawaja 2021 (in press).

The above story exemplifies how theoretical issues such as racism, otherness, whiteness combined with David's confirmative story, leads to strong affective reactions in classroom, and it shows us how these issues is highly politicized and highly personal and sensitive in their nature. Following Khawaja's historical perspectives on "white innocence" many of my ethnical white Danish students often gets offended, irritated or frustrated when we in the class shows how racial practices reveals itself through questions like "Where do you come from?". On the other hand, many of the same students also gets very surprised and caring when they hear, that many of the minority students often have experience discrimination, unjust and racism during their daily life's. They typically reply to these stories with "I didn't know that?" Or "Is this really happening in Denmark?". So besides from the "white innocence" there also seems to be a "blind whiteness" among some of the majority students, who doesn't recognize or is aware of the minority students racialized reality in the Danish Society.

Tolerance Pedagogy and Evaluation

As stated above, my educational objective is to create a space for theoretical and empirical exploration of race, otherness, whiteness and gender through biographical-narrative methods, critical questions, and the pedagogical aim is to work pedagogically towards critical thinking, self-reflection etc. As the story witness, these theoretical concepts and the pedagogical approach can have some serious social consequences among the students in the classroom, which potentially can lead to a continually dichotomization between "us and them" – between the majority and the minority – and where the minority-person is positioned as a victim or blamed for being "violation setted". As a consequence, the minorized person is further marginalized.

Several pedagogical theories about how to work with diversity have had "the diverse" or "the other" (the deviations from the norm) in itself as an object of research, and the focus is on how space can be created for increased diversity by including these in the existing space. This is generally referred to as tolerance pedagogy (Bromseth 2019). The starting point of tolerance pedagogy is that subjects who are said to belong to the majority must be informed and taught about the minorities, in order to create understanding, empathy and acceptance of the minority. The purpose is to encourage the majority subject to show tolerance towards members of a given minority culture (Bromseth 2019; 2021). The major problem with this kind of tolerance strategy is that it firstly confirms and reinforces the 'other' just like the 'other'. Secondly it maintains an understanding of 'them and us'. Likewise, tolerance as a value and action often hides the fact that the majority is in a position to show tolerance towards the minority, and the power relations between the majority and minority is as a consequence not fundamentally shaken. These perspectives on tolerance pedagogy also reveal themselves in the evaluation of the module.

Assessment

At the Social Education in Denmark, it is mandatory that every module is evaluated. The objective of the evaluation is to evaluate the students learning outcomes in relation to every module's educational objective. The educators can decide for themselves how they do the evaluation. At module 2 we always end the module with a final formative oral evaluation. The oral evaluation focus on modules didactics and how the students have worked with the various content elements along the way. Furthermore, we sum up the main points for the oral evaluation in a written formalized evaluation document, which is sent to the administration, as a part of documentation procedure, that secures that the education continuously evaluates.

At module 2 we generally see in the evaluation, that the module, due to its educational objective on gender, sexuality and diversity, to a great extent "awakes" the students in relation to their own identity and development as well as others. Likewise, the module seems to address students who see themselves as "woke". The students emphasize in the evaluation, that the modules concepts, exercises as well as their own experiences invites them in reflexive modes and situations which they not normally think about. In this way the module seems to a large extent to support the important and broader educational objectives such as how the pedagogical work can be investigated from different levels of description - society, institution and individual, as well as how the module's matters can put international and national agendas, political climates and legislation and basics human rights in to perspectives. That being said, the evaluations also show, that the pedagogically strategy to handle issues such social inequality and racial practices in pedagogically settings seems to be informed by ideas from tolerance pedagogy. The students fx emphasizes in the evaluation, that they have become aware how to include members of a minoritized culture in general. Meaning, that being representors of the majority, they need to create "space" so the minority can be included in various social settings. This leads us back to the main critique of tolerance pedagogy which I unfolded in the above, in that way that this toleration strategy among others both confirms and reinforces the 'other' just like the 'other' and maintains an understanding of 'them and us'. So how can we as educators in higher education seek to move beyond tolerance pedagogy and these educational and pedagogical "downfalls" in the classroom?

Norm-Critical and Norm-Creative Inspirations

With the critique towards the tolerance pedagogy in mind, Nordic decolonial and feminist educators including myself, have as a result drawn great inspiration from Swedish gender and race studies and their development of the norm-critique. The norm-critique which originally is developed in a Swedish pedagogical context emerged as an attempt to change perspective and approach to the work of supporting diversity. The norms-critique addresses these issues by changing the perspective. From a norm-critique perspective the focus is not on what breach the 'normal', or on the 'other', which must be included or tolerated. But instead on the existing set of norms, which in different ways stand out from the framework for what is understood as 'the normal' (Frederiksen & Overvad 2020). The primary objective of the norm critique is therefore to shed light on the existing norms, with the aim of deconstructing the norms and showing that norms are not natural, but rather the result of intersubjective negotiations. The norms are historically and culturally conditioned, and the current appearance of the norms should not be understood as necessary. On the contrary, the deconstructive gaze of the norm-critique emphasizes that norms could look different.

The norm-critique, however, does not only seek to show the contingency of the norms. There is also a power-critical perspective embedded in the norm-critique. With a norm-critical perspective one is interested in examining how norms can have a limiting effect on the possibilities of certain subjects to unfold. In addition, the norm-critical perspective also contains an element of constructive norm-creativity, which recognizes the meaning and need for norms in social contexts, where norm-creativity is invited to norm-experiments and building new / other norms, so that the space for the subject's identity-creation and self-determination can be greater. The norm-critique, therefore has a sharpened eye for power relations and hidden privileges (Bruun 2016). The norm criticism is furthermore required by the intersectional epistemology, which means that every individual must be understood through several intertwined social categories such as gender, age, class, ethnicity and sexuality (Bromseth 2019). In this way, norms and consequent power relations must be understood as context-dependent and relationally conditioned. Following the perspectives from the norm-critique, Marta Padovan-Özdemir and Stine del Pin Hamilton (2020) have for example currently studied how educators in pedagogical settings can develop an evaluation culture that illuminates how the norms are in play in pedagogical work, and how the norm-critique and norm-creative pedagogy can lead to the development of more inclusive and diverse norms and opportunities for participation, learning, development and formation in pedagogical settings (Clarup, Hamilton & Padovan-Özdemir 2020).

FUTURE RESEARCH DIRECTIONS

Among the main contributions of this chapter, we highlight the theoretical approach to the state of the art of feminist and decolonial pedagogies, from the dialogue that is established between the approaches presented. In addition, key practical tools are provided to weave visible transformative educational networks around other "possible" assessment methods at the University that generate direct transfers in the construction of feminist and anti-racist citizenships based on social justice and equity. To achieve this, we consider the following:

Why Do We Evaluate?

We evaluate to understand, to learn and to build diverse knowledge. Feminist and decolonial pedagogies place people and their diversities at the center of education instead of discourses and learning based on the reproduction of inequalities.

Education, as the complex act that it is, builds our individual and collective identities, generates spaces for meeting, exchange, and dialogue. However, the wrong approach can lead to reproducing and increasing gaps, violence, and discrimination. For this reason, this first question is essential. We evaluate to build collectively, to accommodate the diversity of knowledge and forms of expression, to dialogue, to transgress and improve, to create, to reflect from a critical perspective and, ultimately, we evaluate to build healthy teaching and learning relationships. All this materialized in clear competences and skills (see Table 1).

Who Do We Evaluate?

All educational agents, all the people involved. This involves questioning the traditional role of the banking educator to promote horizontal and constructive educational relationships. Evaluating cannot remain an isolated mechanism of control, fear, and unequal power.

We evaluate the institution, materials, relationships, spaces, languages, materials, and content, that is, all the curriculum elements that are part of the educational relationship. Feminist and decolonial assessment breaks with the traditional perspective of evaluating the student body as the sole object of the educational process. That is, we evaluate with a community and collective perspective. We start from our own experience, from the situated contexts and the connection with them, as opposed to an external and decontextualized evaluation. Then we add the collective, common, shared learning.

How Do We Evaluate?

Feminist and decolonial assessments recognize multiple ways of knowing and doing. An education based on multiple intelligences, knowledge from the sidelines, education based on experience and universal learning designs. The latter, in its three principles, highlights the need to offer multiple forms of involvement, knowledge access, and the multiple forms of knowledge expression.

Understanding knowledge as diverse, with its multiple forms of action and expression, means rethinking the techniques and assessment methods beyond traditional testing. Narrative, written, oral, memory, experiential, daily, final, processual experiences, field journals, audiovisual techniques, self-evaluation, co-evaluation, among others, are proposed. In other words, an evaluation that is flexible enough to take into account the present heterogeneity in the teaching and learning processes.

We therefore need tools and assessment strategies that are emancipatory, that address the issues of diversity, inequality (identities, roles, stereotypes, norms, differences...), and violence. If we want an inclusive education in which other realities are included, the evaluation methodologies and systems will have to be equally inclusive. No one can be left out of the evaluation process because we would be violating the basic right to education.

The consensual construction of assessment criteria is important, they must be known, clear and consistent with the educational process (with teaching methodologies and styles). Evaluating competences and skills from this perspective is possible and, as we have seen in the previous section, involves trying out diverse and creative evaluation techniques and instruments.

At Whose Service is the Evaluation? What Do We Put at the Center of the Teaching and Learning Process?

Álvarez (2001) already indicated the importance of putting evaluation at the service of the person who learns and education itself. To this we add the contributions of the Pedagogy of Care that places people, well-being, self-care, good treatment, and interdependent relationships at the center. Paraphrasing Paulo Freire (2006), an education that aims not only to transfer knowledge but also to create possibilities for its construction and reflection will be responsible for an evaluation capable of attending to the entire educational process.

Continuing with Freire (2006), evaluating is a process through which certain information is looked for to assess it and make informed and thoughtful decisions that serve to rectify, reform, or revolutionize a process, without the intention of generalizing it. Evaluation should not be confused with qualification (numerical or alphabetical), which implies an immediate judgment on educational actions. Thus, we do not put qualification at the center of the evaluation, but rather the process, reflection, and construction.

An assessment methodology is proposed that puts the following criteria, competences and skills at the center (Table 1): a) contextualized evaluation based on the reality of the participants; b) focused on the basic pillars of education (learning to be, to know, to do, to live together) with special emphasis on learning to learn; c) use of dialogue and critical reflection as the central method; d) promoting evaluation of critical and problematizing education (use of self-evaluation, co-evaluation, learning to ask intelligent questions with complex answers, diverse use of techniques, experiential evaluation, etc.); e) promote diversity of forms of expression and creativity giving rise to the development of affections and feelings; f) promote participation, reflecting on the evaluation itself (for example, group co-evaluation, own group evaluation criteria, collective evaluation dynamics...); g) teachers trained in participatory, inclusive and feminist assessment uses and techniques.

CONCLUSION

The feminist and decolonial evaluation broadens the educational perspective and breaks with the impositions of traditional paradigms. It involves a subversion of closed and decontextualized techniques and turns assessment into a transformative educational moment. Constructing a feminist and decolonial evaluation is a challenge and, in turn, a commitment to an education that places people, their care, the distribution of privileges, and the construction of citizenships in equity and with social justice at the center.

We have analyzed various narratives of assessment processes that break with traditional structures. The biographical-narrative method enabled us to work on an alternative teaching and evaluation model that provided autobiographical accounts. These allowed us to understand the subjectivities and personal experiences of students and teachers that are key to the construction of the educational story. In addition, this model offered a space for further reflection and allowed us to analyze the immediate environment by exploring new teaching and educational practices.

The evaluation of competence in sexuality and equality determined whether university students could acquire a new role when faced with processes of change and social transformation and included scientific knowledge regarding sexuality education and the principle of equality in their learning experiences. It also allowed us to contrast whether or not they were acquiring the necessary skills and attitudes that would allow them to transfer this knowledge to professional contexts. As stated by De Juanas (2010), in the current university context a primary role is given to students in terms of the acquisition and development of competences that makes it easier for students to generalize them to professional situations. The competence approach gives preference to training in some aspects of competence aimed at offering thought structures, tools, and ways of learning adjusted to the reality of the moment, in this case a diverse sexual reality present in all dimensions of the human being. In turn, the skills approach makes it possible to add a global teaching-learning process that takes into account the needs, possibilities, and future projections both in the purely educational as well as in the personal and professional areas of these competences.

The evaluation of skills and competences with a gender and decolonial approach gives us the chance to detect whether students are acquiring these skills in a theoretical-practical way that will allow them to take action in real situations using feminist and anti-racist pedagogies for educational socialization. The evaluation of the presented experiences made it possible for us to observe the procedures of incorporating specific knowledge which was alternative to the one prescribed in the teaching curriculum. For this, it was useful to feed back the skills and competences with a gender and decolonial perspective that they were acquiring and transferring to their professional profiles. This is what we call the educational translation of training effectiveness. There are few studies that have focused on researching self-efficacy beliefs in students despite the multiple benefits, among which we can highlight the improvement in decision-making (Haro-Soler, 2017).

It is a challenge to ask ourselves what a fair evaluation looks like and how we can continue to build teaching and learning processes in the university that transgress the impositions of efficient assessment. However, in this chapter we show that feminist, anti-racist, and decolonial evaluation practices are possible in the university.

REFERENCES

Ahmed, S. (2012). *On being included- Racism and diversity in institutional life*. Duke University Press.

Ahmed, S. (2018). *Killjoy Manifest*. Informations Forlag.

Álvarez, J. M. (2001). *Evaluar para conocer, examinar para excluir*. Morata.

Anguita, R. & Torrego, L. (2009). Género, educación y formación del profesorado. Retos y posibilidades. *Revista interuniversitaria de formación del profesorado*, (64), 17-26.

Ballarín, P., Barranco, E., Gálvez, M. A., Jandali, L., Marín, V., Muñoz, A. M., Ramírez, A., Reyes, M. L., & Soto, P. (2009). *Evaluación de la incidencia de los saberes de las mujeres, feministas y de género en la docencia universitaria: Memoria final 2007-2009*. Ministerio de Trabajo y Asuntos Sociales, Instituto de la Mujer. https://digibug.ugr.es/bitstream/handle/10481/36530/Memoria%20investigacio%CC%81n.pdf?sequence=1

Bandura, A. (1986). *Social Foundations of Thought and Action: A Social Cognitive Theory*. Prentice-Hall.

Bejarano, M. T. & Mateos, A. (2016). Reflexiones y propuestas para mejorar la educación afectivo-sexual en España. In R. Costa, E., Pinheiro de Queiroz, & F. Teixeira, F. (Coord.). Atravessamentos de gêneo, corpos e sexualidades: Linguagens, apelos, desejos, posibilidades e desafíos (pp. 150-172). Editora FURG.

Bejarano, M. T. & Martínez I. (2019). Los cuentos creativos, un recurso didáctico para la igualdad en educación Infantil y Primaria. In Mª. T. Bejarano & R. Marí (Dir.). Educación en sexualidad e igualdad. Discursos y estrategias para la formación docente y educadores sociales (pp. 115-132). Dykinson.

Bejarano, M. T. & Marí, R. (2019). Educación en sexualidad e igualdad. Discursos y estrategias para la formación docente y educadores sociales. Dykinson.

Bejarano, M. (2019). Coeducar hoy. Reflexiones desde las pedagogías feministas para la despatriarcalización del currículum. *Tendencias Pedagógicas*, *34*, 37–50. doi:10.15366/tp2019.34.004

Bejarano, M. T., Téllez, V. & Martínez, I. (2021). Decolonial, Feminist, and Antiracist Pedagogies. In I.M. Barreto (coord.). Promoting Social Justice for Inmigrants and Refugees Through Active Citizenship and Intercultural Education. (pp. 310-320). IGI Global.

Boni, A., Lozano, J. F., & Walker, M. (2010). La educación superior desde el enfoque de capacidades. Una propuesta para el debate. *REIFOP*, *13*(3), 123–131.

Bromseth, J. (2019). Normkritisk pedagogik - rötter och fötter. In J. Bromseth & L. Björkman (Eds.), *Normkritisk pedagogik: Perspektiv, utmaningar och möjligheter* (pp. 41–72). Studentlitteratur AB.

Bromseth, J., & Sörensdötter, R. (2012). Normkritisk pedagogik. In Lundberg. A. & A. Werner (Ed.) Genusvetenskapens pedagogik och didaktik (pp. 43–57). Nationella sekretariatet för genusforskning.

Bruun, T. (2016). Det normales magt. *VERA*, *76*, 4–9.

Butler, J. (1999). *Gender Trouble - Feminism and the Subversion of Identity*. Routledge.

Castagno, A. (2008). "I Don't Want to Hear That!": Legitimating Whiteness through Silence in Schools. *Anthropology & Education Quarterly*, *39*(3), 314–333. doi:10.1111/j.1548-1492.2008.00024.x

Clarup, E., Hamilton, S. D. P., & Padovan-Özdemir, M. (2020). *Normkritisk og normkreativ pædagogik i aktuel praksis: Et forskningsbaseret inspirationskatalog til dagtilbud*. VIA University College.

Crenshaw, K. (1991). Mapping the Margins: Intersectionality, Identity Politics, and Violence against Women of Color. *Stanford Law Review*, *43*(6), 1241–1299. doi:10.2307/1229039

Danbolt, M. (2017). RETRO RACISM - Colonial Ignorance and Racialized Affective Consumption in Danish Public Culture. *Nordic Journal of Migration Research*, *7*(2), 105–113. doi:10.1515/njmr-2017-0013

De Juanas, A. (2010). Aprendices y competencias en el Espacio Europeo de Educación Superior. *Revista de Psicología y Educación*, *1*(5), 171–186.

De Sousa Santos, B. (2011a). Epistemologías del Sur. *Revista Internacional de Filosofía Iberoamericana y Teoría Social*, (54), 17–39.

De Sousa Santos, B. (2012). La universidad en el siglo XXI. Para una reforma democrática y emancipadora de la universidad. In R. Ramírez, Transformar la Universidad para Transformar la Sociedad (pp. 139-194). SENESCYT.

De Sousa Santos, B. (2018). *The End of the Cognitive Empire: The Coming of Age of Epistemologies of the South*. Duke University Press. doi:10.1215/9781478002000

Etxaniz, X. (2011). La transmisión de los valores en la literatura, desde la tradición oral hasta la LIJ. *Ocnos*, *7*(7), 73–83. doi:10.18239/ocnos_2011.07.06

Fanon, F. (1952). *Black Skin, White Masks*. Grove Press.

Frederiksen, J. S., & Overvad, E. (2020). Normkreativ pædagogik og ligestillingsarbejde i skolen. In S. B. Nielsen & G. Riis (Eds.), *Køn, seksualitet og mangfoldighed* (pp. 214–236). Samfundslitteratur.

Freire, P. (2006). *Pedagogía de la indignación*. Editorial Siglo XXI.

Giroux, H. (2018). *Pedagogía crítica para tiempos difíciles*. Mapas colectivos.

Haro-Soler, M. M. (2017). ¿Cómo desarrollar la autoeficacia del estudiantado? Presentación y evaluación de una experiencia formativa en el aula de traducción. *Revista Digital de Docencia Universitaria*, *11*(2), 50–74. doi:10.19083/ridu.11.567

Hipólito, N., & Martínez Martín, I. (2021). Diálogos entre el Buen Vivir, las Epistemologías del Sur, el feminismo decolonial y las pedagogías feministas. Aportes para una educación transformadora. *Estudos Avançados*, (35), 16–28. doi:10.35588/estudav.v0i35.5321

Hooks, B. (2021). *Enseñar a transgredir. Educación como práctica de la libertad*. Capitán Swing.

Isava, L. M. (2009). Breve introducción a los artefactos culturales. *Estudios (Madrid, Spain)*, *17*(34), 441–445.

Khawaja, I. (2022). Memory Work as Engaged Critical Pedagogy: Creating Collaborative Spaces for Reflections on Racialisation, Privilege and Whiteness. *Nordic Journal of Social Research*.

Kishimoto, K. (2018). Anti-racist pedagogy: From faculty's self-reflection to organizing within and beyond the classroom. *Race, Ethnicity and Education*, *21*(4), 540–554. doi:10.1080/13613324.2016.1248824

Latorre, M. (2020). *Evaluación por capacidades y competencias I*. Universidad Marcelino Chaptagnat. https://marinolatorre.umch.edu.pe/wp-content/uploads/2020/09/116_EVALUACI%C3%93N-POR-CAPACIDADES-Y-COMPETENCIAS-I.pdf

Lozano, J. F. (2012). Cómo formar profesionales responsables en la Universidad? In G. Celorio & A. López de Munain (Eds.), *La Educación para el Desarrollo en la Universidad Reflexiones en torno a una práctica transformadora* (pp. 73–81). HEGOA.

Martínez Martín, I. (2016). Construcción de una pedagogía feminista para una ciudadanía transformadora y contra-hegemónica. *Foro de Educación*, *14*(20), 129–151. doi:10.14516/fde.2016.014.020.008

Nussbaum, M. (2005). El cultivo de la humanidad. University of Chicago.

Nussbaum, M. (2006). Education and Democratic Citizenship: Capabilities and Quality Education. *Journal of Human Development*, *7*(3), 385–395. doi:10.1080/14649880600815974

Nussbaum, M. (2016). Educación para el lucro, educación para la libertad. *Nómadas*, (44), 13–25. doi:10.30578/nomadas.n44a1

Padovan-Özdemir, M., & Hamilton, S. D. P. (2020). *Mangfoldighed og ligestilling i dagtilbud: Omfang - Forståelser - Holdninger - Tilgange*. VIA University College.

Ramos, F. J., Martínez, I., & Blanco, M. (2020). Sentido de la educación para la ciudadanía desde pedagogías feministas, críticas y decoloniales. Una propuesta para la formación del profesorado. *Revista Izquierdas*, *49*, 2103–2116.

Said, E. (1978). *Orientalism - Western Conceptions of the Orient*. Penguin Books.

Sancho, J., Hernández, F., Rivas-Flores, J. I., Ocaña, A., & de Pablos, J. (2020). *Caminos y derivas para otra investigación educativa y social*. Octaedro.

UNESCO. (2009). International technical guidance on sexuality education. *Rationale for sexuality education*. UNESCO. https://unesdoc.unesco.org/images/0018/001832/183281e.pdf

Walsh, C. (2013). *Pedagogías Decoloniales. Prácticas insurgentes de resistir, (re) existir y (re) vivir*. Ediciones Abya-Yala.

Wekker, G. (2016). *White innocence: Paradoxes of colonialism and race*. Duke University Press.

KEY TERMS AND DEFINITIONS

Anti-Racist Education: A educational perspective that seeks to show and disrupt the exiting racial stereotypes in the classroom, by fostering the students' analytical skills through collaborative learning techniques, and by addressing the histories and experience of people who normally is left out of the curriculum. Its purpose is to handle equitably with all the cultural and racial differences you find among people and impose social justice and equality among all people.

Biographical-Narrative Educational Method: You invite the personal or lived reality of the student into the classroom, by personal stories from the students and analyze these stories with concepts and theoretical perspectives from the module. In this way, the method seeks through collaboration with the students, to deal with and analyze personal stories on an academic level of critique and reflection.

Competence Assessment: Aims to evaluate cognitive, procedural, and attitudinal knowledge, including practical experiences and professional learning. In addition to evaluating educational practices in pedagogical contexts.

Curriculum Artifact: Analog device used for teaching. Ideal tool to define and organize teaching and learning work in educational contexts.

Education in Equality and Sexuality: Process in which the feminist pedagogical proposal seeks to reformulate the model of transmission of androcentric knowledge incorporating the scientific gender perspective, incorporating sexuality as a central aspect of the human being, present throughout life and in all its dimensions.

Norm-Critical and Norm-Creative Pedagogy: About creating different opportunities for children and help them to see themselves as legitimate participants in pedagogical settings. The pedagogy takes the children's perspective seriously and is engaged in children's change and displacement due to the established norms. Fx gender, age-related or culturally conditioned behavior.

Skills Assessment: Aims to evaluate skills that lead students to achieve higher levels of freedom, other diverse and intercultural knowledge, and the capacity for reflection, global development, and identifying conditions of privilege and oppression.

ENDNOTES

[1] Henry Giroux interview, https://www.lavanguardia.com/vivo/mamas-y-papas/20190506/462 061857522/henry-giroux-examenes-roban-imaginacion-alumnos-pe dagogia.html

[2] Marco Aurelio Denegri https://elcomercio.pe/opinion/columnistas/existe-nombra-marc o-aurelio-denegri-325472-noticia/

Chapter 6
Internal Coherence Between Methodology and Assessment:
Formative and Shared Assessment and Tutored Learning Projects

Carla Fernández Garcimartín
University of Valladolid, Spain

David Hortigüela-Alcalá
University of Burgos, Spain

Teresa Fuentes Nieto
University of Valladolid, Spain

Miriam Molina Soria
University of Valladolid, Spain

Víctor Manuel López-Pastor
University of Valladolid, Spain

Cristina Pascual-Arias
University of Valladolid, Spain

ABSTRACT

The aim of this chapter was to check the importance of the curricular alignment between the teaching methodology and the assessment system used, specifically between the use of tutored learning projects (TLP) and formative and shared-assessment (FandSA) systems, in terms of student participation in assessment. The assessment of students and lecturers on student participation in the FandSA processes is studied when they are associated with active learning methodologies such as TLP. The study sample consisted of 256 students and lecturers from higher education. The results obtained show a high level of satisfaction with the experience of good practice in developing TLP in groups and taking part in the assessment process. One of the advantages found is that student involvement in their learning was high, and an increase was observed in all the subjects. The main disadvantage that the students indicated was the high workload involved.

INTRODUCTION

Firstly, two concepts are described that are basic throughout this study: Tutored Learning Projects (TLP) and Formative and Shared-Assessment (FandSA).

DOI: 10.4018/978-1-6684-3537-3.ch006

According to Meyer (2014), TLP are a working method where students carry out learning related to real situations that may occur in their professional practice in a guided and active way.

On the other hand, "Formative Assessment" seeks to improve student learning, teaching practice and the teaching-learning process that is carried out; therefore, the feedback and feedforward processes that are generated are fundamental. The concept of "Shared-Assessment" is complementary to that of formative assessment and refers to the involvement of students in the assessment processes, through dialogue and decision-making with lecturers on the teaching-learning processes (López-Pastor, 2009; López-Pastor and Pérez-Pueyo, 2017).

Despite the evidence and positive experiences with the application of FandSA in TLP, there is a lack of literature on the curricular alignment between this assessment and TLP. Neither are there many references on the analysis of student participation in FandSA within TLP in relation to its curriculum coherence.

Therefore, the authors consider that it is interesting to analyse the assessment of students as participants in the FandSA system in TLP, in order to check whether there really is curricular alignment. In this regard, the following research objective is proposed: to analyse how the FandSA system and the TLP methodology affect student engagement in learning.

BACKGROUND

Instructional Alignment in Higher Education

Martin (2011) and Polikoff and Porter (2014) define the concept of 'instructional alignment' as the process by which instructional elements are connected to each other, giving coherence and quality to teaching. It is often confused with the concept of curriculum alignment, which is the alignment of particular curricular elements with assessment standards. In this case, instructional alignment can also be defined as the alignment of the curriculum with the curriculum objectives, content, teaching strategies and assessment.

Biggs (2005) discusses the concept of "constructive alignment" in Higher Education, referring to the strong coherence that should exist among objectives, content, methodology and assessment in learning activities, including TLP. Other Spanish authors prefer to refer to "curriculum coherence" (López-Pastor, 2009) and defend the importance of ensuring that all curricular elements have a strong internal coherence in Higher Education (Castejón et al., 2011). By curricular elements they refer to: teaching objectives, methods, teaching-learning activities and the assessment and marking system used. In this respect, Biggs (2005) and López-Pastor (2011) agree that the higher the level of internal coherence between the curricular elements, the greater the chances that what is implemented in the classroom will work and that students will achieve a high degree of learning and better academic performance. In contrast, these authors emphasise that a lack of coherence or incorrect alignment among these elements will result in poor subject performance, problems in student learning and thus, inconsistencies with regard to what is intended to be taught.

Active methodologies are an excellent resource that contributes to developing curricular alignment and, in addition, promotes the acquisition of European Higher Education Area (EHEA) competences (Fortea, 2009). Methodologies that foster student autonomy and the learning of knowledge, skills and attitudes in themselves favour the development of competences (Fernández-March, 2006). According to Riesco (2008), competences are divided into two groups: (1) transversal, which are those common to all

Table 1. Transversal competences of university degrees from the EHEA approach

Transversal competences		
Instrumental	Capacity for analysis and synthesis	
	Organisation and planning	
	Oral and written communication	
	Use of ICT in the study and professional environment	
	Information management	
	Problem solving and decision making	
Interpersonal	Critical and self-critical capacity	
	Ability to integrate and communicate with experts from other areas and contexts.	
	Recognition of and respect for diversity and multiculturalism	
	Interpersonal skills	
	Ethical commitment	
Systemic	Autonomy	
	Adaptability to different situations	
	Creativity	
	Leadership	
	Initiative and entrepreneurial spirit	
	Openness to lifelong learning	
	Commitment to professional identity, development and ethics	
	Process management with quality indicators	

Source: based on Riesco (2008).

degrees; and (2) specific, which are those specific to each degree. Table 1 shows the different transversal competences indicated by Riesco (2008) that are applicable to any degree programme:

Manrique et al. (2010) and Molina et al. (2019) agree that TLP are considered an active methodology, as they meet the following characteristics, among others: the lecturer is a learning guide, learning is meaningful, and student responsibility and autonomy are encouraged. Authors such as López-Pastor and Pérez-Pueyo (2017) emphasise the necessity of a teaching model focused on student learning and participation. Table 2 describes different types of current active teaching and learning methodologies:

Tutored Learning Projects in Higher Education

Since the EHEA Convergence process, the importance of generating learning based on transversal and specific competences and, above all, learning where the role of the university lecturer is to promote the development of competences that help students to be trained in their degree (OECD, 2002), has been emphasised within the educational curricula. In this respect, the active methodologies already defined are a good example of practice. Among them we find the TLP. Gutiérrez (2010), López-Pastor et al. (2019), Luengo and Puente (2017) and Mínguez (2017) define TLP as group activities based on the independent and active learning of students and the monitoring of learning by the tutor. Thus, practices are carried out that aim to develop different professional competences such as: teamwork, critical reasoning, organisational skills, planning and communication, among others.

Table 2. Description of a sample of active teaching and learning methodologies.

ACTIVE METHODOLOGY	DESCRIPTION
Tutored Learning Projects	The TLP are a methodology that links professional development and autonomous learning. In its development, it encourages cooperative, and group learning and facilitates interdisciplinary work. In the TLP, each group of students must carry out an educational intervention proposal and present its corresponding theoretical framework. Students need continuous tutoring to solve problems that arise during their autonomous learning process (Luengo and Puente, 2017).
Project-based learning	This is a teaching-learning methodology based on the elaboration of a final product and the acquisition of skills therein. It encourages individualised and autonomous learning by the student, framed within a work plan with objectives and procedures. All learning is based on the project carried out, without systematic tutoring (Muñoz-Repiso and Gómez-Pablos, 2017).
Cooperative learning	Students work towards a common challenge that can only be achieved if all students reach it. This type of learning involves a series of different interactions among learners that favours their learning (Velázquez, 2010). It is based on five principles outlined by Johnsson and Johnsson (1999; 2014): (1) positive interdependence; (2) individual responsibility; (3) face-to-face interaction; (4) development of interpersonal and small group skills; and (5) group processing.
Problem-based learning	It is a learning method based on problem solving in a coordinated way among students for the acquisition of knowledge. Students work in small groups following a series of phases. Problems are the focus and stimulation of learning. Learning is student-centred and the lecturer will serve as a guide and support during the process (Escribano and del Valle, 2015).
Simulation and gaming	The student learns interactively through a simulated game experience. Learning takes place in a series of steps where students must: discover, problem-solve and problem-solve situations as they experiment (Dempsey, 1993).
Case study	A specific case or situation must be analysed in depth. Students must: interpret the case, generate hypotheses, contrast data, reflect and arrive at a final diagnosis (Fidel, 1984).
Flipped classroom	It is a methodology that proposes that students prepare the learning content outside the classroom and then expound that knowledge and generate learning exchange processes. It facilitates: (1) getting to know each student individually; (2) clarifying incorrect notions that students have; (3) adapting the teaching content to the needs of the students; and (4) deepening scientific terms or ideas based on doubts, interests or errors (Tucker, 2012).
Seminars	The class is organised as a single group. The students have previously had to work at home on the topic the lecturer suggested. They encourage reflection and active listening to the ideas or experiences of classmates (Ospina et al., 2008).

Source. Based on Dempsey (1993), Escribano and del Valle (2015), Fidel (1984), Johnson and Johnson (2014), Luengo and Puente (2017), Muñoz-Repiso and Gómez-Pablos (2017), Ospina et al. (2008), Ruiz-Omeñaca (1999) and Tucker (2012).

Manrique (2017), Manrique et al. (2010), Martínez-Mínguez et al. (2019) and Molina et al. (2019) argue that TLP are perfectly viable for achieving the following objectives related to the implementation of the EHEA: (1) structuring the teaching system around the students' learning processes; (2) carrying out dialogical learning processes; and (3) using formative assessment processes. In this experience, the TLP are carried out in Pre-service Teacher Education. They consist of preparing a practical session of a didactic resource, as well as its theoretical framework.

In Table 3, Lopez-Pastor et al. (2020) describe the development of TLP by outlining the following steps:

Álvarez et al. (2004) consider that TLP should have the following characteristics: (1) they should allow students to learn autonomously and in different contexts, always supervised by a tutor; (2) the basic learning to be acquired with TLP is how to do, to favour the development of professional competences; and (3) the student is the main protagonist and responsible for his or her learning.

Table 3. Steps to carry out TLP and their description

Steps	Description
1	Each group of students chooses a project topic and a date for its completion.
2	The group tutor meets with the students and provides them with the basic bibliography they must read according to their topic. This helps them to start drafting a short theoretical framework of about four pages.
3	Once the group has drafted their theoretical framework, the tutor approves the document, and they make a session plan.
4	Students can attend as many tutorials as they need so that the lecturer can review their drafts, and explain the aspects they need to consider in order to improve.
5	Students conduct the practical session and present the theoretical framework of the topic in a maximum of ten minutes. The presenting group gives a copy of the theoretical framework to each partner.
6	Depending on the subject, and on a voluntary basis, the TLP can be carried out in a pre-school or primary school.
7	One week after implementing the TLP in the school, each group has to hand in the final report of the TLP. In this report the group should reflect on the implementation of the work and carry out a self-evaluation.
8	If the lecturer approves the report, they return it to the group to keep it in their collaborative portfolio. If there are any aspects that need to be improved, they must correct it and hand it in within a maximum period of one week.

Source. Own elaboration.

For their part, Manrique et al. (2010) indicate that, in pre-service teacher education, these TLP are group projects within a subject that can be based on carrying out several practical sessions in real situations in an educational centre, or carrying out these sessions with fellow undergraduate students on the subject.

There are several experiences that indicate that the implementation of TLP in Higher Education is feasible and offers different advantages for students, for example: it improves learning and student involvement in the teaching-learning processes, improves academic performance, etc. (Barba, et al., 2012; Barba-Martín and López-Pastor, 2017; López-Pastor, et al., 2020; Martínez-Mínguez, et al., 2019; Sonlleva, et al. 2019).

Formative and Shared-Assessment in Higher Education

Teaching and assessment models have evolved over the years. The transition to the process of Convergence to EHEA proposes carrying out teaching models where the student is the protagonist of the process. Therefore, the most coherent and logical reasoning is to move from a traditional assessment to a formative assessment model, this being a source of improvement in learning (Álvarez-Méndez, 2001). In this regard, Martínez-Mínguez and Nieva (2017) indicate that the assessment of learning activities in Teacher Education should be oriented towards the acquisition of significant learning and its possible implementation in schools.

Studies and experiences can be found in Higher Education that show some progress in breaking with the repeated traditional culture of assessment, and the positive effects on learning of the application of formative assessment systems (Santos and Martínez, 2006; López-Pastor, 2006; 2009; 2012; López-Pastor and Pérez-Pueyo, 2017).

According to López-Pastor (2009; 2017) and López-Pastor and Pérez-Pueyo (2017), the formative assessment model should be useful in three ways by: (1) improving student learning; (2) improving teaching practice; and (3) improving the explicit teaching-learning process itself. This formative evaluation makes coherent sense as long as the student actively participates in the evaluation process. For this reason, the proposal called FandSA is presented (López-Pastor, 1999, 2009; López-Pastor and Pérez-Pueyo, 2017). FandSA promotes dialogical learning and student participation in their learning and assessment (López-Pastor and Pérez-Pueyo, 2017; Santos-Pastor et al., 2009). López-Pastor and Pérez-Pueyo (2017) indicate that FandSA is composed of: (a) "Formative Assessment": meaning improving the teaching-learning process by involving the student consciously in their learning process and facilitating constant feedback and feedforward processes; (b) "Shared-Assessment": representing the importance of involving students in assessment, through dialogue and tools that facilitate decision-making in the teaching-learning process.

Many studies on formative experiences and positive student and lecturer evaluations of developing FandSA systems in TLP can be found in Teacher Education (TE) (Barba-Martín et al., 2012; Barba-Martín and López-Pastor, 2017; Manrique et al., 2010; Martínez-Mínguez et al., 2019).

MAIN FOCUS OF THE CHAPTER

This section sets out the issues to be analysed and the specific context of the research. In order to facilitate the reading and understanding of the text, the specific context of the study is discussed first, followed by its methodology and, finally, the results obtained in the research.

This is followed by a detailed description of how the FandSA system and the TLP are carried out within the subjects analysed.

FandSA System in Teacher Education

The two subjects analysed in the study are imparted in two different semesters of the year. They are taught by the same lecturers and use the same FandSA system, which focuses on student participation through different techniques (self-assessment, shared assessment, peer assessment, self-marking, and dialogue marking). At the beginning of the course, students are offered a choice of three different assessment pathways (see Table 4).

Table 5 presents the grading criteria according to the learning and assessment pathway chosen by the students, as well as their relation to the different learning activities of the subjects.

Table 6 shows each learning activity with its specific assessment tool to facilitate: (1) student self-assessment; (2) subsequent correction of the work; and (3) lecturer assessment.

These assessment instruments (group and/or individual self-assessment sheets) are graduated scales that develop each assessment criterion in detail. They are broken down into four levels from higher to lower quality (A, B, C, D) according to the quality and degree of achievement of the criterion.

At the end of the course, the student is provided with a guide for the final self-assessment report. Within the report they must self-grade following the evaluation and grading criteria agreed at the beginning of the course. The process of self-assessment and final shared-assessment has three steps:

(1) First, students have to hand in their self-assessment report and their collaborative portfolio with all the physical evidence of learning accumulated throughout the course.
(2) After that, the lecturers correct the portfolios and set the students' marks.
(3) Finally, an interview is held with all the students who make up each collaborative portfolio. The self-assessment reports and the functioning of the group are reviewed (shared assessment) and the final grade of each student is finalised in a consensual manner (dialogue grading).

Table 4. Description of each learning and assessment pathway

Pathways	Conditions
(1) Continued	-All learning activities must be completed as indicated and within the required time frame. If any student does not reach the suggested minimum quality in any learning activity, he/she must correct the activity according to the feedback given by the lecturer. In each activity the student must complete a self-assessment form. The lecturer corrects and returns all work completed within one week. In the self-assessment form, the lecturer adds his or her assessment of the student's evaluation and any decisions that need to be taken. -It is compulsory to work in groups of two to four people, as many of the activities are group activities. -Attendance is compulsory. All absences must be justified, up to a maximum of 15%. -There will be a partial exam at the end of the term, which has a weight in the final grade of two points.
(2) Mixed	-Only the TLP is compulsory for the student. The other assignments are voluntary. -The student can be part of a working group ("collaborative portfolio") or work individually. -Attendance is compulsory for at least 50% of the sessions, mainly the practical sessions. Students do not have to justify their absences. -The student has to take the final exam, which in this case counts for five points in the final grade.
(3) Final	-The student does not have to hand in any compulsory work. -They have to take three final exams: the theory exam, a practical exam and defend a TLP they have done in an early childhood education centre.

Source. Own elaboration.

Table 5. Grading criteria for each learning and assessment pathway

	Learning activity	% of mark	Observations
(1) Continuous Path	TLP	35%	Students will be provided with a descriptive scale detailing the assessment and grading criteria for each instrument and procedure. In order to pass, each section must be passed.
	Dossier and concept maps	10%	
	Practical sessions	20%	
	Group and individual work and discussions	15%	
	Partial exam with co-evaluation	20%	
		Total = 100%	
(2) Mixed Path	TLP	30%	In order to pass the subject, each of the activities must be passed. There will be no averages or compensation among them.
	Written exam	50%	
	Remaining activities and documents from the main system. Proportional to the total, up to a maximum of 20%.	20%	
		Total = 100%	
(3) Final Path	Presentation of a report on the TLP carried out and a public defence of the same.	30%	In order to pass the course, each test must be passed. There will be no averages or compensation between them.
	Written exam	50%	
	Practical exam	20%	
		Total = 100%	

Source. Own elaboration.

Table 6. Assessment techniques and instruments for each learning activity

Learning activity	Techniques	Instruments
TLP	Group self-assessment and peer assessment (inter-group)	Group self-assessment sheet
Practical session sheets	Group self-assessment	Group self-assessment sheet
Recensions	Individual self-assessment	Individual self-assessment sheet
Monographic works	Individual/group self-assessment	Self-assessment sheet
Partial exam	Peer assessment	"Ad hoc" correction template

Source. Own elaboration.

How TLP in Teacher Education Are Conducted

As can be seen in Table 5, the TLP are the learning activity that has the highest weight in the grade for the subject, as it is considered the most important activity for the benefits outlined above.

At the beginning of the course, the lecturers explain the topics to be worked on with the TLP and the dates on which they are to be carried out. Some of the topics to be chosen revolve around different methodologies of Physical Education in Early Childhood Education and teaching styles according to different authors. Some examples of both subjects are: Learning Environments; Motor Tales; Shadow Theatre; Action and Adventure Spaces; Pedagogical Treatment of the Corporeal; Teaching Styles in Physical Education; Physical Education in Bilingual Schools; Motor Wedges; etc.

Once they have been shown the topics to choose from, the students organise themselves into groups of three or four and choose their project. Each topic has a pre-established date for its presentation, so the students choose their project according to the following criteria: (1) depending on their affinity with the topic, and (2) according to the date on which it is expounded. Each lecturer leads a project topic. The tutor meets with the group and provides them with bibliographical references on their topic. The students then work with these publications and develop a theoretical framework. Each time they produce a draft of the project they send it to the tutor, and he/she gives them feedback. The second TLP activity is to develop a practical session for an Early Childhood Education course on their topic.

Students attend as many tutorials as necessary until the whole project is of good quality. The group develops the session and presents the theoretical framework to their peers. The TLP is then peer-assessed. Afterwards, each group has one week to elaborate a reflective report on their TLP and hand it in to the tutor. In one week, the tutor gives it back to them with feedback.

Methodological Approach

This chapter shows a mixed methodology study, combining qualitative and quantitative analysis. Furthermore, this paper should also be considered an Action Research (AR) study because it analyses an experience in which students participate in the assessment of subjects through the TLP where these systematic cycles of action research are carried out. The lecturers follow the process outlined by Kemmis and McTaggart (1988): (1) plan the educational action, (2) carry out the action, (3) observe and, (4) analyse the results obtained. The lecturer then analyses the data obtained and makes decisions for the next cycle. The lecturers present the FandSA system at the beginning of the course and agree on different aspects of it with the students, and also show the teaching-learning activities to be developed throughout the course, including the TLP.

Study Sample

A sample of 254 students was taken from two Teacher Education subjects in the Early Childhood Education specialisation (Table 7): Corporal Expression in Early Childhood Education (S1 - ECE) and Physical Education in Early Childhood Education (from now on, S2 - DD; ECE). Both are taught in the Degree in Early Childhood Education and in the Double Degree in Early Childhood Education and Primary Education.

The subjects were developed over two academic years (year I and year II; see Table 7). Each subject has a load of 6 ECTS credits (60 hours of classroom work and 90 hours of autonomous work outside the classroom). An FandSA system was implemented in all subjects.

Table 7. Study sample, grouped by subject and year

Subject	Year I	Year II	Summation
Corporal Expression in Early Childhood Education (S1 - ECE)	35	37	72
Physical Education in Early Childhood Education in Early Childhood Education (1°DD) (S2 – DD)	52	48	100
Physical Education in Early Childhood Education in Early Childhood Education (3°ECE) (S2 – ECE)	38	43	81
Totals	125	128	253

Source. Own elaboration.

Data Collection Instruments

The data collection instruments were:

(1) A previously standardised and validated good practice report, drawn up by the lecturers before, during and at the end of the subject (Fraile, et al., 2013; Jiménez et al., 2021), dealing with aspects related to the assessment system applied and the results obtained.
(2) An anonymous student questionnaire on the use of FandSA and TLP, validated by Castejón et al. (2011), comprising 28 items with a five-level Likert-type scale: - Not at all, 2- A little, 3- Somewhat, 4- Quite a lot and 5- A lot; and an open-ended question. It is given to students on paper at the end of each subject; they should fill it in at the same time.

Data Analysis

We worked with the good practice report for the qualitative analysis. The data categories were defined and then the units of information were coded using the Atlas.ti V. 9 software programme. Table 8 shows the system of categories used to analyse the qualitative data and their relationship with the objectives of the study.

Table 8. Categories and sub-categories of qualitative analysis of reports.

Objective	Categories	Sub-categories
Analyse how the FandSA system and the TLP methodology influence student engagement in learning.	1-Assessment of students' participation in FandSA systems in TLP.	1.1 Student appreciation
		1.2 Appreciation of the lecturers
	2-Student involvement in TLP learning and participation in FandSA systems.	2.1 Student appreciation
		2.2 Appreciation of the lecturers

Source. Own elaboration.

The quantitative analysis comes from the anonymous student questionnaire and was performed using the SPSS V.22.0 programme. A descriptive analysis was carried out, working with the arithmetic mean and standard deviation of the data. The following items were studied for the quantitative analysis (see Table 9):

Table 9. Items from the anonymous student questionnaires on FandSA and TLP

	Items	Answer
1	Was the use of this experience negotiated at the beginning of the academic year?	Likert-type scale
4	Do you consider what you have learnt from this experience to be useful?	
6	How do you value the help received from the lecturer?	
8	Indicate your overall satisfaction in relation to the experience.	
9	Indicate your overall satisfaction in relation to the assessment.	
10	Indicate the degree of difficulty of the experience.	
Competence 2.8	Involving students in their learning	
WN*	Assessment of the process (TLP and FandSA): advantages and disadvantages.	Open-ended question and Likert-type scale
WN*	Do you have any comments in relation to the experience?	Open-ended question.

*Without Number
Source. Own elaboration.

Table 10 shows the overall reliability index of this questionnaire:

The Cronbach's Alpha test was applied to analyse the reliability of the instrument. According to Castañeda et al. (2010) and Rodríguez-Rodríguez and Reguant-Álvarez (2020), reliability data are expressed in a positive interval between 0.00 and 1.00, the latter being a result of perfect reliability. In this case, the data indicate that the questionnaire given to the students in this study has an overall reliability of 0.624, which is an acceptable result considering the interval indicated above by the authors.

RESULTS

The results are shown in the order of the categories set out in Table 8, which respond directly to the objectives of the study.

Table 10. Reliability statistics for the questionnaire

Reliability statistics		
Cronbach's Alpha	Cronbach's Alpha based on standardised items	N of elements
.544	.624	6

Source. Own elaboration.

Assessment of Student Participation in FandSA Systems in TLP

Student Appreciation

Students show high appreciation of their experience with TLP and FandSA, as well as high satisfaction with the usefulness of the learning gained from the experience. They also value the help received from their lecturers throughout the course with the TLP and their formative assessment for the feedback. On the other hand, there is a variety of results regarding whether the experience was negotiated at the beginning of the course, despite having applied the same FandSA system in all courses and subjects. The results indicate that the difficulty of the experience is medium (see Table 11).

In detail, Table 12 shows that students have very high ratings on four items describing TLP and their evaluation (3.68 being the lowest score, up to 4.69 as the highest score out of 5). They highlight that the experience is innovative and replicable to other contexts.

Appreciation of the Lecturers

They indicate that the way of working and assessing in the TLP moves away from traditional models, and tutorials ensure the quality of the work, although these involve a high workload. Moreover, they agree that this work and assessment experience can be carried out in any subject in Teacher Education:

"Innovative: because it is a big difference to more traditional models of teaching. It is an active methodology and requires strong group collaboration to succeed" (S2 - ECE, I-II; S1, I-II).

"Effective: Because tutorials are compulsory during the development of the project, the quality of the TLP improves considerably" (S2 - DD, I; S1 - I).

"Sustainable: Because it involves a greater workload in the tutorials in the central months, when most of the groups are developing their TLP and require tutorials, but it is perfectly feasible, given that it is carried out during official tutorial hours" (S2 - DD, I-II; S2 - ECE, I-II).

"Replicable: Because it can be used in any subject. In fact, in our school it is a methodology that has been widely used for 15-20 years in many subjects" (S1, I-II; S1, I-II; S2 - DD, I-II).

Table 11. Appreciation of the TLP experience. Anonymous questionnaire for students (Likert scale 1-5).

Subject Items	S1 - ECE		S2 - DD		S2 - ECE	
	Year I	Year II	Year I	Year II	Year I	Year II
	$\bar{x}$	$\bar{x}$	$\bar{x}$	$\bar{x}$	$\bar{x}$	$\bar{x}$
1-Did you negotiate the use of this experience in the subject at the beginning of the academic course?	4.5	4.20	3.41	2.66	3.16	3.59
4- Do you consider what you have learnt from this experience to be useful?	4.48	4.70	4.40	4.19	4.38	4.14
6-How do you assess the support you received from the teacher?	4.48	4.30	4.20	3.16	4.30	3.97
8-State your overall satisfaction with the experience.	4.34	4.43	4.06	3.46	4.09	3.72
9-State your overall satisfaction in relation to the assessment of the experience.	4.03	4.10	3.83	3.37	3.84	3.62
10-What is the degree of difficulty of the experience?	3.15	2.97	3.46	3.49	3.44	3

Source. Own elaboration.

Student Involvement in TLP Learning and Participation in FandSA Systems

Student Appreciation

The data referring to competence 2.8: "Student involvement in their learning" show that in most cases this involvement increased at the end of the subject with respect to the beginning (see Table 13). The subject S1 in the Double Degree stands out in its second year, almost doubling average involvement with respect to the beginning of the subject:

In particular, the students have positive evaluations in this respect. They indicate that participating in the experience offered them much learning and usefulness for their future as teachers. In some cases,

Table 12. Student appreciation of the experience of good practice developed (Likert scale 1-5)

Subject Items	Students					
	S1 - ECE		S2 - DD		S2 - ECE	
	Year I	Year II	Year I	Year II	Year I	Year II
	$\bar{x}$	$\bar{x}$	$\bar{x}$	$\bar{x}$	$\bar{x}$	$\bar{x}$
Innovative	4.27	4.10	4.20	3.70	4.69	3.92
Effective	4.64	4.43	4.23	3.86	4.03	4.03
Sustainable	4.3	4.33	4.06	3.68	4.06	3.89
Replicable	4.58	4.60	4.17	4.11	4.25	4

Source. Own elaboration.

Table 13. Specific competence: student involvement in their learning (average; SD: standard deviation)

Subject	Beginning of subject		End of subject	
	$\bar{x}$	SD	$\bar{x}$	SD
S1, ECE, year I	3,33	,476	3,44	,505
S1, ECE, year II	3,47	,571	3,60	,553
S2, DD, year I	3,22	,637	3,09	,530
S2, DD, year II	2,94	,669	4,03	,523
S2, ECE, year I	3,31	,604	3,29	,693
S2, ECE, year II	3,32	,477	3,55	,568

Source. Own elaboration.

they indicated that the lecturers were not well coordinated because each one applied different assessment criteria:

"A lot of work for a short time. As there were four lecturers, there were times when some had different correction criteria than others. Different corrections depending on the lecturer. A lot of work every week" (S2 - DD, I).

"A lot of learning and a lot of effort too. Uncoordinated in the subject" (S2 - ECE, I).

"It has been a very useful subject for my future. I consider that I have been able to learn a lot and that everything has been put into practice. The most complete and useful subject of the course without a doubt, on a personal and professional level, as well as the most demanding and the one that has taken the most time and dedication. The demand has been commensurate with obtaining greater involvement. That is why I consider that this subject fulfils all the competent qualities" (S1, I).

"I found the way of implementing individualised education and the way of giving so much importance to daily work very good, however, I think that, in most cases, so much weekly work means that you have to do things in a hurry, which is an obstacle for the student (although the work is interesting). In the assessment there should be more margin for absences between continuous and blended assessment. The workload is very unbalanced with the rest of the subjects" (S2 - DD, II).

"This subject requires more credits; a lot of work and effort for 6 credits. Although there are different assessment criteria (classroom and non-classroom), if I hadn't gone to class, I wouldn't have learnt half as much" (S2 - ECE, II).

Appreciation of the Lecturers

For their part, the lecturers assess how the TLP developed in general and how they perceive the students' involvement in them. Most of them indicate that the success rate is high, but they also show differences between groups of students. The DD group stands out for its high academic level in the development of TLP, compared to the ECE group:

"They are first year, Double Degree, and there has been a very high percentage of students who have been dropping out and performing badly. Almost 50% of the group ended up going to the mixed track because they did not work properly during the course. There have been many people who did not contribute to the group; this has generated conflicts when it came to distributing the marks within each group in June" (P-F, DD, I).

"High success rate, despite the low involvement of some students (mostly boys)" (P-F, DD, I-II).

"Very high success rate" (P-CE, I-II; F, ECE, I-II).

"In general, differences can be observed between 3rd ECE and 4th DD, but not in all cases. Pupils in 4th DD tend to have a higher academic level and preparation, which is often noticeable in the development of TLP" (P, CE, I).

SOLUTIONS AND RECOMMENDATIONS

This study has analysed the students' and lecturers' perceptions of student participation in the FandSA processes when they are linked to active learning methodologies such as TLP, as well as student involvement in learning with the application of TLP.

With regard to the objective, the data obtained indicate that students were quite satisfied with the good practice experience (TLP) and its assessment (FandSA). The implementation of the TLP was negotiated with the students at the beginning of the subject. Overall, TLP were quite useful for the students, especially the learning gained from them and the tutor's work during the teaching-learning process.

Lecturers and students valued the combination of FandSA and TLP as an innovative methodology, because it is group work that is different from traditional methods. Moreover, they indicated that TLP are effective and sustainable because: (1) the tutorials favour the acquisition of meaningful learning; (2) they are transferable to any subject; and (3) it is perfectly viable to carry out the tutoring process, given that the different TLP are staggered over three months.

The analysis of the students' assessment of the TLP with the FandSA was positive. The students indicated that there is a transfer of this experience to their future work as teachers. These positive results may be due to several aspects: (1) the flexibility of the lecturers in developing the projects; (2) the involvement of the students.

For students, the most complex aspect of FandSA in TLP was the self-evaluation of the TLP at the end of it. Also, the workload involved in TLP seemed to be high. This may be due to their not being accustomed to participation in FandSA systems as they were in the first year of Teacher Education. In this respect, Barba-Martín and López-Pastor (2017) and López-Pastor et al. (2021) carried out experiments with TLP and FandSA, where they also found that students found the workload to be high, but that it was in line with the hours set in the syllabus.

The success rate and student involvement in this experience was high, although there are differences between the two groups of students in one of the subjects. In this case, it is considered that the difference may be because the students from one year had more experience working with TLP and FandSA than those from the other. Barba-Martín and López-Pastor (2017), also obtain a very high success rate in an FandSA experience in TLP in their group of students; interpreting that this is due to the high involvement of students in these projects. Therefore, it seems that the high success rate may be because the TLP offer more learning and are a very authentic approach with a strong practical orientation. In fact, although the whole subject is based on the use of active learning methodologies, the TLP are the learning activity with the highest weight in the grade given for the subject.

FUTURE RESEARCH DIRECTIONS

The results obtained may be of interest to lecturers who want to implement FandSA systems in Higher Education. It may also be used as a model to start involving students in the assessment of different learning activities and to achieve good curricular alignment between objectives, learning activities, methodology and assessment.

The data analysed indicate possible research directions. Future work could analyse the instructional alignment with longitudinal studies on how students adapt to the TLP methodology and the FandSA system from the beginning of their studies to the end, within Initial Teacher Education. Moreover, it would be interesting to complement these studies with an analysis of how participation in these systems during their initial training influences their subsequent application as teachers. In addition, studies can be carried out on the application of TLP and FandSA in schools with pupils at different educational stages or in schools of different types (rural vs. urban, public vs. subsidised, etc.).

CONCLUSION

The results found are positive in relation to satisfaction with the application of the TLP and the FandSA, and there is a high level of student involvement in the experience. There also seems to be a high instructional alignment in the application of the TLP and the FandSA due to the coherence between the proposed evaluation, the positive results obtained and the satisfaction of the students and lecturers. The implementation of FandSA processes carries with it a transparent reflection of curricular elements; therefore, their development in TLP is key to the development of instructional alignment between learning activities. Findings seem to indicate that there is internal curriculum coherence in the combination of FandSA and TLP. Lecturers and students valued this experience of good practice positively. On the downside, it was found that TLP and FandSA entail a high workload for students. For future research, it might be interesting to carry out a comparative analysis of the application of TLP and FandSA in different Higher Education subjects. It would also be possible to study the assessment of different lecturers according to their professional position.

ACKNOWLEDGMENT

This research was partially supported by the Ministry of Universities of Spain (FPU grant CNU/450/2019: university lecturer training).

This research was supported by the Research, Development, and Innovation (RandDandI) project: "Evaluation of competences in Final Year Projects (Degree and Master's) in the Initial Training of Physical Education Teachers". Call: August 2018 of the State Programme for RandDandI Oriented to the Challenges of Society in the framework of the State Plan for Scientific and Technical Research and Innovation 2017-2020. Reference: RTI2018-093292-B-I00. Duration: 3 years (2019-2021).

REFERENCES

Barba-Martín, J. J., Martínez-Scott, S., & Torrego, L. (2012). El proyecto de aprendizaje tutorado co-operativo: Una experiencia en el grado de maestra de Educación Infantil. *REDU. Revista de Docencia Universitaria, 10*(1), 123–144. doi:10.4995/redu.2012.6125

Barba-Martín, R. A., & López-Pastor, V. M. (2017). Evaluación formativa y compartida en los proyectos de trabajo tutorado, un ejemplo de buena práctica. *Revista Infancia. Educación y Aprendizaje, 3*(2), 66–70.

Biggs, J. (2005). *Calidad del aprendizaje universitario*. Narcea.

Castañeda, M. B., Cabrera, A. F., Navarro, Y., & De Vires, W. (2010). *Procesamiento de datos y análisis estadístico utilizando SPSS*. Edipucrs.

Castejón, F. J., López-Pastor, V. M., Clemente, J. A., & Zaragoza, J. (2011). Evaluación formativa y rendimiento académico en la formación inicial del profesorado de Educación Física. *Revista Internacional de Medicina y Ciencias de la Actividad Física y del Deporte, 11*(42), 328–346.

Dempsey, J. V. (1993). Interactive instruction and feedback. *Technology*.

Escribano, A., & Del Valle, A. (2015). *El aprendizaje basado en problemas (ABP)*. Ediciones de la U.

Fidel, R. (1984). The case study method: A case study. *Library and Information Science Research, 6*(3), 273–288.

Fortea, M. Á. (2009). *Metodologías didácticas para la enseñanza/aprendizaje de competencias*. Unitat de Suport Educatiu de la Universitat Jaume I.

Fraile, A., López-Pastor, V. M., Castejón, J., and Romero, R. (2013). La evaluación formativa en docencia universitaria y el rendimiento académico del alumnado. *Aula abierta, 41*(2), 23-34.

Gutiérrez, M. (2010). Los proyectos de aprendizaje tutorado en la formación universitaria dentro del espacio europeo. *Acción pedagógica, 19*(1), 6-18.

Jiménez, F., Navarro, V., & Pintor, P. (2021). Estado de las vías de opcionalidad de la evaluación en la Red Nacional de Evaluación Formativa y Compartida en la enseñanza universitaria. In *Explorando colaborativamente alternativas de evaluación formativa en la Universidad: el aprendizaje de un grupo de profesores durante el período 2009-2018* (pp. 25–46). Universidad de La Laguna.

Johnson, D. W., & Johnson, R. T. (1999). *Aprender juntos y solos. Aprendizaje cooperativo, competitivo e individualista*. Aique.

Johnson, D. W., & Johnson, R. T. (2014). Cooperative Learning in 21st Century. *L'Année Psychologique*, *30*(3), 841–851.

López-Pastor, V., Molina, M., Pascual, C., & Manrique, J. (2020). La importancia de utilizar la Evaluación Formativa y Compartida en la Formación Inicial del Profesorado de Educación Física: Los Proyectos de Aprendizaje Tutorado como ejemplo de buena práctica. *Retos*, *37*, 620–627.

López-Pastor, V. M. (coord.) (2009). *La Evaluación Formativa y Compartida en Educación Superior: propuestas, técnicas, instrumentos y experiencias*. Narcea.

López-Pastor, V. M. (2011). El papel de la evaluación formativa en la evaluación por competencias: Aportaciones de la red de evaluación formativa y compartida en docencia universitaria. *REDU. Revista de Docencia Universitaria*, *9*(1), 159–173. doi:10.4995/redu.2011.6185

López-Pastor, V. M., & Pérez-Pueyo, A. (Coords.) (2017). *Buenas prácticas docentes. Evaluación formativa y compartida en educación: experiencias de éxito en todas las etapas educativas*. Universidad de León.

Luengo, M. L., & Puente, M. G. (2017). El proyecto de aprendizaje tutorado en la formación científica de maestros de Educación Primaria. *Revista Infancia. Educación y Aprendizaje*, *3*(2), 190–196.

Manrique, J. C., López-Pastor, V. M., Monjas, R., & Real, F. (2010). El potencial de los proyectos de aprendizaje tutorado y los sistemas de evaluación formativa en la mejora de la autonomía del alumnado. Una experiencia interdisciplinar en formación inicial del profesorado. *Revista Española de Educación Física y Deportes*, *14*, 39–57.

Martin, F. (2011). Instructional design and the importance of instructional alignment. *Community College Journal of Research and Practice*, *35*(12), 955–972. doi:10.1080/10668920802466483

Martínez-Mínguez, L., Moya, L., Nieva, C., & Cañabate, D. (2019). Percepciones de Estudiantes y Docentes: Evaluación Formativa en Proyectos de Aprendizaje Tutorados. Perceptions of Students and Teachers: Formative Evaluation in Tutored Learning Projects. *Revista Iberoamericana de Evaluación Educativa*, *12*(1), 59–84.

Mínguez, M. L. M. (2017). Proyectos de Aprendizaje Tutorados y autoevaluación de competencias profesionales en la formación inicial del profesorado. *Retos: nuevas tendencias en educación física, deporte y recreación*, (29), 242-250.

Molina, M., López-Pastor, V. M., Pascual, C., & Barba, R. A. (2019). Los proyectos de aprendizaje tutorado como buena práctica en educación física en primer curso de doble titulación (educación infantil y educación primaria). *Revista de Innovación y Buenas Prácticas Docentes*, *8*(1), 1–14. doi:10.21071/ripadoc.v8i1.11988

Muñoz-Repiso, A. G. V., & Gómez-Pablos, V. B. (2017). Aprendizaje Basado en Proyectos (ABP): Evaluación desde la perspectiva de alumnos de Educación Primaria. *Revista de Investigación Educacional*, *35*(1), 113–131.

OCDE. (2002). *Definition and Selection of Competences*. OCDE.

Ospina, B. E., Aristizábal, C. A., & Toro, J. A. (2008). El seminario de investigación y su relación con las diferentes metodologías y estrategias de enseñanza aprendizaje. *Investigacion y Educacion en Enfermeria*, *26*(2), 72–79.

Polikoff, M. S., & Porter, A. C. (2014). Instructional alignment as a measure of teaching quality. *Educational Evaluation and Policy Analysis*, *36*(4), 399–416. doi:10.3102/0162373714531851

Riesco, M. (2008). El enfoque por competencias en el EEES y sus implicaciones en la enseñanza y el aprendizaje. *Tendencias Pedagógicas*, *13*, 79–105.

Rodríguez-Rodríguez, J., & Reguant-Álvarez, M. (2020). Calcular la fiabilidad de un cuestionario o escala mediante el SPSS: El coeficiente alfa de Cronbach. *REIRE*, *13*(2), 1–13. doi:10.1344/reire2020.13.230048

Romero, M. A., & Crisol, E. (2011). El portafolio, herramienta de autoevaluación del aprendizaje de los estudiantes. Una experiencia práctica en la Universidad de Granada. *Revista Docencia e Investigación*, *21*, 25–50.

Ruiz-Omeñaca, J. V. (1999). *Juegos cooperativos y educación física*. Editorial Paidotribo.

Santos-Pastor, M., Martínez, L. F., & López-Pastor, V. M. (2009). *La innovación docente en el Espacio Europeo de Educación Superior*. Universidad de Almería.

Sonlleva, M. M. S., Martínez, S., & Monjas, R. (2019). Evaluación del proyecto de aprendizaje tutorado en la asignatura de Educación para la Paz y la Igualdad. *Revista Infancia. Educación y Aprendizaje*, *5*(2), 114–120.

Tucker, B. (2012). The flipped classroom. *Education Next*, *12*(1), 82–83.

Velázquez, C. (2010). *Aprendizaje cooperativo en Educación Física*. Inde.

ADDITIONAL READING

Aloi, S. L., Gardner, W. S., & Lusher, A. L. (2003). A framework for assessing general education outcomes within the majors. *The Journal of General Education*, *52*(4), 237–252. doi:10.1353/jge.2004.0009

Andrade, H., & Cizek, G. J. (2010). Students as the definitive source of formative assessment: Academic self-assessment and the self-regulation of learning. In *Handbook of formative Assessment* (pp. 102–117). Routledge. doi:10.4324/9780203874851

Bennett, R. E. (2011). Formative assessment: A critical review. *Assessment in Education: Principles, Policy and Practice*, *18*(1), 5–25. doi:10.1080/0969594X.2010.513678

Biggs, J. (1996). Enhancing teaching through constructive alignment. *Higher Education*, *32*(3), 347–364. doi:10.1007/BF00138871

Biggs, J. (2014). Constructive alignment in university teaching. HERDSA. *Review of Higher Education*, *1*(5), 5–22.

Davis, H. L., & Somerville, M. M. (2006). Learning our way to change: Improved institutional alignment. *New Library World*, *107*(3/4), 127–140. doi:10.1108/03074800610654907

Fuess, S., & Mitchell, N. D. (2011). General education reform: Opportunities for institutional alignment. *The Journal of General Education*, *60*(1), 1–15. doi:10.5325/jgeneeduc.60.1.0001

López-Pastor, V. M. (2011). Best practices in academic assessment in higher education: A Case in formative and shared assessment. *Journal of Technology and Science Education*, *1*(2), 25–39.

Yan, Z., Li, Z., Panadero, E., Yang, M., Yang, L., & Lao, H. (2021). A systematic review on factors influencing teachers' intentions and implementations regarding formative assessment. *Assessment in Education: Principles, Policy and Practice*, *28*(3), 1–33. doi:10.1080/0969594X.2021.1884042

Yorke, M. (2003). Formative assessment in higher education: Moves towards theory and the enhancement of pedagogic practice. *Higher Education*, *45*(4), 477–501. doi:10.1023/A:1023967026413

KEY TERMS AND DEFINITIONS

Higher Education: The last stage of the academic learning process in universities, oriented towards access to the labour system.

Instructional Alignment: The process by which the focus is on establishing the greatest possible coherence between the different curricular elements (objectives, professional competences, contents, assessment criteria, etc.).

Methodology: A set of teaching techniques, methods and strategies that promote the acquisition of learning and skills.

Teacher: A person who has studied for a Teacher Degree and works as a teacher in Early Childhood Education and/or Primary Education schools.

Physical Education: The educational action that frames the work with motor and physical activity to acquire learning and develop different physical and expressive capacities and skills.

Formative evaluation: An evaluation process that focuses on improving the student's learning and teaching-learning processes, as well as the lecturer's teaching quality.

Shared assessment: A dialogical process between lecturer and student to evaluate and improve teaching-learning processes and encourage student participation in assessment.

Chapter 7
Learning to Apply Formative and Shared Assessment Through In-Service Teacher Education and Action Research

Cristina Pascual-Arias
University of Valladolid, Spain

David Hortigüela-Alcalá
University of Burgos, Spain

Teresa Fuentes Nieto
University of Valladolid, Spain

Víctor M. López-Pastor
University of Valladolid, Spain

Carla Fernández-Garcimartín
 https://orcid.org/0000-0002-2171-0293
University of Valladolid, Spain

Miriam Molina Soria
 https://orcid.org/0000-0003-2974-5535
University of Valladolid, Spain

ABSTRACT

This chapter has two clearly defined objectives: (a) to analyse how higher education (HE) teachers participating in an in-service teacher education (ISTE) inter-level seminar evaluated the Action-Research (A-R) processes they carried out; (b) to determine the advantages that HE teachers find after carrying out formative and shared assessment (F&SA) processes, as well as the disadvantages and proposals for improvement to overcome them. For this purpose, a case study was conducted in an ISTE inter-level seminar on F&SA with 10 HE teachers. The teachers found the A-R processes very useful although they believed that they should systematise them continuously during the whole teaching-learning process; moreover, they considered that F&SA practices have many advantages and some disadvantages for which they proposed solutions to overcome them.

DOI: 10.4018/978-1-6684-3537-3.ch007

INTRODUCTION

This chapter considers the importance of applying Formative and Shared Assessment (F&SA) systems successfully in Higher Education (HE), for which In-Service Teacher Education (ISTE) is emphasised through Action-Research (A-R) processes.

F&SA is a proposal that seeks to enhance student learning with their participation (Hortigüela-Alcalá et al., 2015; López-Pastor, 2009). Formative assessment aims to improve three perspectives: (a) student learning; (b) teacher teaching; (c) the teaching-learning process itself (López-Pastor, 2009). In order for Formative Assessment to also be Shared Assessment, student participation in their own assessment should be promoted, individually or in groups, and self-assessment, peer assessment or collaborative assessment processes should be used (López-Pastor, 2009).

This F&SA process is especially significant in HE, because it is based on a continuous process of learning and educational improvement, and in addition, is a learning process in itself for future teachers who are studying Initial Teacher Education. After learning and experiencing these assessment systems, the students can apply them once they have finished their studies and become teachers. However, not all teachers who teach in HE are familiar with F&SA. A good way to obtain this training is through ISTE using A-R processes that allow them to learn continuously in their actual teaching context (Kennedy, 2005).

ISTE seems desirable for developing F&SA in HE. However, there are hardly any references that study how working groups function in ISTE, especially in HE; and even fewer in inter-level working groups, where teachers from all educational stages participate. Therefore, the objectives of this study were as follows:

(a) To analyse how teachers participating in an ISTE group on F&SA value the implementation of Action Research processes in HE.
(b) To determine the advantages and disadvantages of F&SA for HE teachers participating in an ISTE group.

BACKGROUND

Formative and Shared Assessment in Higher Education

Today, education needs a global change towards a quality education system that is constantly being renewed and improved. Teaching in Higher Education (HE) requires the development of ongoing teacher training, adapting to the need for dialogical learning and educational transparency that the European Higher Education Area (EHEA) has been calling for over the last 15-20 years (Aubert et al., 2008; Dochy et al., 1999; López-Pastor, 2009; Santos et al., 2018).

This shift towards a culture of assessment, dialogical learning and competence-based systems can be brought about through formative assessment models that foster learning (Beutel et al., 2017), such as F&SA. This type of assessment provides a tool that meets the need for transparency in the assessment and improvement of the educational process.

The application of F&SA systems has generated very positive results at all educational stages, from Early Childhood and Primary Education (Fernández et al., 2019; Pascual-Arias et al., 2019; Reyes, 2019), to HE (Gallardo and Carter, 2016; Hortigüela-Alcalá et al., 2015; Martínez et al., 2019; Molina et al., 2019; Romero et al., 2014; Sonlleva, 2019). It is also particularly relevant in HE since F&SA is also a learning tool for future teachers. Some of the advantages of applying F&SA systems are (Bores-García, et al. 2021; Falchikov and Boud, 1989; Gallardo et al., 2018; Hortigüela-Alcalá et al., 2015, 2017, 2019a, 2019b; López-Pastor et al., 2020; López-Pastor and Pérez-Pueyo, 2017; Pascual-Arias et al., 2019; Romero et al., 2014):

a) It allows students to be involved in their assessment in an active and egalitarian way, which fosters their motivation and learning. It also improves their personal autonomy, self-regulation and self-criticism, and promotes their responsibility.

b) It improves learning, acquisition of competences and academic performance. In these experiences, the students value the learning, as well as the competences acquired, positively thanks to the F&SA, since they are involved in their own evaluation process and receive feedback from the teacher during the whole teaching-learning process.

c) In the case of Initial Teacher Education, the acquisition of teaching competences related to assessment is fostered and students acquire the potential to develop lifelong learning strategies.

d) There is an increased connection between teacher and learner; the learner feels that their assessment matters and that the teacher takes it into account, which improves the teacher-learner relationship.

e) It allows teachers to reflect on their professional identity, to be self-critical of their own practice and to rethink how they conceive the teaching-learning process, in order to continuously improve it.

Regarding the disadvantages of developing F&SA processes, most research points to these disadvantages as efforts or changes in praxis and teaching-learning systems that need to be made to implement these proposals, compared to more traditional assessment systems (Barba et al. 2010; Gallardo-Fuentes and Carter-Thuillier, 2016; Molina et al. 2019; Pérez-Pueyo et al., 2008; Romero-Martín et al. 2014):

a) It requires a change of mentality in all those involved in the process towards continuous assessment, which fosters learning and takes place throughout the entire process, not only with tests or final exams like traditional assessment.

b) There is an increase in the workload for both students and teachers, compared to more traditional assessment models.

c) There is a certain risk of students' self-assessments being over- or undervalued.

Moreover, it can be deduced that the application of F&SA systems requires some effort, but generates many advantages and positive aspects, both for students and teachers and for the teaching-learning process itself. It is important to point out that F&SA makes it possible to orientate teaching towards the aspects that work in the teaching-learning process and favours the search for alternatives to those aspects that are not so fruitful; thus, developing a truly continuous improvement of the teaching-learning processes (Gutiérrez et al., 2018; Hortigüela-Alcalá et al., 2015; López-Pastor and Pérez-Pueyo, 2017; López-Pastor et al. 2020; Manrique-Arribas et al., 2012).

Numerous research studies with similar results can be found in HE (Gallardo et al., 2016; Hortigüela-Alcalá et al., 2015; Martínez et al., 2019; Romero et al., 2014): students positively value teacher feedback, their involvement in their own assessment, the learning they obtain or the professional competences they have acquired compared to traditional assessment systems (Hortigüela-Alcalá, et al. 2015, 2019; López and Sicilia, 2017; Martínez et al., 2019; Romero et al. 2014). In these experiences, teachers also value positively the fact of developing F&SA processes, even if it is a major change in the whole teaching-learning process, such as in the design of new assessment instruments or processes in which students participate in their own assessment (Pérez-Pueyo, et al., 2008).

Learning About Formative and Shared Assessment in In-Service Teacher Education

Several studies indicate that in order to adapt to the change required by HE towards a learning culture and to carry out F&SA processes, professional development processes linked to ISTE can be implemented to develop F&SA systems with greater confidence and guarantees (Barrientos et al., 2019; Herrero et al., 2021; Molina and López-Pastor, 2019; Palacios and López-Pastor, 2013).

Developing and engaging in ISTE processes implies a commitment to teaching itself (Hamodi et al., 2017; López-Pastor et al. 2011; Margalef, 2005; Pérez-Pueyo, 2008). ISTE should be considered as an irreplaceable condition of teaching tasks (Domínguez and Vázquez, 2015; Imbernón, 2014; Souto-Seijo et al., 2020). As Souto-Seijo et al. (2020, p. 93) state: "knowledge does not have an expiry date, and for this reason, teachers cannot be satisfied with the knowledge they acquired in their initial training stage, as much of it becomes obsolete". Therefore, ISTE is essential for teachers to achieve the necessary educational updating required in HE, in order to adapt to a constantly evolving and changing education and be able to prepare future professionals committed to education, since without this constant preparation it seems difficult to develop quality praxis.

Escudero (1998), defines ISTE as a good scenario of experiences and learning opportunities throughout the teaching career for promoting the reforms and improvements that society demands. It is important to consider ISTE as a reflective learning process in which teachers themselves improve their practice as a result of solving a problem or concern (Nieto, 2000). Serrano (2021) points out that ISTE should encourage teachers' personal, professional and institutional development through collaborative work; in this way, educational practice could be transformed avoiding innovations being limited just to the classroom where they are developed.

The ISTE process should take various factors into account in order to make it as meaningful as possible. Bearing in mind the contributions of various authors such as Imbernón (2014), Margalef (2005), Soto (2002) or Tomas-Folch and Durán-Bellonch (2017), the most decisive ones have been determined as follows: (a) planning the ISTE taking different training strategies, the participants' prior knowledge and their teaching context into account; (b) developing the ISTE based on real contexts, generating collaborative learning, uniting theory and practice and generating reflection and self-criticism based on the teaching practice itself; (c) monitoring the ISTE by accompanying teachers in the subsequent implementation of what they have learned.

The teamwork involved in the ISTE in search of a common goal is essential, even if this goal is achieved individually in each classroom by the teachers who participate in the same ISTE group. In other words, ISTE must be a group endeavour in search of social improvement, and education must meet the demands of a constantly changing society. The advancement of education and society should be two complementary processes.

In-Service Teacher Education and Action-Research

Research in education generates changes and new knowledge that make it possible to advance student learning and teacher training (Andreu and Labrador, 2011). Through research, teachers can develop professionally and build a constantly improving education.

Latorre (2003) points to research as a constitutive element of teachers' professional development. They are interrelated processes, since the teaching profession requires the constant development of new knowledge in order to adapt to the changing nature of society and the education system: "hence, the research action of teachers constitutes its professionalising element" (Latorre, 2003, p. 16). This author states that, through research, teachers acquire educational knowledge to improve their own teaching practice, which leads to: (a) professional self-development; (b) improved professional practice; (c) improvements in the educational institution; and (d) better social conditions. This process allows for reflection on one's own professional identity, which can take place through processes of self-criticism.

One of the most successful ways of developing ISTE processes is Action-Research (A-R). A-R makes it possible to explore, act and evaluate the results obtained in the classroom cyclically (Barbier, 1975; Carr and Kemmis, 1988; Kemmis and McTaggart, 1988, Latorre, 2003). Thus, by carrying out A-R processes, teachers are continuously analysing and improving the teaching-learning process.

Latorre (2003) states that ISTE is understood as a creative and transformative teaching activity; considering that the development of ISTE from A-R contributes to improving the educational practice of teachers from their own praxis.

A-R is undoubtedly a methodology oriented towards educational change, which has an impact on both the researcher and the situations investigated. As Bausela (2004, p. 1) points out: "it is a way of understanding teaching, not only of researching on it. A-R involves understanding teaching as a process of research, of continuous search". It is a process of educational transformation towards the improvement of education, and therefore, towards quality.

At this point, it is necessary to emphasise the collaborative nature of A-R. As Latorre (2003, p. 41) points out, "the goal of A-R is personal improvement for social transformation, so it is essentially collaborative". A-R cannot be carried out in isolation; its collaborative nature is intrinsic to its practice and its purpose of educational improvement. Collaborative A-R makes it possible to explore, act and evaluate the results obtained in the classroom cyclically (Blández, 2021; Carr and Kemmis, 1988; Kemmis and McTaggart, 1988; Latorre, 2003).

ISTE and A-R have a common goal: educational improvement. ISTE developed through collaborative A-R is fundamental to fostering teachers' professional development. Thus, change in the classroom through A-R will contribute to the overall change of the educational system, towards being open, democratic and egalitarian (Latorre, 2003).

Experiences of ISTE groups learning through Action Research (A-Research) (Córdoba et al., 2016; Hamodi et al. 2017; Jiménez, 2021; López-Pastor et al., 2011; Pascual-Arias et al, 2021; Pedraza and López-Pastor, 2015; Pérez-Pueyo et al., 2008) indicate that: (a) the individual learning of each teacher is complemented by the collaborative learning that takes place in the ISTE group; (b) it is based on real conflicts and problems in the classroom, generating reflection based on the practice itself; and (c) positive attitudes towards ISTE and teacher development are enhanced.

All this research seems to indicate that belonging to an ISTE group in which A-R takes place strengthens the research function of the teacher. Thus, given that the A-R process is an exploratory process, the teachers themselves should approach their practice as a constant investigation, this being their own teaching-learning process.

In an in-depth review of different studies, we consider that belonging to an ISTE group that carries out A-R has numerous advantages (Barba-Martín et al., 2016; Córdoba et al., 2016; Ibarra-Sáiz and Rodríguez-Gómez, 2014; Jiménez et al., 2021; López-Pastor et al., 2016; Pascual-Arias et al., 2021; Pedraza and López-Pastor, 2015):

a) There is synergy between individual learning and collaborative learning. Mutual support among teachers leads to the resolution of common problems, the creation of shared knowledge and the reduction of professional isolation.

b) It improves the link between theory and practice, because it broadens the training horizon, which in turn is applied in real contexts to improve educational practice.

c) The work is contextualised on actual practices, as it is based on real conflicts and problems in the classroom, generating reflection based on the educational activity itself.

d) Participating in A-R working groups promotes teachers' autonomy and professional development through the reflection that takes place and, in turn, fosters positive attitudes towards ISTE, while reducing professional isolation.

e) It encourages critical reflection, favouring the formation of a professional who is more reflective and self-critical of his or her own practice.

f) It encourages teachers to innovate autonomously, which generates an emancipatory process thanks to A-R in ISTE. These processes are effective in bringing about educational change and reform at the local level.

MAIN FOCUS OF THE CHAPTER

The context of the research, the methodology used, the data collection techniques and the data analysis will be presented in detail below.

Research Context

The context of the research is an ISTE inter-level seminar on F&SA at the Faculty of Education in Segovia (University of Valladolid, Spain). Teachers from all stages of education, from Early Childhood Education to HE, participate in this inter-level seminar. This means that two-way knowledge transfer is generated: (a) from the university to the schools, since the faculty offers resources and knowledge to develop F&SA experiences; (b) from the schools to the university, since the innovations and practices developed in the schools are useful for training future teachers in HE.

All the teachers participating in the seminar carry out cyclical A-R processes in their classrooms to put F&SA into practice: (a) a first planning phase where they consider what problem they are going to focus their A-R on; (b) a second phase where they get down to business, implementing the actions they have previously planned; (c) a third phase entails observation, where they collect the data on their A-R; (d) an analysis phase where they study what has happened in each F&SA practice (what F&SA techniques and tools have been used, how the students have reacted to them, what improvements have been made, what teaching aspects have been improved or changed...); this is all reflected upon and decisions are made for starting again with another A-R cycle, which will lead to a spiral of A-R cycles implemented by each teacher.

In the development of the inter-level seminar, great importance is given to the collaborative learning that takes place, this being understood as the joint work of the group of teachers to achieve a common goal: to develop their professional competences linked to F&SA. At each monthly meeting, the group works on the doubts, concerns and debates that may arise from these F&SA practices.

Methodological Approach

Qualitative methodology, defined by Taylor and Bodgan (1987, p. 20) as "one that produces descriptive data: people's own words, spoken or written, and observable behaviour" was chosen for this research. Qualitative methodology studies reality in its overall context, trying to interpret what happens in that context together with the implications it has for the people under investigation (Stake, 1998).

Qualitative methodology has been developed through the elaboration of a case study, where the particularity and complexity of a specific reality was analysed in detail, through inductive reasoning, starting from a particular reality, from what happens there, and from the different perspectives of the participants, in order to make judgements (Álvarez and San Fabián, 2012; Stake, 1998).

Study Sample

This research studied 10 HE teachers who were part of the interlevel seminar, these teachers were studied because they were the most relevant and most stable participants during the seminar. The participating teachers have different characteristics, such as different ages and years of teaching experience, some of them new to the teaching profession. This study was carried out during the 2020/2021 academic year.

Data Collection Instruments

The data were collected during the 2020/2021 academic year using two instruments:

a)   "HE good practice reports on F&SA". These reports collected the data related to the F&SA experience of the 2020/2021 academic year, each teacher had to carry out at least one experience during the academic year. The report templates are established by the International Network for Formative and Shared Assessment and the sections that make up the report are: (a) data on the context of the subject in which F&SA has been carried out; (b) learning activities carried out; (c) students' perception of competence acquisition; (d) estimated workload of students and teaching staff; (e) advantages and disadvantages of the F&SA system; and (f) students' academic performance.

b)   "Minutes of seminar meetings". These are a collection of all the discussions at the ISTE seminar meetings of the 2020/2021academic year, a total of eight documents with the following structure: (a) attendance register; (b) questions about F&SA experiences; and (c) discussions and concerns about F&SA based on participants' comments or readings.

Data Analysis

The data analysis was qualitative using a case study, investigating the main themes of the research through the collected annotations and transcriptions (Álvarez and San Fabián, 2012; Coller, 2000; Taylor and Bogdan, 1987).

The participant researcher contrasted the experience during the research through continuous and prolonged observation with the data obtained with the instruments explained above, in this way performing a triangulation between these data that gives the process credibility and consistency (Noreña, 2012).

The data analysis was based on the content analysis of the documents studied was carried out with the Atlas.ti programme after transcription. In this way, the information was reduced for subsequent coding in order to be able to describe and interpret it. This coding was carried out both on the data collection instruments and the participants in the study. In this coding process, the use of the system of categories that arise from the saturation of the data collected and which, moreover, are in line with the research objectives (Bores et al., 2021) was also fundamental. This process has been carried out considering the criteria of scientific rigour (such as transferability, credibility, dependability and confirmability), and methodological ethnical criteria (such as respect for participants' autonomy and privacy).

The category system is shown below in Table 1.

Table 1. Co-relation between the objectives of the study and the categories and subcategories of analysis

Objectives of the study	Categories	Subcategories
a. To analyse how teachers participating in an ISTE group on F&SA valued the implementation of A-R processes in HE.	1. A-R processes of HE teachers participating in the ISTE interlevel seminar.	1.1. Implementation of the A-R processes by HE teachers.
		1.2. Valuation of HE teachers' A-R processes.
b. To determine the advantages and disadvantages of F&SA for HE teachers participating in an ISTE group.	2. F&SA systems of HE teachers participating in an ISTE group.	2.1. Advantages of developing F&SA in HE.
		2.2. Drawbacks and proposed improvements of developing F&SA in HE.

RESULTS

The results are shown below following the categories set out in Table 1, organised according to the objectives of this study.

A-R Processes of the HE Teachers Participating in the ISTE Interlevel Seminar of F&SA

Implementation of A-R Processes of the HE Teachers

The HE teachers who participated in the F&SA interlevel seminar indicated that the A-R processes were more systematic at the beginning and at the end of the subject, since this was when they collected more data; in contrast, during the subject, the A-R process was assimilated and the collection of data on the different A-R phases they carried out was not so systematic and they conceived it as an "automated" process:

"EU8 points out that at the beginning of the course he did collect the notes and personal reflections on the A-R systems that he made in his notebook at the end of each class; but he adds that he only did this at the beginning of the course, after which, due to lack of time, he stopped doing it" (Act 8, 20-21).

Based on these conclusions, the teachers pointed out, as a proposal for improvement, that perhaps the collection of information should be done continuously and systematically throughout the entire academic year or term. In this way, it would be possible to report what has happened with greater accuracy and improve on specific rather than general aspects. In addition, they would be able to make more in-depth reflections. They could also use their own instruments for this purpose in order to systematise the process and be more aware of the progress, changes and achievements made in the FandS systems through the A-R.

"EU7 points out that he believes that the problem we may encounter is that perhaps we do the data collection at the end; he adds that in the A-R process we must respond to the problems immediately, but in his case he does it at the end, he suggests that perhaps the seminar could provide a solution to this problem and focus more on the A-R processes. EU2 replies that this is a reflection that should be made throughout the whole process, since as teachers, we make decisions throughout the whole A-R process and this reflection should not be left to the end because important information would be missing" (Act 8, 20-21).

Valuation of the A-R Processes of HE Teachers

The HE teachers participating in the interlevel seminar gave a very positive assessment of the A-R processes they carried out in order to implement their F&SA systems. Moreover, they pointed out that it was very enriching that this A-R process was complemented by the group work that took place in the seminars; specifically in the discussions and conversations in which concerns were shared with the other seminar participants, whether from HE or from other educational stages.

"EU4 states that in his opinion, A-R processes are being carried out and we are aware of them; but he also comments that it may be that we have systematised the process of collecting information on student assessment more, and paid less attention to the process of teaching, self-assessment and A-R itself" (Act 8, 20-21).

"EU8 points out that he believes that participating in the seminar generates assurance and confidence, as well as being a very powerful tool for resolving doubts among teachers. He considers it to be a very enriching network of resources" (Report 8, 20-21).

F&SA Systems of HE Teachers Participating in an ISTE Group

Advantages of Developing F&SA in HE

The HE teachers participating in the interlevel seminar pointed out that implementing F&SA in HE has multiple advantages.

The first one that stands out is that through F&SA, students can be made co-participants in their own learning and assessment process. Developing F&SA processes fosters students' and capacity for reflection, a very important aspect in HE focused on the training of future teachers, since it serves to develop teachers with the capacity for reflection who are committed to the culture of formative assessment.

"The data collected in the anonymous questionnaire given to students at the end of the term indicate that they are happy with this applied methodological process, as well as noticing that the so-called theoretical classes have lost the directionality of traditional lectures to give way to a greater role for students and their preparation before arriving in the classroom" (EU6 Report, 2020-2021).

HE teachers have seen that the students' academic performance has improved through F&SA.

"Among the main benefits found was a very high success rate. The quality of the mentored learning projects has been extremely good in most of them, due to being well prepared by most groups" (EU1, EU2, EU5, EU8, 2020-2021 report).

Students who experienced F&SA processes indicated that they had acquired the competences to be developed better in the subjects in which these assessment processes were carried out.

"The students indicate that the acquisition of competences has been achieved between a great deal and quite a lot; high percentages of acceptance that contribute to reaffirming the idea that this inductive teaching-learning model facilitates the acquisition of most of the competences required for the Bachelor's degree and enhances the students' training" (EU6 Report, 2020-2021).

Carrying out F&SA processes and the variety of assessment tools allows for continuous assessment of students, improving teaching and the teaching-learning process itself. Futhermore, F&SA fosters a good classroom climate, since it increases student involvement and participation in the sessions; it also foments student motivation and interest in the teaching-learning process.

"One of the most outstanding advantages is the involvement of the pupils both in the group work and the development of the proposal and choice of the subject to be worked on. A good working atmosphere has also been achieved in the classroom, with a high level of participation in the sessions, in which students show motivation and interest in the development of the course" (EU3 Report, EU10, 2020-2021).

Drawbacks and Proposed Improvements for Developing F&SA in HE

The HE teachers participating in the interlevel seminar pointed out that implementing F&SA in HE has some drawbacks such as the difficulty for students to understand the F&SA process at first, the lack of rigour in some cases when carrying out self-assessments, or the increased workload. In order to overcome these drawbacks, they proposed providing more detailed explanations of F&SA to increase students' awareness of the process, or to reduce the workload in some learning activities. These drawbacks and their possible solutions are detailed below.

The first of the disadvantages highlighted by the HE teachers participating in the seminar is that students initially find it difficult to understand the F&SA process, because it is the opposite of the traditional assessment they have predominantly experienced throughout their academic education. The possible solution they proposed to overcome these drawbacks was to explain in more detail what F&SA is all about.

"The problem encountered is the lack of understanding of the formative assessment process, and the possible solution could be to explain what formative assessment is, its purpose and how to carry it out correctly, in more detail" (EU9 Report, 2020-2021).

Another of the disadvantages they found is that self-assessment processes sometimes do not generate self-knowledge because they are not rigorously carried out. The proposal for improvement is to make students aware of the need for this activity to be carried out thoroughly in order to generate as much learning as possible.

"The problem encountered is that self-assessment sometimes does not generate self-knowledge about where they are in their learning process due to a lack of rigour, and the possible solution could be to make students aware of the importance and need for self-assessment to be carried out thoroughly " (EU9 Report, 2020-2021).

The workload generated by F&SA activities for both students and teachers was another drawback reported by HE teachers. There are several possible solutions to this problem: (a) on the one hand, reducing the number of documents or articles on which they have to base these activities; (b) asking students to keep a log of working hours; (c) teaching techniques to improve self-regulated learning in the first sessions.

"The biggest problems reported by the students are centred on the large number of hours they have had to spend on the compulsory activities required to complete the F&SA. Possible solutions would include reducing the number of articles or documents they have to work on, as well as lightening the content of the practical session sheets so that they do not become monotonous and demotivating" (EU6 report, 2020-2021).

"Students complain of having worked a lot. The level of demand of the subject has been high for them. Perhaps they are not aware of the teaching load of autonomous and group work outside the classroom. They will be asked to keep a record of their working hours in order to compare their working hours with the hours they would have to devote to the subject in total according to the teaching project" (EU3 report, EU10, 2020-2021).

The last problem encountered by the HE teachers was that work can accumulate at specific points in the subject, so they proposed allowing postponement of submission or making it more flexible.

"One problem that has arisen is the accumulation of work in some weeks when the submission of the activities that had to be done in a fixed manner coincided with handing in the corresponding content block essay or the development of the tutored learning project to the corresponding group. I therefore propose allowing the groups involved to postpone the handing in of the activities" (EU6 Report, 2020-2021).

SOLUTIONS AND RECOMENDATIONS

The results show that, as far as the HE students' performance of the A-R cycles is concerned, they considered that once the cyclical A-R process (planning, action, observation and analysis) had been assimilated and worked on several times, it became more systematic and simpler. Based on this conclusion, they suggested as a proposal for improvement that the collection of information should be done continuously throughout the course and not only at the beginning and end of the process to help them to be more aware of the progress and changes made in their F&SA systems. The results show that university teachers valued the A-R processes they carried out in the ISTE F&SA seminar very positively, and are able to transfer what they learn with greater assurance and in a longitudinal way (Mahon and Smith, 2020).

They stated that it was very enriching to complement the individual work that each teacher carries out in their classrooms with the group work that takes place in the seminars, thanks to debating and sharing concerns with the rest of their colleagues.

The main advantages found are similar to those of other works mentioned above (Gutiérrez et al., 2018; Hortigüela-Alcalá et al., 2015; López-Pastor and Pérez-Pueyo, 2017): (a) it develops students' self-criticism, reflection and responsibility; (b) it improves the acquisition of the competences of initial teacher training; (c) it improves the classroom climate and students' participation in their own teaching-learning process; (d) the variety of tools used allows for continuous evaluation of student learning, teaching and the teaching-learning process; (e) it improves students' academic performance.

As for the disadvantages, they mentioned: (a) students may find it difficult to understand the F&SA system at the beginning; (b) students' self-regulation with their learning tasks may sometimes not work; (c) students may experience an increased workload; (d) it involves a lot of perseverance in the teaching-learning process on the part of the student and the teacher.

FUTURE RESEARCH DIRECTIONS

As a prospective work, it would be interesting to study other work dynamics, such as training groups, distance meetings, or interlevel training, which are carried out in ISTE groups in HE and the results they obtain. It would also be interesting to test two lines of research on the basis of the results obtained: (a) on the one hand, it would be enriching to see what specific aspects can improve the A-R that takes place within an ISTE interlevel seminar, as well as to check how systematising the A-R processes further affects the F&SA systems that each teacher carries out in their classroom; (b) on the other hand, it would be interesting to check how the proposals for improvement that HE teachers have considered for the disadvantages encountered after carrying out F&SA practices in HE have been implemented. In this respect, it would be enriching to carry out longitudinal studies on the praxis of the teachers in the ISTE internal level seminar.

CONCLUSION

As a conclusion to the objectives proposed in the chapter, the results are very positive. The teachers participating in the seminar point out that A-R is very useful for developing F&SA practices in HE and that the fact of participating in an ISTE group is very positive. Moreover, thanks to the A-R cycles and the spirals that take place during the seminars, teachers learn how to apply and improve F&SA systems, also making proposals for improvement in order to solve these drawbacks.

Regarding the second objective, university teachers consider that F&SA processes have great advantages as well as some disadvantages, for which they propose some solutions.

This study may be of interest to HE teachers who want to learn how to apply F&SA systems and improve their teaching practice through ISTE groups using Action Research as a basic working methodology.

REFERENCES

Álvarez, C., and San Fabián, J. L. (2012). La elección del estudio de caso en investigación educativa. *Gazeta de Antropología, 28*(1), 1-13. http://hdl.handle.net/10481/20644

Andreu, M. A., & Labrador, M. J. (2011). Formación del profesorado en metodologías y evaluación. Análisis cualitativo. *Revista de Investigación Educacional, 9*(2), 236–245. https://reined.webs.uvigo.es/index.php/reined/article/view/127

Aubert, A., Flecha, A., García, C., Flecha, R., & Racionero, S. (2008). *Aprendizaje dialógico en la sociedad de la información.* Hipatia.

Barba, J. J., Manrique, J. C., López-Pastor, V. M., & Gea, J. M. (2010). Garantir l'èxit en la formació inicial del professorat d'educaciò física: Els projectes d'aprenentatge tutelats. *Temps d'Educacio, 39,* 187–206. https://raco.cat/index/php/TempsEducacio/article/view/245016

Barba-Martín, R. A., Barba, J. J. and Martínez, S. (2016). La formación continua colaborativa a través de la investigación-acción. Una forma de cambiar las prácticas de aula. *Contextos educativos, 19,* 161-175. doi:10.18172/con.2769

Barbier, R. (1975). *Le recherche-action dans l'education.*

Barrientos, E. J., López-Pastor, V. M., & Pérez-Brunicardi, D. (2019). ¿Por qué hago Evaluación Formativa y Compartida y/o Evaluación para el Aprendizaje en Educación Física? La influencia en la Formación Inicial y Permanente del profesorado. *Retos, 36,* 37–43. doi:10.47197/retos.v36i66478

Bausela, E. (2004). La docencia a través de la investigación-acción. *Revista Iberoamericana de Educación, 35*(1), 1–9. doi:10.35362/rie3512871

Beutel, D., Adie, L., & Lloyd, M. (2017). Assessment Moderation in an Australian Context: Processes, Practices, and Challenges. *Teaching in Higher Education, 22*(1), 1–14. doi:10.1080/13562517.2016.1213232

Blández, J. (2021). *La investigación-acción: un reto para el profesorado: guía práctica para grupos de trabajo, seminarios y equipos de investigación.* INDE.

Bores-García, D., Hortigüela-Alcalá, D., Hernando-Garijo, A., & González-Calvo, G. (2021). Analysis of student motivation towards body expression through the use of formative and share assessment. *Retos, 1*(40), 198–208. doi:10.47197/retos.v1i40.83025

Carr, W., & Kemmis, S. (1988). *Teoría crítica de la Enseñanza. La Investigación-Acción en la formación del profesorado.* Martínez-Roca.

Coller, X. (2000). *Estudio de casos.* Centro de Investigaciones Sociológicas.

Córdoba Jiménez, T., Carbonero Sánchez, L., Sánchez Aguayo, D., Inglada Moreno, S., Serra Figueroa, M., Blasco, M., Sáez Miota, S., & Ivanco Casals, P. (2016). Educación Física Cooperativa, formación permanente y desarrollo profesional. De la escritura colectiva a un relato de vida compartido. [Cooperative Physical Education, In-service Teacher Education and professional development] *Retos, 29,* 264–269. doi:10.47197/retos/v.i35.60168

Dochy, F., Segers, M., & Dierick, S. (2002). Nuevas vías de aprendizaje y enseñanza y sus consecuencias: Una era de evaluación. *Red Estatal de Docencia Universitaria, 2*(2), 13–30. https://revistas.um.es/redu/article/view/20051/19411

Dochy, F., Segers, M., & Sluijsmans, D. (2002). The use of self, peer and co-assessment in higher education. *Studies in Higher Education, 24*(3), 331–350. doi:10.1080/03075079912331379935

Domínguez, J. and Vázquez, E. (2015). Atención a la diversidad: análisis de la formación permanente del profesorado en Galicia. *Revista Nacional e Internacional de Educación Inclusiva, 8*(2), 139-145.

Escudero, J. M. (1998). Consideraciones y propuestas sobre la formación permanente del profesorado. *Review of Education, 317*, 11–29.

Falchikov, N., & Boud, D. (1989). Student self-assessment in higher education. A meta-analysis comparing peer and teacher marks. *Review of Educational Research, 70*(3), 287–322. doi:10.3102/00346543070003287

Fernández, C., López-Pastor, V. M., & Pascual-Arias, C. (2019). La evaluación formativa y compartida en Educación Infantil. Consecuencias del uso de dos metodologías diferentes. *Infancia* [IEYA]. *Educación y Aprendizaje, 5*(2), 54–59. doi:10.22370/ieya.2019.5.2.1504

Gallardo, F. and Carter, B. (2016). La evaluación formativa y compartida durante el prácticum en la formación inicial del profesorado. Análisis de un caso en Chile. Retos. Nuevas tendencias en educación física, deportes y recreación, 29, 258-263

Gallardo, F., López-Pastor, V. M., & Carter, B. (2018). Efectos de la aplicación de un sistema de evaluación formativa en la autopercepción de competencias adquiridas en formación inicial del profesorado. *Estudios Pedagógicos (Valdivia), 44*(2), 55–77. doi:10.4067/S0718-07052018000200055

Gutiérrez, C., Hortigüela-Alcalá, D., Peral, Z., & Pérez, A. (2018). Percepciones de los alumnos del grado en maestro en Educación Primaria con mención en Educación Física sobre la adquisición de competencias. *Estudios Pedagógicos (Valdivia), 44*(2), 223–239. doi:10.4067/S0718-07052018000200223

Hamodi, C., López-Pastor, V. M., & López, A. T. (2017). If I experience formative assessment whilst studying at university, will I put it into practice later as a teacher? Formative and shared assessment in Initial Teacher Education (ITE). *European Journal of Teacher Education, 40*(2), 171–190. doi:10.1080/02619768.2017.1281909

Herrero, D., Manrique, J. C., & López-Pastor, V. M. (2021). Incidencia de la Formación Inicial y Permanente del Profesorado en la aplicación de la Evaluación Formativa y Compartida en Educación Física. *Retos*, (41), 533–543. doi:10.47197/retos.v0i41.86090

Hortigüela-Alcalá, D., Fernández-Río, J., Castejón, J., & Pérez-Pueyo, A. (2017). Formative assessment, work regulation, organization, engagement, tracking and attendance in Spanish Universities. *Revista Electrónica Interuniversitaria de Formación del Profesorado, 20*(3), 49–63. doi:10.6018/reifop.20.3.268681

Hortigüela-Alcalá, D., Palacios, A., & López-Pastor, V. (2019). The impact of formative and shared or coassessment on the acquisition of transversal competences in higher education. *Assessment and Evaluation in Higher Education, 44*(6), 933–945. doi:10.1080/02602938.2018.1530341

Hortigüela-Alcalá, D., Pérez-Pueyo, A., & González-Calvo, G. (2019). Pero... ¿A qué nos referimos realmente con la Evaluación Formativa y Compartida?: Confusiones Habituales y Reflexiones Prácticas. *Revista Iberoamericana de Evaluación Educativa, 12*(1), 13–27. doi:10.15366/riee2019.12.1.001

Hortigüela-Alcalá, D., Pérez-Pueyo, A., & López-Pastor, V. M. (2015). Implicación y regulación del trabajo del alumnado en los sistemas de evaluación formativa en educación superior. *RELIEVE, 21*(1), 1–15. doi:10.7203/relieve.21.1.5171

Ibarra-Sáiz, M. S., & Rodríguez-Gómez, G. (2014). Formación del profesorado universitario en evaluación: análisis y prospectiva del Programa Formativo EVAPES-DevalSimWeb "Evaluación para el aprendizaje en la Educación Superior". En Congreso Iberoamericano de Ciencia, Tecnología, Innovación y Educación. Buenos Aires. Organización de Estados Iberoamericanos para la Educación, la Ciencia y la Cultura. https://doi.org/ doi:10.13140/RG.2.2.23638-86082

Imbernón, F. (2014). *10 ideas clave. La formación permanente del profesorado. Nuevas ideas para formar en la innovación y el cambio.* Graó.

Imbernón, F. (2014). *10 ideas clave. La formación permanente del profesorado. Nuevas ideas para formar en la innovación y el cambio.* Graó.

Jiménez, F., Navarro, V., and Souto, R. (coord.) (2021). *Explorando colaborativamente alternativas de evaluación formativa en la universidad.* La Laguna (Tenerife): Universidad de La Laguna. https://riull.ull.es/xmlui/handle/915/22232

Kemmis, S., & McTaggart, R. (1988). *Cómo planificar la investigación-acción.* Laertes.

Kennedy, A. (2005). Models of Continuing Professional Development: A framework for analysis. *Journal of In-service Education, 31*(2), 235–250. doi:10.1080/13674580500200277

Latorre, A. (2003). *La investigación-acción. Conocer y cambiar la práctica educativa.* Graó.

López-Pastor, V. M. (Coord.) (2009). *La Evaluación Formativa y Compartida en Educación Superior: propuestas, técnicas, instrumentos y experiencias.* Narcea

López-Pastor, V. M., Molina, M., Pascual, C. and Manrique, J. C. (2020). La importancia de utilizar la Evaluación Formativa y compartida en la formación inicial del profesorado de educación física: los Proyectos de Aprendizaje Tutorado como ejemplo de buena práctica. *Retos, nuevas tendencias en educación física, deporte y recreación, 37,* 680-687. doi:10.47197/retos.v37i37.74193

López-Pastor, V. M., Monjas, R. and Manrique, J. C. (2011). Fifteen years of action research as professional development: seeking more collaborative, useful and democratic system for teachers. *Educational Action Research, 19*(2), 153-170. https://dx.doi.org/. 569190 doi:10.1080/09650792.2011

López-Pastor, V. M., and Pérez-Pueyo, A. (Coords.) (2017). *Evaluación formativa y compartida en Educación: experiencias de éxito en todas las etapas educativas.* Universidad de León. http://buleria.unileon.es/handle/10612/5999

López-Pastor, V. M., & Sicilia-Camacho, A. (2017). Formative and shared assessment in higher education. Lessons learned and challenges for the future. *Assessment and Evaluation in Higher Education, 42*(1), 77–97. doi:10.1080/02602938.2015.1083535

Mahón, K., & Smith, H. (2020). Moving beyond "Methodising" Theory in Preparing for the Profession. *Journal of Adventure Education and Outdoor Learning, 20*(4), 357–368. doi:10.1080/14729679.2019 .1686039

Manrique-Arribas, J. C., Vallés, C., & Gea, J. (2012). Resultados generales de la puesta en práctica de 29 casos sobre el desarrollo de sistemas de evaluación formativa en docencia universitaria. *PYSE Psychology. Social Education, 4*(1), 87–102. doi:10.25155/pyse.v4i1.483

Margalef, L. (2005). La formación del profesorado universitario: Análisis y evaluación de una experiencia. *Revista de Educación, 337*, 389–402. https://hdl.handle.net/11162/68047

Martínez-Mínguez, L., Moya, L., Nieva, C., & Cañabate, D. (2019). Percepciones de Estudiantes y Docentes: Evaluación Formativa en Proyectos de Aprendizaje Tutorados. *Revista Iberoamericana de Evaluación Educativa, 12*(1), 59–84. doi:10.15366/10.15366/riee2019.12.1.004

Molina, M., & López-Pastor, V. M. (2019). ¿Evalúo como me evaluaron en la facultad? Transferencia de evaluación formativa y compartida vivida en la formación Inicial del profesorado a la práctica como docente. *Revista Iberoamericana de Evaluación Educativa, 12*(1), 85–101. doi:10.15366/riee2019.12.1.005

Molina, M., López-Pastor, V. M., Pascual-Arias, C. and Barba, R. A. (2019). Los proyectos de aprendizaje tutorado como buena práctica en educación física en primer curso de doble titulación (educación infantil y educación primaria). *Revista de innovación y buenas prácticas docentes, 8*(1), 1-14. doi:10.21071/ ripadoc.v8i1.11988

Nieto, S. (2000). El discurso del profesorado universitario sobre la evaluación del aprendizaje de los alumnos como estrategia de innovación y cambio profesional: Exposición y análisis de una experiencia. *Review of Education, 322*, 305–324.

Noreña, A., Alcaraz-Moreno, N., Rojas, J., & Rebolledo-Malpica, D. (2012). Aplicabilidad de los criterios de rigor y éticos en la investigación cualitativa. *Aquichan, 12*(3), 263–274.

Palacios, A., & López-Pastor, V. M. (2013). Haz lo que yo digo pero no lo que yo hago: Sistemas de evaluación del alumnado en la formación inicial del profesorado. *Revista de Educación, 361*, 279–305. https://www.educacionyfp.gob.es/dam/jcr:bf834e01-0af8-4400-89fe-5d669ca640ad/re36111-pdf.pdf

Pascual-Arias, C., García-Herranz, S., & López-Pastor, V. M. (2019). What do preschool students want? The role of formative and shared assessment in their right to decide. *CandE, Cultura y Educación, 31*(4), 865–880. Advance online publication. doi:10.1080/11356405.2019.1656486

Pascual Arias, C., López-Pastor, V. M., and Hamodí-Galán, C. (2021). Seminario de formación permanente internivelar en evaluación formativa y compartida en educación. Resultados de trasferencia de conocimiento entre universidad y escuela. En C. Hamodí-Galán y R. Barba-Martín, Evaluación Formativa y Compartida: Nuevas propuestas de desarrollo en Educación Superior (271-285). Dextra.

Pedraza-González, M. A., & López-Pastor, V. M. (2015). Investigación-acción, desarrollo profesional del profesorado de educación física y escuela rural. *Revista Internacional de Medicina y Ciencias de la Actividad Física y del Deporte, 57*(2015), 1–16. doi:10.15366/rimcafd2015.57.001

Pérez-Pueyo, A., Tabernero, B., López-Pastor, V. M., Ureña, N., Ruiz, E., Caplloch, M., González, N., & Castejón, F. J. (2008). Evaluación formativa y compartida en la docencia universitaria y el Espacio Europeo de Educación Superior: Cuestiones clave para su puesta en práctica. *Revista de Educación, 347*, 435–451. https://www.educacionyfp.gob.es/revista-de-educacion/numeros-revista-educacion/numeros-anteriores/2008/re347/re347-20.html

Reyes, V. (2019). Más allá de la calificación: La evaluación formativa y compartida en Educación Física en la etapa de Educación Primaria. *Infancia* [IEYA]. *Educación y Aprendizaje, 5*(2), 161–165. doi:10.22370/ieya.2019.5.2.1505

Romero-Martín, R., Fraile-Aranda, A., López-Pastor, V. M., & Castejón-Oliva, F. J. (2014). Relación entre sistemas de evaluación formativa, rendimiento académico y carga de trabajo del profesor y del alumno en docencia universitaria. *Infancia y Aprendizaje, 37*(3), 491–527. doi:10.1080/02103702.2014.918818

Santos, J. M., Ortiz, E., & Martín, S. (2018). Índices de variación de la nota debidos a la evaluación continua. Contrastación empírica en la enseñanza universitaria. *CandE, Cultura y Educación, 30*(3), 491–527. doi:10.1080/11356405.2018.1488422

Serrano, V. (2012). Actividades de formación permanente del profesorado y educación inclusiva: Análisis de la situación en Castilla y León. *Revista Educación Inclusiva, 5*(3), 119–132.

Simons, H. (2011). *El estudio de caso: teoría y práctica*. Morata.

Sonlleva, M. (2019). La participación de los estudiantes en el proceso de evaluación: Una experiencia en el aula universitaria. *Infancia. Educación y Aprendizaje, 5*(2), 108–113. doi:10.22370/ieya.2019.5.2.1658

Soto, P. (2002). La formación permanente del profesorado. *Cuadernos de pedagogía, 35,* 44-49.

Souto-Seijo, A., Estévez, I., Iglesias, V., & González-Sanmamed, M. (2020). Entre lo formal y lo no formal: Un análisis desde la formación permanente del profesorado. *Educar, 56*(1), 91–107. doi:10.5565/rev/educar.1095

Stake, R. E. (1998). *Investigación con estudio de casos*. Morata.

Taylor, S. J., & Bogdan, R. (1987). *Introducción a los métodos cualitativos de investigación*. Paidós Básica.

Tomas-Folch, M., & Durán-Bellonch, M. (2017). Comprendiendo los factores que afectan a la transferencia de la formación permanente del profesorado. Propuestas de mejora. *Revista Electrónica Interuniversitaria de Formación del Profesorado, 20*(1), 145–157. doi:10.6018/reifop/20.1.240591

ADDITIONAL READING

Álvarez, V., García, E., Gil, J., & Romero, S. (2004). La enseñanza universitaria: Planificación y desarrollo de la docencia. *Eos (Washington, D.C.)*.

Álvarez Méndez, J. M. (2011). *Evaluar para conocer, examinar para excluir*. Morata.

García-Peñalvo, F. J., Corell, A., Abella-García, V., & Grande, M. (2020). La evaluación on-line en la educación superior en tiempos de la COVID-19. *Education in the Knowledge Society, 21*, 26. doi:10.14201/eks.23086

Hamodí-Galán, C., & Barba-Martín, R. (2021). *Evaluación Formativa y Compartida: Nuevas propuestas de desarrollo en Educación Superior*. Dextra.

Li, Y. L. (2008). Teachers in Action Research: Assumptions and potentials. *Educational Action Research, 16*(2), 251–260. doi:10.1080/09650790802011908

Margalef, L. (2005). La formación del profesorado universitario: Análisis y evaluación de una experiencia. *Review of Education, 337*, 389–402.

Martínez, L. F., Santos, M. L., and Castejón, F. J. (2017). Percepciones de alumnado y profesorado en Educación Superior sobre la evaluación en formación inicial en educación física. *Retos, 32*, 76-81. https://doi.org/10.47197/retos.v0i32.52918

Nicol, D. J., & Macfarlanee-Dick, D. (2006). Formative assessment and self-regulated learning: A model and seven principles of good feedback practice. *Studies in Higher Education, 31*(2), 199–218. doi:10.1080/03075070600572090

Sonlleva, M., Martínez, S., & Monjas, R. (2019). Evaluación del proyecto de aprendizaje tutorado en la asignatura de Educación para la Paz y la Igualdad. *Revista Infancia. Educación y Aprendizaje, 5*(2), 114–120.

KEY TERMS AND DEFINITIONS

Collaborative Learning: The process of knowledge acquisition between two or more people in the same group, setting or space; it can be between teachers and/or learners.

Self-Regulation: The ability to control and/or manage a person's work time.

Workload: The amount of work a person has to do (in education this can refer to both the student and the teacher), usually measured in hours.

Higher education: The stage of education that is the last stage of academic learning, which comes after secondary education and usually refers to the university stage.

Shared Assessment: Assessment in which students participate in their own assessment process, sharing it with the teacher, in order to check how they are progressing, their skills and areas for improvement.

Formative Assessment: That which aims to improve student learning, to improve the teaching of the teacher and to improve the teaching-learning process itself.

In-Service Teacher Education: A process of continuous learning for teachers who are already teaching at any stage of education.

Teaching Research: The process of educational enquiry with the aim of improving one's own practice and/or acquiring new knowledge on any educational subject.

Chapter 8

Rethinking Assessment by Creating More Authentic, Learning–Oriented Tasks to Generate Student Engagement

Sally Brown
Independent Researcher, UK

Kay Sambell
 https://orcid.org/0000-0001-8192-8537
University of Cumbria, UK

ABSTRACT

In March 2020, assessment in universities and colleges globally changed in radical and unprecedented ways when the Covid-19 pandemic closed campuses to students and staff, meaning that on-site, unseen, time-constrained exams could not take place. University management and staff had to move very fast to ensure that students could be assessed reliably and validly in crisis conditions. The authors' immediate and widely shared suggestions on pragmatic alternatives incorporating assessment-for-learning principles were well-received and prompted the development of a systematic and practical six-stage 'task-generator' to enable the creation of flexible context/scenario-based assessment activities for use off-campus. This chapter concludes by arguing why some of the changes implemented in crisis conditions have so much value in terms of student learning and engagement that universities must never revert to an over-reliance on former modes of assessment.

INTRODUCTION: A RAPIDLY CHANGING LANDSCAPE

In this chapter we aim to discuss the rethinking of assessment that occurred when the pandemic caused Higher Education Institutions (HEIs) to change from on-campus face-to-face, and in particular, our own rapid response. Next, we discuss the case for alternatives to traditional exams and why we think that

DOI: 10.4018/978-1-6684-3537-3.ch008

authentic assessment approaches that use an *assessment for learning* paradigm work well, before discussing definitions and features of authentic assessment, drawing on global scholarship before making the case for wider adoption of authentic assessment practices, which we argue is as much about advancing self-hood as it about preparing students for graduate employment. We illustrate this with our own six-stage strategic approach to designing authentic assessment tasks, including examples, before pointing readers to further exemplification of these. We conclude with a summary of our argument, together with an exhortation to refuse to revert to former less authentic approaches.

When, in March 2020 the Covid-19 pandemic resulted in the need suddenly to close campuses to students and staff, this meant that on-site, unseen, time-constrained exams could not take place. Given the widespread reliance on in-person invigilated examinations across the tertiary education sector, university management and staff had to move very fast to ensure that, during the enforced rapid pivot to emergency remote teaching, students at the end of the forthcoming semester could be examined in ways that aligned with prior plans.

Different Higher Education Institutions (HEIs) dealt with the situation in different ways: some by shifting planned exams to off-site take-home papers with no changes to the questions asked, some by radically increasing the amount of off-site computer-based assessment and some by moving to alternative forms of assignment which reframed the assessment process altogether. While our chapter deals briefly with these developments, it is this latter area that forms the principal focus, because, we argue, there are considerable benefits to be accrued by using alternative assessment formats instead of traditional exams, both during the challenging period of the pandemic but also, more importantly, in the longer term.

The impetus to move universities towards more authentic, learning-oriented assessment practices underpinned the extensive suite of widely-used, highly pragmatic resources that we produced over time in response to the Covid pandemic. The resources in our Covid Collection were created at rapid pace, because our objective was to support university-based colleagues cope with the range of assessment issues and challenges that emerged during the pandemic as time unfolded (Brown and Sambell 2020, 2021). Our work built on our pioneering involvement in over three decades of research on Assessment for Learning (Sambell et al, 2013). This has convinced us that assessment practices which are fully integrated throughout the learning process have high value in fostering student engagement, resulting in deeper approaches to learning and better ultimate outcomes. Central to this approach is our conviction of the importance of authenticity in assessment as a means of enhancing student learning for the longer term (Boud and Soler, 2014). The main objective of this chapter, then, is to argue that universities would do well to seize the opportunity to make some radical and substantial reconfigurations to assessment in the future to make it more authentic.

To set our recent work on authentic assessment practices in context the chapter will, first, briefly present the timeline against which we created our assessment resources, together with an explanation for the ways in which our Covid Collection evolved as the pandemic unfolded. It will then move on to outline the theoretical rationale for moving towards more authentic assessment tasks, highlighting the significant literature upon which the desirability of this trajectory is based. Next, some of the key defining characteristics of authentic assessment will be indicated. The substantial evidence base highlighting the impact of authentic assessment on students in higher education will be reviewed and key challenges and issues which face course designers who wish to embrace the benefits of authentic assessment will be identified. These include a lack of familiarity among practitioners about methods that move away from well-worn assessment formats towards more authentic assessments targeted on university-based learning which is focused on *subject-knowledge*, in contrast to the relatively well-established authentic assessment formats which are now frequently used in practice-based assessments, or which focus on workplace/practical skills.

This general lack of awareness of the broader possibilities for alternative assessment ultimately led us to propose a pragmatic tool – which we call the task generator – as a means of supporting hard-pressed staff to rethink their assessment designs. It aimed to help those under pressure to create more authentic, learning-oriented tasks to catalyse and foster student engagement with the ways of thinking and practising of their subject areas, as well as to broaden, develop and hone their work-related competencies and skills. Finally, our practical six-step model for generating more authentic tasks will be outlined in full, and illustrative examples drawn from a range of practice across diverse disciplinary, institutional and national contexts will be presented.

COVID RESPONSE TIMELINE

Responding to the changing situation, we incrementally produced a suite of resources in our Covid Assessment Collection, which are still being developed further: a timeline indicating their development can be viewed in Figure 1.

Figure 1. Timeline of outputs in the Covid assessment collection

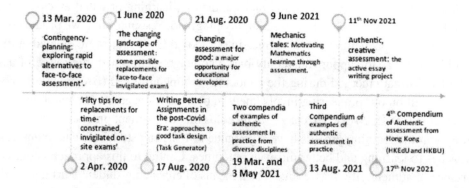

The first two outputs focused on making immediate contingency plans for the substantial diet of time-constrained, in person, invigilated exams which could no longer run as intended in their original format once campuses closed at immensely short notice due to the pandemic. The first suggested a range of rapid adjustments that could be considered at a general and strategic level to avoid disadvantaging students as far as humanly possible. The second focused on providing a range of more detailed reflective prompts for the vast numbers of hard-pressed staff who were being required to move all their traditional unseen time-constrained written exams into an **'open book'** or virtual format at breakneck speed. While many academics were being advised by university leaders to use what was often popularly coined as an 'open-book' approach, in practice we recognised that most were likely to be using what we termed in the resource a **'take-away exam paper'** (in which students were given a week or more as a 'window' in which to complete and submit unseen exam questions or tasks) or **'online exams taken remotely'**

(where students undertook the unseen exam on a specific day with a more stringent set time limit (perhaps five hours) within which the set questions have to be undertaken and submitted). Our second resource therefore outlined some issues it would be wise to consider in this scenario and provided practical suggestions for relatively modest adjustments that might mitigate potential problems. Our focus at this point was on making the best of what could be achieved in extreme circumstances while recognising the need for compassionate practice for all parties in very challenging circumstances.

By summer 2020 it started to become clear that campuses were unlikely to open completely in the following months however, so our resources then focused on helping teams prepare for the upcoming academic year, when they had a slightly longer lead in time for possible changes to assessment practice. The enforced switch to assessment alternatives had sparked fruitful conversations across universities (as discussed in 'Changing assessment for good: a major opportunity for educational developers', August 2021 in the Covid Collection) and increasing numbers of staff (not just the pioneering enthusiasts) had begun to rethink why and how we assess at more fundamental levels. Hence the sector was facing a golden opportunity to bring about more radical assessment reform, at scale, of the kind that the Assessment for Learning (AfL) movement had been arguing for since the 1990s. Because well-worn approaches to assessment, including the substantial diet of traditional exams, still had to be replaced, or some proxy method had to be used to stand in their stead, and conversations had prompted the realisation that alternative ways offered potential learning benefits, many institutions looked to longer term solutions.

We were not alone, however, in our concern that the adjustments to assessment made during the pandemic might be superficial, technical, or temporary (McArthur, 2021), or worse, return to business as usual at the earliest opportunity, rather than rethink fundamental principles. So, that summer we provided a resource ('The changing landscape of assessment: some possible replacements for unseen time-constrained face-to-face invigilated exams', June 2020 in the Covid Collection) which outlined a host of tried and tested alternatives to traditional exams, to support those who were looking for replacements at the point when they had longer time to plan next steps for the 2020-2021 academic year onwards.

QUESTIONING TRADITIONAL, INVIGILATED UNSEEN TIME-CONSTRAINED EXAMS

The Assessment for Learning movement has long been keen to question the orthodoxy of exams as the assumed gold standard of assessment practice. In many ways research has shown them to be deficient. *Inter alia,* the time/place/duration constraints carry high risks which prevent the traditional exam being taken, and thereby jeopardize business continuity and interruption, which would continue to require on-the-hoof mitigations. But arguably more importantly and pedagogically, traditional exams all too often lack authenticity. Poorly designed exam questions risk seeming contrived and irrelevant to students, so that sitting the exam is framed by learners as a matter of compliance, or enacting a drilled routine, rather than connecting in a meaningful way to events and contexts beyond the test itself.

The range of activities that students are asked to do in a traditional written exam tend to be very limited, comprising mainly writing with a pen individually in silence, with no reference to wider resources. In employment and wider contexts, however, most will have internet access and a keyboard to work on, as well as the expectation that they will work as team members, often in interdisciplinary settings. Traditional exams also lack relevance to students' future lives in employment, entrepreneurship, and civil society, since they are rarely in any meaningful way a valid representation of what work or life challenges typically require.

Unfortunately, exams are often viewed by students as memory-tests, so invoke cramming and topic-spotting rather than any sustained effort at authentic achievement of educational outcomes over time. Students may often also feel that success in high stakes tests like this rely on luck (e.g. the right questions come up in an exam, or conversely, bad luck which penalises you for having an off day) or that they privilege those who have higher social and cultural capital and therefore tend to be familiar and well-schooled into dealing with traditional assessment formats, rather than representing a valid evaluation of what a student knows and can do.

Our own early research (Sambell et al, 1997) on the impact of alternative assessment indicated that students frequently felt that the arbitrary and contrived nature of exams 'contaminated' their learning, whereas if students felt alternative assessment tasks were intrinsically useful and worthwhile (for example, they required them to communicate, discuss, defend their ideas, or produce something that felt meaningful to them beyond simply acquiring marks or grades), then they were more likely to invest effort in deep, genuine, lasting learning, rather than simply going through the motions, or submitting whatever they thought their lecturers wanted to hear or see. In this way the assessment tasks we set can send strong backwash messages about the kind of learning that is valued. It is sadly extremely easy for traditional exams to provoke a surface approach to learning focused on reproducing taught material solely to pass the test and, as Ramsden asserts (1992) this sends a very damaging message about appropriate learning.

Alternative assessment (Brown and Knight, 1994; Birenbaum 1996; Sambell et al, 1997) of the sort we outlined in our June 2020 paper (*op cit*), aims, by contrast, to stimulate the deep, complex, high-order learning we value in higher education, which includes meaning-making, criticality, and connectivity, thus potentially changing the very ways in which learners see and interact with their worlds (Ashwin, 2020). While our own empirical research into the impact of assessment on student perceptions (Sambell and McDowell, 1998) revealed that this is by no means straightforward or easy, as assessment messages are filtered and co-constructed variously by individual students, our research generally illuminated that more authentic, learning-oriented assessment formats can have a powerful positive backwash effect on students' approaches to learning and the way they view themselves and approach their studies (Sambell et al, 2013).

Hence, we were keen to challenge the orthodoxy of conventionally-framed exams and so in mid-summer 2020 we published our Changing Landscapes paper to stimulate a wider debate about why we use exams, and challenge university colleagues' beliefs about the purposes of assessment. We saw this as a golden opportunity to encourage practitioners, at scale, to consider the possibility that a different assessment method could enable a better engagement with subject knowledge. Thereby, drawing on 30 decades of the Assessment for Learning (AfL) tradition, we created a table of alternative methods, accompanied by pros and cons for each, as well as areas for further consideration.

DRAWING ON THE WORK OF THE AFL MOVEMENT IN HE

The AfL movement (Boud and Falchikov, 2007) acknowledges that many assessment practices in HE tend not to equip students well for the processes of effective learning post-graduation, including the abilities to undertake those activities that necessarily accompany learning throughout life in formal and informal settings. Assessment tasks and accompanying processes therefore need to play what Boud

(2000) calls 'double duty' – that is both meet the immediate and specific goals of a course as well as establish a basis for students to undertake their own assessment activities in future. In one sense this means creating overall learning, teaching and assessment environments (Sambell et al, 2013) which do not separate out Learning, Teaching and Assessment as discrete events, but constructively align goals, activities and assessment, holistically moving assessment and feedback processes into the hands of learners so they do not learn to depend on others for evaluation and feedback. Hence AfL speaks to the fact that students must become active and engaged participants in the assessment system, rather than passive recipients of others' directives and judgments. It also means we pedagogically create the conditions which enable them to become effective evaluators (Tai et al 2018) and feedback agents (Winstone and Carless, 2019; Nicol 2021) themselves, if they are to be expected to flourish and use assessment and feedback processes productively.

In the mid-2000s AfL practitioners at the University of Northumbria developed a pragmatic model, involving six core conditions (see Sambell et al, 2013) for creating overall AfL environments at module and ideally programme level, which was used to bring about the culture shift required to move away from a testing culture and, instead, to prepare graduates for the learning society (Birenbaum, 1996). While AfL is generally believed to place the spotlight on formative assessment, dialogue and interaction over the duration of a course, it is, we argue, equally important to recognise that if we want to inspire productive student learning, the design of more authentic **summative** assessment tasks is one of the most practical tools we have in our teaching toolbox, because it establishes the overall context for driving learning, priming the engine for student involvement in deep learning and formative assessment.

The design of summative assessment tasks is important because summative assessment provides the *de facto* agenda for learning, publishing the 'deep running sort of ought' (Wolf, 1993) of a disciplinary area and issuing authoritative statements about 'what counts' as achievement. Summative assessment powerfully directs students' attention to those matters. It tells them, in short, what, and to an extent, how to learn. As previously highlighted, conventional assessment has frequently been criticised for embodying a sub-text which communicates the 'wrong' messages to students about how to learn. For example, Entwistle and Entwistle (1991) note how preparation for exams hinders students' efforts towards genuine understanding of course material. So, while they cannot offer a simple panacea, alternative assessment tasks characterised by key features of authenticity can play an important part in inspiring and engaging appropriate and formative learning processes, hence are a key condition for AfL.

AUTHENTIC ASSESSMENT

Alternative assessment is a broad term which is largely defined by what it is trying to provide an alternative to (Fox 2008), (that is, usually a move away from conventional or standardized testing formats). Authentic assessment, by contrast, while still broadly conceived, is a term typically invoked by the AfL movement (see Villarroel et al, 2018) because it focuses explicitly on assessing student performance on challenging, complex and 'worthy intellectual tasks' (Wiggins, 1990, p1). These resemble the types of things that academics and professionals do in the field, rather than relying on indirect or proxy items in traditional tests, which 'tend to reveal only whether the student can recognize, recall or "plug in" what was learned out of context" (*ibid*, p1). Admittedly the established literature on authentic assessment, which is all about all about **preparing students for the reality** of their lives as graduates of their disciplines and the longer term, often emanated from critiques of conventional assessment and its failure to forge links between what was learned in university and the world outside and beyond it. But in the mid-2000s it also became linked in HE to a renewed focus on graduate attributes (Barrie, 2006) and the problems that arise from trying to infer a graduate's capability from a relatively narrow range of paper-based traditional university assessments such as exams and essays.

Authentic assessment usually, then, refers to assessment tasks that are situated within, or correspond to, the 'real world' or appropriate social, professional or disciplinary contexts (Kreber, 2014), implying that assessment should represent the knowledge and skills that are needed in realistic contexts, as opposed to being restricted to the educational context (Segers, Dochy and Gibels, 2010). It typically conveys a sense that what is learned can be *applied* in an analytical and thoughtful way or *used* to solve a problem or meet a need.

Some would argue that there is not time in a busy curriculum to get involved in this kind of assessment activity, since traditional exams are regarded as quick and easy to mark, but we would argue that not only are such assessments less capable of demonstrating students' real capacities, but also the learning gain involved far outweighs any loss of content delivery, particularly since students in the pandemic have become much more used to accessing information in ways other than simply hearing it from their teachers in lectures.

According to Cumming and Maxwell (1999: 2), the first formal use of the term 'authentic' in the context of learning and assessment appears to have been by Archbald and Newmann (1988). Here the focus was on trying to address a lack of connection between educational and lifelong contexts. The authors used the term 'authentic achievement' (p.72) which they regarded as having several characteristics that emulate the `kinds of mastery demonstrated by successful adults' (p.74). These included: production of knowledge instead of reproduction or response only to the produced work of others; disciplined enquiry, dependent on a prior knowledge base (which is used to help to produce knowledge); in-depth understanding (rather than superficial awareness). The production of knowledge requires the ability to 'organize, synthesize, and integrate information in new ways' and holds value beyond assessment's aesthetic, utilitarian, or personal value.' In sum, then, authentic achievement rests upon the extent to which the outcomes measured represent appropriate, meaningful, significant, and worthwhile forms of human accomplishment.

According to Villarroel *et al* (2018), the higher education literature began to associate authentic assessment with high-order thinking, ability to solve problems, and make decisions. Wiggins (1993) and Torrance (1995) introduced the concept of **relevance** – with authentic assessment engaging students with problems or important questions which have worth beyond the classroom – that is, setting ill-defined, divergent tasks which resemble the types of things faced in working life. Because students are often engaged in "**using** and **applying** skills and knowledge to address '**real world**' problems" (Lund 1997) to give the task a sense of authenticity, HE researchers regularly explicitly frame authentic assessment as a strategy to **link learning and work** – forging a correspondence between what students need to do in the workplace and their learning in university. Often this entails explicitly providing a context for assessment or assessing performance in everyday situations. It is scarcely surprising, then, that early research into the impact of authentic assessment in HE (e.g. Gulikers et al, 2004, 2008) tended to focus on vocationally-oriented courses, where alternative assessment had been designed to require students to use the same competencies, or combinations of knowledge, skills, and attitudes that they need to apply in the criterion situation in professional life.

Systematic studies of authentic assessment in HE prior to the pandemic indicated positive influences on learning. For instance, Villarroel et al's (2018) review reported that assessment designs that replicate the tasks and performance standards typically found in the world of work had been found to have a positive impact on student learning, autonomy, motivation, self-regulation and metacognition; abilities highly related to employability. Similarly, a recent systematic literature review (Sokhanvar et al, 2021) of the advantages of implementing authentic assessment highlighted reported benefits on students including:

- Enhanced engagement;
- Improved student satisfaction and contribution to increasing students' efforts to reach educational goals;
- Enhanced employability skills.

However, Villaroel et al (*op cit*) also note significant **barriers** to the implementation of authentic assessment, including a lack of conceptualisation of the term 'authentic assessment' in ways that seemed sufficient to inform the development of practice at individual course level, especially in situations where there was a strong tradition of testing decontextualised subject knowledge. To help address this, and well before the pandemic ensued, these researchers conducted their influential review of existing literature to generate key characteristics which they distilled into **three key conceptual dimensions**. These characteristics formed the basis of their proposal for a **four-step model** to aid the design of authentic assessment, targeted strongly on developing what the authors refer to as students' "'authentic' capabilities for employment." (p.850) This important groundwork has influenced our thinking and the development of our 'task generator', which we outline later, in response to pandemic times.

The key dimensions of authentic assessment according to Villaroel et al's (*op cit*) analysis are:

- **Realism.** This could be the presence of a **real context** or a **task similar** to those encountered in professional or real life, (e.g. cases, problem solving, or questions which act as a close approximation to real world scenarios). Or realism could be achieved through **performance-based** tasks where students produce work or demonstrate knowledge, understanding and skills in activities that are close to the profession (e.g. a true performance in that field of performance, or authentic simulations, or actual professional tasks).
- **Cognitive challenge** implies that assessment tasks require students to go beyond textual reproduction of fragmented and low order content, and move towards understanding, and making relationships between new ideas and previous knowledge, linking theoretical concepts with everyday experience, deriving conclusions from data analysis, examining logic of arguments presented in theory as well as examining its practical scope. These might include critical and reflective analysis and outputs such as a diagnostic report which demonstrate genuine mastery of content. In this way a premium is placed on **application** and **knowledge transfer** skills to solve real problems (rather than just to reproduce knowledge in a decontextualized situation).
- **Evaluative Judgment:** Their analysis importantly highlights the role of authentic tasks which hone learners' evaluative judgment because MacFarlane argues that when evaluative judgement is incorporated into the assessment process, it adds to the authenticity by, firstly, helping students understand the concept of teacher 'quality' and what it means for a task to be 'of excellence' (Nicol and Macfarlane-Dick 2006), and, secondly, by developing the lifelong capability to assess and regulate their learning and performance.

Villarroel *et al's* four-step design model, which begins with 'identifying the graduate profile' and 'workplace context' to inform the authentic assessment; includes methods that require cognitive challenge, application, integration and are useful to third parties to give a purpose to student learning; and involves learning and applying standards and engaging in feedback processes, reflects the breadth of the dimensions which they hope encourages [teachers to consider the] "integration of discipline-specific skills and knowledge with application in the workplace, but also, importantly, with the generic capacity to evaluate and improve performance." The breadth of the dimensions and the four-step model "also highlight the complexity of learning for authentic practice, and the potential of assessment to create a richer learning environment and build capacity for higher order and lifelong learning" (p.850).

TOWARDS MORE AUTHENTIC, LEARNING-ORIENTED TASK DESIGNS DURING THE PANDEMIC

This thinking provided a substratum to our own endeavours to offer alternatives to traditional assessment during pandemic times, not just as an *ad hoc* means of coping with the crisis, but as a way of developing and enabling students to demonstrate personal 'capability' that goes considerably beyond work-related knowledge and skills to provide graduates with a sound foundation for long-term ability relevant to unknown future work and citizenship contexts. In effect, this entailed broadening the notion of authentic assessment to embody more than work-related relevance. Indeed, well before the onset of the pandemic, Arnold (2019) was already usefully drawing attention to the importance of context and realism in assignments but **also** broadening the definition of authentic assessment to include relevance to the **self** (the person a student wishes to become), and relevance to the **discipline**, as well as to work. Building on Villarroel et al's (op cit) review she asserted that:

"Authentic assessment is characterised by **realism***, cognitive challenge and evaluative judgment with* **relevance** *to self, discipline community or professional community"* (Arnold, 2019).

Given current circumstances we caution against adopting too narrow a definition of authentic assessment based on workplace knowledge and skills associated directly and literally with 'employability'. While these have an important overall part to play, alternative views of authenticity have helpfully utilised a much broader notion of relevance (National Forum, 2017). It has been suggested, for instance, that developing a sense of self and ownership through personal meaning and **personal involvement** are crucial for authenticity, whereby personally meaningful experiences are 'about an experience that *the student* determines as significant or worthwhile' (Wald and Harland, 2017, p.757: our emphasis). This frames authenticity as an issue which extends beyond work-related learning *per se*. Similarly, Davison's (2011) research into students' perceptions of assessment's authenticity in non-vocational subjects found authenticity became linked to students' personal interests or issues they have identified for themselves.

So, giving students some degree of choice in the assessment task may also be valuable in some circumstances, for example, allowing them to choose a focus that has a stronger sense of relevance for them. Along similar lines, authentic assessment has been linked to tasks whose purpose students buy into, which generate **intrinsic interest** and enable them to feel that they are making a genuine contribution, for example, by creating a novel product or performance (O'Neill, 2019). By making active choices and having influence, students can be helped to feel that they are engaging in important transformative identity-work that is part of the HE learning experience, including learning to see the world through different eyes.

We believe, then, that authentic assessment can usefully be **defined and positioned along a continuum** from directly work-related competencies to wider characteristics which go beyond an exclusive focus on the 'real world'. These characteristics include, among others; challenge, a concrete outcome such as a performance or a product, transfer of knowledge, collaboration, metacognition, opportunities for feedback (Ashford-Rowe et al, 2014). We see this broader range of assessment characteristics as relative and appropriate to a range of pedagogic contexts/discipline areas, but having equal value in the HE context, rather than assessment necessarily being positioned on a continuum representing 'high' or 'low' levels of authenticity (Mueller, 2006).

Hence the 'task generator' approach we developed during the pandemic aimed to enhance authenticity by encouraging staff to take small manageable steps towards authenticity in their assessment redesigns, (for example, by ensuring that student work demonstrates an awareness of a specific audience for outputs), without requiring assessment designers to go all out to radically change every aspect of their assignments and letting the perfect be the enemy of the good. For us, making marginal gains towards authenticity is worthwhile in itself in terms of motivating and engaging students in a general sense, not purely associated with professionally orientated or explicitly work-related situations.

ADVANCING SELFHOOD

We contend that more authentic, learning-oriented (Carless, 2015) assessments might also be a positive force in fostering, *inter alia*, a student's personal growth, capabilities, development, sense of *belonging and becoming* in disciplinary communities, as well as identity, confidence and self-worth (Arnold, 2021; Brown, 2019; Kreber, 2021). This moves beyond simply conflating realism with the world of work, because, as McArthur (2021) argues: "assessment can be a powerful force in shaping individual students' identity and sense of self-worth….it's about who they are and who they go on to be in our society"

So suitably reframed, more authentic tasks might also play a facilitative role in developing students not only as individuals but also as **active and fulfilled citizens** by, for instance, fostering criticality, divergent thinking, agency, motivation to question commonly held assumptions, creativity, and a sense of pride and value in deeply engaging with complex knowledge, or potential contributions to the broader social good (McArthur, *op cit* 2021). They may also help build capabilities such as confidence to act for social change; empathy, integrity, informed vision and imagination, developing partnerships across status hierarchies, and communicating professional knowledge in accessible ways (Kreber, 2021). They might also activate or nurture learners' sense of university scholarship as community-based engagement (Renwick et al, 2020) whereby students see themselves becoming part of communities' **'mosaic of talent.'**

Seen from the viewpoint of immersing learners in the ways of thinking and practising (McCune and Hounsell, 2005) associated with their chosen discipline, students need chance to become personally invested in the issues they have learned and are assessed on, and need encouragement to reflect on what these issues mean to them on a personal level and how they can contribute (now, and as future graduates), to society and the world (Kreber, 2014). Further, if the goal is to support learning that leads to a deeper understanding of subject matter and of self, students need chance to experience important conceptual shifts (Kreber, 2014). Hence authentic tasks have the opportunity to positively influence students' perceptions of themselves as potential change agents, as well developing their sense of becoming a member of a discipline community with important disciplinary capacities, helping them feel more like, for example, an historian or an engineer (Sambell and McDowell 2013).

So we set about to help staff working under immense pressure to come up with workable alternatives by proposing a systematic approach which we have termed the 'task generator', whereby each aspect of the assessment design is categorised according to function, closely linked to their descriptors in course documentation. Hence busy staff can use similar assignments year on year without a wholesale redesign, by, for example, changing the scenario/plausible context and reusing the same tasks, or keeping the scenario and modifying the tasks.

TAKING A 6-STAGE STEP-BY-STEP APPROACH TO DESIGNING MORE AUTHENTIC ASSESSMENTS

We outlined our systematic approach to designing more authentic and rounded assessment in **'Writing better assignments in the Post-Covid 19 era: approaches to good task design'** https://sally-brown.net/kay-sambell-and-sally-brown-covid-19 -assessment-collection/ 17th August. The second part of the chapter will draw on this work to reprise our six-stage approach to designing authentic assignments to enable curriculum designers to do so systematically and efficiently. We argue that if designers start with the **learning outcomes,** (see Chapter 3 in Brown, 2015) and if they are well written, they are likely to contain one or more powerful, driving **verbs** at their centre to direct student effort, such as 'interpret', 'research and review', 'set up and calibrate', 'evaluate' and 'compile'.

In our approach, this is then followed by identifying the **object of the verb** i.e. what is done to provide a focus for action as illustrated in Table 1 below. Appropriate **outcomes/evidence of achievement** are then needed to demonstrate confidence that the outcome has been achieved.

Students can then be helped to understand what is required of them by providing **modifiers/ developments/ range statements** to provide guidance about the scale and scope of what is required, so they can gauge the amount of work they need to do to do justice to themselves.

Table 1. Illustrative examples of verbs/objects/outcomes/ modifiers

Verb/ educational outcome	What? i.e. object	Outcome/ evidence of achievement	Modifiers/ developments/ range statements
Interpret	complex and sometimes incomplete or conflicting data	compile a summary meaningful for experts and laypersons	leading to a viable action plan for a team to implement.
Review	data from a variety of sources	produce an executive summary	for a specific audience of employers
Set up	specialised equipment appropriately	draw up a 'quick guide' for peers	to enable them to use it safely and appropriately
Evaluate	three proposed solutions to a problem	propose a further two of your own	with suggestions about what might work best
Compile	contingency plans for a professional environment	produce disaster recovery in case of a serious emergency	leading to mitigations and remediation

To make for a well-rounded assignment, this should be prefaced with detail around a **plausible** subject or professional **context** or a **realistic scenario** relevant to the subject area/ discipline/ course to support a student's sense of the relevance of the assessment task. These plausible scenarios and context descriptors can really bring assignments to life for students and help them to appreciate how learning on the course can help them as well-rounded citizens and employable graduates to make sense of the knowledge and capabilities they are acquiring during the course of their learning programmes.

Table 2. Our six-stage approach to designing authentic assessment task

1	Start with consulting or designing the learning outcomes.	This approach is premised around a constructively-aligned curriculum design methodology.
2	Identify powerful, driving verbs at their centre to direct student effort, such as 'interpret', 'research and review', 'set up and calibrate', 'evaluate' and 'compile'.	It's best to avoid vague verbs like 'understand' which are difficult to evidence.
3	Consider the object of the verb i.e. what students do which provides a focus for action e.g. produce a digital learning pack, or provide a professional opinion in the form of a letter with appendices.	Here the assessment designer should aim to draw on a wide range of relevant activities that are fit-for-purpose.
4	Indicate what outcomes/evidence of achievement you require so you could be confident the outcome has been achieved.	These activities then dictate what the student assignment tasks for formative and summative assessment should be.
5	Wrap the task around with detail concerning the subject or professional context/plausible scenario relevant to the subject area/ discipline/ course to bring the assignment to life.	Professional contexts/ plausible scenarios should be drafted to give students enough detail to make the task meaningful, without overwhelming students with detail.
6	Complete it with modifiers/developments/ range statements to guide the students about the scale and scope of what is required of them.	These indicators will let students know, for example, how long the podcast should be, approximately how many bullet points the summary should contain, how many words overall the written assignment should contain. This guidance is especially important for first year students with little experience of HE assessment.

The many proponents who have adopted this kind of approach testify to the benefits of authentic assessment in terms of bringing about more engaged and interactive learning environments. Effective task designs set up helpful possibilities for productive learning processes. They encourage students to spend time and ongoing effort on educationally-purposeful activities (Kuh, 2001) and pave the way for engagement with feedback processes through interaction, classroom dialogue and activity, and ongoing self-evaluation (Sambell et al, 2013; Carless, 2015). Furthermore, getting students involved in their own or each other's assessment through peer discussions, commentary and review, so that gauging the quality of their own work doesn't simply rely on markers' inputs, but instead foregrounds internal feedback (Nicol, 2021).

While it might at first sight look as if this approach to assessment might be more time consuming, the **principal effort is front-loaded**, with year-on year benefits since new assignments can be readily created by changing the plausible context/scenario and retaining the tasks, or re-using the contexts/ scenarios and providing new accompanying tasks.

EXAMPLES

To illustrate our approach, we have collected more than 50 **worked examples** of assignments using this approach as exemplified in our compendia of examples at https://sally-brown.net/kay-sambell-and-sally-brown-covid-19 -assessment-collection/ on 19th March, 3rd May, 9th June, 18 August and 17 November 2021.

These demonstrate how our methodology can be applied to numerous professional, applied and other disciplines at various levels and we are very grateful to their international originators for allowing us to share their original and creative takes on our approach.

Here are three lightly fictionalised examples of this approach in action: note how in each case the verbs in the learning outcomes can lead directly into active and engaging tasks, which involve using classroom and independent learning applied to realistic contexts and plausible scenarios. Note how the tasks inter-relate and build on one another: they can also explicitly involve an element of reflection or similar, which, suitably framed, explicitly helps students recognise their own role in, say, the learning, evaluative or feedback processes which underpin effective AfL designs. These self-contained tasks are often time/word limited to ensure manageability of marking.

Example 1: thanks to Aoife O'Brien of Galway-Mayo Institute of Technology, Ireland

Aoife replaced a traditional paper and pen task and MCQ exam with a descriptive statistics task:

Context:

Students are surveyed regularly for feedback on the course during its delivery. Surveys were used more frequently during the academic year 2020/2021 as the course was delivered entirely online for the first time due to the pandemic. Additionally, normal educational data such as assessment results, online quiz responses, and attendance information is recorded for the students. This data was anonymised, cleaned, and presented to students in 10 Excel worksheets for analysis.

Tasks:

The students work in groups of 4 on the following:

- **Analyse** the data presenting the appropriate descriptive statistics you learned about in the module (up to 300 words). Students should take note of the type of data which is presented and what statistics or summary analysis is appropriate based on the type of variable.
- Format the descriptive statistics in Excel to ensure ease of interpretation.
- **Analyse** and **interpret** the statistics to create a profile of the students themselves based around a particular theme or story, with commentary (500 words).
- **Create** appropriate figures, graphs, and/or tables in Excel, based on the statistics of interest.
- **Create** an A1 poster in PowerPoint to present the information you have found. The poster must have a clear theme, contain images, facts, figures, and text. An element of fun is encouraged.

Example 2: thanks to Gayle Blackburn, University of Sunderland.

On a BA (Hons) Childhood Studies degree Gayle replaced a traditional essay question with a scenario-based task:

Authentic Assessment Example:

As part of your development as an Early Years graduate practitioner, you are **asked to plan, design, produce** and **implement** two resources to support child development, with a clear rationale to explain how each resource supports young children's development and learning in relation to current theory, policy and practice. For your assessment you will:

- **Design and produce two resources** to support children's learning and development and use them in your placement with young children, which should examine the interrelationship between theory, policy and practice.
- **Present your resources to your peers and academic tutor** in a small group (10 minutes) explaining the processes involved with the design of your resource, which learning and development strategies you engaged with during planning, making and implementing these resources. For example, explain what are the links you make to EYFS, consider your choice of materials and why you have used them, as well as the extent to which your resources are inclusive, discuss health and safety considerations, reflect on the success of your implementation, and consider how you will adapt them for future use. Discuss whether the children engaged well with the resources and the extent to which they be used as part of continuous provision. Your peers will be encouraged to ask you questions on this to enable you to have a reflective and professional dialogue on your resources and their implementation.
- **Write a 200-word reflection** about your own learning during fieldwork visits and from comments on your presentation.

Example 3: thanks to Thomas Broderick, Munster Technological University, Ireland.

Thomas replaced a traditional exam/essay question with a scenario-based task:

Context: Envisage that you are working on placement in a local residential home with persons with disability and considering the impacts of Covid, you have been asked to introduce some new health initiatives to support residents in their overall wellness.

Tasks:

1. **Research** what the wellness needs of service-users are, and what kinds of health initiatives are most appropriate to support their wellness at this time. Present this as a set of up to ten bullet points, with a list on one side of A4 of your references (texts, leaflets, websites etc).
2. **Prepare** a plan to implement three health initiatives, one each to support physical, social and occupational/vocational needs of the service user. (One side of A4 for each initiative).
3. **Present** in the form of a table what you think are the principal benefits of the initiatives you are proposing, and any problems or pitfalls you could envisage in implementing each of these.
4. **Provide** a rationale for the recommendations you are making written in the form of an email (up to 300 words) for your busy line manager.
5. In your reflective diary, **comment** on what you have most learned from this assignment and **note** what insights you have developed from undertaking this assignment that you can carry forward into your future working life.

CONCLUSION

Authentic assessments of the kinds described here involve students in tasks they are likely to actually care about beyond merely achieving a mark, thereby ensuring that they can discern relevance to their personal development and their future selves as well as to their employment by applying, in a range of plausible or meaningful contexts, the knowledge, skills and attributes they have worked hard to gain and develop while studying with us, which tends to be both efficacious and fulfilling.

Our multiple examples from diverse subject areas and nations demonstrate that this approach is widely applicable in higher education institutions at different levels: the colleagues who have collaborated with us in collating them are enthusiastic about an approach which encourages students to expend effort on relevant and meaningful activities which reinforce how learning gained through advanced study can be put to work in practical and applied contexts.

Our approach demonstrably builds on the notion that authentic task designs are amongst the most powerful means we have of fostering genuine, worthwhile learning for the longer term, and assumes that the goal of assessment for learning is primarily to promote the development of **capabilities** that transfer effectively from the university to individual's future worlds and lives. We argue that thus assessment activities can be readily and compassionately be designed to be:

- **Cognitively challenging,** in than they foster the development of high order knowledge, capabilities and including synthesis, application, and integration leading to 'authentic achievement' rather than merely demonstrating lower order skills such as recall and memorisation, while being engaging and purposeful, catalysing deep not surface approaches to learning;
- Capable of fostering the **development of evaluative judgment,** that is the ability to make **informed decisions** and gauge the quality of own and others' work, and leading, particularly through the use of reflective elements, leading to enhanced self-regulation;
- **Realistic,** in that tasks represent and prepare students for the reality of their lives as graduates of their discipline as well as advanced concepts of selfhood.

All this has been proved possible under the challenges of unprecedented pandemic circumstances where creative solutions had to be achieved rapidly in crisis conditions. What for some were at first recognised as being workarounds to solve a particular problem have now been recognised to have such transformative potential to integrate learning within assessment tasks, that they have been adopted permanently. These not only add resilience to any future fragile conditions, but also add significantly to student learning to the extent that returning to former, less powerful and less enabling approaches to assessment should be unthinkable. We must change Higher Education assessment for good.

REFERENCES

Archbald, D. A., & Newmann, F. M. (1988). *Beyond standardized testing: Assessing authentic academic achievement in the secondary school*. National Association of Secondary School Principals.

Arnold, L. (2019). Advancing Authentic Assessment Practice. *Arise lecture*. Edinburgh Napier University. https://lydia-arnold.com/2019/11/27/edinburgh-napier-authentic-assessment-and-action-research/

Ashford-Rowe, K., Herrington, J., & Brown, C. (2014). Establishing the critical elements that determine authentic assessment. *Assessment and Evaluation in Higher Education, 39*(2), 205–222. doi:10.1080/02602938.2013.819566

Ashwin, P. (2020). *Transforming university education: a manifesto.* Bloomsbury Publishing. doi:10.5040/9781350157279

Barrie, S. C. (2006). Understanding what we mean by the generic attributes of graduates. *Higher Education, 51*(2), 215–241. doi:10.100710734-004-6384-7

Birenbaum, M. (1996). Assessment 2000: Towards a pluralistic approach to assessment. In *Alternatives in assessment of achievements, learning processes and prior knowledge* (pp. 3–29). Springer. doi:10.1007/978-94-011-0657-3_1

Boud, D. (2000). Sustainable assessment: Rethinking assessment for the learning society. *Studies in Continuing Education, 22*(2), 151–167. doi:10.1080/713695728

Boud, D., & Falchikov, N. (2007). Introduction: Assessment for the longer term. In Rethinking assessment in higher education (pp. 13-23). Routledge.

Boud, D., & Soler, R. (2016). Sustainable assessment revisited. *Assessment and Evaluation in Higher Education, 41*(3), 400–413. doi:10.1080/02602938.2015.1018133

Brown, S. (2015). *Learning, teaching and assessment in higher education: global perspectives.* Macmillan International Higher Education. doi:10.1007/978-1-137-39667-9

Brown, S. (2019). Using assessment and feedback to empower students and enhance their learning. In C. Bryan & K. Clegg (Eds.), *Innovative Assessment in Higher Education* (2nd ed., pp. 50–63). Routledge. doi:10.4324/9780429506857-5

Brown, S., & Knight, P. (1994). *Assessing learners in higher education.* Routledge.

Brown, S., & Sambell, K. (2020). *The Covid Collection.* Sally Brown. https://sally-brown.net/kay-sambell-and-sally-brown-covid-19-assessment-collection/

Carless, D. (2015). Exploring learning-oriented assessment processes. *Higher Education, 69*(6), 963–976. doi:10.100710734-014-9816-z

Cumming, J., & Maxwell, G. S. (1999). Contextualising authentic assessment. *Assessment in Education: Principles, Policy and Practice, 6*(2), 177–194. doi:10.1080/09695949992865

Davison, G. (2011). *Investigating the relationships between authentic assessment and the development of learner autonomy.* University of Northumbria at Newcastle.

Entwistle, N. J., & Entwistle, A. (1991). Contrasting forms of understanding for degree examinations: The student experience and its implications. *Higher Education, 22*(3), 205–227. doi:10.1007/BF00132288

Fox, J. (2008). Alternative assessment. Encyclopedia of language and education, 7, 97-108.

Gulikers, J. T., Bastiaens, T. J., & Kirschner, P. A. (2004). A five-dimensional framework for authentic assessment. *Educational Technology Research and Development, 52*(3), 67–86. doi:10.1007/BF02504676

Gulikers, J. T., Bastiaens, T. J., Kirschner, P. A., & Kester, L. (2008). Authenticity is in the eye of the beholder: Student and teacher perceptions of assessment authenticity. *Journal of Vocational Education and Training*, *60*(4), 401–412. doi:10.1080/13636820802591830

Kreber, C. (2013). *Authenticity in and through teaching in higher education: The transformative potential of the scholarship of teaching*. Routledge. doi:10.4324/9780203072301

Kreber, C. (2014). Rationalising the nature of 'graduateness' through philosophical accounts of authenticity. *Teaching in Higher Education*, *19*(1), 90–100. doi:10.1080/13562517.2013.860114

Kreber, C., Wardley, L., Leviten-Reid, C., & MacPherson, S. (2021). Community-engaged learning in business schools to effect social change: a capabilities perspective. In *Handbook of Teaching and Learning at Business Schools*. Edward Elgar Publishing.

Kuh, G. D. (2001). The National Survey of Student Engagement: Conceptual framework and overview of psychometric properties. *Center of Inquiry*.

Lund, J. (1997). Authentic assessment: Its development and applications. *Journal of Physical Education, Recreation and Dance*, *68*(7), 25–28. doi:10.1080/07303084.1997.10604979

McArthur, J. (2021). *For assessment to count as authentic it must mean something to students*. WONKHE.

McCune, V., & Hounsell, D. (2005). The development of students' ways of thinking and practising in three final-year biology courses. *Higher Education*, *49*(3), 255–289. doi:10.100710734-004-6666-0

Mueller, J. (2006). *Authentic assessment toolbox*. Noctrl.

National Forum for the Enhancement of Teaching and Learning in Higher Education. (2017). Authentic Assessment in Irish Higher education, Dublin: National Forum for the Enhancement of Teaching and Learning in Higher Education. *Forum Insights*. https://www.teaching and learning.ie/publication/authentic-assessment-in-irish-higher-education/NF-2017-Authentic-Assessment-in-Irish-Higher-Education.pdf (teachingandlearning.ie)

Nicol, D. (2021). The power of internal feedback: Exploiting natural comparison processes. *Assessment and Evaluation in Higher Education*, *46*(5), 756–778. doi:10.1080/02602938.2020.1823314

O'Neill, G. (2019). *Authentic assessment: concept, continuum and contested*. Masterclass presented at the Assessment in Higher Education Conference, Manchester. http://tiny.url.com/AHE2019

Reimann, N., Sambell, K., Sadler, I., & Kreber, C. (2021). Addressing the challenges of assessment and feedback in business schools: developing assessment practices which support learning. In *Handbook of Teaching and Learning at Business Schools*. Edward Elgar Publishing.

Renwick, K., Selkrig, M., Manathunga, C., & Keamy, R. K. (2020). Community engagement is…: Revisiting Boyer's model of scholarship. *Higher Education Research and Development*, *39*(6), 1232–1246. doi:10.1080/07294360.2020.1712680

Sambell, K., & McDowell, L. (1998). The construction of the hidden curriculum: Messages and meanings in the assessment of student learning. *Assessment and Evaluation in Higher Education, 23*(4), 391–402. doi:10.1080/0260293980230406

Sambell, K., McDowell, L., & Brown, S. (1997). "But is it fair?": An exploratory study of student perceptions of the consequential validity of assessment. *Studies in Educational Evaluation, 23*(4), 349–371. doi:10.1016/S0191-491X(97)86215-3

Sambell, K., McDowell, L., & Montgomery, C. (2013). *Assessment for learning in higher education.* Routledge.

Sokhanvar, Z., Salehi, K., & Sokhanvar, F. (2021). Advantages of authentic assessment for improving the learning experience and employability skills of higher education students: A systematic literature review. *Studies in Educational Evaluation, 70*, 101030. doi:10.1016/j.stueduc.2021.101030

Tai, J., Ajjawi, R., Boud, D., Dawson, P., & Panadero, E. (2018). Developing evaluative judgement: Enabling students to make decisions about the quality of work. *Higher Education, 76*(3), 467–481. doi:10.100710734-017-0220-3

Torrance, H. (1995). *Evaluating authentic assessment.* Open University Press.

Villarroel, V., Bloxham, S., Bruna, D., Bruna, C., & Herrera-Seda, C. (2018). Authentic assessment: Creating a blueprint for course design. *Assessment and Evaluation in Higher Education, 43*(5), 840–854. doi:10.1080/02602938.2017.1412396

Wald, N., & Harland, T. (2017). A framework for authenticity in designing a research-based curriculum. *Teaching in Higher Education, 22*(7), 751–765. doi:10.1080/13562517.2017.1289509

Wiggins, G. (1990). The case for authentic assessment. *Practical Assessment, Research and Evaluation, 2*(1), 2.

Winstone, N., & Carless, D. (2019). *Designing effective feedback processes in higher education: A learning-focused approach.* Routledge. doi:10.4324/9781351115940

Wolf, D. P. (1993). *Assessment as an episode of teaming. Construction Versus Choice in Cognitive Measurement.* Lawrence Erlbaum Associates.

Chapter 9
The Assessment of Emotional Education in the Training of Social Educators:
A Mixed Method Research

Juan Lirio Castro
University of Castilla-La Mancha, Spain

Luis Medina Bernáldez
Social Services of Mocejón City Council, Spain

Sergio J Fernández Ortega
(iD) https://orcid.org/0000-0003-3911-8308
Complutense University of Madrid, Spain

Esther Portal Martínez
(iD) https://orcid.org/0000-0002-0958-4095
University of Castilla-La Mancha, Spain

ABSTRACT

In this chapter the authors try to delve into the relationship between emotional education and social education in the context of higher education. To do this, the theoretical framework has been developed by referring to the interest of emotional education, as well as the importance of emotional competencies, within the educational work of the 21st century. In this way, the research carried out to know this relationship more in depth is justified, on the one hand, contemplating the perceptions of students and teachers from a questionnaire that raises the perceptions about the importance of this relationship and, on the other hand, identifying the content on education and emotional management in the educational programs of bachelor's degrees in social education at the Spanish universities, highlighting the importance of competencies assessment. The results are discussed with other studies and contributions on emotional education in socio-educational intervention, thus achieving the aims of the research.

DOI: 10.4018/978-1-6684-3537-3.ch009

INTRODUCTION

Emotional competencies are considered important for the success of socio-educational interventions (López, 2007). Thus, there are several university training programs for bachelor's degrees in social education where courses are taught and/or competencies related to emotional intelligence, emotional competencies or emotional education are established.

In addition, there are some works on the emotional management of social education professionals in the field of childhood protection (Lirio & Medina, 2021) where relevant aspects for the emotional management of this professional profile are investigated.

The study of emotions has a longer scope for children, adolescents and young people (Trianes et al., 2003), but it is also of interest to adults and the elderly (López et al., 2008). In this way, information in this social education area of intervention can be found, as in the case of gerontology, where it is determined in a study that the elderly of a residence consider emotional management necessary for both their part and the workers who take care of them (Lirio et al., 2020).

Specifically, this study goes in two directions. On one hand, it shows the considerations made by the students and part of the teaching team of the Bachelor's Degree in Social Education of the Faculty of Social Sciences of Talavera de la Reina, at the University of Castilla-La Mancha, on the emotional management of the social educator. It is confirmed the influence of emotions in the work of the social educator, and the need to develop emotional management and training in this regard.

On the other hand, the analysis of the specific courses, the competences of the degrees and the way in which it is evaluated makes it clear that the contents related to education and emotional management are not yet integrated in a concrete way in most social education programs, although when it is done through specific courses, in most cases, it is used an assessment that shows evidence of the learning of competences.

BACKGROUND: RELATION BETWEEN EMOTIONAL EDUCATION AND SOCIAL EDUCATION

Emotional education is understood, according to Bisquerra (2005), as an educational process that proposes the development of emotions as a means to ensure that the individual is trained to better face the challenges of his life, thus increasing his personal and social well-being.

In addition, emotional education has among its objectives the development of emotional competencies, which are more important than cognitive ones in the development of tasks within a profession because they allow optimizing the potential of the individual (Goleman, 2011).

This educational conception in which emotion is included responds to the challenges of education for the 21st century that are indicated in Delors Report (1996), since two of the four pillars for education are learning to be, to develop one's personality and to be able to act with growing autonomy, judgment and personal responsibility; and learning to live together, by developing an understanding of other people and an appreciation of interdependence, aspects that are linked to emotional and integral development (Bisquerra et al., 2015).

Social education, understood as a profession of a pedagogical nature that enables the incorporation of social networks by the subject of education and its social and cultural promotion (ASEDES, 2007), is in a position to make contributions in relation to emotional competences, which favor social adaptation, communicative capacity and conflict solving of individuals (Bisquerra, 2005). These competencies are at the center of socio-educational action (López, 2017) and influence their success (Rosa et al., 2015).

For Bravo and Del Valle (2009), is there and approached to conflict solving in the field of childhood and adolescence and, especially, in the childhood protection centers within the residential care program. In these centers, social educators must develop emotional education programs and projects (Extremera & Fernández-Berrocal, 2015).

Emotional education, in relation to conflict, proposes an emotional regulation understanding the interrelation between emotion and conflict, as well as emotional regulation and management strategies to face the conflict in a cognitive and affective way (Bisquerra et al. 2015).

A proposal for conflict resolution is the Interpersonal Emotional Management Model (Redorta et al., 2006) where a type of management is established for the emotions that mostly appear in a conflict.

Another field of action of social education is the family (Gómez, 2003; Ronda-Ortín, 2012), which is the first place of development of emotional education, based on parental style. In this regard, it is necessary to implement emotional education programs for parents that enable them to achieve emotional management from pregnancy, since the baby can suffer consequences from prenatal levels as a result of the anxiety or stress that the mother may suffer. Emotional education allows positive emotions, such as happiness or calm, to be experienced in the family and provides benefits for personal and social well-being (Bisquerra et al., 2015).

The *Manual for the social educator* (Costa & Méndez, 1996) affirms that the influence of the social educator on the emotions of the subjects of education allows the development of accurate intervention in specific situations. This aspect is shared by social education professionals who participated in a study on their management of emotions in the field of childhood protection (Lirio & Medina, 2021).

The processes of identification and emotional regulation carried out by the educator is an influential factor in the learning process and in the health of the learner (Martínez-Otero, 2007; Cabello et al., 2010; Barnés, 2017). However, it has been shown in the research by Cameselle (2017) that social educators under study require an improvement in the development of emotional competencies.

The relevance of this study appears because of the scarce research on the role of emotions in education (Puertas et al., 2018) and the conclusions drawn from the study of emotional management of social education professionals (Lirio & Medina, 2021), where it is considered relevant to deepen the vision of university students and professors, as well as the training given in the bachelor's degrees in social education, since emotional management by social educators and their training in this regard are necessary, considering its utility for socio-educational work.

But it is not only important that content related to education and emotional management be taught, but also the assessment that is made of its acquisition by students, that is, the assessment (Fernández, 2011).

In this way, it is interesting to assess the learning of these contents not only from a cognitive approach, but also from a capabilities approach, that is, it is necessary to identify whether students have acquired the abilities to implement these emotional competencies in their future socio-educational interventions.

Thus, we find the approach to learning by competencies, not only in the school stages, but also in the university environment, which come to propose a new way of teaching and learning. suitable when the purpose is to train future professionals.

One of the aspects that must be collected in the planning of the didactic process from a competences approach is the evaluation modality that is going to be implemented (Tardif, 2003), as well as the instruments that are going to be used (Moreno, 2012), since the information that can be collected about the learning carried out will depend on this.

In recent years, one of the most widely used instruments is the self-report, although it has shown that it is not enough to assess the acquisition of emotional competences (Bisquerra et al., 2006) due to the subjective burden it entails, therefore it is necessary to enrich this tool with other instruments, which can start from observation questionnaires applied by professors or other students, or other more innovative instruments, such as the development of projects, problems, case studies, simulations or rubrics, among others (Moreno, 2007), which try to generate educational situations to be observed where competencies may be developed.

MAIN FOCUS OF THE CHAPTER

Knowing More About the Importance of Emotions in Social Education Practice

Due to the interest that a better understanding of the influence of emotional education on social education may arouse, it has been thought as necessary to collect data about the situation, deepening the analysis of the contents on education and emotional management at the university, as well as the perception of students and professors on the subject. This information will lead to being able to affirm in a certain way if social education needs the contents of the emotional education to be able to develop its work.

To reach that, research has been developed. The research design chosen has been the mixed cross-sectional and concurrent method (Creswell, 2009). Two studies are included in this chapter, one of a quantitative type, through which two agents are investigated: students and university professors; and a qualitative study, which analyzes the offer of emotional education training in the study programs of the bachelor's degrees in Social Education at Spanish universities.

The quantitative study that is presented has as study population the students and teaching staff of the Degree in Social Education at the Faculty of Social Sciences of Talavera de la Reina of the University of Castilla-La Mancha. This empirical study consists of a total sample of forty-eight students and five professors.

The general objective is to investigate the importance that students and professors of this Bachelor's Degree give to emotions in the profession of Social Education. Therefore, the following specific aims are established:

- To know the perception that social education students experience about emotions.
- To know the perception that social education professors experience about emotions.
- To identify the training in emotional education in the bachelor's degrees of social education.

The data collection technique chosen in the case of the quantitative study was the questionnaire. The questionnaires were prepared *ad hoc*, and are made up of twelve questions for professors and sixteen questions for students, being prepared with a Likert-type scale. At the first part of the questionnaire, the questions asked are of a sociodemographic nature: age, sex, marital status… and at the second part, the questions inquiry about the emotions experienced by students, the influence of emotions on the work of the social education professional, the emotional impact that exists on that professional, the training in emotional education received in the Bachelor's Degree and the need they think the emotional management has on the social educator work.

Table 1. Age of students and professors

	Age	Percentage
Students	Under 18 years	2.1%
	18-20 years	25%
	21-23 years	52.1%
	24-26 years	14.6%
	27-30 years	2.1%
Professors	31-35 years	4.2%
	36-40 years	40%
	41-45 years	20%
	46-50 years	20%

Source: (Own elaboration, 2021)

The data was collected between May, the 11th and June, the 2nd of 2020, and was analyzed in a descriptive procedure, for which *Google Forms* tool was used, exposing tables and applying percentages for their interpretation.

The qualitative study, for its part, aims to inquiry about the training in emotional education that is developed in the bachelor's degrees of social education in Spain. Thus, three specific aims were established:

- To identify the courses of the bachelor's degrees that contain education and emotional management content.
- To identify the competencies of the bachelor's degrees related to education and emotional management.
- To locate the assessment system proposals related to the emotional education and/or management contents of the degree courses.

The data collection technique used was a grid prepared for this purpose, in which the information given by the bachelor's degrees programs is indicated and which is then subjected to a content analysis.

This grid includes the courses and competences, as well as the evaluation systems indicated related to emotional education and/or management in the courses of these bachelor's degrees.

RESEARCH RESULTS

Emotional Education Is Important in Socio-Educational Practice

The quantitative study collects information about sociodemographic data addressed in the first seven questions for the students and in the first four questions for professors.

Regarding age, as can be seen in Table 1, the students are mainly between 21 and 23 years old, 52.1%, while 25% are between 18 and 20 years old. As for professors, 40% are between 36 and 40 years old.

Regarding the sex of the students surveyed, 91.7% are women and 8.3% are men, while the professors are 60% men and 40% women (Table 2).

Table 2. Sex of students and professors

	Sex	Percentage
Students	Men	8.3%
	Women	91.7%
Professors	Men	60%
	Women	40%

Source: (Own elaboration, 2021)

Table 3. Marital status of students and professors

	Marital Status	Percentage
Students	Married/Partner	35.4%
	Single	64.6%
Professors	Married/Partner	40%
	Separated/Divorced	40%
	Single	20%

Source: (Own elaboration, 2021)

Of these, Table 3 shows that 64.6% of the students are single and 35.4% are married or with a partner. In the case of professors, 40% are married or with a partner, another 40% are separated or divorced and 20% are single.

Regarding the place of residence of the students, 65.9% share an apartment, while 34.1% reside at a family home (Table 4).

Table 4. Residence status of students

Residence Status	Percentage
Family residence	34.1%
Sharing residence	65.9%

Source: (Own elaboration, 2021)

Regarding the level in which the students of the Bachelor's Degree in Social Education are enrolled, 22.9% are on the first level, 27.1% belong to the second level, 16.7% are on the third level and 33.3% are on the fourth level (Table 5).

Regarding participation in training on emotional education, it is observed in Table 6, that most of them have not participated in training in this regard (57.4%), although in some cases where it is verified that they have participated in courses (21.3%) and seminars (19.1%), among others. This question has also been asked to the professors, finding that 60% have not participated in training in emotional education. Even so, it is observed that the modalities in which they have participated are conferences in 40%, seminars in 20%, courses for 20% and working days in another 20%.

Table 5. Social education bachelor's degree level of students

Bachelor's degree Level	Percentage
First level	22.9%
Second level	27.1%
Third level	16.7%
Fourth level	33.3%

Source: (Own elaboration, 2021)

Table 6. Emotional education training of students and professors

	Emotional Education Training	Percentage
Students	Workshop	14.9%
	Courses	21.3%
	Conferences	2.1%
	Seminars	19.1%
	Working days	8.5%
	None	57.4%
Professors	Courses	20%
	Conferences	40%
	Seminars	20%
	Working days	20%
	None	60%

Source: (Own elaboration, 2021)

To find out information related to leisure and spare time activities of the students, a question was asked with the possibility of multiple answers. Thus, among others, 89.6% consist of social relationships, 68.8% go for a walk and 66.7% read (Table 7).

After completing the socio-demographic questions, the information is collected regarding the content and object of study, that is, emotions and their influence.

Thus, about the emotions that they have felt most frequently studying social education (question with the possibility of multiple answers), it is found that 79.2% have felt joy, 58.3% happiness, 54.2% fear, 45.8% sadness, 39.6% love and, to a lesser extent, it is found anger, guilt, empathy, helplessness, frustration and satisfaction (Table 8).

With the interest of knowing the influence of emotions in socio-educational practice, it is collected that 35.4% of the students agree and 58.3% totally agree. As for the professors, they mostly agree (40%) and totally agree (40%) (Table 9).

The influence on the socio-educational work exerted by the emotions experienced by social educators is a statement which students, mostly, totally agree, being this choice the one marked by 52.1%, while another 31.3% just agree. In the case of professors, it is observed that 40% totally agree and another 40% agree, as shown in Table 10.

Table 7. Leisure and spare time activities of students

Leisure and spare time activities	Percentage
Crafting	18.8%
Taking a walk	68.8%
Watching TV	60.4%
Playing games	16.7%
Reading	66.7%
Working in the field	4.2%
Trips and excursions	47.9%
Social relationships	89.6%
Playing sports	52.1%
Cultural activities	20.8%
Drawing	2.1%
Religious practices	2.1%

Source: (Own elaboration, 2021)

Regarding the emotions of the learners, and referring to the affectation that they have in the socio-educational practice carried out by social educators, 6.4% of the students have shown to disagree, 8.5% are undecided, 34% agree and 51.1% totally agree. Professors, for their part, show that they agree in 40% and totally agree in 60% (Table 11).

Regarding the need to carry out emotional management working as a social educator, 83% of the students totally agree, while professors totally agree in 40% and agree in another 40%, as can be seen in Table 12.

Table 8. Emotions felt by students during the program

Felt Emotions	Percentage
Guilt	8.3%
Sadness	45.8%
Fear	54.2%
Anger	27.1%
Happiness	58.3%
Joy	79.2%
Love	39.6%
Empathy	2.1%
Helplessness	2.1%
Frustration	2.1%
Satisfaction	2.1%

Source: (Own elaboration, 2021)

Table 9. Level of agreement of students and professors on emotions influence in socio-educational practice

	Level of agreement	Percentage
Students	Disagree	2.1%
	Undecided	4.2%
	Agree	35.4%
	Totally agree	58.3%
Professors	Undecided	20%
	Agree	40%
	Totally agree	40%

Source: (Own elaboration, 2021)

Table 10. Level of agreement of students and professors on the influence of emotions experienced by social educators on the professional practice

	Level of agreement	Percentage
Students	Disagree	4.2%
	Undecided	12.5%
	Agree	31.3%
	Totally agree	52.1%
Professors	Undecided	20%
	Agree	40%
	Totally agree	40%

Source: (Own elaboration, 2021)

Regarding the need to receive training in emotional education, 83.3% of the students fully agree, 16.7% agree and 40% of the professors fully agree, with 20% agree and 40% disagree with this statement (Table 13).

Table 11. Level of agreement of students and professors on the influence of emotions experienced by learners on the professional practice

	Level of agreement	Percentage
Students	Disagree	6.4%
	Undecided	8.5%
	Agree	34%
	Totally agree	51.1%
Professors	Agree	40%
	Totally agree	60%

Source: (Own elaboration, 2021)

Table 12. Level of agreement of students and professors on the needing of emotional management

	Level of agreement	Percentage
Students	Undecided	2.1%
	Agree	14.9%
	Totally agree	83%
Professors	Disagree	20%
	Agree	40%
	Totally agree	40%

Source: (Own elaboration, 2021)

Table 13. Level of agreement of students and professors on the needing of emotional education training

	Agreement	Percentage
Students	Agree	16.7%
	Totally agree	83.3%
Professors	Disagree	40%
	Agree	20%
	Totally agree	40%

Source: (Own elaboration, 2021)

Regarding the training in emotional education that they have received in the Bachelor's Degree, it is observed in Table 14 that 39.6% of the students affirm not having received such training, 52.1% consider it insufficient, 4.2% is sufficient, 2.1% believe that they have received a lot of training and another 2.1% consider that it is too much. In relation to professors, 60% think that the training in this regard is none, being 20% those who think that it is insufficient and another 20% that consider that it is a lot.

Table 14. Perception of students and professors of the emotional education received training

	Perception	Percentage
Students	None	39.6%
	Insufficient	52.1%
	Enough	4.2%
	A lot	2.1%
	Too much	2.1%
Professors	None	60%
	Insufficient	20%
	A lot	20%

Source: (Own elaboration, 2021)

Table 15. Perception of students and professors of the emotional impact in social educators

	Perception	Percentage
Students	Undecided	16.7%
	Agree	29.2%
	Totally agree	54.2%
	Totally disagree	20%
Professors	Undecided	40%
	Agree	20%
	Totally agree	20%

Source: (Own elaboration, 2021)

Regarding the existence of emotional impact for the Social Education professional, 16.7% of the students are undecided, 29.2% agree and 54.2% fully agree. For professors, 20% totally disagree, 40% are undecided, 20% agree and another 20% affirm they totally agree (Table 15).

Finally, they are asked to indicate how they would complete the training in emotional education of social educators, on which students agree 83.3% of the times in introducing an emotional education course in the program, 37.5% propose complementary training through free courses, summer courses, talks, etc., 2.1% consider that it would be through master and/or postgraduate programs and in 39.6% they would complete the training with the inclusion of this topic in the Practicum seminars and in the End-of-Degree Projects. Regarding professors, 60% indicate that they would choose complementary training, 20% consider master and/or postgraduate programs, 40% would decide to include the topic in the Practicum seminars and/or in the End-of-Degree Projects and another 20% would choose it to be transversal to the program (Table 16).

Table 16. Proposals of students and professors of emotional education training actions for social educators

	Proposals	Percentage
Students	To introduce a course of emotional education in the degree	83.3%
	Complementary training: free courses, summer courses, talks, etc.	37.5%
	Master and/or postgraduate programs	2.1%
	Inclusion of the topic in the Practicum seminars and/or in the End-of-Degree Projects	39.6%
Professors	Complementary training: free courses, summer courses, talks, etc.	60%
	Master and/or postgraduate programs	20%
	Inclusion of the topic in the Practicum seminars and/or in the End-of-Degree Projects	40%
	Transversal to all subjects	20%

Source: (Own elaboration, 2021)

Once the quantitative study was finished, information from the study programs of the different universities where the bachelor's degree in social education is offered was collected and analyzed, with the intention of knowing the consideration that these universities give to emotional education.

For this, ir has been indicated the courses offered with contents on emotional education and/or management, the competences that refer to the capacity related to emotional education that this professional must possess, and, finally, the evaluation system that is indicated. All this information was fed into a grid designed for this purpose, summarized in the following table (table 17).

Table 17. Emotional education at Spanish Campus or University Centers

Campus or University Center	Course, competences and evaluation on emotional education and management.
University of Almería	Neither courses nor related competences are collected.
University of Granada	Course "Social psychology of conflict and resolution techniques: negotiation and mediation". No related competences are collected. Competencies assessment.
University of Málaga	Neither courses nor related competences are collected.
Pablo de Olavide University	Neither courses nor related competences are collected.
University of Huelva	No related courses are collected. Specific competence: E21 - Know, assimilate and master the professional competences that are typical of the social educator, as well as communication techniques with users/learners, emotional control, social skills, etc.
University of Jaén	No related courses are collected. Transversal competence: CT11 - Interpersonal skills understood as the ability to relate positively with other people through empathic listening and the clear and assertive expression of what is thought and/or felt, by verbal and non-verbal means.
University of Córdoba	Neither courses nor related competences are collected.
University of Granada (Ceuta)	Course "Social psychology of conflict and resolution techniques: negotiation and mediation". No related competences are collected. Competencies assessment.
University of Granada (Melilla)	Course "Social psychology of conflict and resolution techniques: negotiation and mediation". No related competences are collected. Competencies assessment.
University of Oviedo – Faculty Padre Ossó	Course "Mediation: scopes and strategies". General competence: CG 16 - Use emotional capacities in social interaction processes. Specific competence: CE 10 - Act with empathy. Competencies assessment.
University of Las Islas Baleares	Course "Techniques and programs of socio-educational intervention in behavior problems". Generic competence CT8 - Empathic capacity and respectful, supportive and trusting attitude with people and institutions. Competencies assessment.
University of Las Palmas	Neither courses nor related competences are collected.
University of Castilla-La Mancha (Cuenca)	Elective course "Emotional intelligence". No related competences are collected. Competencies assessment.
University of Castilla-La Mancha (Talavera de la Reina)	Neither courses nor related competences are collected.
University of Burgos	Elective course "Emotional intelligence in social education". No related competences are collected. Competencies assessment.
University of Salamanca	Neither courses nor related competences are collected.
Pontifical University of Salamanca	Neither courses nor related competences are collected.
University of Valladolid	Elective course "Emotional intelligence and social competence". Interpersonal skills: G8 - Critical and self-critical ability, includes among its elements emotional distance as an aspect to be acquired by students. No assessment information found.
University of León	Elective course "Emotional intelligence and social competence". No related competences are collected. No assessment information found.

continued on following page

Table 17. Continued

Campus or University Center	Course, competences and evaluation on emotional education and management.
University of Valladolid (Palencia)	No related courses are collected. Interpersonal skills: G8 - Critical and self-critical ability, includes among its elements emotional distance as an aspect to be acquired by students.
University of Barcelona	Course "Social skills: intervention and programs". No related competences are collected. Competencies assessment.
Autonomous University of Barcelona	No related courses are collected. Specific competence: Apply the socio-emotional skills necessary to manage human relationships. Transversal competence: Analyze and recognize one's own socio-emotional competencies (in terms of strengths, potentials and weaknesses) to develop those necessary in their performance and professional development.
Ramón LLull University	Course "Practicum I: approach to social action". Course "Management of crisis situations". Competence: C1 - Recognize and accept your own emotions Competence: C2 - Recognize and accept the emotions of the users, recipients of our action / intervention. Competence: C3 - Execute the key elements of emotion management in educational action. No competencies assessment.
University of Lleida	Course "Professional health and well-being". No related competences are collected. No assessment information found.
University of Vic	Elective course "Emotional education and well-being". Specific competence: Be able to develop skills aimed at self-knowledge (maturity, emotional balance, self-control, etc.). No assessment information found.
Rovira i Virgili University	Neither courses nor related competences are collected.
University of de Girona	Neither courses nor related competences are collected.
University of Extremadura	Neither courses nor related competences are collected.
University of Santiago de Compostela	Neither courses nor related competences are collected.
University of La Coruña	Neither courses nor related competences are collected.
University of Vigo	Neither courses nor related competences are collected.
Autonomous University of Madrid – University Studies Center La Salle	Neither courses nor related competences are collected. Specific objective: OE5 - Acquire self-analysis skills and the habit of exercising reflective practice, so that one is permanently attentive to aspects of improvement and personal care, especially emotionally and attitudinal.
University of Alcalá de Henares - University Center Cardenal Cisneros	Neither courses nor related competences are collected.
Complutense University of Madrid	No related courses are collected. Practical module competence: CMP 2 - Show an empathic, respectful, caring and trusting attitude towards the subjects and institutions of Social Education.
Complutense University of Madrid – University Center Don Bosco	Neither courses nor related competences are collected.
University of Murcia	Neither courses nor related competences are collected.
University of País Vasco - EHU (Guipúzcoa)	Neither courses nor related competences are collected.
University of País Vasco - EHU (Vizcaya)	Neither courses nor related competences are collected.
University of Deusto	No related courses are collected. Macro-competence: M.E.1.3 - Become aware and handle personal biases -cognitive, emotional and behavioral- in the interpretation and analysis of situations, developing coping strategies Macro-competence M.E.2.1 - Use different communication and aid skills (listening, empathy, self-messages, emotional control, giving useful information...) adjusting to the specific contexts and the situation of people.
Catholic University of Valencia - San Vicente Mártir	Elective course "Emotional intelligence". No related competences are collected.
University of Valencia	Neither courses nor related competences are collected.

Source: (Own elaboration, 2021)

In total, 22 of the 41 campuses or university centers (since some universities include more than one campus or center) have courses and/or competencies on emotional education and/or management (Table 17). That is, slightly more than half of the total, 53.6%, include either courses or competencies in the bachelor's degree in social education program with references to emotional education and/or management.

Regarding the courses, it is found that 15 of the analyzed campuses or university centers, that is 36.6%, present courses that address, directly or among their courses, emotional education and/or management content.

Of these, it is found that 60% of the cases are compulsory courses, such as "Social psychology of conflict and resolution techniques: negotiation and mediation" at the University of Granada, and its Ceuta and Melilla campuses; "Mediation: scopes and strategies" at the Padre Ossó Faculty of the University of Oviedo; "Techniques and programs of socio-educational intervention in behavior problems" at the University of the Balearic Islands; "Social skills: intervention and programs" at the University of Barcelona; "Practicum I: approach to social action" and "Management of crisis situations" at the Ramón Llul University and "Health and professional well-being" at the University of Lleida.

The remaining 40% are elective courses, that is, not all students are enrolled since they are not compulsory. Among them, it is found "Emotional Intelligence" at Cuenca campus of the University of Castilla La Mancha; "Emotional Intelligence in Social Education" at the University of Burgos; "Emotional Intelligence and social competence" at the University of Valladolid and the University of León; "Emotional education and well-being" at the University of Vic and "Emotional intelligence and education" at the Catholic University of Valencia - San Vicente Mártir.

Referring to competencies, it is found that another 15 of the 41 campuses and/or university centers, that is 36.6% of the total, include among the competencies of their programs some which refer directly to emotional education and/or management.

Thus, they are collected within interpersonal competences in the case of the University of Valladolid and its campus in Palencia, as well as in the University of Barcelona, referring to emotional distance. In other cases, they are collected within specific competencies such as the cases of the University of Huelva, which refers to emotional control, and the University of Vic, which refers to emotional balance. In two other cases, they are included both in general and specific competences, such as in the case of the University of Oviedo or the Autonomous University of Barcelona, which, in addition to a general competence, includes another transversal competence. Finally, the University of Jaén only collects a transversal competence and the Ramón Llul University collects four competences that mention the acceptance and management of one's own emotions, such as emotional containment.

It is also found that 33.33% of the campuses or university centers include both specific courses and competences that refer to emotional education and/or management, specifically the Universities of Oviedo, Balearic Islands, Valladolid, Ramón Llull and Vic.

An interesting aspect to reflect on the programs and courses refers to the learning assessment. For this reason, it has been decided to analyze this issue, identifying those courses that name some type of instrument, tool or method measuring the assessment of acquired learning focusing on abilities, skills and competencies. It has been agreed by the researchers to name these tools or methods as competencies instruments.

On the one hand, 53.3%, slightly more than a half of campuses or university centers have a course where competencies instruments can be found, such as the University of Granada and its Ceuta and Melilla campuses, the Padre Ossó Faculty of the University of Oviedo, the University of the Balearic

Islands, the Cuenca Campus of the University of Castilla-La Mancha, the University of Burgos and the University of Barcelona.

On the other hand, only one campus or university center where the assessment is not developed using any competencies instruments have been found, the Ramón Llul University.

In addition, it is noteworthy that there is a 33.33% of campuses or university centers where there is no specific information on the instruments or methods for the assessment of learning contents, such as the University of Valladolid, the University of León, the University of Lleida, the University of Vic and the Catholic University of Valencia - San Vicente Mártir.

Regarding the specific instruments used to demonstrate the learning of the contents of the courses, Table 18, on the one hand, it is found that in 60% of the total of campuses or university centers with specific courses, the instruments, tools or methods related to competencies assessment focus found are dramatizations, dialogues, debates and experiential exercises, among others. On the other hand, 46.7%, almost a half of the total, use practical group working as assessment instrument. In addition, it is interesting to highlight the 20% of courses identified where the assessment of participation, in person or virtual in forums, is referred as a means to demonstrate the learning acquired.

Table 18. Instruments used in competencies assessment

Instruments	Percentage
Dramatizations, dialogues, debates, experiential exercises…	60%
Group working	46.7%
Participation	20%

Source: (Own elaboration, 2021)

CONCLUSION

Bachelor's Degrees in Social Education Need Emotional Education Training

Regarding the first study of a quantitative nature, relative to the perception of students and professors of the Bachelor's Degree in Social Education of the Faculty of Social Sciences of Talavera de la Reina, it is verified that students award a greater weight and influence to the emotions in all the raised aspects. Thus, 93.7% of the students agree or totally agree that emotions influence socio-educational practice, compared to 80% of the teaching staff.

When asked about the influence of emotions specifically on the educator or social educator, 83.4% of the students agree and totally agree, with 80% of the teaching staff pointing in the same direction.

Regarding the influence of emotions on students, curiously it is observed that professors indicate, in 100%, that they agree and totally agree, compared to 85.1% of the students, this group indicating that the emotions that they experience the most are joy (79.2%) and happiness (58.3%); which are positive emotions according to Bisquerra (2009), although they also say they feel others such as fear (54.2%) and sadness (45.8%), as observed in Table 8.

Referring to the need to carry out emotional management (Table 12), it is found again that 97.9% of the students agree and totally agree, compared to 80% in the case of the teaching staff. This trend is also observed when inquiring about the need for training in emotional education, in which 100% of the students indicate they agree or totally agree, compared to 60% of the teaching staff.

Regarding training in emotional education, 52.1% of the students indicate that it is insufficient, while only 20% of the teaching staff consider it that way; 83.3% of the student body also pointed out the need to include a specific course in undergraduate studies, compared to 60% of the teaching staff who indicated complementary training as the appropriate way to approach these contents.

Finally, referring to the emotional impact on social education professionals, 83.4% of the students agree and totally agree, compared to 40% of the professors.

As a synthesis of this first study, the discrepancy found between professors and students of the Degree in social education can be highlighted, with students being the ones who recognize to a greater extent the influence of emotions in educational practice. Curiously, this same discrepancy was found among social education professionals in the field of socio-educational intervention in the childhood protection system, who think that the educator's emotions have less influence on the socio-educational intervention than the emotions of the students (Lirio & Medina, 2021).

However, professors and students agree that students do not receive training in this regard during the Bachelor's Degree (Table 14) and that the way to include complementary training in emotional education should be through Practicum seminars and End-of-Degree Projects, as shown in Table 16. In this regard, Repetto and Pérez-González (2007) consider that practical training is the ideal period of training for learning the emotional competencies that the development of a profession requires.

The second study, the qualitative one, in which it is analyze the study programs of the degrees of social education in Spain (table 17), highlights that 53.6% include either courses or competencies of the degree related to emotional education and/or management. Specifically, 36.6% include some course, another 36.6% include some of these contents in the competences to be achieved in the study programs and, only 33.33% of the universities include both courses and competences related to emotional education and/or management. Therefore, it is considered an insufficiently developed aspect in the Social Education programs and, due to the importance given by students and professors to its incidence in future socio-educational practice, it would require greater attention in the practice of university teaching.

Regarding the proposals for the assessment of learning in the content of these courses, referring to emotional education and/or management, only half of the courses, 53.3%, use competencies instruments, tools or methods, being only one subject in which it is not evaluated with this approach. It should be noted that there is a third of courses, 33.3%, where this information is not found in the teaching guides or planning of the didactic process, something interesting that may be indicating the little importance that is given to the assessment focuses and methods.

The most used techniques and tools are experiential exercises and activities (60%), where students are able to be involved in an active way, such as dramatizations, debates, dialogues... group working (46.7%) and face-to-face and virtual participation (20%). As already mentioned, other instruments can be used for this purpose, such as projects, problems, case studies, simulations or rubrics (Moreno, 2007).

These data coincide with those of the comparative study carried out by López-Goñi and Goñi (2012), which analyzes the place that emotional competences have in the official proposals for teaching competencies in various countries, including Spain. The study shows that emotional competencies are present among teaching competencies, but have a lesser role compared to other types of competences.

Regarding the Degree in Social Education of the Faculty of Social Sciences of Talavera de la Reina, where the study of the emotions of its students and professors is carried out, neither courses related to emotional education and/or management are offered, nor competencies are proposed in this regard, despite the fact that, as shown in Table 16, 83.3% of the bachelor's students consider it necessary to include an emotional education subject.

In the case of study programs where emotional education is addressed, general, transversal and specific competences are found, and some courses that deal with aspects where emotions are present such as interpersonal communication, social skills and conflict solving, or directly emotional skills such as empathy, which also appears in numerous teaching guides.

Future Research Directions, Some Proposals

Taking into account the results of this research, it is considered necessary to continue the research and assessment on this relationship between social education and emotional education, considering the contributions that these contents can make to the training of future professionals in socio-educational intervention. For this, it is essential to carry out research in different professional fields that explore and describe the importance of adequate education and emotional management and, in addition, make visible the need for accurate training that favors the development of these aspects in the teaching practices of the university degrees so that, finally, these contents can be developed through socio-educational practices.

In this way, research can be directed towards quantitative approaches with larger student and teacher samples, from which more realistic results can be achieved. In addition, the research can be opened to professionals in social education, as well as to the people who receive these interventions, to be able to better understand their approaches and compare them with those of the high education community. It is also possible to delve into the different areas of intervention since, perhaps, some present a greater need than others to have a training in emotional education.

When it comes to improving academic programs, there are different proposals, but one should not be forgotten, the assessment of the training of professors who, on many occasions, do not participate in formative actions in which they can also acquire these emotional skills that they should transmit to students, as can be seen in the results of the investigation.

Likewise, more training actions of different types should be incorporated around education and emotional management, for example, in a specific subject, in the subject of professional practices or, transversally, in different subjects of the degree. It is interesting to note that a high percentage of professors propose the inclusion of emotional education as a transversal content within social education programs, an aspect that can be useful, but its development should prioritize a very detailed planning, since, if not, there is a danger of not guaranteeing the learning.

Other options would be the design of a specific postgraduate program on emotional education, as well as being able to collaborate with professional organizations in permanent training.

In addition, whenever content and competencies related to emotional education are incorporated into the courses of the programs, an assessment by competencies should be planned, helping to accurately measure the acquisition of this learning, taking into account the entire range of competencies instruments that exist nowadays.

Finally, it should be noted that the quantitative study has a clear limitation as a case study: the difficulty of generalizing its results.

ACKNOWLEDGMENT

This research has been supported by Facultad de Ciencias Sociales de Talavera de la Reina, Universidad de Castilla-La Mancha.

REFERENCES

Asociación Estatal de Educación Social - ASEDES. (2007). *Documentos profesionalizadores*. ASEDES.

Barnés, A. (2017). Taller 5. Cómo gestionar nuestras emociones para sentirnos bien como educadoras y educadores sociales. *Revista de Educación Social, 24*, 891–894.

Bisquerra, R. (2005). La educación emocional en la formación del profesorado. *Revista Interuniversitaria de Formación del Profesorado, 19*(3), 95–114.

Bisquerra, R. (2009). *Psicopedagogía de las emociones*. Síntesis.

Bisquerra, R., Martínez, F., Obiols, M., & Pérez-Escoda, N. (2006). Evaluación 360°: Una aplicación a la educación emocional. *Revista de Investigación Educacional, 24*(1), 187–203.

Bisquerra, R., Pérez, J. C., & García, E. (2015). *Inteligencia emocional en educación*. Síntesis.

Bravo, A., & Del Valle, J. (2009). *Intervención socioeducativa en acogimiento residencial*. Gobierno de Cantabria - Consejería de Empleo y Bienestar Social.

Cabello, R., Ruíz, D. & Fernández, P. (2010). Docentes emocionalmente inteligentes. *Revista electrónica interuniversitaria de formación del profesorado, 13*(1), 41-49.

Cameselle, N. (2017). Percepción de la gestión emocional del/a educador/a social [End-of-Postdegree Project, University of Barcelona]. Repository of the University de Barcelona. Retrieved from https://diposit.ub.edu/dspace/bitstream/2445/118320/7/TFP%20Noemi%20Cameselle.pdf

Costa, M. & Méndez, E. (1996). *Manual para el educador social: Habilidades en la relación de ayuda; 2. Afrontando situaciones*. Ministerio de Asuntos Sociales. Centro de publicaciones.

Creswell, J. W. (2009). *Research design: Qualitative, quantitative, and mixed methods approaches*. SAGE Publications.

Extremera, N. & Fernández-Berrocal, P. (2015). *Inteligencia emocional y educación*. Grupo 5.

Fernández, A. (2011). La evaluación orientada al aprendizaje en un modelo de formación por competencias en la educación universitaria. *Revista de Docencia Universitaria, 8*(1), 11–34. doi:10.4995/redu.2010.6216

Goleman, D. (2011). *El cerebro y la inteligencia emocional: nuevos descubrimientos*. Ediciones B.

Gómez, M. (2003). Aproximación conceptual a los sectores y ámbitos de intervención de la educación social. *Pedagogía Social,* (10), 233-251. Retrieved from http://hdl.handle.net/2445/65334

Lirio, J., & Medina, L. (2021). La gestión de las emociones en profesionales de la Educación Social en el ámbito de la protección de menores. *Márgenes. Revista de Educación de la Universidad de Málaga, 2*(1), 112–129.

Lirio, J., Medina, L. & Moreno, M. (2020). La gestión emocional de los adultos mayores: Un estudio de caso. *Revista Euro latinoamericana de Análisis Social y Político, 2*(2), 88-103.

López, B., Fernández, I., & Márquez, M. (2008). Educación emocional en adultos y personas mayores. *Revista Electrónica de Investigación Psicoeducativa, 6*(15), 501–5022.

López, P. (2017). Competencias socioemocionales y salud en educación social. *Educació Social. Revista d'Intervenció Socioeducativa, 66*, 51–69.

López-Goñi, I., & Goñi, J. M. (2012). La competencia emocional en los currículos de formación inicial de los docentes. Un estudio comparativo. *Review of Education*, (0357), 467–489.

Martínez-Otero, V. (2007). *La inteligencia afectiva. Teoría, práctica y programa.* CCS.

Moreno, T. (2012). La evaluación de competencias en educación. *Sinéctica, 39*. http://www.sinectica.iteso.mx/index.php?cur=39&art=39_09

Redorta, J., Obiols, M., & Bisquerra, R. (2006). *Emoción y conflicto. Aprenda a manejar las emociones.* Paidós.

Repetto, E., & Pérez-González, J. C. (2007). Formación en competencias socioemocionales a través de las prácticas en empresas. *Revista Europea de Formación Profesional*, (40), 92–112.

Ronda-Ortín, L. (2012). El educador social. Ética y práctica profesional. *Pedagogía Social. Revista Interuniversitaria, 19*(19), 51–63. doi:10.7179/PSRI_2012.19.04

Rosa, G., Riberas, G., Navarro-Segura, L., & Vilar, J. (2015). El coaching como herramienta de trabajo de la competencia emocional en la formación de estudiantes de educación social y trabajo social de la Universidad Ramón Llull, España. *Formación Universitaria, 8*(5), 77–90. doi:10.4067/S0718-50062015000500009

Tardif, J. (2003). Développer un programme par compétences: de l'intention à la mise en œuvre. *Pédagogie collégiale, 16*(3), 36-44.

Trianes, M. V., Cardelle-Elawar, M., Blanca, M. J., & Muñoz, A. M. (2003). Contexto social, género y competencia social autoevaluada en alumnos andaluces de 11-12 años. *Electronic Journal of Research in Educational Psychology, 1*(2), 37–56.

ADDITIONAL READING

Agulló, M. J., Filella, G., García, E., López-Cassà, E., & Bisquerra, R. (2010). *La educación emocional en la práctica.* Horsori.

Álvarez, M. (2011). *Diseño y evaluación de programa de educación emocional.* Wolters Kluwer.

Álvarez, M., Bisquerra, R., Fita, E., Martínez, F., & Pérez-Escoda, N. (2000). Evaluación de programas de educación emocional. *Revista de Investigación Educacional, 18*(2), 587–599.

Bisquerra, R. (2012). *Cómo educar las emociones? La inteligencia emocional en la infancia y la adolescencia.* Hospital Sant Joan de Déu.

Bisquerra, R., Pérez, J. C., & García Navarro, E. (2015). *Inteligencia emocional en educación.* Síntesis.

Güel, M., & Muñoz, J. (2003). Educación emocional: Programa de actividades para educación secundaria postobligatoria. *Praxis (Bern).*

Gutiérrez-Lestón, C., Pérez-Escoda, N., Reguant, M., & Eroles, M. (2020). Innovación de educación emocional en el ocio educativo: El Método La Granja. *Revista de Investigación Educacional, 38*(2), 495–513. doi:10.6018/rie.405721

Pérez-Escoda, N., Alegre, A., & López-Cassà, E. (2021). Validación y fiabilidad del cuestionario de desarrollo emocional en Adultos (CDE-A35). *Educatio Siglo XXI, 39*(3), 37–60. doi:10.6018/educatio.422081

Soldevila, A. (2009). *Emociónate. Programa de educación emocional.* Pirámide.

KEY TERMS AND DEFINITIONS

Assessment: Process included within the planning of an intervention in which the achievement of certain learning contents by the students is valued, through instruments and methods with different perspectives.

Capabilities: Aspects of the person that allow them to initiate certain behaviors or implement useful actions for the development of their life.

Competences: Set of knowledge, attitudes and skills that are put in place for the development of vital activities in an appropriate way.

Emotional competencies: Set of knowledge, attitudes and skills that are put in place for the identification, regulation, expression and understanding of emotional situations, in oneself and in others.

Emotional Education: Educational intervention that aims to develop emotional competencies in learners.

Emotional Management: Set of skills and abilities people develop to deal with their emotional states, ranging from identification to control of emotions.

Emotions: Set of affective reactions of the organism characterized by an excitement before significant events, internal or external, and a short term.

Profession: Occupation of a person useful for the society in which he lives, for what it is needed a set of knowledge, specialized skills and deontological standards that guide the actions, within an organizational framework.

Social Education: Discipline that is based on the development of educational interventions in different social contexts, using mediation and training to accompany people to achieve optimal life processes in a context of coexistence with other people.

Chapter 10

The Importance of Formative and Shared Assessment Systems in Pre–Service Teacher Education:
Skills Acquisition, Academic Performance, and Advantages and Disadvantages

Miriam Molina Soria
🆔 https://orcid.org/0000-0003-2974-5535
Universidad de Valladolid, Spain

Víctor Manuel López-Pastor
University of Valladolid, Spain

David Hortigüela-Alcalá
University of Burgos, Spain

Teresa Fuentes Nieto
University of Valladolid, Spain

Cristia Pascual-Arias
University of Valladolid, Spain

Carla Fernández-Garcimartín
🆔 https://orcid.org/0000-0002-2171-0293
University of Valladolid, Spain

ABSTRACT

The main objective of the study was to analyse the results of the implementation of formative and shared assessment (F&SA) systems in pre-service teacher education (PTE) classrooms with respect to the acquisition of student competencies, their academic performance and the advantages and disadvantages of the system. It is an "ex post facto" study with a sample of 333 students of a PTE subject in a Spanish public university. The data collection instruments were: (1) a structured report of best practices in higher education (HE); and (2) an anonymous questionnaire for the assessment of the best practice experience carried out and the assessment system used. The results show that F&SA had a positive influence on the acquisition of professional competencies and on the academic performance of students and that these systems present more advantages than disadvantages.

DOI: 10.4018/978-1-6684-3537-3.ch010

INTRODUCTION

The quest to change traditional methods for assessment systems focused on student learning is of particular interest to HE. This research focuses on the implementation and study of a specific assessment system. The system, called "Formative and Shared Assessment" (F&SA), is composed of two mutually related concepts that must be followed. The concept of "Formative Assessment" is characterised by seeking to improve student learning, as well as teaching-learning processes and teaching practice (López-Pastor, 2009; López-Pastor and Pérez-Pueyo, 2017). "Shared Assessment" involves the dialogic processes that take place between the teacher and the student about the assessment (López-Pastor, 2009; López-Pastor and Pérez-Pueyo, 2017). For some time, university teachers have been looking to encourage student participation in the assessment process through different techniques such as self-assessment, peer assessment, shared assessment, self-grading or dialogical grading (López-Pastor, 2009; López-Pastor and Pérez-Pueyo, 2017).

Therefore, this study investigates what results are obtained when students experience F&SA systems during HE, focusing on the acquisition of competencies, academic performance and the advantages and disadvantages.

BACKGROUND

This section contains a theoretical foundation on the research topic. First, a theoretical exposition is made on the concepts of F&SA, as well as on the techniques of student participation in the assessment process. Then, sections are developed on the acquisition of competencies, the influence of F&SA systems on the students' academic performance and the advantages and disadvantages of applying F&SA systems in PTE.

F&SA in PTE

Several research interventions in PTE reinforce the idea of the importance of experimenting with F&SA systems because they improve learning processes, teaching competence and the teaching-learning process (Gallardo & Carter, 2016; Hamodi & López-Pastor, 2012), and because they favour the transfer between what has been experienced in PTE and its application in the near future in early childhood and primary education classrooms (Barrientos et al., 2019; Hamodi et al., 2017; Lorente-Catalán & Kirk, 2013, 2016; Molina & López-Pastor, 2019; Palacios & López-Pastor, 2013). These assessment systems have several advantages, such as improving learning, self-regulation, autonomy, acquisition of personal and professional skills, and academic performance (Arribas, 2012; Bore-García, et al. 2021; Bores-García et al., 2020; Castejón et al., 2011; Delgado et al., 2016; Gallardo et al., 2020; Hortigüela-Alcalá et al., 2021; Hortigüela-Alcalá et al., 2019; Romero-Martín et al., 2014).

F&SA and Skills Acquisition

HE is focused on the development of competencies, so it is also important to take into account the assessment of these competencies. This has meant that teachers have been looking for methodological and assessment alternatives consistent with this change; therefore, for several decades, some PTE teachers have been seeking to overcome the traditional assessment system based on constant and summative grading (López-Pastor & Pérez-Pueyo, 2017). In this sense, Ibarra-Sáiz et al. (2020) claims that a change in assessment is necessary in the current reality of our classrooms, using "Learning Oriented Assessment" and the acquisition of skills.

F&SA systems promote the acquisition of professional competencies (Amor & Serrano, 2019; Castejón et al., 2018; Hortigüela-Alcalá et al., 2019; Gallardo et al., 2020). Several investigations confirm that it is feasible to implement F&SA systems in PTE because it helps in the acquirement of professional competencies thanks to the involvement of the students in the assessment process (Cañadas et al., 2018; Gallardo & Carter, 2016; Manrique et al., 2010; Romero et al., 2016). López-Pastor et al. (2020) mention several reasons why it would be positive to experience F&SA systems in PTE. One of these reasons is because such systems help improve teaching skills. In an intervention using F&SA in five PTE subjects, Hortigüela-Alcalá et al. (2016) found that there was a greater acquisition of teaching skills in the students who had experienced these systems than in the students who had received a traditional grade-based assessment.

F&SA and Academic Performance

Different studies indicate that F&SA seems to positively influence students' academic performance (Angelini, 2016; Buscà et al., 2010; Panadero & Jonsson, 2013; Santos et al., 2009; Vallés et al., 2011). Castejón et al. (2011) found several factors of F&SA use that influence the academic performance of PTE students: continuous monitoring, high class attendance, and student involvement and participation in their assessment process. These same results were obtained by Arribas (2012) and, in turn, corroborated by Fraile et al. (2013) after analysing the academic performance of students in 52 subjects at 19 Spanish universities.

Romero-Martín et al. (2014) reported that students who experience F&SA systems during PTE improve their academic performance and learning and, in addition, are satisfied with this system. In a later study, Romero-Martín et al. (2015) found that students agree with the final grades of the subjects, despite the fact that these assessment systems are demanding. For their part, Molina et al. (2020) conducted a study of the academic performance of a PTE subject in which they implemented an F&SA system. The results show that 97.3% of the students passed the subject, which confirms that these systems seem to improve the students' academic performance. Fraile et al. (2020) asserts that the results of their study show that group work in which students use the assessment criteria and self-regulate their learning has resulted in higher grades.

Advantages and Disadvantages of F&SA Systems

López-Pastor and Pérez-Pueyo (2017) presented successful experiences at all educational stages, from early childhood education to higher education, analysing the advantages and disadvantages encountered in each experience.

Student motivation increases with the use of F&SA in classrooms, which implies greater involvement in their tasks (López-Pastor, 2008; Vallés, et al., 2011); and in turn, the improvement of student autonomy and responsibility (López-Pastor and Pérez-Pueyo, 2017). These systems improve learning (Molina and López, 2017) generating active, functional and meaningful learning (Martínez-Mínguez et al., 2015) thanks to the constant feedback throughout the process, an aspect that has an impact on improved academic performance (Fraile et al., 2013).

The main drawbacks of F&SA systems are the workload, both for students and teachers (Vallés et al., 2011 and López-Pastor. 2008), due to the continuity involved in terms of compulsory and active attendance (Martínez-Mínguez et al., 2015); the lack of habit of this type of assessment and the students' resistance to this change (Hamodi et al., 2017).

Several studies (Atienza et al., 2016; Delgado et al., 2016; Gallardo et al., 2018; Gallardo et al., 2020; Romero-Martín et al., 2017) found that F&SA systems present more advantages than disadvantages, coinciding with those previously mentioned.

For all of the above, the main purpose of this study was to analyse the results obtained when students experience F&SA systems during PTE, with respect to the acquisition of competencies, academic performance and advantages and disadvantages. Therefore, the specific objectives established in this study were: (1) to compare the results of the students' perception of the acquisition of competencies in eight cases of a PTE subject that implemented F&SA systems, between the academic years of 2017 and 2021; (2) to analyse whether the implementation of F&SA systems influences the students' academic performance; and, finally, (3) to present the advantages and disadvantages of the F&SA system used.

MAIN FOCUS OF THE CHAPTER

This section will describe the methodology used in the study, as well as the context of the subject in which it was carried out.

Methodological Approach

This is an "ex post facto" study. This design is used in studies with events that have already occurred, in which the values of the independent variables cannot be manipulated (Montero and León, 2005).

Study Sample

The sample consisted of 333 students of a PTE subject (Fundamentals and Didactics of Children's Physical Education) belonging to eight groups at a Spanish public university during the academic years between 2017 and 2021. The subject is taught in the third year of the Degree in Early Childhood Education (3rdECE) and the first year of the Joint Study Programme of the Degree in Early Childhood Education and Primary Education (1stJSP). Table 1 shows the participants differentiated by academic year and group to which they belonged.

Context: How is the course organised? What is the assessment system used?

On the first day of class, students are presented with the three learning and assessment methods (continuous, mixed and final), together with the grading criteria. The grading criteria for the continuous pathway are established by consensus between teachers and students.

The following table presents in detail the three types of pathways from which students can choose, as well as the requirements that must be met for each of them.

On the first day of class, students are organised in work groups with collaborative folders. They must hand in a folder to the teacher with all the work at the end of the course.

Table 1. Sample of the study

Subject: Fundamentals and didactics of children's physical education	STUDENTS ENROLLED BY GROUPS		TOTALS
	3rdECE	**1stJSP**	
Academic year 2017-2018	43	47	90
Academic year 2018-2019	38	52	90
Academic year 2019-2020	28	44	72
Academic year 2020-2021	37	44	81
TOTALS	146	187	**333**

Source: own elaboration.

The learning activities in the course are very varied involving both individual and group work. All work is accompanied by a student self-assessment form, so that the students are aware of the criteria that are evaluated and that they have fulfilled when they have handed in the document. The following table shows the learning activities and the assessment instrument and/or process for each one.

Students are constantly part of the regularly scheduled assessment process throughout the course: self-assessment (in all work, both individual and group), peer-assessment (in the session sheets and in the partial exam), self-grading (at the end of the course, at the end of the global self-assessment report) and dialogical grading (final interview with each group of students). The teacher corrects each work submitted within one week and provides quality feedback for its improvement. The student has one week after the teacher gives it back to improve any aspect of the document if desired. Also, each submission of improvements must be accompanied by the self-assessment.

At the end of the course each group delivers a collective portfolio containing all the learning activities carried out, which are again reviewed by the teachers, since all the work has been reviewed throughout the process. Subsequently, there is a final shared assessment interview (on the learning processes carried out) and a dialogical grading (on the grade that corresponds to each student).

Table 2. Learning and assessment pathways offered to students

TRACK	Requirements	Rating percentages
Continuous track	-Class attendance is mandatory. -All assignments must be submitted in a timely manner.	30% Tutored Learning Project 20% Dialogical Talks/Discussions 10% Concept maps and monographic works 20% Practical session worksheets 20% Partial test
Mixed track	-In this track it is mandatory to attend at least 50% of the classes, but it is not mandatory to justify any lack of attendance. -The submission of assignments is voluntary.	30% Tutorial Learning Project. 50% Theoretical exam. 20% Rest of the work done.
Final track	-There is no obligation to attend classes.	There are three exams in which the students must demonstrate that they have acquired the contents seen in the course. 50% Theoretical exam. 20% Practical exam: a session on the contents of the course is analysed. 30% Presentation and defence of the Tutorial Learning Project.

Source: own elaboration.

Table 3. Learning activities and assessment of each one

Learning activity	What does it consist of?	Assessment
Concept maps	A concept map is made for each theoretical topic developed in class.	Individual self-assessment sheets
Reviews	Four reviews and dialogical discussions are held on basic books and articles for the subject.	Group self-assessment sheets with graded scale
Session analysis sheets	A report is made for each practical session carried out in the course.	
Monographs	Work on the analysis of the early childhood education curriculum.	
Tutored Learning Project	Theoretical-practical group work on a practical didactic resource. They must present a theoretical framework and a practical session on the topic.	
Partial test	Written test of short questions covering all the topics developed in the course.	Peer-assessment with correction template

Source: own elaboration.

Data Collection Instruments

The data collection instruments were designed and validated by the F&SA Network in Education:

(1)　A structured report of Best Practices in HE (Hortigüela et al., 2018). This report collects subject data on (1) the Good Practice experience; (2) the learning activities carried out; (3) the students' perceived acquisition of competencies; (4) the workload of students and faculty; (5) the advantages and disadvantages of the assessment system that has been developed; and (6) the students' academic performance.

(2)　An anonymous questionnaire for students to evaluate the Good Practice experience carried out and the assessment system of the subject. This instrument was validated by Castejón et al. (2015) with a confirmatory factor analysis of the total number of questions in the different scales, obtaining a high instrument validity index (RMSEA= 0.078) and a reliability index of 0.84. It is a 28-item questionnaire with a five-level Likert-type scale: 1 (not at all), 2 (a little), 3 (somewhat), 4 (quite a lot) and 5 (a lot). In addition, there is an open-ended question for any observations the students may wish to add. This questionnaire is filled out at the end of the course.

(3)　Three scales of self-perception of competencies, made up of 45 items; the first on students' transversal competencies (14 items), the second on teaching competencies (17 items) and the third and last on the specific competencies of physical education teachers (14 items). These scales were validated by Salcines et al. (2018), the internal consistency is Cronbach's alpha of .992. The validity of the scales was confirmed through the Delphi technique to check the content validity. Student rating is also recorded with a four-level scale: (1) (not at all), 2 (a little), 3 (quite a lot), 4 (a lot). This document is also filled out at the end of the course.

Data Analysis

Data analysis was performed with the statistical programme SPSS v.20.0. A descriptive analysis (arithmetic mean and standard deviation) and an inferential analysis through a parametric test (Student's t-test for independent samples) were developed to compare whether there were significant differences between them. The significance level was set at p≤0.05. Academic performance in the subject was also analysed and compared.

RESULTS

The results are organised according to the proposed objectives: (1) analysis of the students' acquisition of competencies; (2) analysis of the academic performance of the different groups; and (3) the students' opinion on the advantages and disadvantages of the implementation of the F&SA system.

Students' Skill Acquisition

In this section, the results will be organised according to the blocks of competencies that make up the instrument: (1) Block I, transversal competencies; (2) Block II, teaching competencies; and (3) Block III, competencies specific to physical education teachers.

The rows of each table correspond to the competencies evaluated, while the columns show the academic years, and in turn, the data on the scale of competencies and Student's t-test for independent samples, which allows us to analyse whether there are significant differences between the means of the data in this scale between the two groups (1stJSP and 3rdECE). It is interesting to compare 1stJSP and 3rdECE because they are two independent groups taking the course at the same time, with the same teachers and the same F&SA system.

Table 8 (in appendix) shows the data related to Block I, transversal competencies. This table shows the data on the scale of competencies (S) in arithmetic mean (B) and standard deviation (⌒), as well as Student's t-test results (T) to compare the means between both groups. Tables 2 and 3 (in appendix) are organised in the same way.

The data in Table 8 (in appendix) show a considerable variety of results. For example, the competency on knowing a foreign language scored the worst averages (between 1 and 2.70 out of 5) throughout the four academic years, followed by the competency on the use of information and communication technologies. The rest of the competencies analysed obtained arithmetic averages higher than 3 points out of 5 in all groups throughout the four academic years.

Students' t-test for independent samples compared the results obtained by the two groups (1stJSP vs. 3rdECE students) in the means of the competencies scale. Many significant differences were observed in the first year (bold), few in the second, none in the third and only one in the fourth year. Almost always on different competencies and in almost all cases with higher values in the 3rdECE students. Therefore, the only logical reason for these differences seems to be the course, in the sense that students in higher courses seem to have a higher self-perception of generic competencies, although these significant differences are different according to the cohort and, in one of them, non-existent.

Table 9 (in appendix) shows the data for Block II, teaching competencies. As can be seen in this table, the averages are quite low, since most of the items obtained averages below 3 out of 5 in all academic years. Two items stand out with averages above 4 in the 2019-2020 academic year in the competencies: Designing learning situations and Involving students in their learning. The teaching competencies included in this table are basic for the PTE and are worked on implicitly throughout all the subjects.

Regarding the significant differences between the 1stJSP and 3rdECE groups, similar results to those in the previous table are evident. In the teaching competencies, many significant differences can be observed in the first and second years (bold), none in the third year and only one in the fourth year. Almost always on different competencies and in almost all cases with higher values in the 3rdECE students. Therefore, the only global logical reason for the differences seems to continue to be the course, in the sense that students in higher courses seem to have a higher self-perception of teaching competencies, although these differences vary according to the cohort.

Table 10 (in appendix) presents the results of Block III: specific physical education teaching competencies across all academic years. As can be seen in this table, the arithmetic mean data are high in almost all competencies. This is due to the fact that the subject under analysis develops physical education contents which are the competencies being evaluated in this table.

Less significant differences can be observed in Student's t-test results than in the previous scales. In the teaching competencies specific to physical education, differences are observed in the second and fourth years (bold) and none in the first and third years. These differences are always with higher values in the 3rdECE group. Therefore, the only global logical reason for these differences seems to continue to be the course, since students in higher courses seem to have a higher self-perception of competencies.

After reviewing the three tables above, it is evident that the averages of the competency scales are generally high, except in Block II on general teaching competencies, which has the lowest averages (around 2.5 points out of 5), since only two items in the same academic year obtain averages higher than 4 out of 5. The highest values are found in the last scale on specific physical education teaching competencies.

Regarding Student's t-test results, it seems that the students in the higher course (3rdECE) have a higher self-perception of competencies in all the scales, compared to the 1stJSP group. There is no logical criterion that is repeated throughout the different academic years in the same competencies analysed, but rather isolated differences in competencies between the two groups.

Academic Performance

This section shows the students' academic performance throughout the four academic years. The grading system used is a 0-100 scale: N.A. (students who did not sit the exam); D (grade between 0 and 49 points, fail); C (grade between 50-69 points, pass); B (grade between 70 and 89 points, good); A (grade between 90 and 100 points, excellent); and A+ (the best 3, outstanding).

The following tables (Tables 4, 5, 6 and 7) present student academic performance data in percentages and learning and assessment paths, organised by groups (3rdECE and 1stJSP). Each table is for one academic year.

The tables show the results of academic performance in these four academic years. As can be seen, the overall academic performance was very good, with very high percentages of students passing the course (between 72-97%). The percentage of dropouts ("No-shows") was very low, ranging between 2-15%, depending on the academic year. The percentage of failures was very low (between 5-17%) and the percentage of C passes ranged between 4-23%. On the other hand, the grade with the highest percentages was almost always the "B", which normally ranged between 50-80%. It can be seen that the highest percentage of Bs during the four academic years was in the 2019-2020 academic year, the year of confinement due to the COVID-19 pandemic. The percentages of As and A+ were very low (between 1-9% and between 2-5%, respectively). As can be seen in the tables, these grades were not always achieved (group 1stJSP academic year 2017-18 and group 3rdECE academic year 2019-2020).

During the 2019-2020 academic year, there was the obligation to suspend the face-to-face classes due to the COVID-19 pandemic, which caused an adaptation of the F&SA system to the distance classes.

Table 4. Academic performance by assessment pathways and by groups, academic year 2017-2018 (in percentages)

Track	Groups	N.A.	D (0-49)	C (50-69)	B (70-89)	A (90-100)	A+ (3mejor)	Totals/ track
Continuous	1stJSP	-	-	-	55.32	-	-	55.32
	3rdECE	-	-	-	53.49	9.30	4.65	67.44
Mixed	1stJSP	-	4.26	12.76	6.98	-	-	24
	3rdECE	-	11.63	4.65		-	-	16.28
Final	1stJSP	8.51	2.13	-	-	-	-	10.64
	3rdECE	6.98	2.32	-	-	-	-	9.3
Totals	1stJSP	8.51	6.39	12.76	62.3	-	-	100
	3rdECE	6.98	13.95	4.65	53.49	9.30	4.65	100

Table 5. Academic performance by assessment pathways and by groups, academic year 2018-2019 (in percentages)

Tracks	Groups	N.A.	D (0-49)	C (50-69)	B (70-89)	A (90-100)	A+ (3 best)	Totals/ tracks
Continuous	1stJSP	-	-	5.77	42.32	1.92	5.77	55.78
	3rdECE	-	-	7.89	50	5.26	2.63	65.78
Mixed	1stJSP	-	11.53	17.30	5.77	-	-	34.6
	3rdECE	-	-	13.17	5.26		2.63	21.06
Final	1stJSP	3.85	5.77	-	-	-	-	9.62
	3rdECE	10.52	2.63	-	-	-	-	13.15
Totals	1stJSP	3.85	17.3	23.07	48.09	1.92	5.77	100
	3rdECE	10.52	2.63	21.06	55.26	5.26	5.26	100

Table 6. Academic performance by assessment pathways and by groups, academic year 2019-2020 (in percentages)

Tracks	Groups	N.A.	D (0-49)	C (50-69)	B (70-89)	A (90-100)	A+ (3best)	Totals/ tracks
Continuous	1stJSP	-	-	4.54	79.35	2.27	4.54	90.7
	3rdECE	-	-	-	82.61	-	-	82.61
Mixed	1stJSP	-	-	2.29	-	-	-	2.29
	3rdECE	-	13.04	4.35	-			17.39
Final	1stJSP	6.83	-	-	-	-	-	6.83
	3rddECE	-	-	-	-	-	-	-
Totals	1stJSP	6.83	-	6.83	79.35	2.27	4.57	100
	3rdECE	-	13.04	2.29	82.61	-	-	100

Table 7. Academic performance by assessment pathways and by groups, academic year 2020-2021 (in percentages)

Tracks	Groups	N.A.	D (0-49)	C (50-69)	B (70-89)	A (90-100)	A+ (3best)	Totals/ tracks
Continuous	1stJSP	-	-	-	72.73	6.81	4.55	84.09
	3rdECE	-		-	57.90	7.89	5.26	65.79
Mixed	1stJSP	2.29	-	6.81	6.81	-	-	15.91
	3rdECE	-	-	-	7.89	-	-	7.89
Final	1stJSP	-	-	-	-	-	-	-
	3rdECE	15.80	5.26	-	-	-	-	21.06
Totals	1stJSP	2.29	-	6.81	79.54	6.81	4.55	100
	3rdECE	15.80	5.26	-	65.79	7.89	5.26	100

Despite this, the results were quite positive. In the continuous track all the students passed the course with high grades. In the mixed pathway the results were very low, as there were both failures and passes. There was only a small percentage who opted for the final pathway, and none of them sat the exam.

If we compare the academic performance according to the assessment pathway, it can be seen that the highest percentage of students were in the continuous pathway, where the best academic results were reflected: passes, excellent and outstanding. However, in the 2017-2018 academic year there were no As or A+ in the 1stJSP group and in the 2019-2020 academic year the same thing happened in the 3rdECE group, a very unusual aspect in this pathway, probably because in that year we were in a period of confinement due to the COVID-19 pandemic.

In the mixed pathway, most of the grades were passes, with a small percentage of passing grades, except in the course 2019-2020, when there were only passing and failing grades in this pathway. Exceptionally, we found 2% of students in the mixed pathway with the grade of outstanding in the 2018-2019 academic year.

No students who had opted for the final pathway managed to pass the subject, either because they did not take the final exam or because they failed it. In all groups throughout the academic years there were usually students in the final pathway, even if it was a small percentage, but in the 2019-2020 academic year no student was included in the 3rdECE group.

As main conclusions after the analysis of the academic performance of the student body according to the chosen learning and assessment pathway, we can state that: (1) the highest grades were obtained through the continuous pathway; (2) no student failed the subject through the continuous pathway; and (3) no student passed the subject through the final pathway.

With regard to the difference between groups, it can be seen that the percentage of students who passed the subject was slightly higher in 1stJSP in almost all academic years. However, the grades tended to be higher in the 3rdECE group. Despite this, the 3rdECE group tended to have a higher percentage of students who failed the course (between 6-15%, compared to 2-8% in 1stJSP).

Regarding the difference between groups by learning and assessment methods, it can be seen that in both groups most of the students preferred the continuous method. Thus, both groups had a higher percentage of students with a grade of "B". However, in the 3rdECE group, they tended to have a slightly lower percentage of "B" grades, but higher percentages of As and A+. As for the mixed pathway, the percentage of students who opted for this pathway was higher in 1stJSP than in 3rdECE, except in the 2019-2020 academic year when the percentage of mixed pathway students in 3rdECE was much higher (2% compared to 17%). This may be due to the lack of experience in F&SA systems in the first year, as students tend to miss more classes and/or not hand in some of the learning activities in a timely manner. Finally, in the final track, there was not a big difference between both groups, since no student was able to pass the subject, either because they did not take the exams or because they them.

Advantages and Disadvantages of the F&SA System

In this section we will present the advantages and disadvantages of the F&SA system implemented in the course according to the students' perceptions. Table 11 (in appendix) shows the students' opinion on the advantages of the F&SA system used in the course throughout the four academic years, differentiating between the two groups.

As can be seen in this table, all the advantages of F&SA system obtained arithmetic means higher than 3 points out of 5, except: (1) The student was more motivated, the learning process was more motivating, which in the 1stJSP group in the 2018-2019 and 2019-2020 academic years obtained a mean of 2.97 and 2.69, respectively; (2) Improved academic tutoring, which scored a mean of 2.85 in the 2019-2020 academic year in the 3rdECE group.

Throughout the four academic years, the students of both groups valued very positively (arithmetic mean higher than 4) the fact that the F&SA system: (1) focused on the process, importance of daily work; (2) allowed the student to perform active learning; (3) proposed team work in a collaborative way; (4) interrelated theory and practice; and (5) gave the possibility of correcting errors in documents and activities. In addition, another advantage that obtained high scores throughout the academic courses is that it required more responsibility.

Next, the students' perceptions of the disadvantages of the F&SA system experienced in the subject are presented in Table 12 (in appendix). The table is organised in the same way as Table 4 on the advantages.

Following the results shown in the previous table, the analysis of these data will be organised in three blocks according to the value of their arithmetic mean.

In the first place, the items with the highest arithmetic mean (between 4 and 4.82) and therefore considered by the students as the main disadvantages of the system were: (1) It required mandatory and active attendance; (2) It required continuity; (3) It required more effort; and (4) It required participating in their own assessment (self-assessment). The data indicate that these means tended to be slightly higher in the 1stJSP group. A logical reason for this is that the 1stJSP students had barely experienced this assessment system in their PTE; they were therefore unfamiliar with the system and its dynamics.

Among the items with intermediate values, the following stand out: It had a little-known work dynamic, and lack of habit, with averages ranging between 3.06 and 3.81 and, in most cases, the highest values always corresponded to the 1stJSP group. Therefore, it seems that the students were not used to assessment systems of this type, which seemed to be a difficulty at the beginning of the term, until they learned to work in this way. The data indicate that this difficulty was higher among first-year students. One possible explanation for this is that in this faculty of education there are more subjects that use F&SA systems, so that third-year students have assimilated it more.

On the other hand, some items had very low ratings (between 2 and 3 out of 5). This means that the students did not consider them a disadvantage of the assessment system. The one with the lowest ratings was: The corrections have been unclear. And in very close assessment, two others can be found: It was unfair compared to other assessment processes, and the assessment of the work was subjective. Of the three, the only one that presented a constant difference between the groups was the last one, which always gives slightly higher values for the third-year group.

After analysing Tables 4 and 5, it can be affirmed that the students considered that the F&SA system used in the subject presented more advantages than disadvantages; since the scale of advantages received very high arithmetic averages, while the scale of disadvantages showed lower averages and much variability, with several items with low values.

SOLUTIONS AND RECOMMENDATIONS

This study analyses the students' perception of the acquisition of competencies in eight cases of a PTE subject after the implementation of F&SA systems. The results show that the means of the competency scale were slightly higher in the specific physical education teaching competencies. In addition, few significant differences between the two groups were apparent (2 or 3 items per academic year), but there was no logical criterion that was repeated every year. Moreover, in the 2019-2020 academic year, no significant differences were revealed.

The second objective was to analyse how F&SA systems influenced student academic performance. In this case, the results show that the F&SA systems seemed to have a positive influence on academic performance. Students who opted for the continuous pathway, linked to the completion of an F&SA, tended to obtain high grades (B and A). In the mixed pathway, students tended to obtain passing grades and a small percentage of Bs and, exceptionally, As. Thus, grades tended to be quite high (B and A). Therefore, grades tended to be much lower in the mixed pathway than in the continuous pathway. Students in the final pathway did not usually pass the course because they did not take the exam or failed it.

F&SA systems help to enhance learning, skills acquisition and improve academic performance thanks to the constant feedback they generate between teacher and student. Feedback must be continuous and of high quality (Nicol et al., 2014).

Finally, the study aimed to analyse the advantages and disadvantages of the F&SA system implemented. We can affirm that according to the students' perceptions there are more advantages than disadvantages to the implementation of F&SA systems. The main advantages are: (1) the improvement of learning, thanks to continuous feedback throughout the process; (2) the interrelation between theory and practice, since all the contents are worked on theoretically in class and practical sessions are held in the gymnasium to consolidate knowledge; and (3) collaborative work is positively valued, because collaborative folders are made from the first day of class to facilitate the organisation of learning activities.

As for the disadvantages, the students highlighted: (1) it requires continuity and greater effort; (2) it requires mandatory and active attendance during the development of the subject if students opt for the continuous way of assessment; (3) it requires participating in their own assessment process through different techniques.

FUTURE RESEARCH DIRECTIONS

As a future study, we could check if the results are similar in other PTE subjects when using this type of assessment systems. The F&SA model could also be transferred to other degrees to ascertain if the results are similar or different.

CONCLUSION

In conclusion, this study seems to indicate that it would be convenient to use F&SA systems during the PTE because it improves learning, the teaching-learning process and the acquisition of competencies, both personal and professional. In addition, the development of these assessment systems improves students' academic performance.

The results seem to indicate that the application of F&SA systems in PTE has a positive influence on students, specifically on the perception of professional competence and learning and on academic performance. It also has a number of important advantages in learning and some disadvantages, especially in terms of workload. In conclusion, it seems advisable to use F&SA systems in higher education, due to the advantages in the variables studied.

The main limitation of the study is the use of a single PTE subject. This study may be of interest to PTE teachers who wish to use FS&A systems in their classrooms, due to the advantages for students' learning and academic performance and their professional development. It may also be of interest to all higher education teachers, in order to transfer this assessment model to their own context.

ACKNOWLEDGMENT

This research was supported by the Research, Development, and Innovation (R&D&I) project: *Evaluation of competencies in Final Year Projects (Degree and Master's) in the Initial Training of Physical Education Teachers*. Call: August 2018 of the State Programme for R&D&I Oriented to the Challenges of Society in the framework of the State Plan for Scientific and Technical Research and Innovation 2017-2020. Reference: RTI2018-093292-B-I00. Duration: 3 years (2019-2021).

REFERENCES

Amor, M. I., & Serrano, R. (2019). The generic competences in the Initial Teacher Training. A comparative study among students, teachers and graduates of university education degree. *Educación XXI*, *21*(1), 239–261. doi:10.5944/educxx1.21341

Angelini-Doffo, M. L. (2016). Estudio sobre la evaluación formativa y compartida en la formación docente en inglés. *Actualidades Investigativas en Educación*, *16*(1), 1–21. doi:10.15517/aie.v16i1.22614

Arribas, J. M. (2012). El rendimiento académico en función del sistema de evaluación empleado. *Relieve*, *1*(18) 1-15. http://hdl.handle.net/10550/29801

Atienza, R., Valencia-Peris, A., Martos-García, D., López-Pastor, V. M., & Devís-Devís, J. (2016). La percepción del alumnado universitario de educación física sobre la evaluación formativa: ventajas, dificultades y satisfacción. *Movimiento, 22*(4), 1033-1048. https://www.redalyc.org/html/1153/115349439002

Barrientos, E., López-Pastor, V. M., & Pérez-Brunicardi, D. (2019). ¿Por qué hago evaluación formativa y compartida y/o evaluación para el aprendizaje en EF? La influencia de la formación inicial y permanente del Profesorado. *Retos, 36*, 37–43. https:// recyt.fecyt.es/index.php/ retos/article/view/66478

Bores-García, D., Hortigüela-Alcalá, D., Fernández-Rio, J., González-Calvo, G., & Barba-Martín, R. (2021). Research on Cooperative Learning in Physical Education. Systematic Review of the Last Five Years. *Research Quarterly for Exercise and Sport, 92*(1), 146–155. doi:10.1080/02701367.2020.1719 276 PMID:32023176

Bores-García, D., Hortigüela-Alcalá, D., González-Calvo, G., & Barba-Martín, R. A. (2020). Peer Assessment in Physical Education: A Systematic Review of the Last Five Years. *Sustainability (Basel), 12*(9233), 1–15. doi:10.3390u12219233

Buscá, F., Pintor, P., Martínez, L., & Peire, T. (2010). Sistemas y procedimientos de Evaluación Formativa en docencia universitaria: Resultados de 34 casos aplicados durante el curso académico 2007-2008. *Estudios Sobre Educación, 18*, 255-276. https://revistas.unav.edu/index.php/estudios-sobre-educacion /article/view/4674

Cañadas, L., Santos-Pastor, M. L., & Castejón, F. J. (2018). Desarrollo de competencias docentes en la Formación Inicial del Profesorado de Educación Física. Relación con los instrumentos de evaluación. *Estudios Pedagógicos (Valdivia), 44*(2), 111–126. doi:10.4067/S0718-07052018000200111

Castejón, F. J., López-Pastor, V. M., Julián, J. A., & Zaragoza, J. (2011). Evaluación formativa y rendimiento académico en la formación inicial del profesorado de educación física. *Revista Internacional de Medicina y Ciencias de la Actividad Física y del Deporte, 11*(42), 328–346. https://www.redalyc. org/articulo.oa?id=54222171007

Castejón, F. J., Santos-Pastor, M. L., & Cañadas, L. (2018). Desarrollo de competencias docentes en la formación inicial del profesorado de educación física. Relación con los instrumentos de evaluación. *Estudios Pedagógicos (Valdivia), 44*(2), 111–126. doi:10.4067/S0718-07052018000200111

Castejón-Oliva, F. J., Santos-Pastor, M. L., & Palacios Picos, A. (2015). Cuestionario sobre metodología y evaluación en formación inicial en educación física. *Revista Internacional de Medicina y Ciencias de la Actividad Física y del Deporte, 15*(58), 245–267. doi:10.15366/rimcafd2015.58.004

Delgado, V., Ausín, V., Hortigüela-Alcalá, D., & Abella, V. (2016). Evaluación entre iguales: Una experiencia de evaluación compartida en Educación Superior. *Educadi, 1*(1), 9–24. doi:10.7770/EDUCADI-V1N1-ART943

Fraile, J., Gil-Izquierdo, M., Zamorano-Sande, D., & Sánchez-Iglesias, I. (2020). Autorregulación del aprendizaje y procesos de evaluación formativa en los trabajos en grupo. *RELIEVE, 26*(1), 1–15. doi:10.7203/relieve.26.1.17402

Fraile-Aranda, A., López-Pastor, V. M., Castejón-Oliva, F. J., & Romero-Martín, R. (2013). La evaluación formativa en docencia universitaria y el rendimiento académico del alumnado. *Revista Aula Abierta, 41*(2), 23-34. https://dialnet.unirioja.es/servlet/articulo?codigo=4239063

Gallardo, F., & Carter, B. (2016). La evaluación formativa y compartida durante el prácticum en la formación inicial del profesorado: Análisis de un caso en Chile. *Retos, 29*(1), 258–263. https://recyt.fecyt.es/index.php/retos/article/view/43550

Gallardo, F. J., López-Pastor, V. M., & Carter, B. (2020). Ventajas e Inconvenientes de la Evaluación Formativa, y su Influencia en la Autopercepción de Competencias en alumnado de Formación Inicial del Profesorado en Educación Física. *Retos, 38*(38), 417–424. https://recyt.fecyt.es/index.php/retos/article/view/75540. doi:10.47197/retos.v38i38.75540

Gallardo-Fuentes, F. J., López-Pastor, V. M., & Carter-Tuhillier, B. (2018). Efectos de la aplicación de un sistema de evaluación formativa en la autopercepción de competencias adquiridas en formación inicial del profesorado. *Estudios Pedagógicos (Valdivia), 44*(2), 55–77. doi:10.4067/S0718-07052018000200055

Gómez, M. A., & Quesada, V. (2017). Coevaluación o evaluación compartida en el contexto universitario: La percepción del alumnado de primer curso. *Revista Iberoamericana de Evaluación Educativa, 10*(2), 9–30. doi:10.15366/riee2017.10.2.001

Hamodi, C., & López, A. T. (2012). La evaluación formativa y compartida en la Formación Inicial del Profesorado desde la perspectiva del alumnado y de los egresados. *Psychology, Society, &. Education, 4*(1), 103–116. https://ojs.ual.es/ojs/index.php/psye/article/view/484

Hamodi, C., López-Pastor, V. M., & López, A. T. (2017). If I experience formative assessment whilst at University will I put it into practice later as a teacher? Formative and shared assessment in Initial Teacher Education. *European Journal of Teacher Education, 40*(2), 171–190. doi:10.1080/02619768.2017.1281909

Hortigüela-Alcalá, D., Abella, V., Delgado, V., & Ausín, V. (2016). Influencia del sistema de evaluación empleado en la percepción del alumno sobre su aprendizaje y las competencias docentes. *Infancia, Educación y Aprendizaje, 2*(1), 20-42. http://revistainfanciaeducacionyaprendizaje.com/

Hortigüela-Alcalá, D., González-Víllora, S., & Hernando-Garijo, A. (2021). Do we really assess learning in Physical Education? Teacher's perceptions at different educational stages. *Retos, 42*, 643–654. doi:10.47197/retos.v42i0.88686

Hortigüela-Alcalá, D., Palacios, A., & López-Pastor, V. M. (2019). The impact of formative and shared or co-assessment on the acquisition of transversal competences in higher education. *Assessment & Evaluation in Higher Education, 44*(6), 933–945. doi:10.1080/02602938.2018.1530341

Hortigüela-Alcalá, D., Pérez-Pueyo, A., & González-Calvo, G. (2019). Pero… ¿A qué nos referimos realmente con la Evaluación Formativa y Compartida?: Confusiones Habituales y Reflexiones Prácticas. *Revista Iberoamericana de Evaluación Educativa, 12*(1), 13–27. doi:10.15366/riee2019.12.1.001

Ibarra-Sáiz, M. S., Rodríguez-Gómez, G., Boud, D., Rotsaert, T., Brown, S., Salinas-Salazar, M. L., & Rodríguez-Gómez, H. M. (2020). El futuro de la evaluación en la educación superior. *RELIEVE, 26*(1), 1–6. doi:10.7203/relieve.26.1.17323

López-Pastor, V. M. (coord.) (2009). *Evaluación formativa y compartida en educación superior. Propuestas, técnicas, instrumentos y experiencias.* Narcea.

López-Pastor, V. M., Molina, M., Pascual, C., & Manrique, J. C. (2020). La importancia de utilizar la Evaluación Formativa y Compartida en la Formación Inicial del Profesorado de Educación Física: los Proyectos de Aprendizaje Tutorado como ejemplo de buena práctica. *Retos, Nuevas tendencias en Educación Física, Deporte y Recreación, 37,* 680-687. https://dialnet.unirioja.es/servlet/articulo?codigo=7243328

López-Pastor, V. M., & Pérez-Pueyo, A. (Coords.) (2017). *Buenas prácticas docentes. Evaluación formativa y compartida en educación: experiencias de éxito en todas las etapas educativas* (e-book). Universidad de León. https://buleria.unileon.es/handle/10612/5999

Lorente, E., & Kirk, D. (2016). Student teachers' understanding and application of assessment for learning during a physical education teacher education course. *European Physical Education Review, 22*(1), 65–81. doi:10.1177/1356336X15590352

Lorente-Catalán, E., & Kirk, D. (2013). Alternative democratic assessment in PETE: An action-research study exploring risks, challenges and solutions. *Sport Education and Society, 18*(1), 77–96. doi:10.1080/13573322.2012.713859

Manrique, J. C., López Pastor, V. M., Monjas, R., & Real, F. (2010). El potencial de los Proyectos de Aprendizaje Tutorado y los sistemas de evaluación formativa en la mejora de la autonomía del alumnado: Una experiencia interdisciplinar en formación inicial del profesorado. *Revista Española de Educación Física y Deportes, 14,* 39-57. https://www.reefd.es/index.php/reefd/article/viewFile/285/276

Martínez-Mínguez, L., Vallés Rapp, C., y Romero-Mínguez, R. (2015). Estudiantes universitarios: ventajas e inconvenientes de la evaluación formativa. *Revista d'Innovació educativa, 14,* 59-70. doi:10.7203/attic.14.4217

Molina, M., & López-Pastor, V. M. (2017). La transferencia de la Evaluación Formativa y Compartida desde la Formación Inicial del Profesorado de Educación Física a la práctica real en Educación Primaria. *Infancia, Educación y Aprendizaje (IEYA), 3*(2), 626-631. https://revistas.uv.cl/index.php/IEYA/index

Molina, M., & López-Pastor, V. M. (2019). ¿Evalúo cómo me evaluaron en la facultad? Transferencia de la evaluación formativa y compartida vivida durante la formación inicial del profesorado a la práctica como docente. *RIEE. Revista Iberoamericana de Evaluación Educativa, 12*(1), 85–101. doi:10.15366/riee2019.12.1.005

Molina, M., Pascual, C., & López-Pastor, V. M. (2020). El rendimiento académico y la evaluación formativa y compartida en formación del profesorado. *Alteridad, 15*(2), 204–215. doi:10.17163/alt.v15n2.2020.05

Montero, I., & León, O. G. (2005). Sistema de clasificación del método en los informes de investigación en Psicología. *International Journal of Clinical and Health Psychology, 5*(1), 115–127. https://www.redalyc.org/articulo.oa?id=33701007

Nicol, D., Thomson, A., & Breslin, C. (2014). Rethinking feedback practice in higher education: A peer revier perspective. *Assessment & Evaluation in Higher Education, 39*(1), 102–122. doi:10.1080/02602938.2013.795518

Palacios, A., & López-Pastor, V. M. (2013). Haz lo que yo digo pero no lo que yo hago: Sistemas de evaluación del alumnado en la formación inicial del profesorado. *Review of Education, 361,* 279–305. doi:10.4438/1988-592X-RE-2011-361-143

Panadero, E., & Jonsson, A. (2013). The use of scoring rubrics for formative assessment purposes revisited: A review. *Educational Research Review, 9,* 129–144. doi:10.1016/j.edurev.2013.01.002

Pastor, V. M. (2008). Desarrollando sistemas de evaluación formativa y compartida en la docencia universitaria. Análisis de resultados de su puesta en práctica en la formación inicial del profesorado. *European Journal of Teacher Education, 31*(3), 293–311. doi:10.1080/02619760802208452

Romero, M. R., Castejón, F. J., López-Pastor, V. M., & Fraile, A. (2017). Evaluación formativa, competencias comunicativas y TIC en la formación del profesorado. *Comunicar, 52*(3) 73-82. https://www.torrossa.com/en/resources/an/4150000

Romero, R., Castejón, F. J., & López, V. M. (2015). Divergencias del alumnado y del profesorado universitario sobre las dificultades para aplicar la evaluación formativa. *Relieve, 21*(1), 1–16. doi:10.7203/relieve.21.1.5169

Romero, R., Fraile, A., López-Pastor, V. M., & Castejón, F. J. (2014). Relación entre sistemas de evaluación formativa, rendimiento académico y carga de trabajo del profesor y del alumno en la docencia universitaria. *Infancia y Aprendizaje, 37*(1), 16–32. doi:10.1080/02103702.2014.918818

Romero-Martín, M. R., Asún, S., & Chivite, M. T. (2016). La autoevaluación en expresión corporal en formación inicial del profesorado de educación física: un ejemplo de buena práctica. *Retos. Nuevas tendencias en Educación Física, Deportes y Recreación, 29,* 236-241. https://www.redalyc.org/pdf/3457/345743464045.pdf

Salcines, I., González-Fernández, N., Ramírez-García, A. & Martínez-Mínguez, L. (2018). Validación de la escala de autopercepción de competencias transversales y profesionales de estudiantes de educación superior. *Currículum y formación del profesorado, 22*(3), 31-51. doi:10.30827/profesorado.v22i3.7989

Santos, M., Martínez, L. F. & López, V. M. (coords.) (2009). *La Innovación docente en el Espacio Europeo de Educación Superior.* Editorial Universidad de Almería.

Vallés, C., Ureña, N., & Ruiz, E. (2011). La evaluación Formativa en Docencia Universitaria. Resultados globales de 41 estudios de caso en su primer año de desarrollo. *Revista de Docencia Universitaria, 9*(1), 135-158. https://riunet.upv.es/handle/10251/141562

ADDITIONAL READING

Atienza, R., Valencia-Peris, A., & López-Pastor, V. M. (2021). Students' experiences during their early schooling – when and who should assess schoolchildren's physical education. *Journal of Physical Education and Sport, 21*(3), 1479–1490. doi:10.7752/jpes.2021.03188

Bores-García, D., Hortigüela-Alcalá, D., Hernando-Garijo, A., & González-Calvo, G. (2021). Analysis of student motivation towards body expression through the use of formative and share assessment. *Retos*, *1*(40), 198–208. doi:10.47197/retos.v1i40.83025

Cañadas, L., Santos-Pastor, M. L., & Ruiz, P. (2021). Percepción del impacto de la evaluación formativa en las competencias profesionales durante la formación inicial del profesorado. *Revista Electrónica de Investigación Educativa*, *23*, 1–14. doi:10.24320/redie.2021.23.e07.2982

Hamodi, C. (2016) (Coord.). *Formar mediante la evaluación en la Universidad. Propuestas prácticas útiles para docentes.* Universidad de Valladolid. https://uvadoc.uva.es/bitstream/handle/10324/42970/EdUVa-Formar-mediante-evaluaci%c3%b3n.pdf?sequence=1&isAllowed=y

Herrero-González, D., Manrique Arribas, J. C., & López-Pastor, V. (2021). Incidencia de la Formación Inicial y Permanente del Profesorado en la aplicación de la Evaluación Formativa y Compartida en Educación Física (Incidence of Pre-service and In-service Teacher Education in the application of Formative and Shared Assessment. *Retos*, (41), 533–543. doi:10.47197/retos.v0i41.86090

Jiménez, F., Navarro, V., Pintor, P., & Souto, R. (2013). Percepción del alumnado de las dimensiones 'proceso', 'aprendizaje' y 'compromiso' en el marco de los sistemas de evaluación formativa. En M. J. Cuéllar y O'Dwyer (Coords.). Innovación en las enseñanzas universitarias. Universidad de La Laguna.

López-Pastor, V. M., Fuentes, T., Pascual Arias, C., Molina Soria, M., & Fernández, C. (2021). La evaluación educativa en la formación inicial del profesorado: Ventajas y posibilidades de la evaluación formativa y compartida. En W. dos Santos. y R. Stieg, (org.). Evaluación educativa en la formación de profesores. (cap.2, pg. 31-52). Appris.

Molina Soria, M. (2020). La influencia de la pandemia COVID19 en la evaluación formativa de una asignatura de la formación inicial del profesorado. En J. A. Marín, J. M. Trujillo, G. González, y M. N. Campos (eds.), Hacia un modelo de investigación sostenible (pp. 599-611). Dykinson.

KEY TERMS AND DEFINITIONS

Academic performance: Grades obtained by students at the end of the course.

Competences: Skills and knowledge to be acquired by students during their training.

Dialogical mark: Process of dialogue between teachers and students to reach an agreed and reasoned final grade, based on the established criteria and the accumulated evidence.

Formative Assessment: Assessment process aimed at improving student learning, teaching practice and the teaching-learning processes carried out.

Initial Teacher Education: Studies undertaken to train professionally as a teacher.

Peer-assessment: Assessment between peers.

Self-Assessment: Assessment of oneself.

Self-Mark: Process performed by oneself on the grade one believes is deserved at the end of the course, taking into account the agreed grading criteria.

Shared Assessment: Dialogic processes between teachers and students on the assessment process, usually based on a previous self-assessment of the students.

APPENDIX

Table 8. Results Block I: transversal competencies

Course	Course 2017-18					Course 2018-19					Course 2019-20					Course 2020-21				
Group	1stJSP		3rdECE		T	1stJSP		3rdECE		T	1stJSP		3rdECE		T	1stJSP		3rdECE		T
	B	S ✓	B	S ✓		B	S ✓	B	S ✓		B	S ✓	B	S ✓		B	S ✓	B	S ✓	
1.1-Analyse and synthesise	3	.508	3.32	.541	**.036***	2.88	.740	3.10	.301	**.007***	4.05	.621	3.5	1.5	1	3.16	.602	3.14	.441	.087
1.2-Organise and plan	3.31	.693	3.52	.508	.889	3.21	.740	3.35	.486	.383	4.33	.471	3.5	1.5	1	3.51	.559	3.55	.506	.336
1.3-Communicate orally and in writing in the native language	3.19	.592	3.35	.551	.596	2.79	.820	3.06	.680	**.016***	3.44	1.212	3.5	1.5	1	3.32	.669	3.41	.501	.100
1.4-Communicate gesturally and corporeally	3.13	.554	3.52	.570	**.006***	2.97	.728	3.19	.749	.531	3.11	1.149	3	1.581	1	3.11	.737	3.41	.568	.962
1.5-Know a foreign language	2.50	.842	2.23	.679	**.031***	1.79	.857	1.94	.727	.508	1	.749	1	0	.678	2.70	.661	2.41	.733	.532
1.6-Use the Information and Communication Technologies in the field of study.	3.03	.695	3.13	.718	.821	2.33	1.080	2.61	.919	.194	2.38	1.208	3	2	1	3.14	.751	3.21	.675	.900
1.7-Work in a team	3.47	.621	3.87	.341	**.000***	3.73	.517	3.65	.486	.513	4.66	.471	4.25	1.299	1	3.70	.520	3.69	.541	.825
1.8-Develop skills in interpersonal relationships (empathy, assertiveness, respect and listening).	3.63	.554	3.84	.374	**.005***	3.27	.674	3.52	.508	.528	4.27	.730	3.75	1.639	1	3.65	.484	3.90	.310	**.000***
1.9-Develop intrapersonal skills (self-esteem, motivation and self-confidence).	3.28	.729	3.67	.479	**.005***	3	.762	3.26	.514	.117	3.5	1.118	3.75	1.639	1	3.19	.660	3.52	.574	.932

The significance level was set at $p \leq 0.05$.

Table 9. Results Block II: teaching competencies

Group	Course 2017-18					Course 2018-19					Course 2019-20					Course 2020-21				
	1stJSP		3rdECE		T	1stJSP		3rdECE		T	1stJSP		3rdECE		T	1stJSP		3rdECE		T
	B	S	B	S		B	S	B	S		B	S	B	S		B	S	B	S	
2.1. Know the organisational characteristics of schools.	2.78	.553	2.90	,473	.156	2.09	.723	2.52	.570	.953	2.27	.989	2.25	1.089	1	2.81	.569	2.79	.620	.640
2.2. Elaborate proposals for change in the educational reality.	2.91	.689	3.03	,657	.205	2.53	.567	2.94	.512	.032*	2.77	1.133	3.5	1.5	1	2.78	.712	2.93	.593	.046*
2.3. Design learning situations.	3.13	.492	3.42	.502	.000*	3	.661	3.45	.675	.935	4	1.000	3	1.581	1	3.03	.687	3.41	.568	.591
2.4. Animate learning situations.	3.13	.562	3.42	.620	.111	3.09	.678	3.29	.529	.007*	3.55	1.300	3	1.581	1	2.97	.645	3.45	.506	.417
2.5. Manage learning progression.	2.81	.535	3.19	.654	.044*	2.66	.545	3.06	.512	.358	3.61	1.208	3.25	1.299	1	2.81	.569	3.10	.489	.158
2.6. Design strategies to attend to diversity.	3.16	.677	3.10	,662	1	2.76	.902	3.13	.763	.128	3.16	1.213	2.75	1.299	1	3.03	.645	3.07	.458	.138
2.7. Implement strategies of attention to diversity	2.81	.896	2.83	,699	.463	2.58	.830	2.90	.700	.078	2.83	1.067	2.25	.433	1	2.95	.705	3.00	.655	.701
2.8. Involve students in their learning 2.9.	3.09	.530	3.29	,693	.005*	4.03	5.235	3.55	.568	.547	3.94	1.129	4.25	.433	1	3.22	.534	3.69	.471	.947
2.9. Involve students in the life of the school.	3	.568	2.97	,605	.778	2.48	.795	2.74	.815	.210	3.38	1.296	2.75	1.299	1	3.00	.707	3.17	.805	.043*
2.10. Participate in the management of the school	2.56	.716	2.39	,761	.131	1.88	.740	2.03	.547	.009*	2.38	1.208	1.75	.433	1	2.76	.760	2.72	.841	.581
2.11. Inform families about their child's progress.	2.97	.816	2.71	,783	.672	2.15	1.004	2.29	.739	.073	2.22	1.181	2.25	1.089	1	3.22	.712	2.86	.915	.134
2.12. Involve families in their child's learning.	2.88	.793	3.03	,657	.924	2.27	.977	2.32	.748	.109	2.38	1.339	1.75	.433	1	3.24	.641	2.97	.906	.240
2.13. Involve families in the life of the school.	2.91	.588	2.74	,773	.024*	2.24	.936	2.19	.792	.000*	2.27	1.282	1.75	.433	1	3.00	.745	2.93	.884	.411
2.14. Face the duties and ethical dilemmas of the profession.	2.94	.680	3.10	,700	.760	2.85	.619	2.90	.597	.005*	2.83	1.213	2.25	1.089	1	2.95	.705	3.10	.618	.803
2.15. Attend to their own professional development (self-assessment, readings, courses…).	2.88	.609	3.26	,631	.643	3	.661	3.45	.506	.935	3.55	1.012	3.75	1.089	1	3.00	.667	3.17	.658	.267
2.16. Develop processes of educational innovation in the classroom.	2.91	.641	3.10	,597	.301	2.61	.609	3.30	.596	.419	3.38	1.422	3	1.581	.799	2.89	.614	3.17	.539	.728
2.17. Implement research processes in the classroom.	2.84	.677	2.74	,729	.790	2.45	.564	2.94	.727	.001*	3.11	1.523	2.25	1.089	1	2.78	.821	2.62	.728	.871

The significance level was set at p≤0.05.

Table 10. Results Block III: specific physical education teaching competencies.

Course	Course 2017-18					Course 2018-19					Course 2019-20					Course 2020-21				
Group	1stJSP		3rdECE		T	1stJSP		3rdECE		T	1stJSP		3rdECE		T	1stJSP		3rdECE		T
	B	S	B	S		B	S	B	S		B	S	B	S		B	S	B	S	
3.1. Design, apply and analyse didactic interventions in the area of Physical Education.	3	.508	3.23	.560	.255	3.03	.585	3.55	.506	.760	3.94	.970	3.75	1.089	1	3.14	.481	3.34	.614	.008*
3.2. Design, develop and evaluate teaching-learning processes related to physical activity and sport with attention to the Specific Needs of Educational Support.	2.88	.554	3.03	.669	.842	2.73	.719	3.03	.605	.373	4.11	1.048	3.75	1.089	1	3.03	.687	3.03	.566	.238
3.3. Know and promote the different motor manifestations that are part of the traditional culture.	2.84	.677	3.03	.547	.084	2.84	.677	3.29	.693	.978	4.33	.745	4.25	.433	1	3.05	.621	3.14	.441	.272
3.4. Know and apply the biological, physiological, evolutionary maturation and psychomotor development fundamentals.	2.88	.609	3.03	.657	.737	2.7	.728	3.26	.729	.498	4.05	.848	3.5	.866	1	2.89	.614	3.28	.455	.692
3.5. Design, modify and/or adapt to the educational context motor situations oriented to the development and improvement of motor skills.	3.16	.677	3.29	.529	.262	2.94	.704	3.58	.502	.805	4.27	.730	3.75	1.089	1	3.03	.600	3.34	.614	.080
3.6. Know the elements and fundamentals of body expression and non-verbal communication and their formative and cultural value.	3.28	.581	3.26	.575	.367	2.88	.600	3.45	.561	.717	3.83	1.118	3.75	1.089	1	3.24	.683	3.34	.614	.705
3.7. Know how to use play as a didactic resource and as teaching content.	3.44	.619	3.65	.551	.115	3.41	.560	3.97	.180	.000*	4.66	.471	4.25	.433	1	3.70	.520	3.86	.351	.004*
3.8. Know the basic fundamentals of school sports initiation and design specific tasks to use them in the teaching environment.	3.09	.588	3.10	.539	.690	2.82	.683	3.37	.556	.001*	4.33	.745	3.75	1.089	1	3.19	.660	3.38	.494	.465
3.9. Identify the risks to health derived from the practice of inadequate physical activities.	3	.762	2.97	.752	.323	2.3	.847	2.55	.888	.195	3.55	1.165	3	1.581	1	3.00	.745	3.14	.581	.569
3.10. Design a plan of healthy lifestyle habits (hygiene and nutrition) and regular physical activity practice.	3.03	.740	3.07	.691	.462	2	.866	2.29	.783	.405	3.72	.989	2.25	1.089	1	3.16	.834	3.14	.639	.071
3.11. Know how to apply the fundamentals (techniques) of physical activities in the natural environment.	2.91	.641	3.10	.790	.328	2.15	.906	3	.683	.597	3.55	1.300	2	0	1	3.03	.687	3.31	.541	.982
3.12. Know how to use different assessment instruments in the area of Physical Education.	3.19	.592	3.16	.583	.665	3.30	.585	3.42	.564	.384	3.88	.936	3	1.581	1	3.08	.682	3.38	.561	.854
3.13. Have the ability to reflect on the teaching/learning process and the different methodologies within the Physical Education classes.	3.16	.583	3.39	.615	.065	3.18	.635	3.42	.502	.567	4.22	.916	3.75	1.089	1	3.30	.571	3.52	.574	.518
3.14. Analyse and communicate, in a critical and well-founded manner, the value of physical activity and sport and their potential to contribute to people's development and well-being.	3.13	.660	3.29	.643	.478	2.97	.637	3.26	.631	.383	4.27	.730	3.75	1.089	1	3.24	.495	3.38	.494	.255

The significance level was set at $p \leq 0.05$.

Table 11. Advantages recognised in the assessment system applied

Aspects to be considered by the pupils	Course 2017-2018				Course 2018-2019				Course 2019-2020				Course 2020-2021			
	3rdECE		1stJSP		3rdECE		1stJSP		3rdECE		1stJSP		3rdECE		1stJSP	
	B	σ	B	σ	B	σ	B	σ	B	σ	B	σ	B	σ	B	σ
1. It offers alternatives to all students	4.06	.998	3.89	1.078	4.13	1.040	3.89	1.048	3.71	1.380	3.38	0.960	4.28	.797	6.62	1.492
2. There is a prior, negotiated and consensual contract of the assessment system.	3.30	1.104	3.74	1.291	4.24	1.200	3.54	1.216	3.71	1.112	3.83	1.391	4.21	.726	4.32	1.029
3. It is focused on the process, importance of daily work.	4.64	.489	4.83	.382	4.67	.540	4.57	.801	4.00	1	4.30	0.854	4.45	.736	4.57	.647
4. The student is an active learner	4.52	.566	4.63	.490	4.58	.561	4.32	.669	4.00	.577	4.2	0.926	4.62	.561	4.59	.551
5. Collaborative teamwork is considered.	4.61	.566	4.74	.505	4.30	.728	4.49	.870	4.14	1.069	4.46	0.518	4.55	.632	4.24	1.038
6. The student is more motivated, the learning process is more motivating.	3.79	.960	3.54	.852	3.45	1.063	2.97	.928	3.42	1.272	2.69	0.751	4.03	1.052	3.41	1.142
7. The grading is fairer	4.15	.972	3.62	.954	3.39	.998	3.46	1.260	3.57	1.272	3.00	0.918	4.17	.928	3.59	1.117
8. It improved academic tutoring (monitoring and assistance to the student).	4.09	.723	4.09	.818	3.91	.914	3.76	1.164	2.85	1.345	3.20	1.154	4.45	.632	3.89	.906
9. It allows functional learning	4.15	.667	4.35	.812	4.00	.791	4.00	.676	3.28	1.113	3.50	1.702	4.41	.632	4.28	.632
10. It generates meaningful learning	4.39	.788	4.21	.687	4.21	.781	4.14	.751	3.71	1.113	3.84	0.989	4.39	.630	4.32	.613
11. Much more is learned	4.18	.769	4.20	.632	3.97	.918	3.95	.743	3.57	1.272	3.58	1.250	4.08	.829	4.06	.795
12. It improves the quality of the work required	3.88	.707	4.43	.884	3.85	1.004	3.70	.968	3.42	1.339	3.83	1.265	4.14	.839	4.08	.917
13. There is an interrelation between theory and practice	4.67	.479	4.66	.591	4.64	.653	4.46	.691	4.14	0.899	4.30	0.630	4.44	.767	4.40	.884
14. It evaluates all possible aspects (in reference to knowledge, know-how and knowing how to be).	4.33	.692	4.31	.676	4.12	.992	3.92	.906	3.66	1.574	3.69	1.109	4.32	.705	4.19	.709
15. There is feedback in documents and activities	4.55	.617	4.74	.561	4.55	.869	4.22	1.084	4.42	0.787	4.07	1.037	4.41	.701	4.30	.723
16. There is the possibility of correcting errors in documents and activities	4.85	.364	4.71	.519	4.79	.485	4.57	.728	4.57	0.534	4.33	1.414	4.45	.637	4.30	.696
17. There is a more individualised follow-up	3.85	.834	4.17	.785	3.58	.969	3.36	.931	4	0.816	3.30	0.947	3.88	.886	3.89	.954
18. It requires more responsibility	4.61	.609	4.86	.355	4.48	.795	4.65	.633	4	1.414	3.90	1.601	4.70	.607	4.64	.715

The significance level was set at $p \leq 0.05$.

Table 12. Disadvantages recognised in the assessment system applied

Aspects to be considered by the pupils	Course 2017-2018				Course 2018-2019				Course 2019-2020				Course 2020-2021			
	3rdECE		1stJSP		3rdECE		1stJSP		3rdECE		1stJSP		3rdECE		1stJSP	
	B	σ	B	σ	B	σ	B	σ	B	σ	B	σ	B	σ	B	σ
1. It requires mandatory and active attendance	4.82	.465	4.74	.561	4.56	.746	4.59	.798	4.42	0.787	4.46	0.776	4.80	.401	4.80	.401
2. It has an unfamiliar work dynamic, lack of habit.	3.41	1.456	3.80	1.106	3.06	1.223	3.81	1.309	3.16	1.603	3.54	1.683	3.39	1.578	3.27	1.603
3. It requires continuity	4.79	.485	4.80	.406	4.65	.544	4.78	.479	4.57	0.534	4.76	0.438	4.85	.402	4.85	.438
4. It is necessary to understand it beforehand	3.76	.867	3.94	.919	4.03	.797	4.25	.874	4.28	0.756	4.23	0.725	4.06	.762	4.05	.711
5. It requires greater effort	4.61	.496	4.71	.572	4.32	1.036	4.67	.632	4.57	0.534	4.53	0.518	4.65	.620	4.79	.412
6. It is difficult to work in a group	2.24	1.200	3.51	1.095	2.94	1.278	3.51	1.367	2.85	1.345	2.53	0.877	2.98	1.307	3.35	1.364
7. A lot of work can accumulate at the end	3.56	1.162	4.14	1.004	4.00	1.044	3.94	1.351	4.28	0.951	3.69	1.250	3.95	1.156	4.48	.846
8. There is a disproportion between work/credits.	4.15	.939	3.91	1.228	4.48	.906	4.62	.639	3	1.527	3.76	1.165	3.82	1.227	4.00	1.123
9. The grading process is more complex and, at times, unclear.	3.15	1.417	2.80	1.279	2.65	1.125	4.05	1.026	3.14	1.069	2.92	1.320	2.92	1.168	3.24	1.110
10. It generates insecurity and uncertainty, doubts about what is to be done.	3.00	1.323	2.86	.974	2.67	1.109	3.86	1.032	2.85	1.215	3.41	1.405	3.02	1.196	3.30	1.037
11. It is unfair compared to other assessment processes	2.58	1.562	2.34	1.474	2.34	1.405	3.42	1.180	2.14	1.215	2.61	1.660	2.71	1.496	3.23	1.497
12. The corrections have been unclear	2.00	1.125	1.97	1.029	2.33	1.216	2.97	1.082	3	1.732	2.92	1.255	2.14	1.162	2.32	1.192
13. The assessment of the work is subjective	2.52	1.372	2.79	1.269	3.06	1.298	3.28	1.323	3	1.527	3.15	1.154	2.88	1.398	3.27	1.342
14. It requires me to participate in my own assessment (self-assessment).	4.27	.761	4.32	.806	4.35	.734	4.30	.812	4	0.816	3.46	1.330	4.67	.564	4.77	.520

The significance level was set at $p \leq 0.05$.

Chapter 11

Tutoring as a Tool for Academic Performance Improvement During the Covid–19 Pandemic:
A Contribution to the Formative and Shared Evaluation in Ecuador

Juan José Rocha Espinoza
https://orcid.org/0000-0001-7886-2194
Universidad Politécnica Salesiana, Ecuador

Nadia L. Soria-Miranda
Universidad de Guayaquil, Ecuador

ABSTRACT

The Covid-19 crisis not only had a global impact on the sanitary services, but also had economic and social repercussions, especially at the educational system; this last apex is to be dealt with in relation to the Ecuadorian higher education level reality. As it is so, this chapter's aim is to collect the tutoring experience as part of the shared and formative evaluation (F&SA) during the pandemic. For this process the phenomenological methodology of research was used, managing to consolidate teachers and university students focus groups, who made a contribution with derivate features from the university educational reality, coming to consider tutoring as a necessary tool to strengthen those weaknesses given during synchronous connections. In this way, it provides an evaluation that promotes participative training process, where favorable learning environments are generated.

INTRODUCTION

As a result of the global pandemic caused by COVID-19, educational processes were affected. This led to decision-making by various nations to implement virtual education. These emerging decisions led

DOI: 10.4018/978-1-6684-3537-3.ch011

to substantial changes in the methodology, evaluation, and academic follow-up. Considering that at the beginning of the pandemic 336,037,719 people around the world were affected by the closure of educational institutions, according to the *United Nations Educational, Scientific and Cultural Organization* (UNESCO). Ecuador reported 4,307,718.

Following Ecuador's case, according to the research published on this country, the education and relationship to COVID-19, it can be found that Sánchez & Catagña (2021), González (2021), Tejedor et al (2020), Palacios et al (2020), Rocha (2020), Vohlonen (2020), who help to understand the educational reality of the country during the pandemic and lockdown, which began as a virtualized education format, but which is beginning to materialize in what is known as a hybrid education.

The teacher's job is fundamental, in fact, in both educational processes, virtual and hybrid, as well as the students, teachers had experienced these changes (in person, virtual, hybrid), and the methodology changes and procedures in the different digital platforms where educational processes have been performed. Accordingly, teachers had to innovate, create, and implement tools to maintain educational quality. For this research, tutoring, its relevance, procedures, efficacy, etc. is taken as the central theme, as part of the shared and formative evaluation.

Tutoring Perspectives and Legal Issues in the Higher Education System in Ecuador

When speaking of *tutoring*, it can be said that it is "(…) recognized as a compensatory strategy that must be implemented to the inside of the school" (p. 91), in this sense, understanding the compensatory term as an addition to the educational process, which must not only consider the contents, but also as expressed by Boroel et al (2018), this must also "(…) must link individual student issues with its social and family context" (p. 91).

In the same vein, Solaguren-Beascoa & Moreno Delgado (2016) discuss several aspects of the tutoring "(…) which can be grouped into three: academic or assistance to the student in the teaching-learning processes, curricular or guidance in the choice of their academic and professional itinerary, and personal or support regarding their integral development" (p. 248). This is how this tool becomes indispensable in the educational field.

In a more real prospect about tutoring Gómez (2012) indicates that tutoring is "(…) acción pedagógica que trata de favorecer las situaciones educativas para generar un modelo educativo que ayude al proceso de enseñanza-aprendizaje de manera individual y grupal" ["(…) pedagogical action that encourages educational situations to generate a model to help the teaching-learning process individually and in groups] (p. 211). Therefore, it is necessary to understand that tutoring is conceived within the educational field, contributes to the teaching-learning process through the meeting between teacher and student, or student group, to seek improvement in the academic performance.

On the objectives of tutoring in an educational context, López Gómez (2017) refers about mentoring mission, which consists of "(…) ayudar al alumnado a lo largo de sus estudios, en el desarrollo de su proceso formativo, en relación a una serie de elementos básicos como son la integración y adaptación al entorno universitario" [(…)help students throughout their studies, in their training process development, in relation to many basic elements such as integration and adaptation to the university environment] (p. 63). To put it another way, there is an important role in the teacher that goes beyond a job or the fulfillment of an objective, since this support is also linked to the students' general formative development, not only in the academic field.

Here it is important to highlight the teachers' role not only as a professional, but also as a companion for the student, since the author postulates it in his research when he writes:

Estos resultados ponen de manifiesto la armonía entre función docente y labor tutorial, que hace posible orientar a los estudiantes en y desde el propio proceso de enseñar, y que permite a su vez avanzar hacia un enfoque profundo en el aprendizaje de los diversos ámbitos disciplinares desde una enseñanza centrada en el estudiante. Esta es una concepción más amplia de la tutoría académica, entendida de modo superficial como aquella que se ofrece para orientar sobre dudas en el aprendizaje (...) la dimensión profesional de la tutoría debe asumirse desde un enfoque transversal, más allá de determinados ámbitos curriculares centrados en la práctica profesional o de los cursos finales de la titulación. [These results show the harmony between teaching function and tutoring work, which makes possible to guide students in and from the teaching process itself, and which allows to move towards a deep focus on the learning of the various disciplinary areas from a student-centered teaching. This is a broader conception of academic tutoring, understood superficially as the offered to guide on doubts in the learning process(...) the professional dimension of tutoring must be assumed from a transversal approach, beyond certain curricular areas focused on professional internships or the final degree courses.] (pp. 70–71)

Tutoring as a concept tries hard to develop, focus and strengthen the student's learning through teaching accompaniment, as a conceptual basis to also talk about the emotional and personal development that is received through teaching. López Gómez (2017) is clear about this, since he does not conceive it as a merely technical strategy, focused on "optimizing" the student's education, but on this support also being relevant to their integral development.

Gabriela de la Cruz Flores et al (2011) also has interesting contributions to the concept of tutoring, but also to the function, definition and characteristics of the tutor as the main element of the process, since she, along with the other authors, conceive it as "(…) una relación entre dos individuos, uno con alto nivel de pericia en un particular setting, o área práctica, y otro con menor habilidad y conocimientos en la comunidad" [(...) a relationship between two individuals, one with a high level of expertise in a particular setting, or practical area, and the other with less skill and knowledge in the community] (de la Cruz Flores et al., 2011, p. 195).

Here the figure of the tutor takes on a lot of relevance at the conceptual level, since it is conceived from the two perspectives that they consider most universalized: the academic tutoring model, whose emphasis is only on the academic development of the student, and the tutoring model of "personal development", where the focus is on the student's academic development: "(…) presta mayor atención al bienestar y al desarrollo personal de sus alumnos" [(...) pays greater attention to the well-being and personal development of its students] (p. 192).

In these two variants, the figure of the tutor acquires great relevance, since he/she is the conductor and executor of the strategies that will be used for the correct development of the tutoring.

Thus, the authors give a series of characteristics of tutoring when conceptualizing it, among which are the following: The skill, dynamism and knowledge that the tutor must have to carry out the tutoring process, since they will be the ones who teach and work directly with the students; their role as guides, with the aim of achieving academic excellence. That is why they must be clear with students regarding the fulfillment of goals and planning of tutoring. This is more noticeable in higher education contexts due to the complexity or difficulties that students may have with the subject matter, within an educational process.

It is also mentioned that they must have different attributes, such as "formative" attributes, as they must have total and absolute understanding of their working area is considered "indispensable" for tutoring to be effective. They must also have "didactic attributes", which complement the previous ones through the execution of their knowledge: they must know methodologies, examples, teaching models or learning strategies that go in line with their discipline and allow students to understand the area of study. finally, they must have "interpersonal attributes" summarized in two: availability and communication skills. The first due to the commitment that is established when the tutor agrees to tutor with the student, and the second so that there is a correct and effective clarification of doubts. (p. 193–194)

For González Palacios et al (2016), tutoring can also be divided into two areas: work-help and strategic tutoring, and three models: integral, peer tutoring, and academic tutoring. (González & Avelino, 2016, p. 63). Work-help tutoring, refers to the processes of direct help to the student to be able to complete a certain subject, making it clear that the focus is only on help, when writing about strategic tutoring: "El segundo modelo, combina elementos de instrucción y tutoría de trabajo-ayuda. (...) Se les enseñan a los estudiantes estrategias para aprender a aprender y llevar a cabo mientras reciben ayuda con las tareas de clase." [The second model combines elements of instruction and work-help tutoring. (...) It is taught to students learning strategies of how to learn and carry out, while receiving help with class assignments.] (p. 63) In strategic tutoring, the help is complemented by different strategies and more comprehensive methodologies, which serve the student not only for the resolution or approval of a course, but to be able to have a more expanded knowledge of the subject to be worked.

The three models, based on Bakaikoa's work, are defined from what they seek to do in the student and their functioning, the three being different in terms of the approach to tutoring. In the integral model, the search for accompaniment is complete, alluding to the academic, professional, and personal work of the student. This is how tutoring becomes a relationship between two or more people, where the axis is the integral growth of the student, and not only the fulfillment of a course.

In the peer model, the authors write that it focuses on the joint work of a student with other students, strengthening the bonds of a student group, and this student, in turn, to serve as a tutor must be from higher courses, precisely so that he can educate his peers in a more complete way.

The third model, finally, focuses only on academic accompaniment, being a model where there is a "(…) intervención formativa destinada al acompañamiento académico de los alumnos, desarrollada en el contexto de la docencia de cada una de las asignaturas que imparte un profesor." ["(...) training intervention aimed at the academic accompaniment of students, developed in the context of the teaching of each of the subjects taught by a teacher] (p. 63).

In the institutional field is important to mention that in Ecuador there are governmental institutions that are responsible for regulating the processes for higher education, and propose quality standards, so there is the *Council of Higher Education* (CES), the *Council for The Quality Assurance of Higher Education* (CACES), and the *National Secretariat of Higher Education, Science and Technology* (SENESCYT). These institutions supervise the educational processes of all higher education institutions (including universities, university technological institutes and graduate institutions) so that they comply with the respective standards of educational quality at a higher level that the country needs.

In this context, the Council of Higher Education in its *Regulations of Academic Regime* article 45, recognizes learning activities, among these, the collaborative type, in which tutoring is included, described as,

Actividades de aprendizaje colaborativo. - Comprenden actividades grupales en interacción con el profesor, incluyendo las tutorías. Están orientadas a procesos colectivos de organización del aprendizaje, que abordan proyectos, con temáticas o problemas específicos de la profesión orientadas al desarrollo de habilidades de investigación para el aprendizaje. [Collaborative learning activities. - They include group activities in interaction with the teacher, including tutoring. They are oriented to collective processes of learning organization, which address projects, with specific themes or problems of the profession oriented to the development of research skills for learning.] (Reglamento de Regimen Academico Consejo Educacion Superior, 2017, p. 8)

The issue of tutoring is inherent in the university system in Ecuador to the point that it is so, that at the particular level of each university institution, there are regulations in which they regulate this proposal, adapting the guidelines or general concepts to their certain contexts, understanding their university population, as well as the challenges and objectives of each faculty or career of the institution.

Tutoring in Higher Education in the Context of Quarantine: Alternatives and Possibilities of Formative Accompaniment

Given to the inevitable change generated by the COVID-19 pandemic at the educational level, the conditions of education and therefore, of the tutoring implicit in these processes, had have to adapt to the current needs and problems. In that regard, it is important to mention what Caram et al (2020) point out about the teachers role within this context when they write:

Así, el rol del docente resulta fundamental en tanto facilitador de esas mediaciones entre estudiantes y tecnologías, de modo que favorezca procesos de construcción de conocimiento horizontales y colaborativos, a través de la interacción entre todos los que participan de una propuesta de enseñanza. [Therefore, the role of the teacher is fundamental as a facilitator of these mediations between students and technologies, so that it favors horizontal and collaborative knowledge construction processes, through the interaction between all those who participate in a teaching proposal.] (Caram et al., 2020, p. 39).

Virtual education, as an alternative to quarantine and the impossibility of face-to-face classes, is taken in the authors as an opportunity for teachers to generate new ways of communication and learning, much more collaborative and interactive, as well as open, for students.

It is important then, to bear in mind that the teacher within this context must have a technological knowledge, which allows him to give that adequate accompaniment within the new media. García et al (2021) complement this idea when they write: "la tutoría debe contener elementos de interactividad como una propuesta pedagógica y el aprendizaje cooperativo en la educación a distancia." [tutoring should contain elements of interactivity such as a pedagogical proposal and cooperative learning in virtual education] (Calderón García et al., 2021, p. 22).

A concept that Caram et al (2020) add for the improvement of tutorials in virtual environments is the called "virtual learning community", summarized as "(…) un grupo de personas con diferentes niveles de experiencia, conocimiento y pericia que aprenden gracias a la colaboración que establecen entre sí" [(…)a group of people with different levels of experience, knowledge and expertise who learn thanks to the collaboration they establish with each other] (p. 39), to which is added the virtual platforms as a meeting space.

Here a relationship can be made with the models of tutoring mentioned above, specifically that of work between equals, since the VLC being communal, is in a horizontal learning space where the tutors can also be the students, and at the same time, it is an approach to the integral model, since in them the complete accompaniment of the students is sought, whether academically, professionally, and personally. That is why the authors emphasize the "(…) necesidad de fortalecer los procesos de intervención tutorial, en las diferentes asignaturas de las carreras de la Facultad para promover una formación personal y profesional, autónoma, crítica y creativa." [(…) the need to strengthen the processes of tutoring intervention, in the different courses of the careers of the Faculty to promote a personal and professional, autonomous, critical and creative training.] (p. 40).

This strengthening of the tutorial intervention processes, in turn, is strongly related to the performance and improvement of the formative processes in students, since, in a virtual education context, learning conditions are often limited. Understanding the geographical context in which the emphasis is placed, the approach to technology and therefore, to learning given thanks to technological tools, can be problematic, especially if it is taken into account that not all students have access to these tools. The VLCs are perfect complements to an improved academic performance, since they enhance the autonomous and collective training, with the help of students and the tutor teacher.

Following the same idea, with technological support, in addition to adequate training, tutoring as a tool can be adapted to new media, thus ensuring that students do not feel abandoned in their classes, improving the formative education processes. This is important, since the general perception of virtual education is problematic according to the authors' results, which demonstrate, among other things, "(…) que los estudiantes valoran la tutoría virtual por debajo de la personal y grupal, a pesar de pertenecer a una generación que está en constante contacto con las TIC." [(…) that students value virtual tutoring below personal and group tutoring, despite belonging to a generation that is in constant contact with ICTs."] (Calderón García et al., 2021, p. 23).

Despite of this conclusion, they also add that tutoring within a virtual context can serve as a "(…) doble factor de calidad (…) siempre y cuando la tutoría, independientemente de su modalidad, sea un acompañamiento integral" [(…) double quality factor (…) as long as the tutoring, regardless of its modality, is an integral accompaniment] (p. 23). This is how, el éxito de la virtual tutoring depends on how successful the accompaniment of it is in students, and within a virtual space, the difficulties of doing it without actors being present is the first problem to solve.

The Formative and Shared Evaluation, Perspectives

Faced with COVID-19 situation and the implementation of virtual education, it has been necessary to incorporate other evaluation models, shared and formative evaluation (F&SA) is considered as an option to carried out this process. Taking into consideration that Hortigüela et al (2019) when reflecting on this evaluation form indicates that, "(…) si bien no es el predominante en el ámbito educativo, ha experimentado un avance notorio en los últimos años". ["(…) although it is not the predominant one in the educational field, it has experienced notable progress in recent years".] (p. 14).

However, it is possible to very well define shared and formative evaluation, as López & Pérez (2017) case evaluation gets to conceptualize different evaluation types (co-evaluation, self-evaluation, integrated evaluation, etc.), between formative evaluation and shared evaluation.

For Lopez & Pérez (2017) talking about comparative evaluation requires to refer to:

"(…) los procesos dialógicos que mantiene el profesor con su alumnado sobre la evaluación de los aprendizajes y los procesos de enseñanza-aprendizaje que tienen lugar. Este tipo de "diálogos" pueden ser individuales o grupales. También pueden estar basados o relacionados con procesos previos de autoevaluación y/o coevaluación, así como con procesos paralelos o complementarios de autocalificación y calificación dialogada". ["(…) the dialogic processes that the teacher maintains with students on the learning evaluation and the teaching-learning processes that take place. This type of "dialogue" can be individual or groupal. They can also be based on or related to previous self-assessment and / or co-assessment processes, as well as parallel or complementary self-assessment and dialogue assessment processes."] (p. 43).*

Therefore, it should be understood when talking about evaluation is a process of dialogue between teacher and student, in relation to any type of evaluation already performed, referring to the difference between evaluation and qualification that López & Pérez (2017) constantly question in the paper. Expressing that "es fundamental entender que podemos y debemos evaluar sin necesidad de calificar ni poner notas, y que es precisamente cuando hacemos eso cuando la evaluación tiene una mayor repercusión en el aprendizaje de nuestro alumnado". ["it is essential to understand that it is a possible and a must to evaluate without the need to score or grade, and that precisely when this is done the evaluation has a greater learning impact on the students".] (p. 35).

In this aspect, the comparative evaluation specifically should not have previously established a score, but rather the dialogic process should be carried out to be able to review the student's improvements in the teaching-learning process and after that accompaniment, to be able to establish a score.

Regarding formative assessment, López Pastor et al (2006) define it as:

"(…) todo proceso de evaluación cuya finalidad principal es mejorar los procesos de enseñanza-aprendizaje que tienen lugar. Es todo proceso de evaluación que sirve para que el alumnado aprenda más (y/o corrija sus errores) y para que el profesorado aprenda a trabajar mejor (a perfeccionar su práctica docente)". ["(…) any evaluation processes whose main purpose is to improve the teaching-learning processes that take place. It is any evaluation process that help students learn more (and / or correct their mistakes) and so that teachers learn to work better (to improve their teaching practice".] (p. 37).*

It is interesting how the formative evaluation is proposed not only for student's academic performance improvement but also caring for the teaching practice improvement. It is necessary that the teaching team is available to provide feedback as proposed from the student's perspective.

Formative Evaluation and its Relationship With Pedagogical Orientation and the Educational Formative Process

Another interpretation on the same concept of formative evaluation by Allal (2014), "(…) refers to the type of assessment used by the teacher to adapt pedagogic action to students' learning processes and learning problems. In this sense, its function is to regulate instruction procedures used by the educational system". (p. 4).

For López Pastor (2012), formative evaluation is a complex process, in which factors such as observation, assessment and decision-making are what determine the effectiveness of the teaching process (p.

121), therefore being a type of constant work evaluation and rapid adaptability, which has as actors the students and the teacher, from a position of mutual learning and constant change.

It also lists a series of advantages that exist within this model, among which stand out: 1. The motivation and involvement of students in the learning process; 2. Within the student-centered pedagogical models it is the most functional and effective method; 3. enhances criticism and self-criticism in the student; and 4. It builds a sense of responsibility and autonomy in students much greater than with another type of process or evaluation (p. 122). As can be seen, the formative evaluation model strengthens the relationship between the tutor and the student, which allows the guidance that can be given to the student to help improve his or her training process, regardless of the educational context in which he or she finds him or herself.

In higher education, this model is more applicable, due to the communication facilities that students have with the teacher in charge. The guiding function of the latter is better received by the student, who understands well that tutoring will represent an improvement in their education. In this aspect, the aforementioned criticism and self-criticism become the fundamental basis of the tutoring process, which is enhanced by the different pedagogical models and tools that the tutoring teacher can offer to the student.

All these advantages are the result of a type of methodology where great effort is made to make students aware of their own qualifications, making the performance and the formative process of the students have a remarkable improvement, being the teacher the one who, as support for them, gives them the necessary tools at a pedagogical and personal level, so that this happens. Then, it becomes an integral model, but also shared, since students are not the "other", but share learning and teaching. López Pastor (2012) emphasizes this when he writes:

Implica poner el énfasis en utilizar la evaluación para mejorar los procesos de enseñanza-aprendizaje que tienen lugar, así como implicar al alumnado en el proceso de evaluación, de manera que la mayor parte del tiempo dedicado a la evaluación se convierta en un proceso de diálogo y toma de decisiones mutuas, orientadas a la mejora. [It implies placing the emphasis on using evaluation to improve the teaching-learning processes that take place, as well as involving students in the evaluation process, so that most of the time dedicated to evaluation becomes a process of dialogue and mutual decision-making, oriented to improvement.] (p. 24).

The author adds some that can be considered as results of the evaluation models, and from which can be taken those that can be considered most relevant for this analysis: 1. They help in the correction of problems or the resolution of gaps within the subject or course where they are applied, so that the learning process is greatly improved; 2. It generates collective responsibility, since the evaluation processes are joint, which allows a development of permanent learning strategies; and 3. The performance and grades of the students improve significantly, due to the permanent and collective accompaniment of all (Lopez, 2009, p. 49).

Under this perspective, the relationship between an educational orientation, as it can be in higher education, with the formative process of their students, is strengthened by having a tutor to guide them in the process of solving problems, gaps or misunderstandings within their subjects. If joint evaluation is characterized, the perception that a classroom has as a collective is strengthened, as well as the group capabilities they possess. This relationship, intimately linked to the shared evaluation process, will end up improving the grades and skills of the students, precisely because of the tutor's accompaniment and guidance with them.

For Laura Cañadas (2020), formative evaluation is more structural, and proposes a systematization that helps the understanding of the concept as such. For it, the F&SA can be defined as:

As the way in which, based on pre-established and planned criteria, information is gathered during the formative process on student learning and professor teaching with the aim of improving the teaching and learning process . (Cañadas, 2020, p. 4)

She adds a series of fundamental characteristics to understand globally the process of formative evaluation, and especially the scoring process that it has. She points out, for example, that it must be systematic and planned, since the effectiveness and positive consequences of the process will depend on an adequate planning that prevents and adapts any problem that will arise:

it must be planned in advance, deciding what goals are to be achieved in the plan or program, how it will be assessed, when and how the information will be collected, what will be done with that information or who will be in charge of doing it. (Cañadas, 2020, p. 4)

The evaluation, in addition, must be constant, and applied permanently in the process. Cañadas (2020) defines three recommended moments to do so: initial, procedural, and final. The initial assessment is a diagnostic evaluation, which allows the teacher to recognize the skills of students and serves as an initial model for all evaluation. The processual is more formative and can happen at any time in the learning process, or at certain times, either to reinforce content or to help students refresh the course; and the final evaluation is of a summative nature, so it is considered as an exhibition of the knowledge acquired by the student.

In relation to educational guidance, and above all, to the role of the student in this, Cañadas (2020) talks a lot about student participation and considers it a fundamental characteristic of formative evaluation. This is how she mentions that the creation of activities external to the scoring process that highlight the student's learning is an indispensable attribute, since this way the teacher can know what the students know and is in lack of. (p. 5). Consequently, there is an involvement of the student within the formative process, which Cañadas (2020) points out that it can generate "place through self-assessment and co-assessment or peer assessment processes." (p. 6), where the student can self-evaluate, help evaluate their peers, or do it in the company of the teacher.

With this said, the student acquires a means to personally recognize to what extent his process has been a success, where he needs teaching support to improve, and how his study group is at an academic level, endowing him, and providing the course, with a shared responsibility in the process.

Among the perspectives of the different authors on the F&SA, the term of *improvement of the teaching-learning processes* is constantly repeated, so this proposal of the formative and shared evaluation provides the educational quality, since the figure of the teacher goes beyond the traditional one: it no longer intends to establish a numerical grading, but it becomes a kind of companion in the teaching and learning process (Ibarra Ruiz, Lukas Mujika, Ponce-González, Rodríguez Gómez, 2023), in this it engages in the respective dialogues and feedbacks towards the students and in the same way from the students to the teacher. The teacher also plays the role of a tutor, that is where the tutoring process contributes to the F&SA, promoting a friendlier environment both inside and outside the classroom.

Consequently, the relationships that may arise between educational guidance through tutoring, with the formative development in an educational context can be given in several ways. The figure of the tutor becomes a fundamental part of this whole process, since it is he who will be in charge of managing the information given to the students; he will guide them in the resolution of problems or doubts they may have and will give them greater autonomy within their subjects.

In a higher education context, these functions become more relevant, due to the ease with which students can discuss their educational problems with the tutor. Similarly, the tutor can define and select both the students and the elements to be offered to his or her students.

The question of the link, then, becomes important, and the formative evaluation that has been presented is the best way to improve the teaching and learning processes. The evaluation is not categorical or numerical, moving away from traditionalism, forgetting that hierarchical relationship where the teacher is the one who commands the student, but it becomes a direct and constant dialogue, which helps the student's development in his specialty.

This will help him not only in the context of the subject as such, but also, being at an age and with a greater educational commitment to his future professionalism, it will help him to understand how to manage and solve on his own, the different problems he has at the level of academic discipline. It will not only be the tutor of a specific subject, but the bulk of the teaching population of his career, which will help him with the implementation of different types of educational guidance, acting as tutors throughout his higher educational experience.

Study Participants and Results

For the development, it was decided to analyze the different opinions, criteria and perceptions held by the student body, as well as the teachers, of the different concepts previously addressed: how they define the concept of mentoring, their functions and personal experiences about them; what they represent within the context generated by Covid-19, and how they can define formative and shared evaluation. Emphasis is also placed on the relationship between this type of orientation and their own formative developments in the universities where they study.

For the exploration of the analysis, two types of groups were taken as participants: teachers specialized in their area, mostly with master's and doctoral degrees, as well as students from different areas. Both groups are taken from mostly humanistic disciplines: psychology, education, arts, administration, as well as certain engineering disciplines. Although the diversity of disciplines may generate discussions or limitations, the study was based on the general perception of two concepts, and their relationship with the experiences that both teachers and students have had in order to define the analysis technique.

In order to have a better control of the data, it was decided to use focus groups as a technique for data collection and interpretation. Hamui-Sutton and Varela-Ruiz define the importance of this technique in the qualitative interpretation of the results as follows: "qualitative epistemology defends the constructive-interpretative character of knowledge, which implies emphasizing that knowledge is a human production, not something that is ready to be identified in an ordered reality" (p. 56). In this sense, the interpretation of each group of participants is highlighted for the analysis and conclusion of the study.

Similarly, the singularity of each response and group is considered, as well as the dialogic process that characterizes the focus groups. The authors mention that these two characteristics make it possible to generate an "instance of scientific knowledge production" (Hamui-Sutton & Varela-Ruiz, 2013), or in other words, a process of direct communication of the study between the groups and the researcher.

For this reason, taking focus groups as a research and analysis technique, the following references and characteristics were used to define each group:

Table 1. Structure of the focus groups

Focus Group	Group characteristics	Average ages	Disciplines
Teachers	Teachers specialized in areas of knowledge and education. With fourth level degrees such as masters, doctorates or specializations in their respective areas.	Undefined ages	Psychology, Pedagogy, Education, Arts, Engineering, Administration, Humanities.
Students	University students, from public and private universities, in different semesters of various careers, who have had experiences of educational accompaniment and guidance.	Between 20-27 years old	Psychology, Pedagogy, Education, Arts, Engineering, Administration, Humanities.

Analysis of Results

The exploratory analysis allowed to know the main terms associated with tutoring and formative and shared evaluation. The results are presented from the perspective of the participants, who were quite differentiated between teachers and students.

While the narratives of the teachers were characterized by the use of complex terms, questions, theoretical and legal foundations on the topics of discussion and could even speak of a lack of knowledge in the question of definition of terminology, the students revealed simpler and more practical meanings when referring to the tutorials. In what corresponds to the F&SA, they responded that they had no knowledge of the concept, however, at the moment in which the meaning was revealed they came to understand and express better with examples of the application of the F&SA, with a comparison on the experiences in the classes before and during the pandemic.

Undoubtedly, we can talk about a tutoring task in the context of the pandemic where the complexity of the situations occurred in an emerging way, and in this case, the teacher became an important support to the student. The issue of the pandemic plays an important role in the development of tutoring spaces, as there are factors that arise as a result of this event, such as mourning, economic concerns, difficulty in internet connections due to internet access and equipment, etc. In this sense, the categorization carried out by Solaguren-Beascoa & Moreno Delgado (2016) of the types of tutoring, contributes to understanding the importance of this accompaniment of the teacher in "personal or support regarding their integral development" (p. 248) is how it is mentioned in the focus groups,

IL: "the situation of the pandemic led to being able to provide comprehensive accompaniment help to students, since situations such as loss of relatives, and job losses, became common problems in which they accompanied and gave flexibility".

Results on the Definition of *Tutoring*

Students define tutorials as a space of trust and closeness between the teacher and the student or at least a small group of students, who can be heard and guided to understand the topics they review in classes. They assigned a high importance to the tutorials to improve academic performance, although it is recognized that not all teachers perform tutorials as part of the activities of the subjects.

Figure 1. Recurring terms among students to refer to tutoring and formative and shared assessment

H-A: *"not all teachers are in this to quote in a classroom to be able to clear the doubts of the classmates ... in the case of teachers who usually summon a tutor in a zoom room to clear doubts in themselves, in this case I think it works"*

This answer indicates two things: that tutorials in certain contexts are not usually presented to students, a fact that can be interpreted from the educational context that universities have, as well as a lack of knowledge of the teacher, or students, about this tool. Additionally, it is inferred that teachers who do tutoring adapt their tools to virtuality.

Speaking about the tutoring space, it is open to all students, both with those with good performance and those who do not. It is important to note that, just as there are teachers who do not offer tutoring spaces, there are also students who do not access them and are in the category of not having good performance.

P-M: *"the tutorials are open, not everyone accesses this space that has been taken by zoom, however, something interesting is that those who access seek an improvement in their skills despite having acceptable qualifications".*

Among the technological tools used by teachers for tutoring, students identified three mainways, 1) Forums created on educational platforms. 2) Chats on educational platforms and WhatsApp and 3) Zoom meetings.

Thus, the forums created in this case are given on Moodle platform (it is important to clarify that in focus groups the use of this platform is constant) and serve for the raising of doubts or discussion of the subject, one of the main limitations is the scarce feedback that teachers provide by these means, because there are delays in response time, or simply the concerns were not addressed. So they cataloged it as an ineffective strategy for tutoring.

On the other hand, tutoring by WhatsApp is perceived by students as more interactive and immediate, because messages and podcasts help with faster attendance, although it does not always contribute to the understanding of content, it helps the informative function on general activities of the subject, and even to solve concerns that were not solved in class spaces.

The third tool used for tutoring and referred to by the students as the most effective, was the creation of zoom meetings in small groups or in a personalized way. In this space the closeness and trust allow a listening between the teacher and the student, where the small number of people allows the respective feedback that contributes to the improvement of the learning process. In this sense, it can be said that the zoom space allows an accompaniment quite similar to that generated in face-to-face education.

M-L: *"tutoring has helped me a lot, I think virtual education does have barriers... the teacher does not know does not know the student, from the beginning until the end of the semester, because he has the camera off"*

M-M: *"Then we created student rooms, then from 5 students we all started to create... it's quite interactive and especially most of us as we are in small rooms, it's like we turn on the cameras and we are more confident"*

These responses show the direct relationship between a virtual tool adapted to educational guidance, such as Zoom's personalized meetings, with the interest, participation and positive perception of students, strengthening the bond they have with both the teacher and the subject of study.

It is important to highlight the other two tools, which fulfill a different function: the Moodle platform works as a manager of the course information, poor to give an educational orientation but good in the categorization of data, while Whatsapp helps the effective communication of such data, as well as linking the teacher and the student outside the educational context.

Results on *Formative* and *Shared* Evaluation

On the formative and shared evaluation, the students expressed the ignorance on the subject, however, they associated it with those activities that the teacher proposes in order to make a qualitative assessment without the need to assign a grade.

M-C: *"In my career, it is interesting how the teacher is attentive to each exercise we perform, makes an accompaniment and as a talk is indicating what things I should correct, what techniques I should use".*

In the same perspective, this evaluation is perceived as a space for dialogue and feedback that contributes to reducing stress and improving academic performance.

H-A: *"for example, recently we had a class in which all the classmates could write about a topic that was being seen, and the teacher was feeding back the comments of each group, the positive points and the negative points, and the activity was not qualified"*

L-C: *"the process we carry out is to perform the task, that task in principle has no qualification, but we receive the respective feedback that leads us to know our progress in the subject, later the teacher proposes tutorials for those students who want to improve this process and because it has helped me a lot to correct the weaknesses"*

Figure 2. Meanings that teachers and students about the

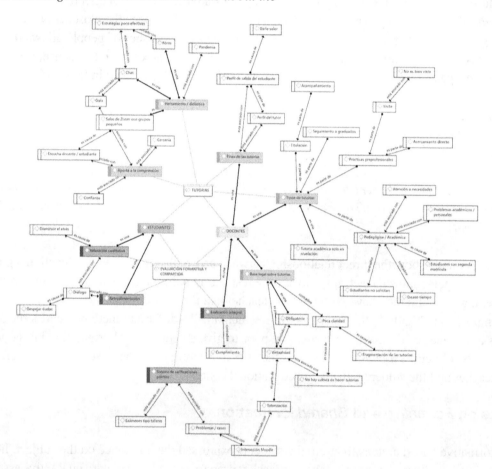

Results from the Teaching Perspective

From the teaching perspective, as mentioned, the responses were more complex, on the tutorials defined three topics of discussion: the types of tutoring, its legal basis and the purpose of the tutorials, the whole discourse focused on the experiences lived during virtual education and the crisis generated by the pandemic.

This last topic is the most controversial, because the teaching task at all educational levels had to be reinforced in technological issues, use of educational platforms such as Moodle, the use of communication applications such as Zoom, Google Meet, Microsoft Teams, etc.

During the dialogue carried out in the focus group, the teachers categorized the types of tutorials they have worked: 1) pedagogical or academic tutorials, 2) tutorials of professional practices and 3) tutoring of degree. They also mention having carried out similar spaces in the follow-up to graduates for the accompaniment in the labor insertion and in the process of leveling for the entrance to the careers.

The pedagogical or academic tutorials were related to the direct attention to students with academic or personal needs, students who are with second / third enrollments and those who request them for some specific doubt. These tutorials, although recognized as necessary, are perceived as not feasible to execute, due to the limited time and lack of clarity about the role of the tutor teacher.

The tutorials of pre-professional practices are the most common, although not preferred by the teachers, they associate them with the direct approach to the student and the visit in situ in the place of practice. In this same line, the degree tutorials are identified with well-defined activities that lead to the development of the final degree project.

From the types of tutoring, the teachers generated a discussion about the purpose of the tutorials, in this sense, they proposed that to give greater value to this activity it is essential to understand the student's exit profile and define the profile of the tutor that contributes to the development of the skills that the professional future will require.

Finally, on formative and shared evaluation, in this research space it was possible to determine some critical points on this subject, for example, 1) the clarity when defining the term on the part of the teachers, 2) rigidity of the evaluation system of the various universities and 3) the application of the F&SA in the teaching-learning processes at the university level.

On the other hand, it is mentioned that the evaluation system of the different universities in question does not allow the flexibility proposed by the Shared and Formative Evaluation, in addition, that they maintain that not all subjects can land their evaluation in the F&SA. However, they expressed in which subjects can be applied.

When talking about the feasibility of the application of F&SA in teaching-learning processes, they recognized that it is not a very common method of evaluation that the pressure to settle a grade, the excess of students in the classrooms, do not allow it to be applied optimally. However, it was discussed in which fields of knowledge can be used, for example, in processes of education in the humanities.

P-M: "in the field of arts and humanities I have been able to apply this type of evaluation, in subjects such as diagnostic laboratory and interdisciplinary laboratory, because by the nature of these subjects it is possible to do that accompaniment in the field of action".

The case of applicability is more common in subjects of pre-professional practices, since it is commented that this, by its nature needs the accompaniment of the teacher constantly, this leads to a greater number of tutorials and conversations to go molding final works.

It would be important to problematize about the application of formative and shared evaluation in the different areas of knowledge, since it would be a mistake to maintain that it would only be for the area of humanities.

Finally, in the process of dialogue, there was an agreement on the need to generate a comprehensive evaluation, and at the same time, a practical grading system that allows greater interaction with the student and assessment from a perspective of problem solving and the assessment of the student's abilities.

CONCLUSION

In this paper it has been possible to know about the perspective of formative and shared evaluation, through the process of tutoring in university education that during these times in Ecuador is mostly virtualized as a result of the pandemic produced by COVID-19. In this sense, the conclusive factors are the following:

While it is true that the issue of virtualization of education has caused its common havoc in the educational process, The results have shown that the incorporation of different complementary tools to the tutoring process, such as personalized zoom meetings or the Moodle platform, have helped to understand the virtual process of educational guidance.

In addition, the evaluation processes commented on by the students, demonstrate that must be proposed in a more open way without losing the quality of the teaching-learning process, but through the F&SA that process of improvement centered on the student can take place.

Beyond the modality in which the teaching-learning processes can be carried out at a higher level, and in tune with the students' responses in the focus group analysis, it is prudent to recognize the importance of the application of a formative and shared evaluation, since this is centered on the student, proposes a firmer commitment of the teacher in the accompaniment, integrates the student in the process of improvements of the teaching task; it does not propose to establish a grade a priori, but it looks at the process and progress of the recipient.

The results have also shown that from a teaching perspective, F&SA is mostly applicable in pre-professional contexts, or humanistic disciplines. This can be considered a limitation for the application of this methodology, something that is pertinent to analyze in future studies, due to the nature of the focus groups studied. However, it stands out, with respect to the relationship between F&SA and teachers, that they do consider its application relevant for the improvement of tutoring in the virtual context.

In addition, it has also been found how tutoring has been adapting to external factors that can limit learning in a virtual context, such as several connections at the same time in relation to people who study in the same home, students who are working while listening to their classes, etc., factors that do not allow the complete understanding of the contents by the students, an where the tutoring manages to complement that space that is given as a result of the various factors.

In this sense, it has been concluded that the tutoring contributes to strengthening the execution of a formative and shared evaluation, since the accompaniment of the teacher to the student proposes a process of dialogue in which the shortcomings of these can be identified, improvements are proposed and even that dialogue allows the teacher to know their performance and rethink more effective methodologies.

REFERENCES

Allal, L. (2014). Estrategias de evaluacion formativa: concepciones psicopedagógicas y modalidades de aplicación. *Journal for the Study of Education and Development, 3*(11), 4–22. doi:10.1080/021037 02.1980.10821803

Boroel, B. I., Sánchez-Santamaría, J., Morales Gutiérrez, K. D., & Henríquez Ritchie, P. S. (2018). Successful education for all: Tutoring as a process of school support from the perspective of educational equity. *Revista Fuentes, 20*(2), 91–104. doi:10.12795/revistafuentes.2018.v20.i2.06

Calderón García, R., González Fernández, M. O., & Torres Valencia, B. (2021). La percepción docente sobre las tutorías en el contexto del COVID 2019. *Revistas.Upch.Edu.Pe, 14*(1), 21–28. doi:10.20453/rph.v14i1.4030

Cañadas, L. (2020). Evaluación formativa en el contexto universitario: Oportunidades y propuestas de actuación. *Revista Digital de Investigación En Docencia Universitaria, 14*(2), e1214–e1214. doi:10.19083/10.19083/ridu.2020.1214

Caram, G., Naigeboren Guzmán, M., Gil De Asar, M., & Bordier, M. S. (2020). *Enseñanza y tutoría en el contexto de la virtualidad.* 37–42. Acta Académica. https://www.aacademica.org/000-007/786.pdf

Ibarra Ruiz, M. S., Lukas Mujika, J.-F., Ponce-González, N., & Rodríguez Gómez, G. (2023). Percepción del profesorado universitario sobre la calidad de las tareas de evaluación de los resultados de aprendizaje. RELIEVE - Revista Electrónica De Investigación Y Evaluación Educativa, 29(1). https://doi.org/10.30827/relieve.v29i1.27404

de la Cruz Flores, G., Chehaybar, Y., Kury, E., & Abreu, L. F. (2011). Tutoría en educación superior: una revisión analítica de la literatura. *Revista de la Educación Superior.* Vol. XL (1), No. 157, 189-209. https://www.scielo.org.mx/pdf/resu/v40n157/v40n157a9.pdf

Gómez-Collado, M. E. (2012). *La percepción de los estudiantes sobre el Programa de Tutoría Académica The perception of students on the Academic Tutelage.* 58, 209–233.

González, J. (2021). *Educación virtual y satisfacción estudiantil durante la pandemia de Covid-19 en una universidad de Ecuador 2021.* Repositorio Institucional - UCV. https://repositorio.ucv.edu.pe/handle/20.500.12692/69339

González Palacios, A., & Avelino, I. (2016). Tutoría: Una revisión conceptual. *Smip.Udg.Mx,* 57–68. http://smip.udg.mx/sites/default/files/38_gonzalez_palacios.pdf

Guamán, R., Villareal, Á., & Cedeño, E. (2020). La Educación Híbrida como alternativa frente al Covid -19 en el Ecuador. *Tse'De, 3*(1). http://tsachila.edu.ec/ojs/index.php/TSEDE/article/view/27

Hortigüela, D., Pérez-Pueyo, Á., & González-Calvo, G. (2019). Pero… ¿A qué nos Referimos Realmente con la Evaluación Formativa y Compartida?: Confusiones Habituales y Reflexiones Prácticas Reflections. *Revista Iberoamericana de Evaluación Educativa, 12*(1), 13–27. doi:10.15366/riee2019.12.1.001

López, V. (2009). Evaluación formativa y compartida en Educación Superior: Propuestas, técnicas, instrumentos y experiencias. Narcea.

López, V. (2012). Evaluación formativa y compartida en la universidad: clarificación de conceptos y propuestas de intervención desde la Red Interuniversitaria de Evaluación. *Psychology, Society, and Education, 4*(1). http://repositorio.ual.es/bitstream/handle/10835/2887/vista%20Lopez%20Pastor.pdf

López, V., & Pérez, Á. (2017). *Evaluación formativa y compartida en educación: experiencias de éxito en todas las etapas educativas.* Universidad de León.

López-Gómez, E. (2017). El concepto y las finalidades de la tutoría universitaria : Una consulta a expertos. *Revista Española de Orientación y Psicopedagogía, 28*(2), 61–78. doi:10.5944/reop.vol.28.num.2.2017.20119

López Pastor, V. M., Monjas Aguado, R., Gómez García, J., López Pastor, E. M., Martín Pinela, J. F., González Badiola, J., Barba Martín, J. J., Aguilar Baeza, R., González Pascual, M., Heras Bernardino, C., Martín, M. I., Manrique Arribas, J. C., Subtil Marugán, P., & Marugán García, L. (2006). La evaluación en educación física. Revisión de modelos tradicionales y planteamiento de una alternativa. La evaluación formativa y compartida. *Retos, 10,* 31–41. https://doi.org/10.47197/retos.v0i10.35061

Palacios-Dueñas, A. I., Michell Loor-Peña, J. I., Mabel Macías-Macías III, K., & Roberth Ortega-Macías, W. I. (2020). Incidencia de la tecnología en el entorno educativo del Ecuador frente a la pandemia del covid-19. *Polo Del Conocimiento: Revista Científico – Profesional, 5*(10), 754-773. https://doi.org/doi:10.23857/pc.v5i10.1850

Reglamento De Regimen Academico Consejo Educacion Superior. (2017). [Testimony of Consejo de Educación Superior]. Reglamento De Regimen Academico Consejo Educacion Superior. www.lexis.com.ec

Rocha, J. J. (2020). Metodologías activas, la clave para el cambio de la escuela y su aplicación en épocas de pandemia. *INNOVA Research Journal 5*(3), 2. doi:10.33890/innova.v5.n3.2.2020.1514

Sánchez, L. A. C., & Catagña, S. M. C. (2021). La educación virtual implementada por la pandemia de la COVID-19 y el derecho a la educación superior. *Revista Jurídica Crítica y Derecho, 2*(3), 44–56. doi:10.29166/cyd.v2i3.3188

Solaguren-Beascoa, M., & Moreno Delgado, L. (2016). Escala de actitudes de los estudiantes universitarios hacia las tutorías académicas. *Redalyc. Org, 19*(1), 247–266. doi:10.5944/educXX1.14479

Tejedor, S., Cervi, L., Tusa, F., & Parola, A. (2020). Educación en tiempos de pandemia: reflexiones de alumnos y profesores sobre la enseñanza virtual universitaria en España, Italia y Ecuador. *Revista Latina de Comunicación Social, 78,* 1–21. doi:10.4185/RLCS-2020-1466

UNESCO. (2021). *Seguimiento mundial de los cierres de escuela causados por el COVID-19.* UNESCO. https://es.unesco.org/covid19/educationresponse

Vohlonen, A. (2020). *COVID-19: Cómo asegurar el aprendizaje de los niños sin acceso a Internet.* UNICEF Ecuador. https://www.unicef.org/ecuador/historias/covid-19-c%C3%B3mo-asegurar-el-aprendizaje-de-los-ni%C3%B1os-sin-acceso-internet

Compilation of References

Ahmed, S. (2012). *On being included- Racism and diversity in institutional life*. Duke University Press.

Ahmed, S. (2018). *Killjoy Manifest*. Informations Forlag.

Ajjawi, R., & Boud, D. (2017). Researching feedback dialogue: An interactional analysis approach. *Assessment & Evaluation in Higher Education, 42*(2), 252–265. doi:10.1080/02602938.2015.1102863

Alba-Pastor, C., Zubillaga del Río, A., & Sánchez-Serrano, J. M. (2015). Technology and Universal Design for Learning (UDL): Experiences in the university context and implications for teacher training. *Revista Latinoamericana de Tecnología Educativa-Relatec, 14*(1), 89–100. doi:10.17398/1695-288X.14.1.89

Albert, M. J. (2007). *La Investigación Educativa: Claves Teóricas*. McGraw Hill.

Alderfer, C. (2014). Clarifying the meaning of mentor-protégé relationships. *Consulting Psychology Journal, 66*(1), 6–19. doi:10.1037/a0036367

Allal, L. (2014). Estrategias de evaluacion formativa: concepciones psicopedagógicas y modalidades de aplicación. *Journal for the Study of Education and Development, 3*(11), 4–22. doi:10.1080/02103702.1980.10821803

Alsina, J. (2010). *Evaluación por competencias en la universidad: las competencias transversales. Cuadernos de docencia universitaria*. Octaedro.

Álvarez Méndez, J. M. (2011). *Evaluar para conocer. Examinar para excluir*. Ediciones Morata.

Álvarez, C., and San Fabián, J. L. (2012). La elección del estudio de caso en investigación educativa. *Gazeta de Antropología, 28*(1), 1-13. http://hdl.handle.net/10481/20644

Álvarez, J. M. (2001). *Evaluar para conocer, examinar para excluir*. Morata.

Amhag, L., Hellström, L., & Stigmar, M. (2019). Teacher Educators' Use of Digital Tools and Needs for Digital Competence in Higher Education. *Journal of Digital Learning in Teacher Education, 35*(4), 203–220. doi:10.1080/21532974.2019.1646169

Amor, M. I., & Serrano, R. (2019). The generic competences in the Initial Teacher Training. A comparative study among students, teachers and graduates of university education degree. *Educación XXI, 21*(1), 239–261. doi:10.5944/educxx1.21341

Anderson, O., El Habbal, N., & Bridges, D. (2020). A peer evaluation training results in high-quality feedback, as measured over time in nutritional sciences graduate students. *Advances in Physiology Education, 44*(2), 203–209. doi:10.1152/advan.00114.2019 PMID:32243221

Andrade, H. (2019). A Critical Review of Research on Student Self-Assessment. *Frontiers in Education, 4*, 87. doi:10.3389/feduc.2019.00087

Andrade, H. L., Bennet, R., & Cizek, G. J. (2019). *Handbook of formative assessment in the disciplines*. Routledge. doi:10.4324/9781315166933

Andreu, M. A., & Labrador, M. J. (2011). Formación del profesorado en metodologías y evaluación. Análisis cualitativo. *Revista de Investigación Educacional, 9*(2), 236–245. https://reined.webs.uvigo.es/index.php/reined/article/view/127

Angelini-Doffo, M. L. (2016). Estudio sobre la evaluación formativa y compartida en la formación docente en inglés. *Actualidades Investigativas en Educación, 16*(1), 1–21. doi:10.15517/aie.v16i1.22614

Anguita, R. & Torrego, L. (2009). Género, educación y formación del profesorado. Retos y posibilidades. *Revista interuniversitaria de formación del profesorado*, (64), 17-26.

Archbald, D. A., & Newmann, F. M. (1988). *Beyond standardized testing: Assessing authentic academic achievement in the secondary school*. National Association of Secondary School Principals.

Area, M., & Adell, J. (2009). E-Learning: Enseñar y aprender en espacios virtuales. In J. De Pablos (Ed.), *Tecnología educativa: la formación del profesorado de la era de internet* (pp. 391–424). Ediciones Aljibe.

Arnold, L. (2019). Advancing Authentic Assessment Practice. *Arise lecture*. Edinburgh Napier University. https://lydia-arnold.com/2019/11/27/edinburgh-napier-authentic-assessment-and-action-research/

Arribas, J. M. (2012). El rendimiento académico en función del sistema de evaluación empleado. *Relieve, 1*(18) 1-15. http://hdl.handle.net/10550/29801

Asghar, M. (2012). The lived experience of formative assessment practice in a British university. *Journal of Further and Higher Education, 36*(2), 205–223. doi:10.1080/0309877X.2011.606901

Ashford-Rowe, K., Herrington, J., & Brown, C. (2014). Establishing the critical elements that determine authentic assessment. *Assessment and Evaluation in Higher Education, 39*(2), 205–222. doi:10.1080/02602938.2013.819566

Ashwin, P. (2020). *Transforming university education: a manifesto*. Bloomsbury Publishing. doi:10.5040/9781350157279

Asociación Estatal de Educación Social - ASEDES. (2007). *Documentos profesionalizadores*. ASEDES.

Asún-Dieste, S., Rapún, M., & Romero-Martín, M. R. (2019). Percepciones de Estudiantes Universitarios sobre una Evaluación Formativa en el Trabajo en Equipo. *Revista Iberoamericana de Evaluación Educativa, 12*(1), 175–192. doi:10.15366/10.15366/riee2019.12.1.010

Atienza, R., Valencia-Peris, A., Martos-García, D., López-Pastor, V. M., & Devís-Devís, J. (2016). La percepción del alumnado universitario de educación física sobre la evaluación formativa: ventajas, dificultades y satisfacción. *Movimiento, 22*(4), 1033-1048. https://www.redalyc.org/html/1153/115349439002

Atienza, R., Valencia-Peris, A., Martos-García, D., López-Pastor, V. M., & Devís-Devís, J. (2016). La percepción del alumnado universitario de educación física sobre la evaluación formativa: Ventajas, dificultades y satisfacción. *Movimento (Porto Alegre), 22*(4), 1033–1048. doi:10.22456/1982-8918.59732

Aubert, A., Flecha, A., García, C., Flecha, R., & Racionero, S. (2008). *Aprendizaje dialógico en la sociedad de la información*. Hipatia.

Autissier, D. (2013). *L'intelligence de situation - Savoir exploiter toutes les situations*. Ed. d'Organisation.

Ayala, M. (2015). *Evaluación según sus agentes*. Atencion. https://n9.cl/0gdu6

Baird, J., Andrich, D., Hopfenbeck, T., & Stobart, G. (2017). Assessment and learning: Fields apart? *Assessment in Education: Principles, Policy & Practice, 24*(3), 317–350. doi:10.1080/0969594X.2017.1319337

Ballarín, P., Barranco, E., Gálvez, M. A., Jandali, L., Marín, V., Muñoz, A. M., Ramírez, A., Reyes, M. L., & Soto, P. (2009). *Evaluación de la incidencia de los saberes de las mujeres, feministas y de género en la docencia universitaria: Memoria final 2007-2009*. Ministerio de Trabajo y Asuntos Sociales, Instituto de la Mujer. https://digibug.ugr.es/bitstream/handle/10481/36530/Memoria%20investigacio%CC%81n.pdf?sequence=1

Bandura, A. (1986). *Social Foundations of Thought and Action: A Social Cognitive Theory*. Prentice-Hall.

Barba, J. J., Manrique, J. C., López-Pastor, V. M., & Gea, J. M. (2010). Garantir l'èxit en la formació inicial del professorat d'educaciò física: Els projectes d'aprenentatge tutelats. *Temps d'Educacio, 39*, 187–206. https://raco.cat/index/php/TempsEducacio/article/view/245016

Barba-Martín, R. A., Barba, J. J. and Martínez, S. (2016). La formación continua colaborativa a través de la investigación-acción. Una forma de cambiar las prácticas de aula. *Contextos educativos, 19*, 161-175. doi:10.18172/con.2769

Barba-Martín, J. J., Martínez-Scott, S., & Torrego, L. (2012). El proyecto de aprendizaje tutorado cooperativo: Una experiencia en el grado de maestra de Educación Infantil. *REDU. Revista de Docencia Universitaria, 10*(1), 123–144. doi:10.4995/redu.2012.6125

Barba-Martín, R. A., & López-Pastor, V. M. (2017). Evaluación formativa y compartida en los proyectos de trabajo tutorado, un ejemplo de buena práctica. *Revista Infancia. Educación y Aprendizaje, 3*(2), 66–70.

Barbier, R. (1975). *Le recherche-action dans l'education*.

Barnés, A. (2017). Taller 5. Cómo gestionar nuestras emociones para sentirnos bien como educadoras y educadores sociales. *Revista de Educación Social, 24*, 891–894.

Barragán, E., & Ahmad, R. Morales, M., & Cinthya, I. (2014). Psicología de las emociones positivas: generalidades y beneficios. *Enseñanza e Investigación en Psicología*. Consejo Nacional para la Enseñanza en Investigación en Psicología. https://www.redalyc.org/pdf/292/29232614006.pdf

Barreto, I. M. G., Fernandez, R., Sánchez-Santamaría, J., & Fernández, C. (2021). A Global Competence Approach to Teaching Development for Intercultural Education. In Barreto, I.M.G. (ed) Handbook of Research on Promoting Social Justice for Immigrants and Refugees Through Active Citizenship and Intercultural Education (pp. 268-287). https://doi.org/10.4018/978-1-7998-7283-2.ch014

Barrientos, E. J., López-Pastor, V. M., & Pérez-Brunicardi, D. (2019). ¿Por qué hago Evaluación Formativa y Compartida y/o Evaluación para el Aprendizaje en Educación Física? La influencia en la Formación Inicial y Permanente del profesorado. *Retos, 36*, 37–43. doi:10.47197/retos.v36i66478

Barrientos, E., López-Pastor, V. M., & Pérez-Brunicardi, D. (2019). ¿Por qué hago evaluación formativa y compartida y/o evaluación para el aprendizaje en EF? La influencia de la formación inicial y permanente del Profesorado. *Retos, 36*, 37–43. https:// recyt.fecyt.es/index.php/ retos/article/view/66478

Barrie, S. C. (2006). Understanding what we mean by the generic attributes of graduates. *Higher Education, 51*(2), 215–241. doi:10.100710734-004-6384-7

Bausela, E. (2004). La docencia a través de la investigación-acción. *Revista Iberoamericana de Educación, 35*(1), 1–9. doi:10.35362/rie3512871

Bejarano, M. T. & Marí, R. (2019). Educación en sexualidad e igualdad. Discursos y estrategias para la formación docente y educadores sociales. Dykinson.

Bejarano, M. T. & Martínez I. (2019). Los cuentos creativos, un recurso didáctico para la igualdad en educación Infantil y Primaria. In Mª. T. Bejarano & R. Marí (Dir.). Educación en sexualidad e igualdad. Discursos y estrategias para la formación docente y educadores sociales (pp. 115-132). Dykinson.

Bejarano, M. T. & Mateos, A. (2016). Reflexiones y propuestas para mejorar la educación afectivo-sexual en España. In R. Costa, E., Pinheiro de Queiroz, & F. Teixeira, F. (Coord.). Atravessamentos de gêneo, corpos e sexualidades: Linguagens, apelos, desejos, posibilidades e desafíos (pp. 150-172). Editora FURG.

Bejarano, M. T., Téllez, V. & Martínez, I. (2021). Decolonial, Feminist, and Antiracist Pedagogies. In I.M. Barreto (coord.). Promoting Social Justice for Inmigrants and Refugees Through Active Citizenship and Intercultural Education. (pp. 310-320). IGI Global.

Bejarano, M. (2019). Coeducar hoy. Reflexiones desde las pedagogías feministas para la despatriarcalización del currículum. *Tendencias Pedagógicas, 34*, 37–50. doi:10.15366/tp2019.34.004

Beutel, D., Adie, L., & Lloyd, M. (2017). Assessment Moderation in an Australian Context: Processes, Practices, and Challenges. *Teaching in Higher Education, 22*(1), 1–14. doi:10.1080/13562517.2016.1213232

Biggs, J. (2005). *Calidad del aprendizaje universitario*. Narcea.

Biggs, J. B. (2003). *Teaching for quality learning at university*. The Open University Press.

Birenbaum, M. (1996). Assessment 2000: Towards a pluralistic approach to assessment. In *Alternatives in assessment of achievements, learning processes and prior knowledge* (pp. 3–29). Springer. doi:10.1007/978-94-011-0657-3_1

Bisquerra, R. (2012). *¿Cómo educar las emociones? La inteligencia emocional en la infancia y la adolescencia.* Espligues de Llobregat (Barcelona): Hospital San Joan de Déu.

Bisquerra, R. (2005). La educación emocional en la formación del profesorado. *Revista Interuniversitaria de Formación del Profesorado, 19*(3), 95–114.

Bisquerra, R. (2009). *Psicopedagogía de las emociones*. Síntesis.

Bisquerra, R., Martínez, F., Obiols, M., & Pérez-Escoda, N. (2006). Evaluación 360°: Una aplicación a la educación emocional. *Revista de Investigación Educacional, 24*(1), 187–203.

Bisquerra, R., Pérez, J. C., & García, E. (2015). *Inteligencia emocional en educación*. Síntesis.

Black, P., Harrison, C., Lee, C., Marshall, B., & Wiliam, D. (2002). *Working inside the black box: assessment for learning in the classroom.* King's College.

Black, P., McCormick, R., James, M., & Pedder, D. (2006). Learning How to Learn and Assessment for Learning: A theoretical inquiry. *Research Papers in Education, 21*(2), 119–132. doi:10.1080/02671520600615612

Black, P., & William, D. (2009). Developing the theory of formative assessment. *Educational Assessment, Evaluation and Accountability, 21*(1), 5–31. doi:10.100711092-008-9068-5

Blández, J. (2021). *La investigación-acción: un reto para el profesorado: guía práctica para grupos de trabajo, seminarios y equipos de investigación.* INDE.

Bloxham, S., & Boyd, P. (2007). *Developing effective assessment in higher education: A practical guide.* Open University Press.

Boni, A., Lozano, J. F., & Walker, M. (2010). La educación superior desde el enfoque de capacidades. Una propuesta para el debate. *REIFOP, 13*(3), 123–131.

Bonicoli, M. P. (2008). How to change learning process: Representation in Higher Education via distance-learning technology: the case study of a French continuing education center. In *Proceedings of the 2nd International Multi-Conference on Society, Cybernetics and Informatics: IMSCI 2008*. IIIS.

Bores-García, D., Hortigüela-Alcalá, D., Fernández-Rio, J., González-Calvo, G., & Barba-Martín, R. (2021). Research on Cooperative Learning in Physical Education. Systematic Review of the Last Five Years. *Research Quarterly for Exercise and Sport, 92*(1), 146–155. doi:10.1080/02701367.2020.1719276 PMID:32023176

Bores-García, D., Hortigüela-Alcalá, D., González-Calvo, G., & Barba-Martín, R. A. (2020). Peer Assessment in Physical Education: A Systematic Review of the Last Five Years. *Sustainability (Basel), 12*(9233), 1–15. doi:10.3390u12219233

Bores-García, D., Hortigüela-Alcalá, D., Hernando-Garijo, A., & González-Calvo, G. (2021). Analysis of student motivation towards body expression through the use of formative and share assessment. *Retos, 1*(40), 198–208. doi:10.47197/retos.v1i40.83025

Borjas, M. (2017). Ludoevaluación en Educación Infantil. *Verbum.*

Boroel Cervantes, B. I., Sánchez-Santamaría, J., Morales Gutiérrez, K. D., & Henríquez Ritchie, P. S. (2018). Educación exitosa para todos: La tutoría como proceso de acompañamiento escolar desde la mirada de la equidad educativa. *Revista Fuentes, 20*(2), 91–104. doi:10.12795/revistafuentes.2018.v20.i2.06

Boud, D., & Falchikov, N. (2007). Introduction: Assessment for the longer term. In Rethinking assessment in higher education (pp. 13-23). Routledge.

Boud, D. (2000). Sustainable assessment: Rethinking assessment for the learning society. *Studies in Continuing Education, 22*(2), 151–167. doi:10.1080/713695728

Boud, D. (2020). Challenges in reforming higher education assessment: A perspective from afar. *RELIEVE, 26*(1), M3. Advance online publication. doi:10.7203/relieve.26.1.17088

Boud, D., & Dawson, P. (2021). What feedback literate teachers do: An empirically-derived competency framework. *Assessment & Evaluation in Higher Education.* doi:10.1080/02602938.2021.1910928

Boud, D., & Molloy, E. (2013). *Feedback in Higher and Professional Education. Understanding it and doing it well.* Routledge.

Boud, D., & Soler, R. (2016). Sustainable assessment revisited. *Assessment and Evaluation in Higher Education, 41*(3), 400–413. doi:10.1080/02602938.2015.1018133

Brackett, M. A., Rivers, S. E., & Salovey, P. (2011). Emotional Intelligence: Implications for Personal, Social, Academic, and Workplace Success. *Social and Personality Psychology Compass, 5*(1), 88–103. doi:10.1111/j.1751-9004.2010.00334.x

Bravo, A., & Del Valle, J. (2009). *Intervención socioeducativa en acogimiento residencial.* Gobierno de Cantabria - Consejería de Empleo y Bienestar Social.

Breuleux, A., Laferrière, T., & Lamon, M. (2002). Capacity building within and across countries into the effective uses of ICTs. In *Pan-Canadian Education Research Agenda Symposium*. Information Technology and Learning.

Broadbent, J., Panadero, E., & Boud, D. (2018). Implementing summative assessment with a formative flavour: A case study in a large class. *Assessment & Evaluation in Higher Education, 43*(2), 307–322. doi:10.1080/02602938.2017.1343455

Bromseth, J., & Sörensdötter, R. (2012). Normkritisk pedagogik. In Lundberg. A. & A. Werner (Ed.) Genusvetenskapens pedagogik och didaktik (pp. 43–57). Nationella sekretariatet för genusforskning.

Bromseth, J. (2019). Normkritisk pedagogik - rötter och fötter. In J. Bromseth & L. Björkman (Eds.), *Normkritisk pedagogik: Perspektiv, utmaningar och möjligheter* (pp. 41–72). Studentlitteratur AB.

Brown, S., & Sambell, K. (2020). *The Covid Collection.* Sally Brown. https://sally-brown.net/kay-sambell-and-sally-brown-covid-19-assessment-collection/

Brown, G. T. L. (2018). *Assessment of student achievement.* Routledge.

Brown, G. T. L., Hui, S. K. F., Yu, F. W. M., & Kennedy, K. J. (2011). Teachers' conceptions of assessment in Chinese context: A tripartite model of accountability, improvement, and irrelevance. *International Journal of Educational Research, 50*(5-6), 307–320. doi:10.1016/j.ijer.2011.10.003

Brown, S. (2015). *Learning, teaching and assessment in higher education: global perspectives.* Macmillan International Higher Education. doi:10.1007/978-1-137-39667-9

Brown, S. (2019). Using assessment and feedback to empower students and enhance their learning. In C. Bryan & K. Clegg (Eds.), *Innovative Assessment in Higher Education* (2nd ed., pp. 50–63). Routledge. doi:10.4324/9780429506857-5

Brown, S., & Knight, P. (1994). *Assessing learners in higher education.* Routledge.

Bruun, T. (2016). Det normales magt. *VERA, 76,* 4–9.

Buscá, F., Pintor, P., Martínez, L., & Peire, T. (2010). Sistemas y procedimientos de Evaluación Formativa en docencia universitaria: Resultados de 34 casos aplicados durante el curso académico 2007-2008. *Estudios Sobre Educación, 18,* 255-276. https://revistas.unav.edu/index.php/estudios-sobre-educacion/article/view/4674

Butler, J. (1999). *Gender Trouble - Feminism and the Subversion of Identity.* Routledge.

Cabello, R., Ruíz, D. & Fernández, P. (2010). Docentes emocionalmente inteligentes. *Revista electrónica interuniversitaria de formación del profesorado, 13*(1), 41-49.

Calderón García, R., González Fernández, M. O., & Torres Valencia, B. (2021). La percepción docente sobre las tutorías en el contexto del COVID 2019. *Revistas.Upch.Edu.Pe, 14*(1), 21–28. doi:10.20453/rph.v14i1.4030

Calderón, C., & Escalera, G. (2008). La evaluación de la docencia ante el reto del Espacio Europeo de Educación Superior. *Educación (Lima), XXI*(0), 11, 237–256. doi:10.5944/educxx1.11.0.316

Cameselle, N. (2017). Percepción de la gestión emocional del/a educador/a social [End-of-Postdegree Project, University of Barcelona]. Repository of the University de Barcelona. Retrieved from https://diposit.ub.edu/dspace/bitstream/2445/118320/7/TFP%20Noemi%20Cameselle.pdf

Campbell, J. (2008). *The hero with a thousand faces* (3rd ed.). New World Library.

Cañadas, L. (2018). *La evaluación formativa en la adquisición de competencias docentes en la formación inicial del profesorado de Educación Física.* [Tesis Doctoral Inédit,. Universidad Autónoma de Madrid].

Cañadas, L. (2021). Contribution of formative assessment for developing teaching competences in teacher education. *European Journal of Teacher Education.* Taylor and Francis. https://doi.org/ doi:10.1080/02619768.2021.1950684

Cañadas, L. (2020). Evaluación formativa en el contexto universitario: Oportunidades y propuestas de actuación. *Revista Digital de Investigación En Docencia Universitaria, 14*(2), e1214–e1214. doi:10.19083/10.19083/ridu.2020.1214

Cañadas, L., & Lobo-de-Diego, F. E. (2021). Desarrollo de competencias en docencia online y semipresencial en la formación en fundamentos en educación física. *Journal of Supranational Policies of Education, 14,* 57–70. doi:10.15366/jospoe2021.14.004

Cañadas, L., Santos-Pastor, M. L., & Castejón, F. J. (2019). Competencias docentes en la formación inicial del profesorado de educación física, *Retos. Nuevas Tendencias en Educación Física. Deportes y Recreación, 35*, 284–288. doi:10.47197/retos.v0i35.64812

Cañadas, L., Santos-Pastor, M. L., & Castejón, J. (2018). Desarrollo de competencias docentes en la formación inicial del profesorado de Educación Física. Relación con los instrumentos de evaluación. *Estudios Pedagógicos (Valdivia), 44*(2), 111–126. doi:10.4067/S0718-07052018000200111

Cañadas, L., Santos-Pastor, M. L., & Ruíz, P. (2021). Percepción del impacto de la evaluación formativa en las competencias profesionales durante la formación inicial del profesorado. *Revista Electrónica de Investigación Educativa, 23*(e03), 1–14. doi:10.24320/redie.2021.23.e07.2982

Cano, E., Pons-Seguí, L., & Lluch, L. (2020). ['*Educació Superior*. Universitat de Barcelona.]. *Feedback*, l.

Caram, G., Naigeboren Guzmán, M., Gil De Asar, M., & Bordier, M. S. (2020). *Enseñanza y tutoría en el contexto de la virtualidad*. 37–42. Acta Académica. https://www.aacademica.org/000-007/786.pdf

Carless, D. (2015). Exploring learning-oriented assessment processes. *Higher Education, 69*(6), 963–976. doi:10.100710734-014-9816-z

Carless, D., & Boud, D. (2018). The development of student feedback literacy: Enabling uptake of feedback. *Assessment & Evaluation in Higher Education, 43*(8), 1315–1325. doi:10.1080/02602938.2018.1463354

Carpenter, J. P., Krutka, D. G., & Trust, T. (2021). Continuity and change in educators' professional learning networks. *Journal of Educational Change, 23*(1), 85–113. doi:10.100710833-020-09411-1

Carrillo, C., & Flores, M. A. (2020). COVID-19 and teacher education: A literature review of online teaching and learning practices. *European Journal of Teacher Education, 43*(4), 466–487. doi:10.1080/02619768.2020.1821184

Carr, W., & Kemmis, S. (1988). *Teoría crítica de la Enseñanza. La Investigación-Acción en la formación del profesorado*. Martínez-Roca.

Casanova, M. A. (2011). Evaluación para la Inclusión Educativa. *Revista Iberoamericana de Evaluación Educativa, 4*(1), 78–89.

Castagno, A. (2008). "I Don't Want to Hear That!": Legitimating Whiteness through Silence in Schools. *Anthropology & Education Quarterly, 39*(3), 314–333. doi:10.1111/j.1548-1492.2008.00024.x

Castañeda, M. B., Cabrera, A. F., Navarro, Y., & De Vires, W. (2010). *Procesamiento de datos y análisis estadístico utilizando SPSS*. Edipucrs.

Castejón, F. J., López-Pastor, V. M., Clemente, J. A., & Zaragoza, J. (2011). Evaluación formativa y rendimiento académico en la formación inicial del profesorado de Educación Física. *Revista Internacional de Medicina y Ciencias de la Actividad Física y del Deporte, 11*(42), 328–346.

Castejón, F. J., López-Pastor, V. M., Julián, J. A., & Zaragoza, J. (2011). Evaluación formativa y rendimiento académico en la formación inicial del profesorado de educación física. *Revista Internacional de Medicina y Ciencias de la Actividad Física y del Deporte, 11*(42), 328–346. https://www.redalyc.org/articulo.oa?id=54222171007

Castejón-Oliva, F. J., Santos-Pastor, M. L., & Palacios Picos, A. (2015). Cuestionario sobre metodología y evaluación en formación inicial en educación física. *Revista Internacional de Medicina y Ciencias de la Actividad Física y del Deporte, 15*(58), 245–267. doi:10.15366/rimcafd2015.58.004

Cendon, E. (2016). Bridging Theory and Practice – Reflective Learning in Higher Education. In W. Nuninger & J.-M. Châtelet (Eds.), *Quality Assurance and Value Management in Higher Education*. IGI Global., doi:10.4018/978-1-5225-0024-7.ch012

Chabot, D., & Chabot, M. (2014). *Pedagogía Emocional. Sentir para Aprender*. Alfaomega.

Chareanpunsirikul, & Wood, R. C. (2002). Mintzberg, managers, and methodology: some observations from a study of hotel general managers. *Tourism Management, 23*(5), 551–556. doi:10.1016/S0261-5177(02)00016-X

Clark, I. (2012). Formative assessment: Assessment is for self-regulated learning. *Educational Psychology Review, 24*(2), 205–249. doi:10.100710648-011-9191-6

Clarup, E., Hamilton, S. D. P., & Padovan-Özdemir, M. (2020). *Normkritisk og normkreativ pædagogik i aktuel praksis: Et forskningsbaseret inspirationskatalog til dagtilbud*. VIA University College.

Cohen, L., Manion, L., & Morrison, K. (2018). *Research Methods in Education*. Routledge.

Coller, X. (2000). *Estudio de casos*. Centro de Investigaciones Sociológicas.

Córdoba Jiménez, T., Carbonero Sánchez, L., Sánchez Aguayo, D., Inglada Moreno, S., Serra Figueroa, M., Blasco, M., Sáez Miota, S., & Ivanco Casals, P. (2016). Educación Física Cooperativa, formación permanente y desarrollo profesional. De la escritura colectiva a un relato de vida compartido. [Cooperative Physical Education, In-service Teacher Education and professional development] *Retos, 29*, 264–269. doi:10.47197/retos/v.i35.60168

Costa, M. & Méndez, E. (1996). *Manual para el educador social: Habilidades en la relación de ayuda; 2. Afrontando situaciones*. Ministerio de Asuntos Sociales. Centro de publicaciones.

Crenshaw, K. (1991). Mapping the Margins: Intersectionality, Identity Politics, and Violence against Women of Color. *Stanford Law Review, 43*(6), 1241–1299. doi:10.2307/1229039

Creswell, J. W. (2009). *Research design: Qualitative, quantitative, and mixed methods approaches*. SAGE Publications.

Cruz, P., Borjas, M. P., & López, M. (2020). Ludoevaluación de la emoción del miedo en educación infantil. *Revista Latinoamericana De Ciencias Sociales, Niñez Y Juventud, 19*(1), 1–21. doi:10.11600/rlcsnj.19.1.4184

Cumming, J., & Maxwell, G. S. (1999). Contextualising authentic assessment. *Assessment in Education: Principles, Policy and Practice, 6*(2), 177–194. doi:10.1080/09695949992865

Cumming, T. M., & Rodriquez, C. D. (2017). A meta-analysis of mobile technology supporting individuals with disabilities. *The Journal of Special Education, 51*(3), 164–176. doi:10.1177/0022466917713983

Danbolt, M. (2017). RETRO RACISM - Colonial Ignorance and Racialized Affective Consumption in Danish Public Culture. *Nordic Journal of Migration Research, 7*(2), 105–113. doi:10.1515/njmr-2017-0013

Davies, A., Fidler, D., & Gorbis, M. (2011). *Future Work Skills 2020*. Institute for the Future for University of Phoenix Research Institute. www.iftf.org/uploads/media/SR-1382A_UPRI_future_work_skills_sm.pdf

Davies, P. (2007). *The Bologna Process and University Lifelong Learning: The State of Play and future Directions, Final report BeFlexPlus*. EUCEN Retrieved from http://www.eucen.eu/BeFlex/FinalReports/BeFlexFullReportPD.pdf

Davison, G. (2011). *Investigating the relationships between authentic assessment and the development of learner autonomy*. University of Northumbria at Newcastle.

De Juanas, A. (2010). Aprendices y competencias en el Espacio Europeo de Educación Superior. *Revista de Psicología y Educación, 1*(5), 171–186.

de la Cruz Flores, G., Chehaybar, Y., Kury, E., & Abreu, L. F. (2011). Tutoría en educación superior: una revisión analítica de la literatura. *Revista de la Educación Superior.* Vol. XL (1), No. 157, 189-209. https://www.scielo.org.mx/pdf/resu/v40n157/v40n157a9.pdf

De Miguel Díaz, M. (2006). Metodologías para optimizar el aprendizaje. Segundo objetivo del Espacio Europeo de Educación Superior. *Revista Interuniversitaria de Formación de Profesorado*, 20-41. https://www.redalyc.org/pdf/274/27411311004.pdf

De Sousa Santos, B. (2012). La universidad en el siglo XXI. Para una reforma democrática y emancipadora de la universidad. In R. Ramírez, Transformar la Universidad para Transformar la Sociedad (pp. 139-194). SENESCYT.

De Sousa Santos, B. (2011a). Epistemologías del Sur. *Revista Internacional de Filosofía Iberoamericana y Teoría Social*, (54), 17–39.

De Sousa Santos, B. (2018). *The End of the Cognitive Empire: The Coming of Age of Epistemologies of the South.* Duke University Press. doi:10.1215/9781478002000

Delgado, V., Ausín, V., Hortigüela-Alcalá, D., & Abella, V. (2016). Evaluación entre iguales: Una experiencia de evaluación compartida en Educación Superior. *Educadi*, *1*(1), 9–24. doi:10.7770/EDUCADI-V1N1-ART943

Dembo, M.-H., & Seli, H.-P. (2004). Student's Resistance to Change in Learning Strategies Courses. *Journal of Developmental Education*, *27*(3), 2–11.

Dempsey, J. V. (1993). Interactive instruction and feedback. *Technology.*

Dille, K. B., & Røkenes, F. M. (2021). Teachers' professional development in formal online communities: A scoping review. *Teaching and Teacher Education*, *105*, 103431. doi:10.1016/j.tate.2021.103431

Dochy, F., Segers, M., & Dierick, S. (2002). Nuevas vías de aprendizaje y enseñanza y sus consecuencias: Una era de evaluación. *Red Estatal de Docencia Universitaria*, *2*(2), 13–30. https://revistas.um.es/redu/article/view/20051/19411

Dochy, F., Segers, M., & Sluijsmans, D. (2002). The use of self, peer and co-assessment in higher education. *Studies in Higher Education*, *24*(3), 331–350. doi:10.1080/03075079912331379935

Domínguez, J. and Vázquez, E. (2015). Atención a la diversidad: análisis de la formación permanente del profesorado en Galicia. *Revista Nacional e Internacional de Educación Inclusiva*, *8*(2), 139-145.

Dunning, J. K., Ehrlinger, J., & Kruger, J. (2003). Why People Fail to Recognize Their Own Incompetence. *Current Directions in Psychological Science*, *12*(3), 83–87. doi:10.1111/1467-8721.01235

Durand, M.-J., & Chouinard, R. (2012). *L'évaluation des apprentissages. De la planification de la démarche à la communication des résultats.* Éditions Hurtubise.

Elliot, N., & Higgins, A. (2005). Self and peer assessment – does it make a difference to student group work? *Nurse Education in Practice*, *5*(1), 40–48. doi:10.1016/j.nepr.2004.03.004 PMID:19038177

Entwistle, N. J., & Entwistle, A. (1991). Contrasting forms of understanding for degree examinations: The student experience and its implications. *Higher Education*, *22*(3), 205–227. doi:10.1007/BF00132288

Escribano, A., & Del Valle, A. (2015). *El aprendizaje basado en problemas (ABP).* Ediciones de la U.

Escudero, J. M. (1998). Consideraciones y propuestas sobre la formación permanente del profesorado. *Review of Education*, *317*, 11–29.

Esteve, F., & Llopis, M. A. (2018). Experiencia con GSuite en los grados de Maestro/a de Educación Infantil y Primaria. In *II Jornadas de innovación educativa DIMEU*. Universitat Jaume I.

Etxaniz, X. (2011). La transmisión de los valores en la literatura, desde la tradición oral hasta la LIJ. *Ocnos, 7*(7), 73–83. doi:10.18239/ocnos_2011.07.06

European Association for Quality Assurance in Higher Education - ENQA. (2015). *Standards and Guidelines for Quality Assurance in the European Higher Education Area (ESG)*. ENQA. www.enqa.eu/index.php/home/esg/

Extremera, N. & Fernández-Berrocal, P. (2015). *Inteligencia emocional y educación*. Grupo 5.

Falchikov, N., & Boud, D. (1989). Student self-assessment in higher education. A meta-analysis comparing peer and teacher marks. *Review of Educational Research, 70*(3), 287–322. doi:10.3102/00346543070003287

Fanon, F. (1952). *Black Skin, White Masks*. Grove Press.

Fernandez, N. (2015). Évaluation et motivation, un couple gagnant pour soutenir l'apprentissage. Dans J. L. Leroux (dir.), Évaluer les compétences au collégial et à l'université: un guide pratique (p. 479-500). Montréal, QC: Chenelière Éducation/Association québécoise de pédagogie collégiale

Fernández, A. (2011). La evaluación orientada al aprendizaje en un modelo de formación por competencias en la educación universitaria. *Revista de Docencia Universitaria, 8*(1), 11–34. doi:10.4995/redu.2010.6216

Fernández, C., López-Pastor, V. M., & Pascual-Arias, C. (2019). La evaluación formativa y compartida en Educación Infantil. Consecuencias del uso de dos metodologías diferentes. *Infancia* [IEYA]. *Educación y Aprendizaje, 5*(2), 54–59. doi:10.22370/ieya.2019.5.2.1504

Fidel, R. (1984). The case study method: A case study. *Library and Information Science Research, 6*(3), 273–288.

Flick, U. (2014). *Qualitative Data Analysis*. SAGE Publications.

Flores, M. A. (2020). Preparing Teachers to Teach in Complex Settings: Opportunities for Professional Learning and Development. *European Journal of Teacher Education, 43*(3), 297–300. doi:10.1080/02619768.2020.1771895

Flores, M. A., & Gago, M. (2020). Teacher Education in Times of COVID-19 Pandemic in Portugal: National, Institutional and Pedagogical Responses. *Journal of Education for Teaching, 46*(4), 507–516. doi:10.1080/02607476.2020.1799709

Fortea, M. Á. (2009). *Metodologías didácticas para la enseñanza/aprendizaje de competencias*. Unitat de Suport Educatiu de la Universitat Jaume I.

Fox, J. (2008). Alternative assessment. Encyclopedia of language and education, 7, 97-108.

Fraile, A., López-Pastor, V. M., Castejón, J., and Romero, R. (2013). La evaluación formativa en docencia universitaria y el rendimiento académico del alumnado. *Aula abierta, 41*(2), 23-34.

Fraile-Aranda, A., López-Pastor, V. M., Castejón-Oliva, F. J., & Romero-Martín, R. (2013). La evaluación formativa en docencia universitaria y el rendimiento académico del alumnado. *Revista Aula Abierta, 41*(2), 23-34. https://dialnet.unirioja.es/servlet/articulo?codigo=4239063

Fraile, J., Gil-Izquierdo, M., Zamorano-Sande, D., & Sánchez-Iglesias, I. (2020). Autorregulación del aprendizaje y procesos de evaluación formativa en los trabajos en grupo. *RELIEVE, 26*(1), 1–15. doi:10.7203/relieve.26.1.17402

Frederiksen, J. S., & Overvad, E. (2020). Normkreativ pædagogik og ligestillingsarbejde i skolen. In S. B. Nielsen & G. Riis (Eds.), *Køn, seksualitet og mangfoldighed* (pp. 214–236). Samfundslitteratur.

Freire, P. (2006). *Pedagogía de la indignación*. Editorial Siglo XXI.

Gallardo, F. and Carter, B. (2016). La evaluación formativa y compartida durante el prácticum en la formación inicial del profesorado. Análisis de un caso en Chile. Retos. Nuevas tendencias en educación física, deportes y recreación, 29, 258-263

Gallardo, F., & Carter, B. (2016). La evaluación formativa y compartida durante el prácticum en la formación inicial del profesorado: Análisis de un caso en Chile. *Retos, 29*(1), 258–263. https://recyt.fecyt.es/index.php/retos/article/view/43550

Gallardo, F., & Carter, B. (2016). La evaluación formativa y compartida durante el prácticum, en la formación inicial del profesorado: Análisis de un caso en Chile. *Retos, 29*(29), 258–263. doi:10.47197/retos.v0i29.43550

Gallardo-Fuentes, F. J., López-Pastor, V. M., & Cartier-Thuillier, B. (2020). Ventajas e Inconvenientes de la Evaluación Formativa, y su Influencia en la Autopercepción de Competencias en alumnado de Formación Inicial del Profesorado en Educación Física. *Retos, 38*(38), 417–424. doi:10.47197/retos.v38i38.75540

Gallardo-Fuentes, F., López-Pastor, V. M., & Carter-Thuillier, B. (2018). Efectos de la Aplicación de un Sistema de Evaluación Formativa en la Autopercepción de Competencias Adquiridas en Formación Inicial del Profesorado. *Estudios Pedagógicos (Valdivia), 44*(2), 55–77. doi:10.4067/S0718-07052018000200055

Gambarini, M. F., & Cruz, P. (2019). Habilidades docentes en comunicación eficaz. Ejercicio de liderazgo centrado en la misión docente. *Aularia, 8*(1), pp. 9-20. http://cort.as/-ME77

Gibbs, G., & Simpson, C. (2009). *Condiciones para una evaluación continuada favorecedora del aprendizaje*. Octaedro.

Girardet, C., & Mottier Lopez, L. (2020). *La bienveillance à l'épreuve de l'évaluation entre pairs à l'université*. Revue Suisse des Sciences de l'Education.

Giroux, H. (2018). *Pedagogía crítica para tiempos difíciles*. Mapas colectivos.

Goleman, D. (2007). Social intelligence: the new science of human relationships. Reprint Editdion: Bantam

Goleman, D. (2006). *Inteligencia social*. Kairós.

Goleman, D. (2011). *El cerebro y la inteligencia emocional: nuevos descubrimientos*. Ediciones B.

Gómez, M. (2003). Aproximación conceptual a los sectores y ámbitos de intervención de la educación social. *Pedagogía Social*, (10), 233-251. Retrieved from http://hdl.handle.net/2445/65334

Gómez-Collado, M. E. (2012). *La percepción de los estudiantes sobre el Programa de Tutoría Académica The perception of students on the Academic Tutelage. 58*, 209–233.

Gómez, M. A., & Quesada, V. (2017). Coevaluación o evaluación compartida en el contexto universitario: La percepción del alumnado de primer curso. *Revista Iberoamericana de Evaluación Educativa, 10*(2), 9–30. doi:10.15366/riee2017.10.2.001

González Palacios, A., & Avelino, I. (2016). Tutoría: Una revisión conceptual. *Smip.Udg.Mx*, 57–68. http://smip.udg.mx/sites/default/files/38_gonzalez_palacios.pdf

González, J. (2021). *Educación virtual y satisfacción estudiantil durante la pandemia de Covid-19 en una universidad de Ecuador 2021*. Repositorio Institucional - UCV. https://repositorio.ucv.edu.pe/handle/20.500.12692/69339

Grzega, J. (2007). *Learning By Teaching: The Didactic Model LdL in University Classes*. http://www.joachim-grzega.de/ldl-engl.pdf

Guamán, R., Villareal, Á., & Cedeño, E. (2020). La Educación Híbrida como alternativa frente al Covid -19 en el Ecuador. *Tse'De, 3*(1). http://tsachila.edu.ec/ojs/index.php/TSEDE/article/view/27

Gulikers, J. T., Bastiaens, T. J., & Kirschner, P. A. (2004). A five-dimensional framework for authentic assessment. *Educational Technology Research and Development, 52*(3), 67–86. doi:10.1007/BF02504676

Gulikers, J. T., Bastiaens, T. J., Kirschner, P. A., & Kester, L. (2008). Authenticity is in the eye of the beholder: Student and teacher perceptions of assessment authenticity. *Journal of Vocational Education and Training, 60*(4), 401–412. doi:10.1080/13636820802591830

Gutiérrez, M. (2010). Los proyectos de aprendizaje tutorado en la formación universitaria dentro del espacio europeo. *Acción pedagógica, 19*(1), 6-18.

Gutiérrez, C., Hortigüela-Alcalá, D., Peral, Z., & Pérez, A. (2018). Percepciones de los alumnos del grado en maestro en Educación Primaria con mención en Educación Física sobre la adquisición de competencias. *Estudios Pedagógicos (Valdivia), 44*(2), 223–239. doi:10.4067/S0718-07052018000200223

Hamodi, C., & López, A. T. (2012). La evaluación formativa y compartida en la Formación Inicial del Profesorado desde la perspectiva del alumnado y de los egresados. *Psychology, Society, &. Education, 4*(1), 103–116. https://ojs.ual.es/ojs/index.php/psye/article/view/484

Hamodi, C., López-Pastor, V. M., & López, A. T. (2017). If I experience formative assessment whilst studying at university, will I put it into practice later as a teacher? Formative and shared assessment in Initial Teacher Education (ITE). *European Journal of Teacher Education, 40*(2), 171–190. doi:10.1080/02619768.2017.1281909

Hamodi, C., López, V. L., & López, A. T. (2015). Medios, técnicas e instrumentos de evaluación formativa y compartida en Educación Superior. *Perfiles Educativos, XXXVII*(147), 146–161. doi:10.22201/iisue.24486167e.2015.147.47271

Haro-Soler, M. M. (2017). ¿Cómo desarrollar la autoeficacia del estudiantado? Presentación y evaluación de una experiencia formativa en el aula de traducción. *Revista Digital de Docencia Universitaria, 11*(2), 50–74. doi:10.19083/ridu.11.567

Hattie, J. (2008). *Visible Learning: A Synthesis of Over 800 Meta-Analyses Relating to Achievement.* Routledge. doi:10.4324/9780203887332

Hattie, J., & Timperley, H. (2007). The Power of Feedback. *Review of Educational Research, 77*(1), 81–112. doi:10.3102/003465430298487

Henderson, M., Ryan, T., & Phillips, P. (2019). The challenges of feedback in higher education. *Assessment & Evaluation in Higher Education, 44*(8), 1237–1252. doi:10.1080/02602938.2019.1599815

Hepplestone, S., & Chikwa, G. (2016). Exploring the processes used by students to apply feedback. *Student Engagement and Experience Journal, 5*(1), 1–15. doi:10.7190eej.v5i1.104

Hernández Sampieri, R., & Mendoza, C. P. (2008). El matrimonio cuantitativo cualitativo: el paradigma mixto. En *6º Congreso de Investigación en Sexología. Congreso efectuado por el Instituto Mexicano de Sexología.* A. C. y la Universidad Juárez Autónoma de Tabasco, Villahermosa, Tabasco, México.

Hernández, R. (2002). El juego en la infancia. *Revista Chilena de Pediatria, 4*(21-22), 134–137. doi:10.4067/S0370-41062008000500014

Herrero, D., Manrique, J. C., & López-Pastor, V. M. (2021). Incidencia de la Formación Inicial y Permanente del Profesorado en la aplicación de la Evaluación Formativa y Compartida en Educación Física. *Retos*, (41), 533–543. doi:10.47197/retos.v0i41.86090

Hipólito, N., & Martínez Martín, I. (2021). Diálogos entre el Buen Vivir, las Epistemologías del Sur, el feminismo decolonial y las pedagogías feministas. Aportes para una educación transformadora. *Estudos Avançados*, (35), 16–28. doi:10.35588/estudav.v0i35.5321

Hooks, B. (2021). *Enseñar a transgredir. Educación como práctica de la libertad.* Capitán Swing.

Hortigüela-Alcalá, D., Abella, V., Delgado, V., & Ausín, V. (2016). Influencia del sistema de evaluación empleado en la percepción del alumno sobre su aprendizaje y las competencias docentes. *Infancia, Educación y Aprendizaje, 2*(1), 20-42. http://revistainfanciaeducacionyaprendizaje.com/

Hortigüela-Alcalá, D., Fernández-Río, J., Castejón, J., & Pérez-Pueyo, A. (2017). Formative assessment, work regulation, organization, engagement, tracking and attendance in Spanish Universities. *Revista Electrónica Interuniversitaria de Formación del Profesorado, 20*(3), 49–63. doi:10.6018/reifop.20.3.268681

Hortigüela-Alcalá, D., González-Víllora, S., & Hernando-Garijo, A. (2021). Do we really assess learning in Physical Education? Teacher's perceptions at different educational stages. *Retos, 42*, 643–654. doi:10.47197/retos.v42i0.88686

Hortigüela-Alcalá, D., Pérez-Pueyo, A., & González-Calvo, G. (2019). Pero… ¿A qué nos referimos realmente con la Evaluación Formativa y Compartida?: Confusiones Habituales y Reflexiones Prácticas. *Revista Iberoamericana de Evaluación Educativa, 12*(1), 13–27. doi:10.15366/riee2019.12.1.001

Hortigüela-Alcalá, D., Pérez-Pueyo, A., & López-Pastor, V. M. (2015). Implicación y regulación del trabajo del alumnado en los sistemas de evaluación formativa en educación superior. *RELIEVE, 21*(1), 1–15. doi:10.7203/relieve.21.1.5171

Hortigüela, D., Palacios, A., & López-Pastor, V. M. (2018). The impact of formative and shared or co-assessment on the acquisition of transversal competences in higher education. *Assessment & Evaluation in Higher Education, 44*(6), 933–945. doi:10.1080/02602938.2018.1530341

Hortigüela, D., Pérez-Pueyo, Á., & Abella, V. (2015). ¿De qué manera se implica el alumnado en el aprendizaje? Análisis de su percepción en procesos de evaluación formativa. *Revista de Investigación Educacional, 13*(1), 88–104.

Ibarra Ruiz, M. S., Lukas Mujika, J.-F., Ponce-González, N., & Rodríguez Gómez, G. (2023). Percepción del profesorado universitario sobre la calidad de las tareas de evaluación de los resultados de aprendizaje. RELIEVE - Revista Electrónica De Investigación Y Evaluación Educativa, 29(1). https://doi.org/10.30827/relieve.v29i1.27404

Ibarra-Sáiz, M. S., & Rodríguez-Gómez, G. (2014). Formación del profesorado universitario en evaluación: análisis y prospectiva del Programa Formativo EVAPES-DevalSimWeb "Evaluación para el aprendizaje en la Educación Superior". En Congreso Iberoamericano de Ciencia, Tecnología, Innovación y Educación. Buenos Aires. Organización de Estados Iberoamericanos para la Educación, la Ciencia y la Cultura. https://doi.org/ doi:10.13140/RG.2.2.23638-86082

Ibarra-Sáiz, M. S., Rodríguez-Gómez, G., Boud, D., Rotsaert, T., Brown, S., Salinas-Salazar, M. L., & Rodríguez-Gómez, H. M. (2020). El futuro de la evaluación en la educación superior. *RELIEVE, 26*(1), 1–6. doi:10.7203/relieve.26.1.17323

Ibarrola, B. (2013). *Aprendizaje emocionante. Neurociencia para el aula.* SM.

Imbernón, F. (2014). *10 ideas clave. La formación permanente del profesorado. Nuevas ideas para formar en la innovación y el cambio.* Graó.

Isava, L. M. (2009). Breve introducción a los artefactos culturales. *Estudios (Madrid, Spain), 17*(34), 441–445.

Jensen, L., Bearman, M., & Boud, D. (2021). Understanding feedback in online learning - A critical review and metaphor analysis. *Computers & Education, 173*, 104271. doi:10.1016/j.compedu.2021.104271

Jerez-Gómez, P., Céspedes-Lorente, J., & Valle-Cabrera, R. (2005). Organizational learning capability: A proposal of measurement. *Journal of Business Research, 58*(6), 715–725. doi:10.1016/j.jbusres.2003.11.002

Jiménez, F., Navarro, V., and Souto, R. (coord.) (2021). *Explorando colaborativamente alternativas de evaluación formativa en la universidad.* La Laguna (Tenerife): Universidad de La Laguna. https://riull.ull.es/xmlui/handle/915/22232

Jiménez, F., Navarro, V., & Pintor, P. (2021). Estado de las vías de opcionalidad de la evaluación en la Red Nacional de Evaluación Formativa y Compartida en la enseñanza universitaria. In *Explorando colaborativamente alternativas de evaluación formativa en la Universidad: el aprendizaje de un grupo de profesores durante el período 2009-2018* (pp. 25–46). Universidad de La Laguna.

Johnson, S. (2011). Making teamwork work: decreasing conflicts in Teams. In Orange Journ., 7(1), 1-14

Johnson, D. W., & Johnson, R. T. (1999). *Aprender juntos y solos. Aprendizaje cooperativo, competitivo e individualista.* Aique.

Johnson, D. W., & Johnson, R. T. (2014). Cooperative Learning in 21st Century. *L'Année Psychologique, 30*(3), 841–851.

Karim, B. H. H. (2015). The impact of teachers' beliefs and perceptions about formative assessment in the university ESL class. *International Journal of Humanities, Social. Sciences and Education, 2*(3), 108–115.

Kemmis, S., & McTaggart, R. (1988). *Cómo planificar la investigación-acción.* Laertes.

Kennedy, A. (2005). Models of Continuing Professional Development: A framework for analysis. *Journal of In-service Education, 31*(2), 235–250. doi:10.1080/13674580500200277

Khawaja, I. (2022). Memory Work as Engaged Critical Pedagogy: Creating Collaborative Spaces for Reflections on Racialisation, Privilege and Whiteness. *Nordic Journal of Social Research.*

Kishimoto, K. (2018). Anti-racist pedagogy: From faculty's self-reflection to organizing within and beyond the classroom. *Race, Ethnicity and Education, 21*(4), 540–554. doi:10.1080/13613324.2016.1248824

Knight, P. (2006). The local practices of assessment. *Assessment & Evaluation in Higher Education, 31*(4), 435–452. doi:10.1080/02602930600679126

Kolb, A. Y., & Kolb, D. A. (2005). Learning Styles and Learning Spaces: Enhancing Experiential Learning in Higher Education. *Academy of Management Learning & Education, 4*(2), 193–212. doi:10.5465/amle.2005.17268566

Kreber, C. (2013). *Authenticity in and through teaching in higher education: The transformative potential of the scholarship of teaching.* Routledge. doi:10.4324/9780203072301

Kreber, C. (2014). Rationalising the nature of 'graduateness' through philosophical accounts of authenticity. *Teaching in Higher Education, 19*(1), 90–100. doi:10.1080/13562517.2013.860114

Kreber, C., Wardley, L., Leviten-Reid, C., & MacPherson, S. (2021). Community-engaged learning in business schools to effect social change: a capabilities perspective. In *Handbook of Teaching and Learning at Business Schools.* Edward Elgar Publishing.

Kuh, G. D. (2001). The National Survey of Student Engagement: Conceptual framework and overview of psychometric properties. *Center of Inquiry.*

Lambert, V. A., & Lambert, C. E. (2012). Qualitative descriptive research: An acceptable design. *Pacific Rim International Journal of Nursing Research, 16*, 255–256.

Latorre, M. (2020). *Evaluación por capacidades y competencias I.* Universidad Marcelino Chaptagnat. https://marinolatorre.umch.edu.pe/wp-content/uploads/2020/09/116_EVALUACI%C3%93N-POR-CAPACIDADES-Y-COMPETENCIAS-I.pdf

Latorre, A. (2003). *La investigación-acción. Conocer y cambiar la práctica educativa.* Graó.

Leclercq, D., & Poumay, M. (2008). The 8 Learning Events Model and its principles. *LabSet.* http://www.labset.net/media/prod/8LEM.pdf

Leduc, M., & Molinié, A. (2020). *Les publications à l'heure de la science ouverte. Ethics Committee Report.* CNRS: France. ww.ouvrirlascience.fr/wp-content/uploads/2020/02/COMETS_Les-publications-a-lheure-de-la-science-ouverte_Avis-2019-40-1.pdf

Lee, S. J., & Reeves, T. C. (2007). Edgar Dale: A significant contributor to the field of educational technology. *Educational Technology, 47*(6), 56.

Legendre, R. (2005). Dictionnaire actuel de l'éducation (3e éd.). Montréal, QC: Guérin.

Lirio, J., Medina, L. & Moreno, M. (2020). La gestión emocional de los adultos mayores: Un estudio de caso. *Revista Euro latinoamericana de Análisis Social y Político, 2*(2), 88-103.

Lirio, J., & Medina, L. (2021). La gestión de las emociones en profesionales de la Educación Social en el ámbito de la protección de menores. *Márgenes. Revista de Educación de la Universidad de Málaga, 2*(1), 112–129.

López Pastor, V. M., Monjas Aguado, R., Gómez García, J., López Pastor, E. M., Martín Pinela, J. F., González Badiola, J., Barba Martín, J. J., Aguilar Baeza, R., González Pascual, M., Heras Bernardino, C., Martín, M. I., Manrique Arribas, J. C., Subtil Marugán, P., & Marugán García, L. (2006). La evaluación en educación física. Revisión de modelos tradicionales y planteamiento de una alternativa. La evaluación formativa y compartida. *Retos, 10,* 31–41. https://doi.org/10.47197/retos.v0i10.35061

López, V. (2009). Evaluación formativa y compartida en Educación Superior: Propuestas, técnicas, instrumentos y experiencias. Narcea.

López, V. (2012). Evaluación formativa y compartida en la universidad: clarificación de conceptos y propuestas de intervención desde la Red Interuniversitaria de Evaluación. *Psychology, Society, and Education, 4*(1). http://repositorio.ual.es/bitstream/handle/10835/2887/vista%20Lopez%20Pastor.pdf

López, B., Fernández, I., & Márquez, M. (2008). Educación emocional en adultos y personas mayores. *Revista Electrónica de Investigación Psicoeducativa, 6*(15), 501–5022.

López-Gómez, E. (2017). El concepto y las finalidades de la tutoría universitaria : Una consulta a expertos. *Revista Española de Orientación y Psicopedagogía, 28*(2), 61–78. doi:10.5944/reop.vol.28.num.2.2017.20119

López-Goñi, I., & Goñi, J. M. (2012). La competencia emocional en los currículos de formación inicial de los docentes. Un estudio comparativo. *Review of Education,* (0357), 467–489.

López, P. (2017). Competencias socioemocionales y salud en educación social. *Educació Social. Revista d'Intervenció Socioeducativa, 66,* 51–69.

López-Pastor, V. M. (2017). Evaluación formativa y compartida: Evaluar para aprender y la implicación del alumnado en los procesos de evaluación y aprendizaje. In V. M. López-Pastor & A. Pérez-Pueyo (Coords.), Evaluación formativa y compartida en Educación: experiencias de éxito en todas las etapas educativas (pp. 34–68). Universidad de León.

López-Pastor, V. M. (coord.) (2009). *Evaluación formativa y compartida en educación superior. Propuestas, técnicas, instrumentos y experiencias.* Narcea.

López-Pastor, V. M. (Coord.) (2009). *La Evaluación Formativa y Compartida en Educación Superior: propuestas, técnicas, instrumentos y experiencias.* Narcea

López-Pastor, V. M. (coord.) (2009). *La Evaluación Formativa y Compartida en Educación Superior: propuestas, técnicas, instrumentos y experiencias.* Narcea.

López-Pastor, V. M., & Pérez-Pueyo, A. (Coords.) (2017). *Buenas prácticas docentes. Evaluación formativa y compartida en educación: experiencias de éxito en todas las etapas educativas* (e-book). Universidad de León. https://buleria.unileon.es/handle/10612/5999

López-Pastor, V. M., & Pérez-Pueyo, A. (Coords.) (2017). *Buenas prácticas docentes. Evaluación formativa y compartida en educación: experiencias de éxito en todas las etapas educativas.* Universidad de León.

López-Pastor, V. M., and Pérez-Pueyo, A. (Coords.) (2017). *Evaluación formativa y compartida en Educación: experiencias de éxito en todas las etapas educativas.* Universidad de León. http://buleria.unileon.es/handle/10612/5999

López-Pastor, V. M., Molina, M., Pascual, C. and Manrique, J. C. (2020). La importancia de utilizar la Evaluación Formativa y compartida en la formación inicial del profesorado de educación física: los Proyectos de Aprendizaje Tutorado como ejemplo de buena práctica. *Retos, nuevas tendencias en educación física, deporte y recreación, 37,* 680-687. doi:10.47197/retos.v37i37.74193

López-Pastor, V. M., Molina, M., Pascual, C., & Manrique, J. C. (2020). La importancia de utilizar la Evaluación Formativa y Compartida en la Formación Inicial del Profesorado de Educación Física: los Proyectos de Aprendizaje Tutorado como ejemplo de buena práctica. *Retos, Nuevas tendencias en Educación Física, Deporte y Recreación, 37,* 680-687. https://dialnet.unirioja.es/servlet/articulo?codigo=7243328

López-Pastor, V. M., Monjas, R. and Manrique, J. C. (2011). Fifteen years of action research as professional development: seeking more collaborative, useful and democratic system for teachers. *Educational Action Research, 19*(2), 153-170. https://dx.doi.org/. 569190 doi:10.1080/09650792.2011

López-Pastor, V. M. (2011). El papel de la evaluación formativa en la evaluación por competencias: Aportaciones de la red de evaluación formativa y compartida en docencia universitaria. *REDU. Revista de Docencia Universitaria, 9*(1), 159–173. doi:10.4995/redu.2011.6185

López-Pastor, V. M., Kirk, D., Lorente-Catalán, E., MacPhail, A., & Macdonald, D. (2013). Alternative assessment in physical education: A review of international literature. *Sport Education and Society, 18*(1), 57–76. doi:10.1080/13573322.2012.713860

López-Pastor, V. M., & Sicilia, Á. (2017). Formative and shared assessment in higher education. Lessons learned and challenges for the future. *Assessment & Evaluation in Higher Education, 42*(1), 77–97. doi:10.1080/02602938.2015.1083535

López-Pastor, V., Molina, M., Pascual, C., & Manrique, J. (2020). La importancia de utilizar la Evaluación Formativa y Compartida en la Formación Inicial del Profesorado de Educación Física: Los Proyectos de Aprendizaje Tutorado como ejemplo de buena práctica. *Retos, 37,* 620–627.

López, V., & Pérez, Á. (2017). *Evaluación formativa y compartida en educación: experiencias de éxito en todas las etapas educativas.* Universidad de León.

Lorente-Catalán, E., & Kirk, D. (2013). Alternative democratic assessment in PETE: An action-research study exploring risks, challenges and solutions. *Sport Education and Society, 18*(1), 77–96. doi:10.1080/13573322.2012.713859

Lorente-Catalán, E., & Kirk, D. (2016). Student teachers' understanding and application of assessment for learning during a physical education teacher education course. *European Physical Education Review, 22*(1), 65–81. doi:10.1177/1356336X15590352

Lozano, J. F. (2012). Cómo formar profesionales responsables en la Universidad? In G. Celorio & A. López de Munain (Eds.), *La Educación para el Desarrollo en la Universidad Reflexiones en torno a una práctica transformadora* (pp. 73–81). HEGOA.

Luengo, M. L., & Puente, M. G. (2017). El proyecto de aprendizaje tutorado en la formación científica de maestros de Educación Primaria. *Revista Infancia. Educación y Aprendizaje, 3*(2), 190–196.

Lund, J. (1997). Authentic assessment: Its development and applications. *Journal of Physical Education, Recreation and Dance, 68*(7), 25–28. doi:10.1080/07303084.1997.10604979

Mahón, K., & Smith, H. (2020). Moving beyond "Methodising" Theory in Preparing for the Profession. *Journal of Adventure Education and Outdoor Learning, 20*(4), 357–368. doi:10.1080/14729679.2019.1686039

Manrique, J. C., López Pastor, V. M., Monjas, R., & Real, F. (2010). El potencial de los Proyectos de Aprendizaje Tutorado y los sistemas de evaluación formativa en la mejora de la autonomía del alumnado: Una experiencia interdisciplinar en formación inicial del profesorado. *Revista Española de Educación Física y Deportes, 14*, 39-57. https://www.reefd.es/index.php/reefd/article/viewFile/285/276

Manrique-Arribas, J. C., Vallés, C., & Gea, J. (2012). Resultados generales de la puesta en práctica de 29 casos sobre el desarrollo de sistemas de evaluación formativa en docencia universitaria. *PYSE Psychology. Social Education, 4*(1), 87–102. doi:10.25155/pyse.v4i1.483

Manrique, J. C., López-Pastor, V. M., Monjas, R., & Real, F. (2010). El potencial de los proyectos de aprendizaje tutorado y los sistemas de evaluación formativa en la mejora de la autonomía del alumnado. Una experiencia interdisciplinar en formación inicial del profesorado. *Revista Española de Educación Física y Deportes, 14*, 39–57.

Margalef, L. (2005). La formación del profesorado universitario: Análisis y evaluación de una experiencia. *Revista de Educación, 337*, 389–402. https://hdl.handle.net/11162/68047

Marina, J. A. (2011). Los secretos de la motivación. *Ariel.*

Martínez Martín, I. (2016). Construcción de una pedagogía feminista para una ciudadanía transformadora y contra-hegemónica. *Foro de Educación, 14*(20), 129–151. doi:10.14516/fde.2016.014.020.008

Martínez-Mínguez, L., Vallés Rapp, C., y Romero-Mínguez, R. (2015). Estudiantes universitarios: ventajas e inconvenientes de la evaluación formativa. *Revista d'Innovació educativa, 14*, 59-70. doi:10.7203/attic.14.4217

Martínez-Mínguez, L., Moya, L., Nieva, C., & Cañabate, D. (2019). Percepciones de Estudiantes y Docentes: Evaluación Formativa en Proyectos de Aprendizaje Tutorados. Perceptions of Students and Teachers: Formative Evaluation in Tutored Learning Projects. *Revista Iberoamericana de Evaluación Educativa, 12*(1), 59–84.

Martínez-Mínguez, L., Moya, L., Nieva, C., & Cañabate, D. (2019). Percepciones de Estudiantes y Docentes: Evaluación Formativa en Proyectos de Aprendizaje Tutorados. *Revista Iberoamericana de Evaluación Educativa, 12*(1), 59–84. doi:10.15366/10.15366/riee2019.12.1.004

Martínez-Mínguez, L., Vallés, C., & Romero-Martín, R. (2015). Estudiantes universitarios: Ventajas e inconvenientes de la evaluación formativa. *@tic. Revista d'Innovació Educativa, 14*, 59–70.

Martínez-Otero, V. (2007). *La inteligencia afectiva. Teoría, práctica y programa.* CCS.

Martin, F. (2011). Instructional design and the importance of instructional alignment. *Community College Journal of Research and Practice, 35*(12), 955–972. doi:10.1080/10668920802466483

Martos-García, D., Usabiaga, O., & Valencia-Peris, A. (2017). Percepción del alumnado sobre la evaluación formativa y compartida: Conectado dos universidades a través de la Blogosfera. *Journal of New Approaches in Educational Research*, *6*(1), 68–74. doi:10.7821/naer.2017.1.194

McArthur, J. (2021). *For assessment to count as authentic it must mean something to students*. WONKHE.

McAteer, M. (2013). *Action Research in Education*. Sage. doi:10.4135/9781473913967

McConlogue, T. (2020). *Assessment and feedback in Higher Education: A Guide for Teachers*. UCL Press. doi:10.2307/j.ctv13xprqb

McCune, V., & Hounsell, D. (2005). The development of students' ways of thinking and practising in three final-year biology courses. *Higher Education*, *49*(3), 255–289. doi:10.100710734-004-6666-0

Medina, A., Herrán, A., & Domínguez, M. C. (2014). *Fronteras en la investigación de la Didáctica*. UNED.

Meissonier. (2017). Évaluer un article: quels syndromes éviter? *Systèmes d'information & management, 22*(4), 3-8. doi:10.3917/sim.174.0003

Miles, M. B., & Huberman, A. M. (1994). *Qualitative data analysis*. Sage Publications.

Mínguez, M. L. M. (2017). Proyectos de Aprendizaje Tutorados y autoevaluación de competencias profesionales en la formación inicial del profesorado. *Retos: nuevas tendencias en educación física, deporte y recreación*, (29), 242-250.

Molina, M., & López-Pastor, V. M. (2017). La transferencia de la Evaluación Formativa y Compartida desde la Formación Inicial del Profesorado de Educación Física a la práctica real en Educación Primaria. *Infancia, Educación y Aprendizaje (IEYA), 3*(2), 626-631. https://revistas.uv.cl/index.php/IEYA/index

Molina, M., & López-Pastor, V. M. (2019). ¿Evalúo como me evaluaron en la facultad? Transferencia de evaluación formativa y compartida vivida en la formación Inicial del profesorado a la práctica como docente. *Revista Iberoamericana de Evaluación Educativa*, *12*(1), 85–101. doi:10.15366/riee2019.12.1.005

Molina, M., López-Pastor, V. M., Pascual, C., & Barba, R. A. (2019). Los proyectos de aprendizaje tutorado como buena práctica en educación física en primer curso de doble titulación (educación infantil y educación primaria). *Revista de Innovación y Buenas Prácticas Docentes*, *8*(1), 1–14. doi:10.21071/ripadoc.v8i1.11988

Molina, M., Pascual, C., & López-Pastor, V. M. (2020). El rendimiento académico y la evaluación formativa y compartida en formación del profesorado. *Alteridad*, *15*(2), 204–215. doi:10.17163/alt.v15n2.2020.05

Montero, I., & León, O. G. (2005). Sistema de clasificación del método en los informes de investigación en Psicología. *International Journal of Clinical and Health Psychology*, *5*(1), 115–127. https://www.redalyc.org/articulo.oa?id=33701007

Mora, F. (2017). *Sólo se puede aprender aquello que se ama*. Alianza Editorial.

Moreno-Olivos, T. (2021). Cambiar la evaluación: Un imperativo en tiempos de incertidumbre. *Alteridad*, *16*(2), 223–234. doi:10.17163/alt.v16n2.2021.05

Moreno, T. (2012). La evaluación de competencias en educación. *Sinéctica*, *39*. http://www.sinectica.iteso.mx/index.php?cur=39&art=39_09

Morris, R., Perry, T., & Wardle, L. (2021). Formative assessment and feedback for learning in higher education: A systematic review. *Review of Education*, *9*(3). doi:10.1002/rev3.3292

Morrissette, J. (2010). Un panorama de la recherche sur l'évaluation formative des apprentissages. *Mesure et Évaluation en Éducation*, *33*(3), 1–27. doi:10.7202/1024889ar

Mottier Lopez, L., Girardet, C., Bendela, P., Constenla Martinez, N., Elisme Pierre, E., Gibert, S., Lyu, X., Roth, M., Sauret, O., & Seguel Tapia, F. (2022). Quand la co-construction d'un référentiel devient un moyen d'apprendre. Expériences de doctorants et de doctorantes, le cas d'un référentiel pour évaluer des textes scientifiques. *La Revue LEeE, 3.* https://revue.leee.online/index.php/info/article/view/136

Mottier Lopez, L., Girardet, C., Broussal, D., & Demeester, A. (2021). EOC – une Evaluation Ouverte et Collaborative entre pairs: analyse critique du dispositif de La Revue LEeE. *La Revue LEeE, Numéro spécial.* doi:10.48325/rleee.spe.01

Mueller, J. (2006). *Authentic assessment toolbox.* Noctrl.

Muñoz-Repiso, A. G. V., & Gómez-Pablos, V. B. (2017). Aprendizaje Basado en Proyectos (ABP): Evaluación desde la perspectiva de alumnos de Educación Primaria. *Revista de Investigación Educacional, 35*(1), 113–131.

Murillo, F. J. (2010). *Retos en la evaluación de la calidad de la educación en América Latina.* CUTT. https://cutt.ly/RePXTI0

Myyry, L., Karaharju-Suvanto, T., Virtala, A.M., Raekallio, M., Salminen, O., Vesalainen, M. & Nevgi, A. (2022). How self-efficacy beliefs are related to assessment practices: a study of experienced university teachers, *Assessment & Evaluation in Higher Education, 47*(1), 155-168. doi:10.1080/02602938.2021.1887812

National Forum for the Enhancement of Teaching and Learning in Higher Education. (2017). Authentic Assessment in Irish Higher education, Dublin: National Forum for the Enhancement of Teaching and Learning in Higher Education. *Forum Insights.* https://www.teaching and learning.ie/publication/authentic-assessment-in-irish-higher-education/NF-2017-Authentic-Assessment-in-Irish-Higher-Education.pdf (teachingandlearning.ie)

Nicol, D. (2021). The power of internal feedback: Exploiting natural comparison processes. *Assessment and Evaluation in Higher Education, 46*(5), 756–778. doi:10.1080/02602938.2020.1823314

Nicol, D., Thomson, A., & Breslin, C. (2014). Rethinking feedback practice in higher education: A peer revier perspective. *Assessment & Evaluation in Higher Education, 39*(1), 102–122. doi:10.1080/02602938.2013.795518

Nieto, S. (2000). El discurso del profesorado universitario sobre la evaluación del aprendizaje de los alumnos como estrategia de innovación y cambio profesional: Exposición y análisis de una experiencia. *Review of Education, 322*, 305–324.

Noreña, A., Alcaraz-Moreno, N., Rojas, J., & Rebolledo-Malpica, D. (2012). Aplicabilidad de los criterios de rigor y éticos en la investigación cualitativa. *Aquichan, 12*(3), 263–274.

Nuninger, W. (2017). Integrated Learning Environment for blended oriented course: 3-year feedback on a skill-oriented hybrid strategy. HCI International, 9-14 July. In: Zaphiris P., Ioannou A. (eds). Learning and Collaboration Technologies. Novel Learning Ecosystems. Springer, Cham. doi:10.1007/978-3-319-58509-3_13

Nuninger, W., & Châtelet, J. (2016). Hybridization-Based Courses Consolidated through LMS and PLE Leading to a New Co-Creation of Learning: Changing All Actors' Behavior for Efficiency. In D. Fonseca & E. Redondo (Eds.), *Handbook of Research on Applied E-Learning in Engineering and Architecture Education* (pp. 55–87). IGI Global. doi:10.4018/978-1-4666-8803-2.ch004

Nuninger, W., & Châtelet, J. (2020). Key Processes for the Performance of Work-Integrated Learning in HE: Focusing on Talents with a Winning-Foursome. In W. Nuninger & J. Châtelet (Eds.), *Handbook of Research on Operational Quality Assurance in Higher Education for Life-Long Learning* (pp. 101–132). IGI Global. doi:10.4018/978-1-7998-1238-8.ch005

Nussbaum, M. (2005). El cultivo de la humanidad. University of Chicago.

Nussbaum, M. (2006). Education and Democratic Citizenship: Capabilities and Quality Education. *Journal of Human Development, 7*(3), 385–395. doi:10.1080/14649880600815974

Nussbaum, M. (2016). Educación para el lucro, educación para la libertad. *Nómadas*, (44), 13–25. doi:10.30578/nomadas.n44a1

O'Neill, G. (2019). *Authentic assessment: concept, continuum and contested.* Masterclass presented at the Assessment in Higher Education Conference, Manchester. http://tiny.url.com/AHE2019

OCDE. (2002). *Definition and Selection of Competences.* OCDE.

Orsmond, P., Merry, S., & Reiling, K. (2000). The use of student derived marking criteria in peer and self-assessment. *Assessment & Evaluation in Higher Education*, *25*(1), 23–38. doi:10.1080/02602930050025006

Osorio González, R., & Castro Ricalde, D.Osorio – González. (2021). Aproximaciones a una metodología mixta. *Novarua*, *13*(22), 65–84. doi:10.20983/novarua.2021.22.4

Ospina, B. E., Aristizábal, C. A., & Toro, J. A. (2008). El seminario de investigación y su relación con las diferentes metodologías y estrategias de enseñanza aprendizaje. *Investigacion y Educacion en Enfermeria*, *26*(2), 72–79.

Padovan-Özdemir, M., & Hamilton, S. D. P. (2020). *Mangfoldighed og ligestilling i dagtilbud: Omfang - Forståelser - Holdninger - Tilgange.* VIA University College.

Palacios, A., & López-Pastor, V. M. (2013). Haz lo que yo digo pero no lo que yo hago: Sistemas de evaluación del alumnado en la formación inicial del profesorado. *Review of Education*, *361*, 279–305. doi:10.4438/1988-592X-RE-2011-361-143

Palacios, A., & López-Pastor, V. M. (2013). Haz lo que yo digo pero no lo que yo hago: Sistemas de evaluación del alumnado en la formación inicial del profesorado. *Revista de Educación*, *361*, 279–305. https://www.educacionyfp.gob.es/dam/jcr:bf834e01-0af8-4400-89fe-5d669ca640ad/re36111-pdf.pdf

Palacios-Dueñas, A. I., Michell Loor-Peña, J. I., Mabel Macías-Macías III, K., & Roberth Ortega-Macías, W. I. (2020). Incidencia de la tecnología en el entorno educativo del Ecuador frente a la pandemia del covid-19. *Polo Del Conocimiento: Revista Científico – Profesional*, *5*(10), 754-773. https://doi.org/ doi:10.23857/pc.v5i10.1850

Panadero, E., Broadbent, J., Boud, D., & Lodge, J. M. (2018). Using formative assessment to influence self- and co-regulated learning: The role of evaluative judgement. *European Journal of Psychology of Education*, *34*(3), 535–557. doi:10.100710212-018-0407-8

Panadero, E., & Brown, G. T. L. (2017). Teachers' reasons for using peer assessment: Positive experience predicts use. *European Journal of Psychology of Education*, *32*(1), 133–156. doi:10.100710212-015-0282-5

Panadero, E., & Jonsson, A. (2013). The use of scoring rubrics for formative assessment purposes revisited: A review. *Educational Research Review*, *9*, 129–144. doi:10.1016/j.edurev.2013.01.002

Pascual Arias, C., López-Pastor, V. M., and Hamodí-Galán, C. (2021). Seminario de formación permanente internivelar en evaluación formativa y compartida en educación. Resultados de trasferencia de conocimiento entre universidad y escuela. En C. Hamodí-Galán y R. Barba-Martín, Evaluación Formativa y Compartida: Nuevas propuestas de desarrollo en Educación Superior (271-285). Dextra.

Pascual-Arias, C., García-Herranz, S., & López-Pastor, V. M. (2019). What do preschool students want? The role of formative and shared assessment in their right to decide. *CandE, Cultura y Educación*, *31*(4), 865–880. Advance online publication. doi:10.1080/11356405.2019.1656486

Pastor, V. M. (2008). Desarrollando sistemas de evaluación formativa y compartida en la docencia universitaria. Análisis de resultados de su puesta en práctica en la formación inicial del profesorado. *European Journal of Teacher Education*, *31*(3), 293–311. doi:10.1080/02619760802208452

Paudel, P. (2021). Online education: Benefits, challenges and strategies during and after COVID-19 in higher education. [IJonSE]. *International Journal on Studies in Education*, *3*(2), 70–85. doi:10.46328/ijonse.32

Pedraza-González, M. A., & López-Pastor, V. M. (2015). Investigación-acción, desarrollo profesional del profesorado de educación física y escuela rural. *Revista Internacional de Medicina y Ciencias de la Actividad Física y del Deporte*, *57*(2015), 1–16. doi:10.15366/rimcafd2015.57.001

Pérez-Escoda, A., Lena-Acebo, F., & García-Ruíz, R. (2021). Digital Competences for Smart Learning During COVID-19 in Higher Education Students from Spain and Latin America. *Digital Education Review*, *40*(40), 122–140. doi:10.1344/der.2021.40.122-140

Pérez-Pueyo, A., Tabernero, B., López-Pastor, V. M., Ureña, N., Ruiz, E., Caplloch, M., González, N., & Castejón, F. J. (2008). Evaluación formativa y compartida en la docencia universitaria y el Espacio Europeo de Educación Superior: Cuestiones clave para su puesta en práctica. *Revista de Educación*, *347*, 435–451. https://www.educacionyfp.gob.es/revista-de-educacion/numeros-revista-educacion/numeros-anteriores/2008/re347/re347-20.html

Pla-Campas, G., Arumí-Prat, J., Senye-Mir, A. M., & Ramírez, E. (2016). Effect of using formative assessment techniques on students' grades. *Procedia: Social and Behavioral Sciences*, *228*, 190–195. doi:10.1016/j.sbspro.2016.07.028

Polikoff, M. S., & Porter, A. C. (2014). Instructional alignment as a measure of teaching quality. *Educational Evaluation and Policy Analysis*, *36*(4), 399–416. doi:10.3102/0162373714531851

Porto, M. (2006). *La evaluación de estudiantes universitarios vista por sus protagonistas*. Educatio Siglo XXI, 24, 167–188. https://revistas.um.es/educatio/article/view/156

Raelin, J. A. (2008). *Work-based Learning. Bridging Knowledge and Action in the Workplace*. San Francisco, CA: Jossey-Bass.

Ramos, F. J., Martínez, I., & Blanco, M. (2020). Sentido de la educación para la ciudadanía desde pedagogías feministas, críticas y decoloniales. Una propuesta para la formación del profesorado. *Revista Izquierdas*, *49*, 2103–2116.

Redecker, C., & Punie, Y. (2017). European Framework for the Digital Competence of Educators. DigCompEdu. JRC Science Hub, European Commission.

Redorta, J., Obiols, M., & Bisquerra, R. (2006). *Emoción y conflicto. Aprenda a manejar las emociones*. Paidós.

Reglamento De Regimen Academico Consejo Educacion Superior. (2017). [Testimony of Consejo de Educación Superior]. Reglamento De Regimen Academico Consejo Educacion Superior. www.lexis.com.ec

Reimann, N., Sambell, K., Sadler, I., & Kreber, C. (2021). Addressing the challenges of assessment and feedback in business schools: developing assessment practices which support learning. In *Handbook of Teaching and Learning at Business Schools*. Edward Elgar Publishing.

Renwick, K., Selkrig, M., Manathunga, C., & Keamy, R. K. (2020). Community engagement is…: Revisiting Boyer's model of scholarship. *Higher Education Research and Development*, *39*(6), 1232–1246. doi:10.1080/07294360.2020.1712680

Repetto, E., & Pérez-González, J. C. (2007). Formación en competencias socioemocionales a través de las prácticas en empresas. *Revista Europea de Formación Profesional*, (40), 92–112.

Reyes, V. (2019). Más allá de la calificación: La evaluación formativa y compartida en Educación Física en la etapa de Educación Primaria. *Infancia* [IEYA]. *Educación y Aprendizaje*, *5*(2), 161–165. doi:10.22370/ieya.2019.5.2.1505

Ricoy, M., & Fernández-Rodríguez, J. (2013). The University students» perception of the evaluation: a case study. *Educación XXI*. *16*(2), 321-341. doi: 10.5944/educxx1.16.2.2645

Riesco, M. (2008). El enfoque por competencias en el EEES y sus implicaciones en la enseñanza y el aprendizaje. *Tendencias Pedagógicas, 13*, 79–105.

Rocha, J. J. (2020). Metodologías activas, la clave para el cambio de la escuela y su aplicación en épocas de pandemia. *INNOVA Research Journal 5*(3), 2. doi:10.33890/innova.v5.n3.2.2020.1514

Rodríguez-Rodríguez, J., & Reguant-Álvarez, M. (2020). Calcular la fiabilidad de un cuestionario o escala mediante el SPSS: El coeficiente alfa de Cronbach. *REIRE, 13*(2), 1–13. doi:10.1344/reire2020.13.230048

Roegiers, X. (2012). *Quelles réformes pédagogiques pour l'enseignement supérieur*. De Boeck.

Romero, M. R., Castejón, F. J., López-Pastor, V. M., & Fraile, A. (2017). Evaluación formativa, competencias comunicativas y TIC en la formación del profesorado. *Comunicar, 52*(3) 73-82. https://www.torrossa.com/en/resources/an/4150000

Romero, M. A., & Crisol, E. (2011). El portafolio, herramienta de autoevaluación del aprendizaje de los estudiantes. Una experiencia práctica en la Universidad de Granada. *Revista Docencia e Investigación, 21*, 25–50.

Romero-Martín, M. R., Asún, S., & Chivite, M. T. (2016). La autoevaluación en expresión corporal en formación inicial del profesorado de educación física: un ejemplo de buena práctica. *Retos. Nuevas tendencias en Educación Física, Deportes y Recreación, 29*, 236-241. https://www.redalyc.org/pdf/3457/345743464045.pdf

Romero-Martín, M. R., Castejón-Oliva, F. J., López-Pastor, V. M., & Fraile-Aranda, A. (2017). Evaluación formativa, competencias comunicativas y TIC en la formación del profesorado. *Comunicar, 52*. Advance online publication. doi:10.3916/C52-2017-07

Romero-Martín, R., Fraile-Aranda, A., López-Pastor, V. M., & Castejón-Oliva, F. J. (2014). Relación entre sistemas de evaluación formativa, rendimiento académico y carga de trabajo del profesor y del alumno en docencia universitaria. *Infancia y Aprendizaje, 37*(3), 491–527. doi:10.1080/02103702.2014.918818

Romero, R., Castejón, F. J., & López, V. M. (2015). Divergencias del alumnado y del profesorado universitario sobre las dificultades para aplicar la evaluación formativa. *Relieve, 21*(1), 1–16. doi:10.7203/relieve.21.1.5169

Ronda-Ortín, L. (2012). El educador social. Ética y práctica profesional. *Pedagogía Social. Revista Interuniversitaria, 19*(19), 51–63. doi:10.7179/PSRI_2012.19.04

Rosa, G., Riberas, G., Navarro-Segura, L., & Vilar, J. (2015). El coaching como herramienta de trabajo de la competencia emocional en la formación de estudiantes de educación social y trabajo social de la Universidad Ramón Llull, España. *Formación Universitaria, 8*(5), 77–90. doi:10.4067/S0718-50062015000500009

Roy, M. et Michaud, N. (2018). Self-Assessment and Peer-Assessment in Higher Education: Promises and Challenges. *Formation et profession, 26*(2), 54-65. doi:10.18162/fp.2018.458

Ruiz-Omeñaca, J. V. (1999). *Juegos cooperativos y educación física*. Editorial Paidotribo.

Sadler, D. R. (2010). Beyond feedback: Developing student capability in complex appraisal. *Assessment & Evaluation in Higher Education, 35*(5), 535–550. doi:10.1080/02602930903541015

Said, E. (1978). *Orientalism - Western Conceptions of the Orient*. Penguin Books.

Salcines, I., González-Fernández, N., Ramírez-García, A. & Martínez-Mínguez, L. (2018). Validación de la escala de autopercepción de competencias transversales y profesionales de estudiantes de educación superior. *Currículum y formación del profesorado, 22*(3), 31-51. doi:10.30827/profesorado.v22i3.7989

Saldaña, J. (2009). *The coding manual for qualitative researchers*. Sage Publications Ltd.

Sá, M. J., & Serpa, S. (2020). COVID-19 and the Promotion of Digital Competences in Education. *Universal Journal of Educational Research*, 8(10), 4520–4528. doi:10.13189/ujer.2020.081020

Sambell, K., & McDowell, L. (1998). The construction of the hidden curriculum: Messages and meanings in the assessment of student learning. *Assessment and Evaluation in Higher Education*, 23(4), 391–402. doi:10.1080/0260293980230406

Sambell, K., McDowell, L., & Brown, S. (1997). "But is it fair?": An exploratory study of student perceptions of the consequential validity of assessment. *Studies in Educational Evaluation*, 23(4), 349–371. doi:10.1016/S0191-491X(97)86215-3

Sambell, K., McDowell, L., & Montgomery, C. (2013). *Assessment for learning in higher education*. Routledge.

Sanahuja, A., & Escobedo, P. (2021). Seminario de innovación educativa sobre formación para una ciudadanía crítica: la evaluación entre iguales en el aula universitaria. In *M. Pallarés, J. Gil-Quintana y A. Santiesteban (Coord.), Docencia, ciencia y humanidades: hacia un enseñanza integral en la universidad del siglo XXI* (pp. 610–631). DYKINSON.

Sanahuja, A., & Sánchez-Tarazaga, L. (2018). La competencia evaluativa de los docentes: Formación, dominio y puesta en práctica en el aula. *Revista Iberoamericana de Educación*, 76(2), 95–115. doi:10.35362/rie7623072

Sánchez, L. A. C., & Catagña, S. M. C. (2021). La educación virtual implementada por la pandemia de la COVID-19 y el derecho a la educación superior. *Revista Jurídica Crítica y Derecho*, 2(3), 44–56. doi:10.29166/cyd.v2i3.3188

Sánchez-Tarazaga, L., Ruiz-Bernardo, R., Viñoles Cosentino, V., & Esteve-Mon, F. (2022). University teaching induction programmes. A systematic literature review. *Professional Development in Education*, 1–17. doi:10.1080/19415257.2022.2147577

Sancho, J., Hernández, F., Rivas-Flores, J. I., Ocaña, A., & de Pablos, J. (2020). *Caminos y derivas para otra investigación educativa y social*. Octaedro.

Sanmartí, N. (2020). *Evaluar y aprender: un único proceso*. Octaedro.

Santiuste, V., & Arranz, M.ª L. (2009). Nuevas perspectivas en el concepto de evaluación. *Review of Education*, 350, 463–476.

Santos, M., Martínez, L. F. & López, V. M. (coords.) (2009). *La Innovación docente en el Espacio Europeo de Educación Superior*. Editorial Universidad de Almería.

Santos, J. M., Ortiz, E., & Martín, S. (2018). Índices de variación de la nota debidos a la evaluación continua. Contrastación empírica en la enseñanza universitaria. *CandE, Cultura y Educación*, 30(3), 491–527. doi:10.1080/11356405.2018.1488422

Santos-Pastor, M., Martínez, L. F., & López-Pastor, V. M. (2009). *La innovación docente en el Espacio Europeo de Educación Superior*. Universidad de Almería.

Scharmer, C. O. (2009). *Theory U: Leading from the Future as It Emerges*. Berrett-Koeheler Publishers.

Schein, E. H. (2013). Humble Inquiry: The Gentle Art of Asking Instead of Telling. Berrett-Koehler Publishers.

Serrano, V. (2012). Actividades de formación permanente del profesorado y educación inclusiva: Análisis de la situación en Castilla y León. *Revista Educación Inclusiva*, 5(3), 119–132.

Sheila Group Concept Mapping study-GCM. (2019). 99 learning analytics policy feature statements. *Sheila Project*. https://sheilaproject.eu/wp-content/uploads/2019/07/PolicyMatters99GCMstatements.pdf

Simons, H. (2011). *El estudio de caso: teoría y práctica*. Morata.

Societé des Ingénieurs et Scientifiques de France-IESF. (2001). *Engineer Charter of Ethics*. IESF. https://www.iesf.fr/752_p_49680/charte-ethique-de-l-ingenieur.html

Sokhanvar, Z., Salehi, K., & Sokhanvar, F. (2021). Advantages of authentic assessment for improving the learning experience and employability skills of higher education students: A systematic literature review. *Studies in Educational Evaluation*, *70*, 101030. doi:10.1016/j.stueduc.2021.101030

Solaguren-Beascoa, M., & Moreno Delgado, L. (2016). Escala de actitudes de los estudiantes universitarios hacia las tutorías académicas. *Redalyc. Org*, *19*(1), 247–266. doi:10.5944/educXX1.14479

Sonlleva, M. (2019). La participación de los estudiantes en el proceso de evaluación: Una experiencia en el aula universitaria. *Infancia. Educación y Aprendizaje*, *5*(2), 108–113. doi:10.22370/ieya.2019.5.2.1658

Sonlleva, M. M. S., Martínez, S., & Monjas, R. (2019). Evaluación del proyecto de aprendizaje tutorado en la asignatura de Educación para la Paz y la Igualdad. *Revista Infancia. Educación y Aprendizaje*, *5*(2), 114–120.

Soto, P. (2002). La formación permanente del profesorado. *Cuadernos de pedagogía, 35*, 44-49.

Souto-Seijo, A., Estévez, I., Iglesias, V., & González-Sanmamed, M. (2020). Entre lo formal y lo no formal: Un análisis desde la formación permanente del profesorado. *Educar*, *56*(1), 91–107. doi:10.5565/rev/educar.1095

Stake, R. E. (1998). *Investigación con estudio de casos*. Morata.

Stone, D., & Heen, S. (2014). Thanks for the feedback: The Science and Art of Receiving Feedback. Viking.

Tai, J., Ajjawi, R., Boud, D., Dawson, P., & Panadero, E. (2018). Developing evaluative judgement: Enabling students to make decisions about the quality of work. *Higher Education*, *76*(3), 467–481. doi:10.100710734-017-0220-3

Tardif, J. (2003). Développer un programme par compétences: de l'intention à la mise en œuvre. *Pédagogie collégiale*, *16*(3), 36-44.

Tashakkori, A., & Teddlie, Ch. (Eds.). (2003). *Handbook of mixed methods in social and behavioral research*. Sage.

Taylor, S. J., & Bogdan, R. (1987). *Introducción a los métodos cualitativos de investigación*. Paidós Básica.

Tejedor, S., Cervi, L., Tusa, F., & Parola, A. (2020). Educación en tiempos de pandemia: reflexiones de alumnos y profesores sobre la enseñanza virtual universitaria en España, Italia y Ecuador. *Revista Latina de Comunicación Social, 78*, 1–21. doi:10.4185/RLCS-2020-1466

Thielfoldt, D., & Scheef, D. (2004). Generation X and the Millennials: What You Need to Know About Mentoring the New Generations (pp. 1-7). The Learning Café.

Thomas, G., Martin, D., & Pleasants, K. (2011). Using self- and peer-assessment to enhance students' future-learning in higher education. *Journal of University Teaching & Learning Practice*, *8*(1), 1–17. http://ro.uow.edu.au/cgi/viewcontent.cgi?article=1112&context=jutlp. doi:10.53761/1.8.1.5

Tlaseca, M. (2010). *La evaluación del aprendizaje vista por los estudiantes: Aportes para la didáctica*. Universidad Autónoma de Querétaro.

Todd, Z., & Low, G. (2010). A selective survey of research practice in published studies using metaphor analysis. In L. Cameron & R. Maslen (Eds.), *Metaphor analysis: Research practice in applied linguistics, social sciences and the humanities* (pp. 26–41). Equinox.

Tomás, U. (2013). *Neuroeducación. Educar con emociones*. Alianza editorial. https://www.alianzaeditorial.es/primer_capitulo/neuroeducacion.pdf

Tomas-Folch, M., & Durán-Bellonch, M. (2017). Comprendiendo los factores que afectan a la transferencia de la formación permanente del profesorado. Propuestas de mejora. *Revista Electrónica Interuniversitaria de Formación del Profesorado, 20*(1), 145–157. doi:10.6018/reifop/20.1.240591

Topping, K. (2009). Peer Assessment. *Theory into Practice, 48*(1), 20–27. doi:10.1080/00405840802577569

Torrance, H. (1995). *Evaluating authentic assessment.* Open University Press.

Tortosa, M. T., Grao, S., & Álvarez, J. D. (coords.). (2016). *XIV Jornadas de Redes de Investigación en Docencia Universitaria. Investigación, innovación y enseñanza universitaria: enfoques pluridisciplinares.* Universitat d'Alacant, Institut de Ciències de l'Educació, pp. 1466-1480. http://hdl.handle.net/10045/57093

Trianes, M. V., Cardelle-Elawar, M., Blanca, M. J., & Muñoz, A. M. (2003). Contexto social, género y competencia social autoevaluada en alumnos andaluces de 11-12 años. *Electronic Journal of Research in Educational Psychology, 1*(2), 37–56.

Trust, T., & Horrocks, B. (2019). Six key elements identified in an active and thriving blended community of practice. *TechTrends, 63*(2), 108–115. doi:10.100711528-018-0265-x

Tucker, B. (2012). The flipped classroom. *Education Next, 12*(1), 82–83.

UNESCO. (2009). International technical guidance on sexuality education. *Rationale for sexuality education.* UNESCO. https://unesdoc.unesco.org/images/0018/001832/183281e.pdf

UNESCO. (2020). *COVID-19 Educational disruption and response.* UNESCO. https://en.unesco.org/themes/educationemergencies/coronavirus-school-closures

UNESCO. (2021). *Seguimiento mundial de los cierres de escuela causados por el COVID-19.* UNESCO. https://es.unesco.org/covid19/educationresponse

Vallés, C., Ureña, N., & Ruiz, E. (2011). La evaluación Formativa en Docencia Universitaria. Resultados globales de 41 estudios de caso en su primer año de desarrollo. *Revista de Docencia Universitaria, 9*(1), 135-158. https://riunet.upv.es/handle/10251/141562

Velázquez, C. (2010). *Aprendizaje cooperativo en Educación Física.* Inde.

Verdaguer, S. (2017). *El arte de dar clases.* Plaza y Valdes.

Viau, R. (2009). La motivation en contexte scolaire. De Boeck.

Villarroel, V., Bloxham, S., Bruna, D., Bruna, C., & Herrera-Seda, C. (2018). Authentic assessment: Creating a blueprint for course design. *Assessment and Evaluation in Higher Education, 43*(5), 840–854. doi:10.1080/02602938.2017.1412396

Viñoles Cosentino, V., Esteve-Mon, F. M., Llopis-Nebot, M. A., & Adell-Segura, J. (2021). Validación de una plataforma de evaluación formativa de la competencia digital docente en tiempos de Covid-19. *RIED. Revista Iberoamericana de Educación a Distancia, 24*(2), 87–106. doi:10.5944/ried.24.2.29102

Vohlonen, A. (2020). *COVID-19: Cómo asegurar el aprendizaje de los niños sin acceso a Internet.* UNICEF Ecuador. https://www.unicef.org/ecuador/historias/covid-19-c%C3%B3mo-asegurar-el-aprendizaje-de-los-ni%C3%B1os-sin-acceso-internet

Wald, N., & Harland, T. (2017). A framework for authenticity in designing a research-based curriculum. *Teaching in Higher Education, 22*(7), 751–765. doi:10.1080/13562517.2017.1289509

Walsh, C. (2013). *Pedagogías Decoloniales. Prácticas insurgentes de resistir, (re) existir y (re) vivir.* Ediciones Abya-Yala.

Wekker, G. (2016). *White innocence: Paradoxes of colonialism and race*. Duke University Press.

Wenger, E. (2000). Communities of Practice and Social Learning Systems. *Organization, 7*(2), 225–246. doi:10.1177/135050840072002

Wiggins, G. (1990). The case for authentic assessment. *Practical Assessment, Research and Evaluation, 2*(1), 2.

Wiklund, H., & Wiklund, P. S. (2002). Widening the Six Sigma concept: An approach to improve organizational learning. *Total Quality Management, 13*(2), 233–239. doi:10.1080/09544120120102469

Wiliam, D., & Thompson, M. (2007). Integrating assessment with instruction: What will it take to make it work? In C.A. Dwyer (Coord), The Future of Assessment: Shaping Teaching and Learning (pp. 53-82). Lawrence Erlbaum Associates.

Wiliam, D. (2018). Feedback: At the heart of - but definitely not all of - formative assessment. In A. Lipnevic & J. Smith (Eds.), *The Cambridge handbook of instructional feedback* (pp. 3–28). Cambridge University Press. doi:10.1017/9781316832134.003

Wiliam, D., & Leahy, S. (2015). *Embedding formative assessment: Practical techniques for K-12 classrooms*. Learning Sciences International.

Winstone, N., & Carless, D. (2019). *Designing effective feedback processes in higher education: A learning-focused approach*. Routledge. doi:10.4324/9781351115940

Winstone, N., & Carless, D. (2020). *Designing Effective Feedback Processes in Higher Education: A Learning-Focused Approach*. Routledge.

Wolf, D. P. (1993). *Assessment as an episode of teaming. Construction Versus Choice in Cognitive Measurement*. Lawrence Erlbaum Associates.

Yankovic, B. (2011). *Emociones, sentimientos, afecto. El desarrollo emocional*. CUTT. https://cutt.ly/0eOnvtT

Younès, N., Gremion, C. & Sylvestre, E. (2020). *L'évaluation, source de Synergies*. Presses de l'ADMEE

Zabalza, M. A., & Lodeiro Enjo, L. (2019). El Desafío de Evaluar por Competencias en la Universidad. Reflexiones y Experiencias Prácticas. *Revista Iberoamericana De Evaluación Educativa, 12*(2), 29–48. doi:10.15366/riee2019.12.2.002

About the Contributors

José Sánchez Santamaría has a Ph.D. in Pedagogy. Associated Professor in Pedagogy and Didactic Coordinator of Social Education at the University of Castilla-La-Mancha (Spain). Full-time researcher at the Research Group of Guidance, Quality and Equity in Education (). His research interest include educational equity and guidance/career, educational assessment, reflective practice. He is committed to working pedagogical practice evidence-informed from the perspective of equity.

* * *

María Teresa Bejarano Franco is a PhD Professor in Women's Studies (U. Granada). Doctor professor. Department Pedagogy. Coordinator Pedagogy at the Faculty of Education of Ciudad Real. It belongs to the research group GIES (UCLM) and History of didactics of the U. of Buenos Aires. Lines of research are: gender-education and sexuality; educational innovation; history of didactics. Dirección. Ronda de Calatrava, 3, 13071 Ciudad Real, Cdad. Real

Sally Brown is an Independent Consultant in Learning, Teaching and Assessment and Emerita Professor at Leeds Beckett University where she was, until 2010, Pro-Vice-Chancellor. She is also Visiting Professor at Edge Hill University and formerly at the Universities of Plymouth, Robert Gordon, South Wales and Liverpool John Moores and at Australian universities James Cook Central Queensland and the Sunshine Coast. She holds Honorary Doctorates from the universities of Plymouth, Kingston, Bournemouth, Edinburgh Napier and Lincoln. She is a Principal Fellow of the Higher Education Academy, a Staff and Educational Development Association (SEDA) Senior Fellow and a National Teaching Fellow. She is widely published on learning, teaching and particularly assessment and enjoys working with institutions and teams on improving the student learning experience.

Laura Cañadas is a teacher in the Department of Physical Education, Sport and Human Movement at Autonomous University of Madrid. International PhD in Physical Activity and Sport Sciences. Her research is focused on teacher competences and formative assessment in Education.

Purificación Cruz Cruz is an Early Childhood Education Teacher. Doctor in Psychopedagogy. Early Childhood and Family Education Program. Associate Professor at the Faculty of Education of Toledo. University of Castilla la Mancha. Coordinator of the Final Course Work of the Postgraduate Course on Disability, Inclusion and Citizenship. Professor of the Master of Secondary Education. Invited professor of the Master of Neuropedagogy of the University of Cordoba. Invited professor of the Master's Degree in Evaluation through ITC resources at the Universidad del Norte. Co-direction of several doctoral theses. Lecturer at many conferences, parenting schools, schools, universities and various entities. Associate Researcher of the Universidad del Norte de Barranquilla (Colombia) and Universidad Autónoma de Zacatecas (Mexico).

Francesc M. Esteve-Mon is a Lecturer in educational technology in the Department of Pedagogy and Rector's Commissioner for Digital Affairs at Universitat Jaume I (Castelló, Spain). He leads the Teaching, Learning and Technology Research Group (GREAT) and his research interests include digital competence, teacher professional development and design-based research.

Carla Fernández is a pre-doctoral contract teacher at the Faculty of Education in Segovia (University of Valladolid). Doctoral candidate in the PhD in Transdisciplinary Research in Education (University of Valladolid). Master's degree in Research in Social Sciences, Education, Audiovisual Communication, Economics and Business from the University of Valladolid. Graduate in Primary Education and Early Childhood Education (University of Valladolid). Member of the International Network of Formative and Shared Assessment in Education. Main lines of research: physical education, formative and shared assessment, initial teacher training, Final Degree Projects.

Sergio Fernández-Ortega is a social educator and pedagogue, as well as a postgraduate degree in "Educational intervention in social contexts", specializing in "Childhood and adolescence in social difficulty". His lines of teaching and research are school social education, childhood and adolescence in social difficulty and sociocultural animation. He has participated in various teaching innovation and knowledge transfer projects, as well as in various conferences, seminars, academic articles and book chapters; the last ones on school participation and older people in Castilla-La Mancha.

Teresa Fuentes Nieto is an Associate Professor at the University of Valladolid, Faculty of Education, Segovia. Member of the International Network of Formative and Shared Assessment in Education. Teacher of Secondary Physical Education and of the Higher Cycle in Teaching and Socio-sporting Animation at the IES La Albuera (Segovia). Doctor and graduate in Physical Activity and Sport Sciences. Extraordinary Doctorate Award (University of Las Palmas, 2011). Research interests: Didactics of Physical Education, Physical Education in Secondary and Vocational Training and Formative Assessment in Education.

Natalia Hipólito Ruiz is a social educator in different socio-educational resources from 2002 to 2013. Lecturer in the degree of Social Education at the Faculty of Social Sciences of Talavera de la Reina, from 2008 to the present. Diploma in Social Education, Degree in Psychopedagogy, Master in e-learning and social networks, PhD in Humanities, Art and Education from the University of Castilla-La Mancha. Participation in research projects: Sexuality and equality education in the initial training of teachers and social educators. Comparative Analysis Spain, Portugal and Brazil. The development of social education and the professional insertion of social educators in Castilla-La Mancha. European project, Shelter. Support and counseling through the health system to victims of hate crimes. Evaluation of the implementation, processes and impact of the plan of citizen guarantees of Castilla -La Mancha. Lines of research: Educational Information and Communication Technologies; Education for development and Emancipatory Education; Culture, Sociocultural Animation and Social Education.

Frédéric Hoogstoel (Dr.). His research work at URM 9189 CRIStAL has focused since 1991 on computer-mediated human activity, especially cooperative work and learning, collective intelligence. It is based on cultural historical activity and instrumental theory. He has developed radically tailorable environments and have studied the behavior of learners in these environments.

David Hortigüela-Alcalá is a Professor at the University of Burgos. Director of the Department of Specific Didactics. Director of the Area of Didactics of Corporal Expression. Director of the Teaching and Research Group in Physical Education (ENIEF). Member of the International Network of Formative and Shared Assessment in Education. Author of more than 250 publications in the field of education. His lines of research deal with pedagogical models of teaching, formative and shared assessment, action research and physical education pedagogy.

Luigi Lancieri is a Professor of the University of Lille (URM 9189 CRIStAL). His research interests include social computing and computer-supported cooperative work (CSCW) (recommendation systems, reuse of collective intelligence and computer-supported creativity), and measure and analysis of human factors in computer-mediated communication (structure of social interactions, sentiments analysis, users' mobility behavior, learning analytics).

Juan Lirio Castro has a PhD in Pedagogy and is a professor at the Faculty of Social Sciences of Talavera de la Reina. Director of the Research Group in Social and Educational Gerontology (GESED) of the UCLM. Collaborator of the Official Master in Gerontology of the University of Deusto and founding member of the RIPUAM. He has published books, chapters and articles in national and international journals. His lines of research are educational and social gerontology, as well as the analysis of socio-educational processes.

Félix E. Lobo de Diego holds an International PhD in Education from the University of Valladolid and his main research focus on Models based practice, youth development interventions and formative assessment in Education.

Lorena López is a teacher of primary education. English Philologist. PhD in Applied Linguistics (Faculty of Philology- Complutense University of Madrid). Part-time professor at the Faculty of Education of Toledo. University of Castilla La Mancha. Speaker at conferences, universities and other institutions. Research stay at Cambridge University (England) and Kansai University (Japan).

Víctor López-Pastor has a PhD in Education since 1998, University Professor and full-time lecturer at the Faculty of Education in Segovia. Coordinator of the International Network of Formative and Shared Assessment in Education. Director of 15 doctoral theses and author of numerous books and scientific articles. Main lines of research: formative and shared assessment, pre-service and in-service teacher education, action-research and teaching innovation, didactics of physical education and early childhood education.

Irene Martínez Martín PhD in Education Cum Laude with European mention. Lecturer at the Complutense University of Madrid, Faculty of Education, Department of Educational Studies since 2015. Degree in Psychopedagogy and Diploma in Social Education at the same university, as well as a pre-doctoral scholarship for the completion of the Thesis: Rebuilding basic education for girls: education, cooperation and development under a gender perspective. A study focused on Mozambique. She collaborates in the INDUCT group of the UCM and the GIES group of the UCLM in research lines dedicated to sexuality and equality education and feminist pedagogies, teacher training, inclusion, universal design for learning, diversities and social education. She has published scientific articles and book chapters, the most significant being in publishing houses such as Síntesis, Grao and IGI-Gloabl and in journals indexed in SCOPUS, Emerging Sources Citation Index and WOS such as Sex Education (2021), Educación XX1 (2017), Athena (2021), RIEJS (2017) and Foro de Educación (2016). It also participates in national and international conferences of interest to the field, as well as in training activities, scientific dissemination and media outreach.

Luis Medina Bernáldez is a social educator. Collaborator of the Research Group on Social and Educational Gerontology UCLM, Spain.

Miriam Molina Soria has a master's degree in research in social sciences: education, audiovisual communication, economics, and business from the University of Valladolid. PhD student in Transdisciplinary Research in Education at the University of Valladolid. Pre-doctoral contract holder at the University of Valladolid in the Faculty of Education of Segovia (Department of Didactics of Musical, Plastic and Corporal Expression). Member of the International Network of Formative and Shared Evaluation in Education. Main lines of research: formative and shared assessment, initial lecturer training, in-service teacher training, early childhood education.

Walter Nuninger (Senior Lecturer) is a Chartered Engineer (1993) with a PhD in Automatic Control awarded in 1997. He further worked as a research engineer at ALSTOM where he developed his skill on friction and traction for trains. Since 1999, he has been an Associate Professor at the University of Lille. He was commissioned for management and financial control in the framework of Continuing Education (2011-2014), then was a member of the Harassment Prevention Unit, offering advice and guidance to students and staff (2014-2019). He works in the Engineering School of Polytech Lille where he directed the Production Department dedicated to Life Long Learning with Work Integrated Learning (2008-2011). He teaches automatic control, computer science and mathematics... He is involved in learner-centered pedagogy and is a tutor of learners in Formative Work Situations in the industry, guiding their reflective attitude. His research work with URM 9189 CRIStAL focuses on Computer Environments for Human Learning. Through the years he has had several experiences in management, leadership and financial control in a quality framework. He is interested in organization, interculturalism and excellence. Since 2023, he has been an Internal Quality Auditor.

Cristina Pascual-Arias is a pre-doctoral contract lecturer at the Faculty of Education in Segovia (University of Valladolid). Doctoral candidate in the PhD in Transdisciplinary Research in Education at the University of Valladolid. Master's degree in Research in Social Sciences, Education, Audiovisual Communication, Economics and Business from the University of Valladolid. Graduate in Early Childhood Education from the University of Valladolid. She is a member of the International Network of Formative and Shared Evaluation in Education. Main lines of research: formative and shared assessment, initial teacher training, in-service teacher training, early childhood education, university education.

Esther Portal Martínez (PhD) is a full-time professor at University of Castilla-La Mancha, Faculty of Social Sciences (Spain) and has been compensatory education teacher, math teacher and social and labour guidance. She has participated in various national and international research projects and her line of research focuses on teaching methodologies, conceptions of learning, employment and labour market. She is a member of the board of directors of Acción Educativa, Educative Renovation Movement.

Pia Rauff Krøyer is an assistant professor at VIA University College, Dep. of Social Education and the research program of Society and Diversity, FLOS Research and teaching areas: My main academical field of research and teaching is gender, sexuality and diversity, and how to strengthen gender equality in pedagogical and educational settings. My main focus is how social and societal circumstances and power dynamics can lead to discrimination, marginalization, racism and sexisme among minority persons and how educators and professionals through perspectives on social justice in general can strengthen social and gender equality. Main academic subjects: cultural theory and decolonial studies, gender and feminist studies, intecultural pedagogy and inclusivness in social work, childhood pedagogy and childrens perspectives.

Juan José Rocha Espinoza is concerned regarding educational change from the transformative proposal of artistic methodologies. University teacher, enemy of linearity, I propose to think from the complex. I seek academic quality, without half measures.

Javier Rodriguez Torres is on a tenured track in Education at the University. of Castilla-La Mancha. Doctor in Pedagogy from the University of Alcalá (Spain) in the line of teacher training and ICT. Teacher of Early Childhood and Primary Education with several specialties, Master of School Psychology at the Complutense University of Madrid. Member of the CIBERIMAGINARIO-UCLM Research Group. He is currently coordinator of the Master's Degree in Secondary Education at the Toledo Campus and director of the postgraduate courses on Disability, Inclusion and Citizenship. New Approaches and Augmentative and Alternative Communication mediated with technologies. The lines of research, with respect to ICT, are its curricular integration, gender differences in its inclusion and curriculum, the discourses of power - knowledge that are generated in the use and application of technologies.

Kay Sambell is widely known internationally for her contributions to the Assessment for Learning (AfL) movement in Higher Education, which seeks to emphasize the ways in which assessment processes can be designed to support and developing students' learning, as well as measure it. For over two decades she has spearheaded a range of pragmatic innovations, research projects and initiatives focused on improving university student learning via assessment. She is a UK National Teaching Fellow (2002) and a Principal Fellow of the Higher Education Academy. She is currently an independent consultant and Visiting Professor of Assessment for Learning at the University of Sunderland and the University of Cumbria. Kay combines her longstanding interest in AfLwith over twenty-five years' experience as a practising lecturer and course leader in the interdisciplinary area of Childhood and Youth Studies, where she specialises in Children's Literature. She continues to teach undergraduates and enjoys the opportunity to work collaboratively with students on pedagogic action research projects. Kay also helped to establish and support a series of international conferences aimed at rethinking assessment practice. She is currently President of the vibrant Assessment in Higher Education (AHE) conference series, (.) which leads the development of assessment for learning. Her interests range broadly, however, and, she has focused on academic literacy, the first year experience, widening participation and student engagement.

Aida Sanahuja Ribés is a Lecturer in the Department of Pedagogy at the Universitat Jaume I. Master's Degree in Secondary Education Teacher. University Master's Degree in Family Intervention and Mediation, Degree in Psychopedagogy and Diploma in Teaching. She is a member of the Educational Improvement and Critical Citizenship Research Group (MEICRI) and collaborates with the Laboratoire International sur l'inclusion scolaire (LISIS). Her current lines of research are inclusive and democratic classroom practices, the school included in the territory and participatory action research processes.

Lucía Sánchez-Tarazaga is a Lecturer on assessment and innovation at the Universitat Jaume I. She belongs to the research group IDOCE (Innovation, Development and Competences in Education) and her lines of research focus on teacher training, professional development of teachers, teacher competences and educational policy. She is also active member of different European associations of teacher education.

Nadia L. Soria-Miranda developed her teaching work in the Universidad de Guayaquil, Ecuador. Her work is focused on gender equity and evaluation issues.

Index

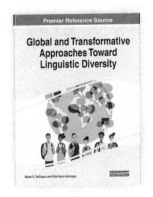
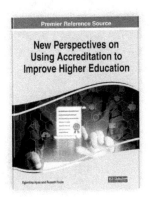

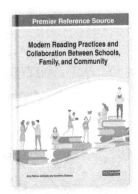
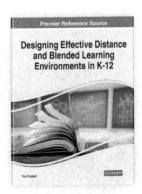

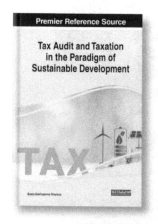

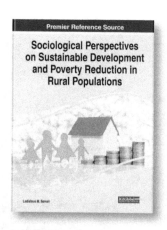

9 781668 435373